Healthcare in the United States

Healthcare in the United States

Clinical, Financial, and Operational Dimensions

Stephen L. Walston | Kenneth L. Johnson

GATEWAY
TO HEALTHCARE MANAGEMENT

HAP

AUPHA

Health Administration Press, Chicago, Illinois
Association of University Programs in Health Administration, Washington, DC

Library of Congress Cataloging-in-Publication Data

Names: Walston, Stephen Lee, author. | Johnson, Kenneth L., 1957– author. | Association of University Programs in Health Administration, issuing body.
Title: Healthcare in the United States : clinical, financial, and operational dimensions / Stephen L. Walston, Kenneth L. Johnson.
Other titles: Gateway to healthcare management.
Description: Chicago, Illinois : Health Administration Press ; Washington, DC : Association of University Programs in Health Administration, [2021] | Series: Gateway to healthcare management | Includes bibliographical references and index. | Summary: "This book offers an introductory overview of the American healthcare system by exploring its many organizations, populations, professions, finance structures, and delivery models, as well as their impact. The authors delve into the many conflicting issues related to cost, access, and quality"— Provided by publisher.
Identifiers: LCCN 2020032834 (print) | LCCN 2020032835 (ebook) | ISBN 9781640551459 (paperback ; alk. paper) | ISBN 9781640551497 (epub) | ISBN 9781640551480 (mobi)
Subjects: MESH: Delivery of Health Care | Health Services Administration | Health Care Sector—economics | Health Care Sector—organization & administration | Health Policy | United States
Classification: LCC RA971.3 (print) | LCC RA971.3 (ebook) | NLM W 84 AA1 | DDC 362.1068/1—dc23
LC record available at https://lccn.loc.gov/2020032834
LC ebook record available at https://lccn.loc.gov/2020032835

Acquisitions editor: Janet Davis; Manuscript editor: Deborah Ring; Project manager: Andrew Baumann; Cover designer: James Slate; Layout: Integra

Health Administration Press
A division of the Foundation of the American
   College of Healthcare Executives
300 S. Riverside Plaza, Suite 1900
Chicago, IL 60606-6698
(312) 424-2800

Association of University Programs
   in Health Administration
1730 M Street, NW
Suite 407
Washington, DC 20036
(202) 763-7283

To our wives, children, and grandchildren, for your support and love

BRIEF CONTENTS

DETAILED CONTENTS

PREFACE

The United States does not have a single "system" of healthcare but rather many over-lapping systems. This textbook will examine and elaborate on these components, trace their development, and assess their impact on the people of the United States. The book will also address the many challenges and conflicted assumptions that undergird the way healthcare in the United States operates.

Chapter 1 explores the history of US healthcare and the challenges of balancing cost, access, and quality. It also discusses trends associated with aging and diversity throughout the US population, variances in costs and outcomes from one part of the country to another, the importance of lifestyle factors, and the impact of emerging diseases and health threats.

Chapter 2 provides an overview of the healthcare professions and occupations. It includes information about the education and training required for various roles, median salaries, and likely future demand.

Chapter 3 describes acute care organizations, including hospitals, in the United States. It looks at their leadership structure and importance to healthcare.

Chapter 4 explores the pharmaceutical and medical device industries, which account for a significant portion of US healthcare costs. These industries are global in scope and present a number of challenges associated with costs and sustainability.

Chapter 5 focuses on long-term care. It presents the background and history of long-term care services in the United States, along with the organization and function of long-term care today and the challenges for long-term care in the future.

Chapter 6 seeks to foster a greater understanding of the country's mental health care industry. Readers will learn of the serious mental health challenges facing Americans, along with the history of mental health services and the various categories of providers.

Chapter 7 examines the role of the US government in healthcare, health insurance, and the licensure of health professionals. It also provides an overview of the major agencies that regulate healthcare.

Chapter 8 presents basic economic principles and concepts as they apply to healthcare. It discusses topics such as diminishing returns, opportunity costs, adverse selection, and the impact of preexisting conditions on insurance costs.

Chapter 9 delves into health insurance and its various options and components. It emphasizes the importance of risk and the use of risk pools, along with impact of deductibles, coinsurance, and copays. The chapter concludes with a look at future options for health insurance in the United States.

Chapter 10 is devoted to the issue of quality in US healthcare. It defines quality, discusses safety concerns and medical errors, and reviews concepts of quality improvement as they apply to healthcare.

Chapter 11 focuses on the uses and implications of information technology in healthcare. The chapter discusses electronic medical records, cloud computing, and issues of privacy and security. It then reflects on the future impact of information technology in the field.

Chapter 12 explores the principles of population health. Social determinants of health, health disparities, and positive health outcomes are reviewed and discussed in detail.

Chapter 13 compares the US healthcare system with the systems found in other countries. Readers will learn the four basic models on which most healthcare systems are created, and they will see how the US system incorporates elements of each. The chapter also compares the United States with other countries in terms of costs and health outcomes.

Chapter 14 considers the future of the US healthcare delivery system. It highlights the many challenges facing the current system, the need for greater integration of healthcare services, the growing impact of chronic conditions, and the philosophies behind the major political groups seeking to guide the system's direction.

In each chapter, key terms in **bold type** are accompanied by concise definitions in the margins (and in the glossary near the end of the book). Questions, assignments, and cases are provided to enhance and assess learning.

After completing this text, readers will have a better understanding of healthcare in the United States across its clinical, financial, and operational dimensions. Readers should be well versed in the system's history, its present state, and the emerging strategies for addressing the complexities and challenges that lie ahead.

INSTRUCTOR RESOURCES

This book's Instructor Resources include a test bank, PowerPoint presentations, answer guides for the chapter-end questions, and case study instructions.

For the most up-to-date information about this book and its Instructor Resources, go to ache.org/HAP and browse for the book's title, author names, or order code (2408I).

This book's Instructor Resources are available to instructors who adopt this book for use in their courses. For access information, please email hapbooks@ache.org.

CHAPTER 1

THE HISTORY OF US HEALTHCARE AND THE DEMOGRAPHICS OF DISEASE

The delivery and funding of healthcare in the United States are complex and uncertain for many people. In fact, Americans experience vastly different levels of care, depending on their age, race/ethnicity, socioeconomic status, and geographic location. These differences are products of the convoluted development of healthcare in the United States. Today, whether healthcare is a right or a privilege for those who can afford it is one of the most pressing questions in American society.

"Is healthcare a privilege or a right? That may be the most contentious question in the whole healthcare debate. When he was president, George W. Bush felt the need to address this question by saying we have universal care in this country because everyone can 'just go to an emergency room.' But there is a big difference between going to the ER because you have no insurance versus having health insurance that allows you to go to a doctor or clinic of your choice when you are sick or think you might have a problem. In general, people with health insurance tend to get help earlier, when it is less costly and more effective. In fact, one Harvard study suggests that 45,000 Americans die prematurely every year because they lack health insurance. . . . There is no such thing as an American healthcare system. . . . What we have instead is a hodgepodge of private and public insurance plans with cracks between them" (Johnson 2017).

LEARNING OBJECTIVES

After reading this chapter, you will be able to

➤ Identify the key historical events that shaped the US healthcare system.

➤ Explain how healthcare access, quality, and cost are interrelated.

➤ Discuss how age and chronic disease affect healthcare use, cost, and access.

➤ Understand how the diversity of the US population influences healthcare.

➤ Explain why healthcare costs vary so widely in the United States.

➤ Identify the factors that affect life expectancy and explain why life expectancy in the United States has declined.

➤ Understand the dangers of new and emerging diseases.

THE HISTORY OF THE US HEALTHCARE SYSTEM

Healthcare in the United States and elsewhere in the world was primitive and lacked sophisticated technology until the beginning of the twentieth century. Before then, the training and practice of medicine was not standardized, and most practitioners were unlicensed. Between 1760 and 1850, some educated doctors sought to establish special recognition for their profession and organized medical schools. However, US state legislatures consistently rejected the need to professionalize medicine, and many states even eliminated what little medical licensure existed. During this time, lay practitioners with little or no formal medical education proliferated, many of whom practiced herbal and folk remedies. Some physicians even denigrated the value of medical training, suggesting that "professional knowledge and training were unneeded in treating most diseases" (Starr 1982, 33).

American physicians initially sought to model their profession after England's Royal Society of Medicine, which set physicians apart as an elite order. Physicians did not physically examine patients but primarily recommended courses of treatment. Physicians at first were distinguished from surgeons, who came from the same guild as barbers and primarily performed manual tasks, such as draining wounds and pulling teeth. Another important group in the medical establishment was apothecaries, who prescribed and charged for medicines, which they made by hand. By the late 1700s, these roles began to converge, with physicians both examining and treating patients as well as creating and dispensing their own medications. Few, however, had any formal training: At this time, only about 200 of 4,000 physicians in the United States held medical degrees. The rest were lay personnel, who were inconsistently trained (at best) in areas such as childbirth, bone setting, cancers, inoculations, and abortions (Starr 1982).

By the early 1800s, medical schools were being established in the United States. By the mid-1850s, 42 US medical schools were in operation. Most were located in rural areas that lacked hospitals and clinical facilities. A degree from such a school was generally considered sufficient training to practice medicine without state licensure. Hospitals also began to emerge during this time. Some communities opened hospitals and "pesthouses" to isolate those with contagious diseases, and every state had at least one mental asylum. By 1850, the number of physicians had increased eightfold, to about 40,000.

Medical care typically was provided on credit. Physicians billed their patients directly, but patients often paid only a fraction of their charges, or they provided goods in kind or bartered for the medical services they received. The increase in the number of physicians saturated many markets. As a result, many doctors chose to relocate to rural areas, while others took second jobs to make a living.

The lack of transportation infrastructure was a major factor that constrained the use of medical care. Most of the US population lived in rural areas, where transportation was relatively inaccessible. In 1850, 84.6 percent of the US population was rural; by 1900, this number had decreased to 60.4 percent (US Census Bureau 1993). In both rural and urban areas, most physician consultations took place in patients' homes rather than in offices, and physicians generally charged according to the distance they had to travel. Before the invention of the telephone, families had to travel to find a doctor; because most doctors were out visiting patients, they were difficult to locate. As a result, families in rural areas sought a doctor only for very serious conditions. The advent of railroads and canals, followed later by the automobile and the telephone, facilitated greater access to care by lowering the cost and time required to obtain healthcare services (Starr 1982).

In the early 1800s, Americans perceived little need for hospitals, as most people received healthcare services in their homes. The few hospitals that did exist generally provided poor and dirty conditions and were primarily designed to isolate the sick from their communities. Hospitals were most often established by religious and charitable organizations as holding institutions for the sick, rather than as places for curing illness. Mental asylums, likewise, were created as holding facilities for the mentally ill. These places were frequently dangerous, however, and most patients felt safer at home (see sidebar).

 THE ORIGIN OF NEW YORK CITY'S BELLEVUE HOSPITAL

In 1736, the New York Almshouse was founded as a pest and death house for people suffering from communicable diseases such as cholera and yellow fever. The poor and the mentally ill were treated with experimental care there—often without the use of anesthesia. For those who could not afford a private doctor, the almshouse sometimes was their only choice for medical care. Later, the facility was used as a "dumping ground" for many patients who were terminally ill or otherwise unwanted.

Because of the diversity of cases treated there, the Almshouse—renamed Bellevue Hospital in 1824—provided an ideal setting for clinical training and research. Training for physicians as interns began there in 1856, and the first professional nursing school opened at Bellevue in 1873. In the twentieth century, the hospital continued to improve its quality of care and professionalization, and it become known as one of the premier training and treatment centers in the United States (Howe 2016).

Advances in transportation and technology made the centralization of patients into hospitals and physician offices more practical. Both the automobile and the telephone allowed patients to more easily schedule and access medical care. Physicians could practice in their offices, rather than travel to patients' homes. This concentration of practice allowed greater efficiencies of scale for medical personnel, as physicians could see greater numbers of patients in a day. This practice also gave rise to specialization. Still, however, few physicians in the 1800s could become wealthy practicing medicine.

Toward the end of the nineteenth century, most states had implemented medical licensure for physicians. Initially, licensure laws allowed anyone graduating from any operating medical school to practice medicine. Gradually, these laws changed to allow only those who graduated from recognized, accredited medical schools to practice medicine. These stricter regulations led many poorly trained and marginally competent physicians to stop practicing.

American Medical Association (AMA)
The largest professional association of physicians and medical students in the United States, founded in 1847.

The rapid expansion of the **American Medical Association (AMA)**, along with local medical societies, had a powerful influence on physician training by organizing and standardizing it throughout the country. In the early 1900s, the AMA helped reform medical school education, requiring a minimum number of years of high school education and medical training, in addition to a test for licensure. The AMA also began to grade medical schools. Ultimately, the AMA facilitated the greatest change in medical school education by sponsoring a research group from the Carnegie Foundation that examined and recommended changes to medical training. The issuance of the so-called **Flexner Report** (named for its lead author, Abraham Flexner) in 1910 resulted in the closure of about 35 percent of existing medical schools by 1915 and decreased the number of medical school graduates from 5,440 to 3,536 (Starr 1982, 120). The higher standards may have improved the quality of practitioners, but they also increased the cost of medical education and resulted in a greater concentration of physicians in urban settings, which exacerbated the physician shortages in rural and poor areas.

Flexner Report
A study published in 1910 by the Carnegie Foundation that evaluated medical education in the United States and prompted major changes in the way physicians were educated.

Hospitals also benefited from the recommendations of the Flexner Report and the changes it spurred in medical education. More and more physicians began to train in hospitals. In 1902, about 50 percent of physicians trained in hospitals; by 1912, the share had risen to almost 80 percent (Starr 1982, 124). In addition, advances in bacteriology and antibiotics dramatically expanded the range of surgical operations. This, coupled with developments in diagnostic testing that required expensive equipment, reinforced the importance of medical practice in hospitals. Patients began to use hospitals for more complicated medical treatments, rather than simply for isolation for acute illnesses.

As healthcare education and practice moved toward standardization in the early twentieth century, the structures of hospitals and the roles of healthcare professionals evolved as well. The roles of physicians and nurses were defined more clearly, especially as these professionals began to specialize in areas such as surgery, children, adult medicine, and so on. Nonphysician providers, such as pharmacists, laboratory assistants, and dieticians, were trained to take over some of the tasks that traditionally had been done by physicians. Advances in surgery, as a result of the discovery of effective anesthetics and antibiotics, drew many physicians to hospitals. Doctors began treating patients in these facilities and relying on them for much of their income. However, because physicians typically did not own the facilities, nor were they employed or paid by hospitals, they retained a high degree of autonomy and could bill patients directly for their services.

Gradually, hospitals shifted from organizations funded by charities to institutions financed by patients, insurance companies, and employers. Hospitals became one of the main employers in the United States and centers for the practice of medicine. From their humble beginnings, hospitals have grown into a mammoth industry, now accounting for $1.1 trillion in healthcare spending each year in the United States (AHA 2020).

The same developments that shaped the delivery of healthcare also influenced the pharmaceutical industry. Prior to the twentieth century, the quality and composition of drugs sold to the public were unreliable. Many so-called **patent medicines** were composed of proprietary, or secret, compounds. The pharmaceutical industry emerged as a result of efforts by the AMA to make physicians the preferred prescribers of drugs as well as investigative journalism that exposed dangerous, unregulated drugs. Many of these products, as seen in exhibit 1.1, contained toxic, addictive, or dangerous ingredients. By the early 1900s, the public was being encouraged to obtain their medications from doctors (see sidebar). Further, new discoveries, such as vaccines and antibiotics, bolstered the reputation of the nascent industry.

patent medicines
Nonprescription drugs made of proprietary, or secret, compounds that were sold to the public in the early 1900s.

Norodin—a methamphetamine product that promised to dispel the shadows of depression
Laudanum—an opium mix used to treat everything from meningitis to yellow fever
Cigares de Joy—tobacco to treat asthma
Quaalude 300—a sedative used to treat insomnia
Mrs. Winslow's Soothing Syrup—a morphine concoction given to teething children
Kimball White Pine & Tar Cough Syrup—a chloroform syrup for colds and bronchitis
Bayer Heroin Hydrochloride—a heroin product used as a cough suppressant
Cocaine Toothache Drops—a cocaine product for children's toothaches

Exhibit 1.1
Dangerous Patent Medicines in the 1800s and Early 1900s

Source: Amondson (2013).

By the mid-twentieth century, laws had been passed that outlined the formal approval process for drugs and designated which drugs required written prescriptions from physicians and which could be sold "over the counter" (Rahalkar 2012). Since then, the pharmaceutical industry has become a trillion-dollar global industry. North America alone accounts for almost half (48.9 percent) of all prescription costs (Mikulic 2019). Almost 300,000 pharmacists are now working in the United States, filling almost 4.4 billion prescriptions annually (Shahbandeh 2019; Venosa 2016).

THE "IRON TRIANGLE" OF HEALTHCARE

Iron Triangle of Healthcare
A concept introduced by William Kissick describing three competing dimensions of healthcare: access, cost, and quality.

As medical technology has advanced, governments around the world have struggled to balance three dimensions of healthcare: providing adequate access to care, containing the cost of care, and improving the quality of care. As shown in exhibit 1.2, access, cost, and quality make up the **Iron Triangle of Healthcare**.

The concept of the Iron Triangle was introduced by William Kissick in his 1994 book *Medicine's Dilemmas: Infinite Needs Versus Finite Resources*. Kissick, a physician, public health official, and scholar, argued that the three dimensions of access, cost, and quality necessarily compete with one another—that is, a change in one factor must have an

EXHIBIT 1.2
The Iron Triangle of Healthcare

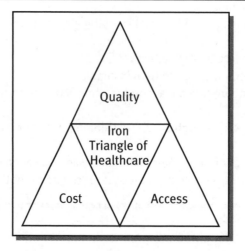

impact on the others. For instance, increasing the quality of care requires increasing costs, because quality requires the allocation of more resources, including people and equipment, to improve clinical processes and outcomes. Likewise, increasing access to care requires providing more services at more locations, which also increases costs. Conversely, cutting costs, which might mean limiting resources or minimizing operational locations, hours, equipment, and clinicians, decreases quality and access. This trade-off is a key principle of the Iron Triangle: Healthcare organizations can improve only two of the three dimensions while sacrificing the third. Many, like Kissick, argue that these trade-offs are inevitable.

However, others believe that all three of the dimensions of care can be pursued concurrently (IHI 2020). They propose that achieving access, cost, and quality can be accomplished by improving healthcare efficiencies, changing the way healthcare is paid for, and fostering disruptive innovations (Berwick, Nolan, and Whittington 2008).

The Institute for Healthcare Improvement (IHI), a national healthcare organization that is focused on improving healthcare in the United States, has proposed a modified version of the Iron Triangle called the **Triple Aim**, which highlights the interdependencies of population health, quality, and cost. The Triple Aim was developed to help healthcare organizations focus on these three dimensions simultaneously. The IHI does not regard the three components of the Triple Aim as independent of one another; rather, it recommends that healthcare organizations pursue a balanced approach to reducing cost while increasing quality among at-risk populations and addressing communities' health concerns (Berwick, Nolan, and Whittington 2008). As shown in exhibit 1.3, the Triple Aim differs slightly from the Iron Triangle of Healthcare. The Triple Aim focuses on three factors:

> *Triple Aim*
> A modified version of the Iron Triangle that highlights the interdependencies of population health, quality of care, and cost; it refers to the simultaneous pursuit of three goals: improving the health of populations, improving the patient experience of care, and reducing the per capita cost of healthcare.

- ◆ *Population health.* Population health centers on improving the health of entire populations. Identifying populations to work with, especially at-risk populations, is essential to addressing the Triple Aim.

- ◆ *Experience of care.* This component includes quality of care but is broken down into two measures: patient satisfaction and clinical quality of care.

- ◆ *Per capita cost.* This factor refines healthcare costs by measuring them on a per capita, or per person, basis. The Triple Aim seeks to lower, or at least maintain, actual costs for individuals while improving care outcomes (Galvin 2018).

The US healthcare system has struggled to balance the three dimensions of access, quality, and cost. Healthcare spending has risen steadily over the last century. As shown in exhibit 1.4, by the middle of the twentieth century, healthcare spending accounted for 4.5 percent of US gross domestic product (GDP). By 1980, this figure had reached 8.9 percent, and by 2018, it stood at 17.8 percent (Statista 2019, 2020). Much of the increase in healthcare spending is attributable to increases in the price and intensity of healthcare, higher rates of chronic diseases, and higher expenditures on pharmaceuticals (Scutti 2017).

Exhibit 1.3
The IHI Triple Aim

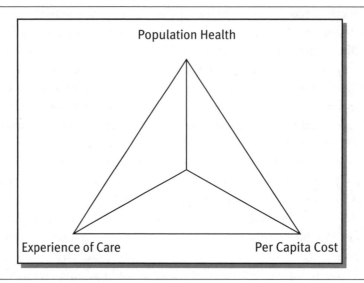

Affordable Care Act (ACA)
A federal law passed in 2010 to reform the US healthcare system.

The **Affordable Care Act (ACA)** of 2010 sought to address the three aims of the Iron Triangle by simultaneously improving healthcare access and quality while reducing the cost of care. However, the expansion of access and quality came at a cost. The implementation of the ACA increased the costs of compliance and thus contributed to a rise in healthcare costs and insurance premiums, as predicted by the Iron Triangle of Healthcare (Godfrey 2012; Manchikanti et al. 2017; Weiner, Marks, and Pauly 2017).

Exhibit 1.4
US National Healthcare Expenditures as a Percentage of GDP, 1950–2019

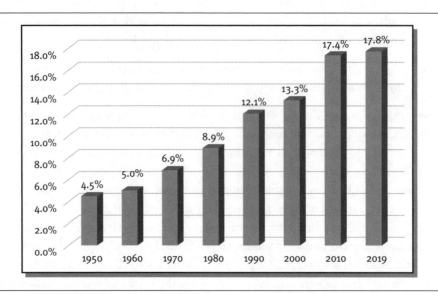

Source: Data from Statista (2019, 2020).

Dr. Aaron Carroll (2012), a pediatrician and healthcare researcher at Indiana University, summarized the trade-off in this way:

> I can make the healthcare system cheaper (improve cost), but that can happen only if I reduce access in some way or reduce quality. I can improve quality, but that will either result in increased costs or reduced access. And of course, I can increase access . . . but that will either cost a lot of money (it does) or result in reduced quality. . . . The lesson of the iron triangle is that there are inherent trade-offs in health policy.

Healthcare remains a top concern for Americans. A 2019 survey showed that healthcare was the top concern for 36 percent of the US population, followed by the economy at 26 percent. In addition, 67 percent of respondents agreed that the US healthcare system is broken or not working well (Cannon 2019). Americans perceive the quality and cost of healthcare as the most significant concerns. (See chapter 10 for an in-depth discussion of efforts to improve healthcare quality in the United States.)

Escalating healthcare costs in the United States have affected both access to and the quality of care. As the Institute of Medicine (2001, 1) stated two decades ago, "The U.S. healthcare delivery system does not provide consistent, high-quality medical care to all people. . . . Healthcare harms patients too frequently and routinely fails to deliver its potential benefits." Yet 20 years later, healthcare disparities persist, which have direct effects on Americans' life expectancy. As a National Academy of Medicine report noted more recently, "Despite the magnitude of national spending, unacceptable disparities still exist in the health experiences of different population groups, and, for certain groups, those disparities are increasing to the point that life spans are actually decreasing" (Whicher et al. 2018, xi)

Employers, politicians, insurance companies, and providers continue to struggle with the Iron Triangle of Healthcare and achieving the Triple Aim of controlling costs without unreasonably affecting quality and access. Nevertheless, increasing costs have forced many Americans to give up their health insurance (see sidebar), leaving them vulnerable to higher healthcare expenses and, potentially, decreased access to and quality of care.

AGING AND CHRONIC DISEASE

Statistics show a direct correlation between age and the amount of healthcare an individual uses. As in most industrialized nations, the population of the United States is aging rapidly. Demographers estimate that by 2030, about 20 percent of the US population will be over the age of 65, an increase from 12 percent in 2000. Between 2000 and 2016, the median age of the US population rose 2.5 years, from 35.3 to 37.9 (Chappell 2017).

Aging puts people at greater risk of developing a **chronic disease**, which, in turn, increases the use, cost, and intensity of healthcare. In 1900, infectious diseases such as

chronic disease
A disease that persists for three months or longer that generally cannot be prevented by vaccines or cured by medication.

⊛ **DEBATE TIME** A Retiree's Difficult Decision

In 2018, Dana Farrell, a 54-year-old retired social worker, had to make a difficult decision. Her monthly health insurance premiums had jumped to about $600 per month. Even with coverage, she still had to pay $80 per doctor visit. This expense, coupled with her many other bills and limited savings, made her health insurance unaffordable, so she made the difficult decision to drop it. Dana was nervous about not having coverage. Although she hoped she would not get sick or have an accident, she felt she simply did not have a choice (Bazar 2018).

Why do people choose not to have health insurance? What happens when people drop their health insurance? What options might a person have to retain some form of health insurance?

---

pneumonia, tuberculosis, and gastrointestinal infections were the leading causes of death (Statista 2020). The twentieth century saw a major shift as chronic diseases, such as heart disease, stroke, cancer, and diabetes, became the leading causes of death in the United States (Rutledge et al. 2018).

Today, as shown in exhibit 1.5, about 60 percent of adults in the United States have one or more chronic diseases, and 40 percent have two or more. The most prevalent chronic diseases are heart disease, cancer, chronic lung disease, stroke, Alzheimer's disease, diabetes, and chronic kidney disease. Furthermore, 40 percent of all adults in the United States are obese, and more than one-third of adults who are obese have diabetes, which is the leading cause of kidney failure, limb amputations, and blindness. Tobacco use, poor

EXHIBIT 1.5
Most Prevalent
Chronic Diseases
Among Americans

Source: CDC (2020c).

nutrition, lack of physical activity, and excessive alcohol use contribute to many of these chronic diseases (CDC 2020c).

Among the elderly, those who are sicker spend much more money on healthcare. In 2016, 1 percent of the elderly accounted for 12 percent of healthcare costs, and 10 percent of the elderly accounted for 50 percent of healthcare expenses. People aged 65 and older make up 13 percent of the US population, but they account for 34 percent of total healthcare spending—$18,424 per person—and spend three times more, on average, than adults under age 65 (Sawyer and Claxton 2019). Healthcare use—and hence cost—continues to rise with age: Healthcare spending for an 85-year-old, for example, is 2.5 times more than that of a 66-year-old, and for a 95-year-old, it is three times more (Neuman et al. 2015). A couple who retired in 2019 at age 65 can expect to spend $285,000 on healthcare during their retirement (O'Brien 2019).

DIVERSITY AND HEALTHCARE

As the United States becomes a more diverse country, its healthcare needs are changing as well. Although non-Hispanic/Latino whites still make up a majority of the US population, accounting for 60.4 percent (198 million people), Hispanics/Latinos have become the second-largest population, accounting for 18.3 percent (60 million), and Blacks and African Americans are the third-largest population, with 13.4 percent (44 million) (Chappell 2017; US Census Bureau 2019).

The composition of the US population is projected to continue these trends over the next several decades, as shown in exhibit 1.6. Demographers forecast that by 2055,

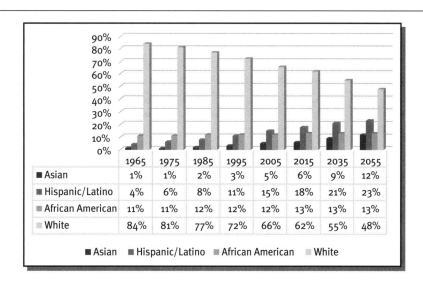

EXHIBIT 1.6

Historical and Projected Racial/Ethnic Composition of the US Population, 1965–2055

	1965	1975	1985	1995	2005	2015	2035	2055
■ Asian	1%	1%	2%	3%	5%	6%	9%	12%
■ Hispanic/Latino	4%	6%	8%	11%	15%	18%	21%	23%
▨ African American	11%	11%	12%	12%	12%	13%	13%	13%
▨ White	84%	81%	77%	72%	66%	62%	55%	48%

■ Asian   ■ Hispanic/Latino   ▨ African American   ▨ White

Source: Data from Pew Research Center (2015).

the United States will not have a single racial or ethnic majority, as the white population is expected to shrink to 48 percent of the total population, while Hispanics/Latinos are projected to make up nearly one-quarter of the population (Cohn and Caumont 2016).

Historically, people of African American and Hispanic/Latino backgrounds in the United States have experienced greater difficulty accessing healthcare services and health insurance than whites, and they have tended to receive lower-quality care and experience worse healthcare outcomes (Hayes et al. 2017). These outcomes are attributable to two factors: These groups tend to have lower incomes compared with whites, and they are more likely to work for businesses that do not provide health insurance. Both of these factors limit access to healthcare, which leads to untreated health conditions and exacerbates health problems.

As shown in exhibit 1.7, African Americans earn 32 percent less than whites, and Hispanics/Latinos earn 42 percent less. In addition, about 20 percent of Hispanics/Latinos in 2017 did not have health insurance, and 26 percent used emergency rooms as their primary source of care (Artiga and Orgera 2019).

Even though most African American and Hispanic/Latino families have at least one full-time worker, they are twice as likely as whites to be living under the federal poverty level. For this reason, many more African American and Hispanic/Latino families qualify for and receive health coverage from Medicaid. In fact, among these groups, Medicaid covers more than half of all children. In 2016, more than 55 percent of Black children

EXHIBIT 1.7

Earnings by Racial/
Ethnic Group

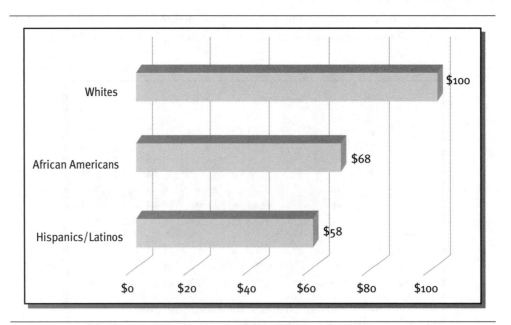

Source: Data from Martinovich (2017).

and 56 percent of Hispanic/Latino children received Medicaid versus 32 percent of white children (Child Trends 2019).

Although having Medicaid coverage has been shown to improve children's health, many states have implemented rules to reduce coverage for this population. For instance, from 2018 to 2019, enrollment of children in Medicaid declined by 840,000 nationwide. Many prominent national organizations, including the American Hospital Association, the American Academy of Family Physicians, and the American Academy of Pediatrics, have warned that the loss of Medicaid coverage will have negative effects on the health of these children and hurt physicians' ability to serve low-income populations (Kaiser Family Foundation 2013; Meyer 2019).

In addition, people with Medicaid coverage have a harder time finding a doctor who will accept them as a patient. Across the United States, about 30 percent of all physicians and 65 percent of psychiatrists refuse to accept new Medicaid patients (King 2019).

People of color are more likely to have co-occurring behavioral health illnesses and chronic medical conditions (see chapter 6 for a more in-depth discussion of mental health). The combination of these conditions increases the severity of disease and accentuates the effects of reduced access to care and lower income. The percentage of low-income individuals who have both a chronic disease and serious psychological stress is more than four times the rate of higher-income individuals (29 percent versus 7 percent), and this population spends over three times more on inpatient and emergency care each year. In addition, low-income individuals with chronic conditions are about 2.5 times more likely not to obtain medical care than those with higher incomes (22 percent versus 9 percent) (Cunningham 2018).

HEALTHCARE COST VARIATIONS

Research has shown significant differences in healthcare spending by geographic location. The reasons for these spending differences depend on whether the healthcare users are Medicare patients or private or commercial payers. For Medicare patients, about 73 percent of higher costs were tied to greater use of postacute services, such as skilled nursing and home health care, while about 70 percent of higher private/commercial costs were attributable to higher prices. In some US cities, Medicare costs are higher because of the greater intensity and volume of services used (see sidebar). Higher costs for commercial payers appear to be driven primarily by higher prices charged in different locations. High-cost areas are less likely to provide preventive services, such as vaccinations, but they also have much longer physician office waits and more emergency room visits. High-cost areas also use postacute services to a greater extent (Fisher and Skinner 2013; Institute of Medicine 2013).

(✱) COST VARIANCE BY GEOGRAPHIC LOCATION

Studies show that higher healthcare costs are largely attributable to the number of healthcare providers and other "supply-side" factors that permit providers to establish higher prices and operate less efficient clinical practices (Callison, Kaestner, and Ward 2018). For example, McAllen, Texas, had one of the most expensive healthcare markets for Medicare in the United States. In 2006, Medicare paid almost twice as much per beneficiary there (about $15,000) as the US average, primarily because of spending on postacute services. McAllen's per capita income was only $12,000—meaning that Medicare paid more than the average resident of McAllen earned.

Patients in McAllen received more treatment and services than patients in other areas of the country. Medicare patients had about 50 percent more specialist visits, and two-thirds saw ten or more specialists. McAllen's physicians ordered 20 to 60 percent more diagnostic tests (Gawande 2009), such as ultrasounds, bone density testing, echocardiography, nerve conduction, and urine flow studies. As a result, this population had a higher likelihood of undergoing more surgeries and invasive procedures, such as gallbladder operations, knee replacements, breast biopsies, pacemaker and defibrillator implantations, and cardiac bypass operations.

The same thing occurs with private and commercial payers, who pay very different amounts for similar services, depending on geographic location. For instance, in 2016, the cost of a knee replacement in South Carolina was $47,000 but only $24,000 in New Jersey. Similarly, a fetal ultrasound cost $522 in Cleveland but only $183 in Canton, Ohio (Herman 2016). Difference in what is paid is due mainly to differences in prices set by providers rather than to differences in the use of healthcare services.

Charges for services provided to patients can vary dramatically by location. For example, as seen in exhibit 1.8, in 2016, the median price for a cesarean (C-section) delivery was $7,742 in Oklahoma City, Oklahoma, but $20,721 in San Francisco, California (Kennedy et al. 2019). The prevalence of preventive care also varies by geography in the United States. For example, in 2015, children's immunization rate for hepatitis was 88 percent in North Dakota but only 49 percent in Vermont (Hill et al. 2016).

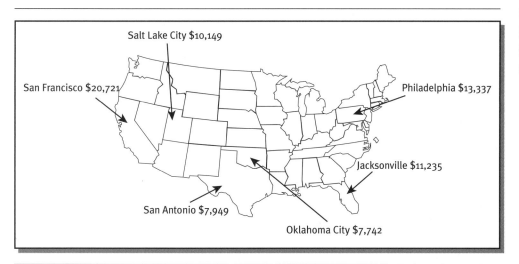

EXHIBIT 1.8
Price Differences for C-Section in the United States

LIFE EXPECTANCY, LIFESTYLE, AND CHRONIC DISEASE

Between 2010 and 2019, **life expectancy** in the United States declined for the first time since the early twentieth century, and in 2020, it stood at 78.9 years. As illustrated in exhibit 1.9, US life expectancy has dropped below the average for countries belonging to the Organisation for Economic Co-operation and Development (OECD). In 1960, the United States had the highest life expectancy in the world, but by 1998, it had fallen below

life expectancy
The average number of years a person is expected to live.

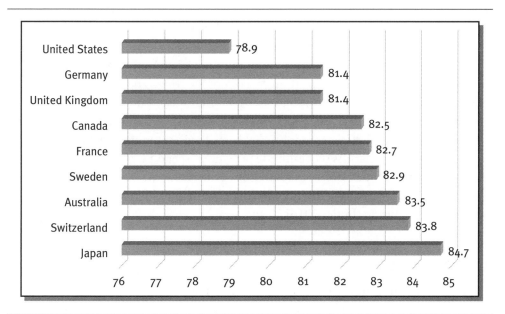

EXHIBIT 1.9
Life Expectancy at Birth by Nation, 2020

Source: Data from Macrotrends (2020).

the OECD average. While US life expectancy rose between 1998 and 2012, it plateaued in 2012 and then declined from 2010 to 2019.

Americans' lower life expectancy compared with OECD countries is attributable to overall poorer health and to factors such as worse birth outcomes and higher numbers of injuries at birth, as well as increasing rates of obesity, diabetes, heart disease, drug overdose, and homicide.

Americans are more likely than people in other nations to eat too many calories, abuse drugs, and misuse firearms. On average, Americans eat more than 3,600 calories each day, far beyond the 2,000 calories recommended (Renee 2018), and do not exercise as much as recommended. As a result, by 2020, the CDC reported that 42 percent of adults in the United States were obese, and 9 percent were severely obese (Hill et al. 2020). In 2017 alone, more than 70,000 Americans died from drug overdoses (National Institute on Drug Abuse 2019). And, almost 40,000 people die each year from gun-related injuries, including almost 24,000 suicides (Gramlich 2019). Americans also drive cars more often, thereby getting less exercise from walking; they have weaker social networks that help support and maintain healthy lifestyles; and many people lack health insurance (Woolf and Aron 2018).

Americans' unhealthy lifestyles encourage the onset and severity of disease. In 2014, Dr. David Katz, director of Yale University's Prevention Research Center, stated that "We have known now for decades that the 'actual' causes of premature death in the United States are not the diseases [written] on death certificates, but factors that cause those diseases" (Park 2014).

Researchers believe that about 40 percent of the major causes of death in the United States, such as heart disease, stroke, cancer, lower respiratory illness, and unintentional injuries, could be prevented by modifying bad habits. Reducing or eliminating smoking and drinking, increasing exercise, and eating a healthier diet, coupled with a decrease in obesity, could dramatically improve Americans' life expectancy, experts say (CDC 2020b).

The comparative decline in life expectancy in the United States is also directly related to the lower amount of money spent on social services. There appears to be a trade-off between money spent on healthcare and social services, such as housing assistance, food assistance, and child support services. The United States spends only about 56 cents on social services for each dollar it spends on healthcare services. On the other hand, OECD countries, which spend far less on healthcare per citizen, spend $1.70 on average on social services for each healthcare dollar. Based on this evidence, some believe that the United States could lower its healthcare costs by investing more in social services to prevent disease and related expenditures (Butler 2016).

NEW DISEASES

In addition to meeting the current challenges of healthcare in the United States and around the world, countries and healthcare systems must also anticipate new diseases whose source and timing are uncertain. For example, antibiotic-resistant infections have already become a serious concern. Because bacteria are constantly mutating, existing antibiotics may eventually become ineffective; this has already occurred with infectious diseases such as gonorrhea and tuberculosis. In 2018, more than 2 million Americans became infected with antibiotic-resistant germs, and 23,000 die from these infections each year (Scutti 2018).

The twenty-first century already has seen global outbreaks of new diseases such as the bird flu, Zika, Ebola, and COVID-19. Many of these diseases originate in the exchange of bacteria or viruses from animals to people. For example, the bird flu (avian influenza, also known as H5N1) first spread from birds to humans in 2013 and has continued to resurface since them. The disease has been devastating to bird populations; in humans, it has a 40 percent mortality rate and has killed more than 600 people (Liu 2017; McKenna 2016). Zika, originally identified in Uganda, is a type of virus that mutates frequently and spreads from a species of mosquito. The virus, which causes severe birth defects, became an epidemic in Brazil in 2015 and 2016 and quickly extended to most of the Americas (Musso 2015). Ebola, a virus that is endemic in many African countries, exploded between 2014 and 2016, with fatalities ranging from 25 to 90 percent of those infected (WHO 2020). COVID-19 exploded across the globe in 2019 and 2020, which caused the World Health Organization (WHO) to declare a public health emergency of international concern. The virus is suspected to have originated in bat populations and can cause severe respiratory problems, especially among the elderly and infirm (CDC 2020a).

The United Nations has warned that other new diseases are likely to emerge and that a pandemic sweeping across the globe could kill up to 80 million people. Aside from waiting for a global disease that will kill many, the WHO is constantly battling epidemics across the world. Between 2011 and 2018, the WHO has worked to contain nearly 1,500 epidemics worldwide (Garrett 2019).

The WHO has identified a list of unknown diseases that require accelerated research (exhibit 1.10). The last disease on that list, labeled "Disease X," represents the next big epidemic, which will come from a completely unexpected source, a pathogen, or vector that is currently unknown. To prepare for Disease X, countries need to take the following steps (Lee 2018):

1. Improve surveillance systems to detect new diseases.

2. Increase access to healthcare to ensure that diseases are identified and controlled quickly.

3. Set aside funds to fight the next big disease.

4. Establish research and development systems to rapidly develop new vaccines and medications to combat emerging diseases.

5. Ensure that supply chain and delivery systems work for the distribution of vaccines and medications.

- Crimean-Congo hemorrhagic fever
- Ebola virus disease and Marburg virus disease
- Lassa fever
- Middle East respiratory syndrome (MERS) and severe acute respiratory syndrome (SARS)
- Nipah and henipaviral diseases
- Rift Valley fever
- Zika
- Disease X

Source: WHO (2019).

SUMMARY

The complicated system of healthcare in the United States has its roots in the early days of the nation, when healthcare was fragmented among a variety of unlicensed practitioners who may or may not have received formal medical training. During the late nineteenth and early twentieth centuries, healthcare professions, licensure, and hospitals gained prominence as scientific discoveries improved health outcomes and as organizations such as the American Medical Association (AMA) helped standardize medical education based on the recommendations of the Flexner Report. The creation of railroads, canals, telephones, and automobiles facilitated greater access to care by lowering the cost and time to obtain healthcare services.

These developments allowed more people to access healthcare and bolstered the central role of hospitals. By the early 1900s, most physicians were receiving their education in hospitals. Advances in medical technology for diagnosis and treatment required expensive equipment that was concentrated in hospitals. With the growth of hospitals, the roles of healthcare professionals became more clearly defined. Over time, funding for hospitals shifted from charitable organizations to patients, insurance companies, and employers.

The pharmaceutical industry also emerged during this period. By the middle of the twentieth century, laws had been passed to require prescriptions from physicians for designated drugs. Patent drugs with secret ingredients were eliminated, and the safety of drugs was regulated.

As the US healthcare system developed, the struggle to balance access, cost, and quality became apparent. These three dimensions, known as the "Iron Triangle" of Healthcare, are interrelated—that is, a change in one dimension necessarily affects the others.

The rising cost of healthcare, especially since the middle of the twentieth century, has put pressure on access and quality of care.

The struggle to balance access, cost, and quality becomes more difficult as Americans grow older and sicker. The United States, like most industrialized countries, has an aging population with ever more chronic illnesses. Obesity, which is linked to diabetes and other chronic diseases, affects almost one-third of US adults. As a result, the elderly and those with chronic diseases spend much more on healthcare services.

People of color have historically had more difficulty accessing healthcare services and health insurance. As a result, they have traditionally received lower-quality care and experienced worse health outcomes. African Americans and Hispanics/Latinos are more frequently covered by government healthcare programs, with Medicaid covering more than half of African American and Hispanic/Latino children. These groups also tend to have a higher incidence of behavioral health illness and chronic disease.

Research has shown that healthcare spending varies by geographic location. Higher costs for Medicare patients are tied to greater use of postacute services, while higher costs for private and commercial payers are attributable to higher prices.

Life expectancy in the United States reached a plateau in 2012 and has declined since then. Americans' life expectancy, at 78.6 years in 2016, is now well below that of other industrialized nations. The decline is the result of worse birth outcomes and higher injuries at birth; conditions such as obesity, diabetes, and heart disease, as well as drug overdose and homicide; and a weaker social support system. Countries with higher social support services appear to spend less money on healthcare services. In addition, unhealthy behaviors cause the onset and severity of chronic diseases. Almost 40 percent of disease, it is estimated, could be prevented by modifying bad habits.

In addition to these challenges, the United States—with the rest of the world—faces the threat of new diseases that could have serious effects on the healthcare system. Physicians are already seeing antibiotic-resistant infections. Other global outbreaks are expected, with new diseases originating in almost any location. The World Health Organization and other public health agencies are preparing for new, unknown diseases in the future.

QUESTIONS

1. How did improvements in transportation facilitate the expansion of healthcare in the United States?
2. Before the 1700s, how was the role of the physician distinguished from that of a surgeon or an apothecary?
3. How did the American Medical Association, along with local medical societies, help organize and standardize medical training?
4. What was the Flexner Report, and what changes resulted from it?
5. What was a "patent" medicine?

6. What are the three dimensions of the "Iron Triangle" of Healthcare? How are they related?
7. What are the three components of the IHI Triple Aim? How does the Triple Aim differ from the Iron Triangle of Healthcare?
8. What are two reasons why minorities have greater difficulty obtaining healthcare services and health insurance in the United States?
9. Why are costs for Medicare patients and for private and commercial payers higher in some parts of the country than in others?
10. What are some of the reasons for the decline in US life expectancy?
11. What can be done to prepare for new diseases in the future?

ASSIGNMENTS

1. Why does the United States spend so much more on healthcare? Read the following article: "Why Does the U.S. Spend So Much More on Healthcare? It's the Prices," *Modern Healthcare*, April 7, 2018, available at www.modernhealthcare.com/article/20180407/NEWS/180409939. Write a one-page essay that answers the following questions:
   a. What are some of the reasons for the healthcare spending gap between the United States and other countries?
   b. Why are healthcare administrative costs so much higher in the United States than in other countries?
   c. What actions does the author suggest to control US healthcare costs? If these actions are taken, what impact to you think they would have on healthcare quality and access?
2. How are companies such as Amazon and Walmart working to change the US healthcare system? Read the following article: "Amazon Could Do a Lot to Fix the U.S. Healthcare System—but Walmart Could Do More," CNBC, April 4, 2018, available at www.cnbc.com/2018/04/04/walmart-has-more-power-to-fix-us-health-care-system-than-walmart.html. Write a one-page essay explaining why Walmart might be more effective in changing the US healthcare system than Amazon.

CASES

NURSING AND PHYSICIAN POWER

Jim is a registered nurse who recently completed his degree. He took his first nursing job at University Specialty Hospital, where he was excited to contribute to improving the health of his patients.

On his first day after orientation, Jim was assigned to a medical floor with eight patients in his care. One of his patients, Flora, was quite ill, and Jim thought that he should contact her attending physician to change her medication. One of the other nurses cautioned him about calling her doctor, Dr. Tall, as he had a reputation of being rather short with nurses and quite arrogant. Jim felt that it was important for the medication administration to take place soon and, disregarding his colleague's advice, called Dr. Tall. Jim introduced himself and started telling the doctor about his suggested change in the medication. Jim was unable to finish, as Dr. Tall cut him off in the middle of a sentence and started yelling: "Understand—YOU DO NOT PRACTICE MEDICINE! Never question my orders!" The doctor hung up.

Jim was embarrassed and disappointed. He questioned why the doctor had such power over him and why he would not listen.

Discussion Questions

1. Based on what you learned in chapter 1, what historical developments shaped the dominant role that doctors play in healthcare?
2. What could Jim do the next time he encounters a problem with a patient?
3. What could Jim do to change the dynamic with Dr. Tall?

DIVERSITY IN HEALTHCARE

By 2020, more than half of US children will belong to a minority racial or ethnic group, and by 2060, this share will increase to 64 percent. At the same time, health professionals are transitioning to a more patient-centered model of care, as patients demand more personalized services and want to be comfortable with their healthcare providers and care teams. Although studies have shown that greater representation of minorities in healthcare professions improves access to care for those minority communities (NCSL 2014), only about 5 percent of doctors, dentists, and nurses now come from minority racial and ethnic groups.

Discussion Questions

1. What are some reasons why minorities lack equal representation in healthcare professions?
2. How might having more minorities in healthcare professions affect access to healthcare for those populations?
3. What actions would you take to improve opportunities for minorities to enter healthcare professions?

REFERENCES

American Hospital Association (AHA). 2020. "Fast Facts on U.S. Hospitals, 2020." Accessed March 3. www.aha.org/statistics/fast-facts-us-hospitals.

Amondson, C. 2013. "10 Dangerous Drugs Once Marketed as Medicine." Published April 8. www.bestmedicaldegrees.com/10-dangerous-drugs-once-marketed-as-medicine.

Artiga, S., and K. Orgera. 2019. "Key Facts on Health and Healthcare by Race and Ethnicity." Kaiser Family Foundation. Published November 12. www.kff.org/disparities-policy/report/key-facts-on-health-and-health-care-by-race-and-ethnicity/.

Bazar, E. 2018. "Without Obamacare Penalty, Think It'll Be Nice to Drop Your Plan? Better Think Twice." Kaiser Health News. Published December 5. https://khn.org/news/without-obamacare-penalty-think-itll-be-nice-to-drop-your-plan-better-think-twice/.

Berwick, D. W., T. W. Nolan, and J. Whittington. 2008. "The Triple Aim: Care, Health and Cost." *Health Affairs* 27 (3): 759–69.

Butler, S. M. 2016. "Social Spending, Not Medical Spending, Is Key to Health." Brookings Institution. Published July 13. www.brookings.edu/opinions/social-spending-not-medical-spending-is-key-to-health/.

Callison, K., R. Kaestner, and J. Ward. 2018. "A Test of Supply-Side Explanations of Geographic Variation in Health Care Use." Vox. Published October 13. https://voxeu.org/article/explaining-geographic-variation-health-care-use.

Cannon, C. M. 2019. "Medicare for All Support Is High . . . but Complicated." RealClear Opinion Research. Published May 15. www.realclearpolitics.com/real_clear_opinion_research/new_poll_shows_health_care_is_voters_top_concern.html.

Carroll, A. 2012. "The 'Iron Triangle' of Healthcare: Access, Cost and Quality." news@JAMA. Published October 3. https://newsatjama.jama.com/2012/10/03/jama-forum-the-iron-triangle-of-health-care-access-cost-and-quality/.

Centers for Disease Control and Prevention (CDC). 2020a. "Coronavirus 2019 (COVID-19) Situation Summary." Updated March 9. www.cdc.gov/coronavirus/2019-nCoV/summary. html.

———. 2020b. *Morbidity and Mortality Weekly Report*. Accessed April 2. www.cdc.gov/ mmwr/index.html.

———. 2020c. "National Center for Chronic Disease Prevention and Health Promotion." Accessed March 10. www.cdc.gov/chronicdisease/about/index.htm.

Chappell, B. 2017. "Census Finds a More Diverse America, as Whites Lag Growth." National Public Radio, June 22. www.npr.org/sections/thetwo-way/2017/06/22/533926978/ census-finds-a-more-diverse-america-as-whites-lag-growth.

Child Trends. 2019. "Trends in Children's Health Care Coverage." Accessed October 6. www. childtrends.org/indicators/health-care-coverage.

Cohn, D., and A. Caumont. 2016. "10 Demographic Trends That Are Shaping the U.S. and the World." Pew Research Center. Published March 31. www.pewresearch.org/ fact-tank/2016/03/31/10-demographic-trends-that-are-shaping-the-u-s-and-the-world/.

Cunningham, P. J. 2018. "Income Disparities in the Prevalence, Severity, and Costs of Co-occurring Chronic and Behavioral Health Conditions." Commonwealth Fund. Published February 26. www.commonwealthfund.org/publications/in-the-literature/2018/feb/ income-disparities-chronic-behavioral-health.

Fisher, E., and J. Skinner. 2013. "Making Sense of Geographic Variation in Healthcare: The New IOM Report." *Health Affairs Blog*. Published July 24. www.healthaffairs.org/ do/10.1377/hblog20130724.033319/full/.

Galvin, G. 2018. "Population Health: The 'North Star' of the Triple Aim." *U.S. News & World Report*. Published May 25. www.usnews.com/news/healthiest-communities/ articles/2018-05-25/a-decade-later-triple-aim-health-care-framework-offers-lessons-promise.

Garrett, L. 2019. "The World Knows an Apocalyptic Pandemic Is Coming." *Foreign Policy*. Published September 20. https://foreignpolicy.com/2019/09/20/the-world-knows-an-apocalyptic-pandemic-is-coming/.

Gawande, A. 2009. "The Cost Conundrum." *New Yorker*. Published June 1. www.newyorker.com/magazine/2009/06/01/the-cost-conundrum.

Godfrey, T. 2012. "What Is the Iron Triangle of Healthcare?" *Penn Square Post*. Published March 3. http://pennsquarepost.com/what-is-the-iron-triangle-of-health-care/.

Gramlich, J. 2019. "What the Data Says About Gun Deaths in the U.S." Pew Research Center. Published August 15. www.pewresearch.org/fact-tank/2019/08/16/what-the-data-says-about-gun-deaths-in-the-u-s/.

Hayes, S. L., P. Riley, D. C. Radley, and D. McCarthy. 2017. "Reducing Racial and Ethnic Disparities in Access to Care: Has the Affordable Care Act Made a Difference?" Commonwealth Fund. Published August 24. www.commonwealthfund.org/publications/issue-briefs/2017/aug/racial-ethnic-disparities-care.

Herman, B. 2016. "The Striking Variation of Commercial Healthcare Prices." *Modern Healthcare*. Published April 27. www.modernhealthcare.com/article/20160427/NEWS/160429918.

Hill, C., M. Carroll, C. Fryar, and C. Ogden. 2020. "Prevalence of Obesity and Severe Obesity Among Adults: United States, 2017–2018." Centers for Disease Control and Prevention. National Center for Health Statistics Data Brief No. 360. Published February. www.cdc.gov/nchs/products/databriefs/db360.htm.

Hill, H., L. Elam-Evans, D. Yankey, J. Singleton, and V. Dietz. 2016. "Vaccination Coverage Among Children 15–39 Months, United States, 2015." *Morbidity and Mortality Weekly Report*. Published October 7. www.cdc.gov/mmwr/volumes/65/wr/mm6539a4.htm.

Howe, C. 2016. "How Bellevue Went from a Desolate New York Almshouse and Mental Hospital to Top Medical Facility." *Daily Mail*. Published November 22. www.dailymail.co.uk/news/article-3938852/How-Bellevue-went-desolate-New-York-almshouse-medical-facility.html.

Institute for Healthcare Improvement (IHI). 2020. "The IHI Triple Aim." Accessed June 1. www.ihi.org/Engage/Initiatives/TripleAim/Pages/default.aspx.

Institute of Medicine. 2013. *Variation in Healthcare Spending: Target Decision Making, Not Geography*. Washington, DC: National Academies Press.

———. 2001. *Crossing the Quality Chasm: A New Health System for the 21st Century*. Washington, DC: National Academies Press.

Johnson, T. 2017. "Analysis: Healthcare Should Be a Right, but the U.S. Doesn't Have a System." ABC News. Published November 23. http://abcnews.go.com/Health/analysis-health-care-us-system/story?id=51281693.

Kaiser Family Foundation. 2013. "Health Coverage by Race and Ethnicity: The Potential Impact of the Affordable Care Act." Published March 13. www.kff.org/disparities-policy/issue-brief/health-coverage-by-race-and-ethnicity-the-potential-impact-of-the-affordable-care-act/.

Kennedy, K., W. Johnson, S. Rodriguez, and N. Brennan. 2019. "Past the Price Index: Exploring Actual Prices Paid for Specific Services by Metro Area." Health Cost Institute. Published April 30. https://healthcostinstitute.org/in-the-news/hmi-2019-service-prices.

King, R. 2019. "Medicaid Enrollees Last in Line When Docs Accepting New Patients." *Modern Healthcare*. Published January 14. www.modernhealthcare.com/article/20190124/NEWS/190129962/medicaid-enrollees-last-in-line-when-docs-accepting-new-patients.

Kissick, W. 1994. *Medicine's Dilemmas: Infinite Needs Versus Finite Resources*. New Haven, CT: Yale University Press.

Lee, B. Y. 2018. "Disease X Is What May Become the Biggest Infectious Threat to Our World." *Forbes*. Published March 10. www.forbes.com/sites/brucelee/2018/03/10/disease-x-is-what-may-become-the-biggest-infectious-threat-to-our-world/#12e010be2cd7.

Liu, M. 2017. "Is China Ground Zero for a Future Pandemic?" *Smithsonian Magazine*. Published November. www.smithsonianmag.com/science-nature/china-ground-zero-future-pandemic-180965213/.

Macrotrends. 2020. "US Life Expectancy 1950–2020." Accessed June 1. www.macrotrends. net/countries/USA/united-states/life-expectancy.

Manchikanti, L., L. Helm, R. Benyamin, and J. Hirsch. 2017. "A Critical Analysis of Obamacare." *Pain Physician* 20 (3): 111–38.

Martinovich, M. 2017. "Significant Racial and Ethnic Disparities Still Exist, According to Stanford Report." *Stanford News*. Published June 16. https://news.stanford.edu/2017/06/16/report-finds-significant-racial-ethnic-disparities/.

McKenna, M. 2016. "The Looming Threat of Avian Flu." *New York Times*. Published April 17. www.nytimes.com/2016/04/17/magazine/the-looming-threat-of-avian-flu.html.

Meyer, H. 2019. "Medicaid, CHIP Enrollment for Kids Dropped by 840,000 in 2018." *Modern Healthcare*. Published April 25. www.modernhealthcare.com/government/medicaid-chip-enrollment-kids-dropped-840000-2018.

Mikulic, M. 2019. "Global Pharmaceutical Industry—Statistics & Facts." Statista. Published August 13. www.statista.com/topics/1764/global-pharmaceutical-industry/.

Musso, D. 2015. "Zika Virus Transmission from French Polynesia to Brazil." *Emerging Infectious Diseases* 21 (10): 1887.

National Conference of State Legislatures (NCSL). 2014. "Diversity in Healthcare Workshop." Published August. www.ncsl.org/documents/health/workforcediversity814.pdf.

National Institute on Drug Abuse. 2019. "Overdose Death Rates." Revised January. www.drugabuse.gov/related-topics/trends-statistics/overdose-death-rates.

Neuman, T., J. Cubanski, J. Huang, and A. Damico. 2015. "The Rising Cost of Living Longer: Analysis of Medicare Spending by Age for Beneficiaries in Traditional Medicare." Kaiser Family Foundation. Published January 14. www.kff.org/medicare/report/the-rising-cost-of-living-longer-analysis-of-medicare-spending-by-age-for-beneficiaries-in-traditional-medicare/.

O'Brien, S. 2019. "Health-Care Costs for Retirees Climb to $285,000." CNBC. Published April 2. www.cnbc.com/2019/04/02/health-care-costs-for-retirees-climb-to-285000.html.

Park, A. 2014. "Nearly Half of U.S. Deaths Can Be Prevented with Lifestyle Changes." *Time*. Published May 1. http://time.com/84514/nearly-half-of-us-deaths-can-be-prevented-with-lifestyle-changes/.

Pew Research Center. 2015. "Immigration's Impact on Past and Future U.S. Population Change." Published September 28. www.pewresearch.org/hispanic/2015/09/28/chapter-2-immigrations-impact-on-past-and-future-u-s-population-change/.

Rahalkar, H. 2012. "Historical Overview of Pharmaceutical Industry and Drug Regulatory Affairs." *Pharmaceutical Regulatory Affairs* S11-002. https://doi.org/10.4172/2167-7689.S11-002.

Renee, J. 2018. "The Average Calorie Intake by a Human per Day Versus the Recommendation." *San Francisco Chronicle*. Published December 2. https://healthyeating.sfgate.com/average-calorie-intake-human-per-day-versus-recommendation-1867.html.

Rutledge, G., K. Lane, C. Merlo, and J. Elmi. 2018. "Coordinated Approaches to Strengthen State and Local Public Health Actions to Prevent Obesity, Diabetes, and Heart Disease and Stroke." *Public Health Research Practice and Policy* 15 (E14): 1–7. www.cdc.gov/pcd/issues/2018/pdf/17_0493.pdf.

Sawyer, B., and G. Claxton. 2019. "How Do Health Expenditures Vary Across the Population?" Peterson-KFF Health System Tracker. Published January 16. www.healthsystemtracker.org/chart-collection/health-expenditures-vary-across-population/#item-start.

Scutti, S. 2018. "Unusual Forms of 'Nightmare' Antibiotic Resistant Bacteria Detected in 27 States." CNN. Published April 3. www.cnn.com/2018/04/03/health/nightmare-bacteria-cdc-vital-signs/index.html.

———. 2017. "4 Reasons Why U.S. Healthcare Is So Expensive." CNN. Published November 7. www.cnn.com/2017/11/07/health/health-care-spending-study/index.html.

Shahbandeh, M. 2019. "Total Number of Retail Prescriptions Filled Annually in the U.S." Statista. Published November 12. www.statista.com/statistics/261303/total-number-of-retail-prescriptions-filled-annually-in-the-us.

Starr, P. 1982. *The Social Transformation of American Medicine*. New York: Basic Books.

Statista. 2020. "Top 10 Causes of Death in the U.S. in 1900 and 2018 (per 100,000)." Accessed June 1. www.statista.com/statistics/235703/major-causes-of-death-in-the-us/.

———. 2019. "U.S. National Health Expenditure as Percent of GDP from 1960 to 2019." Accessed June 1, 2020. www.statista.com/statistics/184968/us-health-expenditure-as-percent-of-gdp-since-1960/.

Turow, J. 2010. *Playing Doctor: Television, Storytelling and Medical Power*. Ann Arbor: University of Michigan Press.

US Census Bureau. 2019. "Quick Facts." Accessed June 1, 2020. www.census.gov/quickfacts/fact/table/US/RHI225218#RHI225218.

———. 1993. "Population: 1790 to 1990." Accessed March June 1, 2020. www.census.gov/population/censusdata/table-4.pdf.

Venosa, A. 2016. "History of the Pharmacy: How Prescription Drugs Began and Transformed into What We Know Today." *Medical Daily*. Published March 16. www.medicaldaily.com/pharmacy-prescription-drugs-378078.

Weiner, J., C. Marks, and M. Pauly. 2017. "Effects of the ACA on Healthcare Cost Containment." Issue Brief, University of Pennsylvania, Leonard Davis Institute of Health Economics. Published March 2. https://ldi.upenn.edu/brief/effects-aca-health-care-cost-containment.

Whicher, D., K. Rosengren, S. Siddiqi, and L. Simpson (eds.). 2018. *The Future of Health Services Research: Advancing Health Systems Research and Practice in the United States*. Washington, DC: National Academy of Medicine. https://nam.edu/wp-content/uploads/2018/11/The-Future-of-Health-Services-Research_web-copy.pdf.

Woolf, S., and L. Aron. 2018. "Failing Health of the United States." *BMJ* 360: k496.

World Health Organization (WHO). 2020. "Ebola Virus Disease: Fact Sheet." Updated February 10. www.who.int/mediacentre/factsheets/fs103/en/.

——. 2019. "Prioritizing Diseases for Research and Development in Emergency Contexts." Accessed March 3, 2020. www.who.int/blueprint/priority-diseases/en/.

CHAPTER 2

HEALTHCARE PROFESSIONS

Many different types of professionals participate in taking care of our health. Physicians, nurses, respiratory therapists, nurse aides, lab workers, radiology technicians, clergy members, social workers, and other professionals visit and care for patients. Behind the scenes, law enforcement personnel, carpenters, housekeepers, engineers, computer scientists, educators, chefs, accountants, and many other professionals provide direct and indirect support to patients as well. As the US population ages, the demand for healthcare and those who provide it will only continue to grow. "The U.S. will need to hire 2.3 million new healthcare workers by 2025 in order to adequately take care of its aging population, a new report finds. But a persistent shortage of skilled workers—from nurses to physicians to lab technicians—will mean hundreds of thousands of positions will remain unfilled" (Kavilanz 2018).

The aging of the healthcare workforce will require replacements with new healthcare experts in all areas (Harrington and Heidkamp 2013; Institute of Medicine 2008).

◆ By 2020, nearly half of all registered nurses reached traditional retirement age.

◆ Nearly one-quarter of physicians in 2007 nationwide were 60 or older.

◆ In 2001, more than 80 percent of dentists in the United States were older than 45.

LEARNING OBJECTIVES

After reading this chapter, you will be able to

➤ Describe key clinical care personnel, their educational requirements, and their median salaries.

➤ Identify some of the careers in allied health professions.

➤ Compare the educational requirements of healthcare professionals in administrative (nonclinical) positions.

➤ Understand the future demand for and growth of health professions.

Healthcare occupations are among the fastest-growing jobs in the United States, projected to increase 18 percent from 2016 to 2026. Over that ten-year period, about 2.4 million new jobs are expected to be created. A 2018 study conducted by the global healthcare consulting firm Mercer reported that by 2025, the United States will face an estimated shortage of 446,300 home health aides, 98,700 medical and lab technologists and technicians, 95,000 nursing assistants, and 29,400 nurse practitioners.

The healthcare workforce encompasses a wide variety of careers, employing more than 18 million people in relatively well-paying jobs. According to the US Bureau of Labor Statistics, median wages for workers in the healthcare industry tend to be higher compared with the entire US workforce (BLS 2020). Healthcare jobs can be divided into two categories: clinical care positions and administrative positions, both of which are explored in this chapter.

CLINICAL CARE POSITIONS

PHYSICIANS

A physician in the United States typically completes one of two types of clinical training. Most physicians attend an allopathic medical school and graduate as a doctor of medicine (MD), while a smaller number attend an osteopathic medical school and graduate as a doctor of osteopathic medicine (DO). Graduates of both types of schools are licensed to practice medicine in the United States. Both groups are similarly educated and certified, but they are distinguished by differences in their training and their philosophies of treatment, which are explained here.

More than 90 percent of physicians in the United States practice **allopathic medicine**. These physicians receive a doctor of medicine degree and are designated as medical doctors, or MDs (Salsberg and Erikson 2017). As discussed in chapter 1, during the early twentieth century, doctors came from different backgrounds in terms of their education, philosophy, and perspective on medicine. However, after the publication of the Flexner Report in 1910 (discussed in chapter 1), most medical schools became standardized as allopathic teaching institutions. Allopathic medicine, also called "conventional" or "mainstream" medicine, refers to healing through opposites. It focuses on treating disease through medication, surgery, or other interventions. For example, if a person has swelling and too much water in the body, an appropriate treatment would be a drug that increases urination. This system of medicine became known for using treatments that had scientific value. Of the 25,955 medical school graduates in 2018, 19,533 completed

allopathic medicine
A system of medical practice that focuses on treating disease through medication, surgery, or other interventions; also called *conventional medicine* or *mainstream medicine*.

allopathic medical education, while 6,402 graduated from osteopathic medical schools (Kaiser Family Foundation 2018).

osteopathic medicine
A system of medicine that originated in the manipulation of the musculoskeletal system and that emphasizes preventive medicine while taking a holistic approach to health.

Osteopathic medicine, although it is not recognized in many countries outside the United States, is one of the fastest-growing healthcare professions. These physicians are designated as doctors of osteopathic medicine, or DOs. Most DOs serve in primary care, which includes family medicine, internal medicine, and pediatrics. About 44 percent of DOs specialize in emergency medicine, general surgery, obstetrics and gynecology, anesthesiology, and psychiatry (American Osteopathic Association 2018). Like their MD counterparts, they are licensed to perform surgery and prescribe medications.

Dr. Andrew Taylor Still, a physician in Kansas, is credited with developing the philosophy of osteopathic medicine in the 1870s. Osteopathic medicine is grounded in the view that all of the body's systems are interrelated and dependent on one another for good health. Still advocated the idea of preventive medicine and taught physicians to focus on treating the whole patient, not just the disease. He believed in using osteopathic manipulative medicine to allow the body to better heal itself. Today, DOs provide comprehensive medical care throughout the United States. Like their MD colleagues, DOs are healthcare policy leaders at all levels of government and pursue careers in medical research (American Association of Colleges of Osteopathic Medicine 2020).

MDs made up 91.3 percent of actively licensed physicians in the United States in 2016, while DOs accounted for 8.5 percent. More than 75 percent of licensed physicians were graduates of medical schools in the United States and Canada, while around 23 percent received training from a school elsewhere in the world (Young et al. 2017).

primary care physician (PCP)
A physician who typically serves as the first contact for patients with basic medical needs; treats acute and chronic ailments and illnesses; and focuses on health promotion, disease prevention, health maintenance, and counseling. PCPs primarily practice family medicine, internal medicine, and pediatrics.

Primary care physicians (PCPs) are typically the first contact for patients with basic medical needs. They practice family medicine, internal medicine, and pediatrics. Some insurers also identify gynecologists as PCPs, while others include geriatric physicians. These doctors treat a variety of ailments and illnesses, both acute and chronic. They also focus on health promotion, disease prevention, health maintenance, and counseling. PCPs practice in private offices, hospitals, long-term care facilities, home care agencies, and other settings (American Academy of Family Physicians 2020a).

Data from the Kaiser Family Foundation on state licensing in the United States (see exhibit 2.1) in March 2020 report more internal medicine physicians (199,683) than any other specialty. The second-largest group is family practice physicians (141,417), followed by pediatricians (89,168) and obstetric and gynecology physicians (54,718) (Kaiser Family Foundation 2020). The data show very few geriatricians (1,419). The aging US population is expected to demand more care in the future,

A 2018 snapshot report in *USA Today* indicated that Washington, DC, had the highest number of physicians per residents in the United States, at 8.24 per 1,000. In comparison, the Association of American Medical Colleges reported in 2019 that the total rate for the United States was 2.8 physicians per 1,000 population.

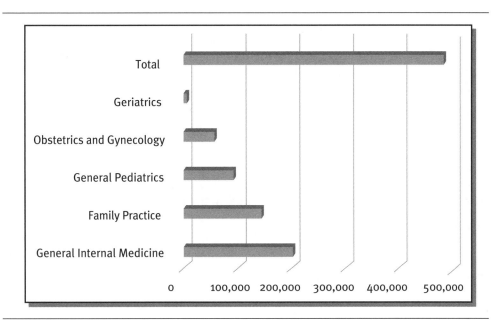

EXHIBIT 2.1
Active Primary
Care Physicians by
Specialty, March
2020

Source: Kaiser Family Foundation (2020).

however, and by 2030, the country is expected to face a shortage of PCPs. Estimates suggest that between 8,700 and 43,100 more primary care doctors will be needed (Mann 2017).

While PCPs are often the first providers to treat patients, medical and surgical specialists treat a variety of specific illnesses and injuries. Diagnostic specialists focus on identifying conditions, diseases, and injuries.

Medical specialists include, but are not limited to, cardiologists (dealing with diseases of the heart and blood vessels), dermatologists (skin), emergency medicine specialists, endocrinologists (hormones and metabolism), gastroenterologists (stomach, bowels, pancreas, liver, and gallbladder), hospitalists (inpatient care), infectious disease specialists, nephrologists (kidneys), neurologists (brain and nervous system), oncologists (cancer), ophthalmologists (eyes), otolaryngologists (ear, nose, and throat), palliative care specialists (pain management and hospice care), podiatrists (feet), proctologists (anal and rectal diseases), psychiatrists (mental and behavioral disorders), pulmonologists (lungs), rehabilitation specialists, rheumatologists (rheumatism, arthritis, and other disorders of the joints, muscles, and ligaments), and urologists (urinary tract).

Surgical specialists include anesthesiologists (physicians who administer local or general anesthesia during surgery), cardiovascular surgeons (heart surgery), general surgeons, neurosurgeons (surgery on the brain and nervous system), oral surgeons (surgery on the teeth, mouth, and jaw), orthopedic surgeons (bones, joints, ligaments, tendons and muscles), plastic surgeons (cosmetic and reconstructive surgery), transplant surgeons (organ transplants), and vascular surgeons (surgery on the arteries and veins).

Finally, pathologists (physicians who examine bodily tissues and fluids) and radiologists (physicians who examine X-rays and other imaging tests) are physicians who diagnose disease and injury. Exhibit 2.2 reports the number of physicians in non–primary care specialties in the United States in 2015.

In 2015, the United States had 153 allopathic medical schools (Association of American Medical Colleges 2020) and 36 osteopathic medical schools (American Association of

EXHIBIT 2.2

Number of Physicians in Non–Primary Care Specialties, 2015

Specialty	Total Active Physicians
Anesthesiology	41,351
Psychiatry	37,736
Radiology	27,522
General surgery	25,254
Cardiovascular disease	22,058
Orthopedic surgery	19,145
Ophthalmology	18,593
Hematology and oncology	14,476
Gastroenterology	14,126
Neurology	13,392
Pathology	13,286
Dermatology	11,706
Critical care medicine	10,158
Nephrology	10,083
Urology	9,808
Ear, nose, and throat (otolaryngology)	9,411
Physical medicine and rehabilitation	9,164
Child and adolescent psychiatry	8,736
Infectious disease	8,515
Plastic surgery	7,020
Endocrinology	6,968

Source: Data from Association of American Medical Colleges (2015).

Colleges of Osteopathic Medicine 2020). Medical students typically complete a bachelor's degree and then a four-year program of study at a medical school. Many hours of medical school are completed in clinical settings working with patients. After medical school—depending a student's chosen specialty—most physicians spend at least three years in a residency program, and some complete more specialized fellowships. Family physicians, for example, complete a three-year residency program after medical school (American Academy of Family Physicians 2020b). Cardiac or heart surgeons require more training, typically completing a five-year general surgery residency and then a two- to three-year specialized cardiac or cardiothoracic fellowship.

Wages for physicians and surgeons are among the highest of all occupations, according to the Bureau of Labor Statistics. Exhibit 2.3 shows the median annual compensation for selected healthcare specialties in the United States in 2017.

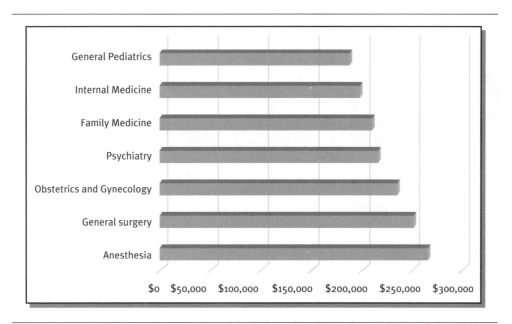

EXHIBIT 2.3
Median Annual Compensation for Selected Healthcare Specialties in the United States, 2017

Source: Data from US Bureau of Labor Statistics, *Occupational Outlook Handbook*, 2018.

PHYSICIAN EXTENDERS

In the 1980s, the term **physician extender** was introduced to identify nonphysician providers who perform medical activities typically done by physicians. Nurse practitioners, physician assistants, and certified nurse midwives, in particular, practice in a variety of healthcare settings alongside or sometimes geographically quite distant from physicians.

physician extender
A healthcare provider who is not a physician but performs medical activities typically done by a physician; most physician extenders are nurse practitioners or physician assistants.

A *nurse practitioner (NP)* is an advanced practice registered nurse who can examine patients, diagnose illnesses, prescribe medicines, and provide treatment. Twenty-eight US states allow NPs "full practice authority," or the license to practice without the supervision of a doctor (Rappleye 2019) (see sidebar).

✴ PRACTICE SCOPE OF NURSE PRACTITIONERS

Each US state defines the practice authority of nurse practitioners (American Association of Nurse Practitioners 2018):

- *Full practice.* State law licenses NPs to evaluate, diagnose, treat, and prescribe on their own.

- *Reduced practice.* State law requires NPs to work with a physician to provide patient care and limits some of what they do.

- *Restricted practice.* State law requires supervision, delegation, or team management by a physician to provide patient care.

According to a Kaiser Family Foundation report, NPs can manage 80 to 90 percent of the care typically provided by PCPs, with comparable care outcomes. Typically, NPs earn a bachelor's degree from a four-year college or university and then complete a master's degree. These providers can help meet the increasing demand for primary care (Van Vleet and Paradise 2015).

NPs hold advanced degrees, either a master of science in nursing (MSN) or a doctor of nursing practice (DNP). Individual states license these providers and have different requirements for national certification and the nature or specialization of education needed. Typically, NPs focus on one or more patient populations, such as families and individuals across the life span, pediatrics, adult geriatrics, neonatal care, women's health, or mental health (*Nurse Journal* 2020b). The DNP is a terminal professional degree in nursing, along with the doctor of nursing (ND), doctor of nursing science (DNSc), and doctor of nursing philosophy (PhD) degrees. NPs must complete 100 hours of continuing education and 1,000 clinical hours every five years (American Association of Nurse Practitioners 2020).

More than 248,000 NPs are licensed in the United States, and nearly 87 percent are certified in an area of primary care. They work in hospitals, clinics, private group practices, long-term care facilities, and psychiatric and mental health clinics. In 2017, the mean full-time base salary for an NP was $105,500 (American Association of Nurse Practitioners 2020).

A *physician assistant (PA)* is a medical professional who can diagnose illness, determine the appropriate treatment for patients, and prescribe medications. Some individuals choose PAs as their principal healthcare providers. PAs work in a variety of settings, including hospitals and clinics (American Academy of Physician Assistants 2020) (see sidebar).

More than 123,000 PAs are practicing in all 50 states and Washington, DC. About 12 percent of PAs work in rural settings, most of whom practice primary care. PAs tend to have a wider scope of practice and often see uninsured individuals or those covered by Medicaid or Medicare. Rural patients seen by PAs frequently have chronic conditions (Cawley et al. 2016).

 PHYSICIAN ASSISTANTS: A Growing Profession

Between 2010 and 2016, the number of certified physician assistants grew 44 percent, and according to the US Department of Labor, employment for PAs will likely increase 31 percent between 2018 and 2024. The number of nurse practitioners is also expected to grow, from 128,000 in 2008 to 244,000 by 2025 (Young et al. 2017). In 2020, *U.S. News & World Report* rated physician assistant as the third-best job in the United States (Roberson 2020).

PAs hold master's degrees, completing programs that typically take three years and include 2,000 hours or more of clinical rotations. These rotations include family medicine, internal medicine, general surgery, pediatrics, obstetrics and gynecology, emergency medicine, and psychiatry. They are trained as medical generalists (American Academy of Physician Assistants 2020).

In most cases, state medical boards regulate and license PAs. Five states—Arizona, Iowa, Massachusetts, Rhode Island, and Utah—have separate PA board exams. PAs must complete 100 hours of continuing medical education every two years and recertify every ten years.

In 2016, the median salary for a PA was $101,480, while the highest-paid PAs made $142,210 (*U.S. News & World Report* 2018). In 2019, the median salary grew to $112,260. The number of jobs for PAs is predicted to grow 31 percent between 2018 and 2028—much faster than the average for all occupations (BLS 2020).

Nurse midwives are advanced practice registered nurses who specialize in the management of women's reproductive health and the care of women during pregnancy, labor, and childbirth. In 2020, there were 40 accredited schools for nurse midwives in the United States. After finishing their education (typically an MSN), nurses take an exam to become a certified nurse midwife. Nurse midwives earn salaries between $90,000 and $100,000 per year and often work in private birthing centers, hospitals, and clinics. Some also participate in home births. In 2020, there were more than 12,000 certified nurse midwives in the United States, who attended more than 330,000 births, most occurring in hospitals (American Midwifery Certification Board 2020; *Nurse Journal* 2020c).

The ability to practice varies by state law. Twenty-four states allow certified nurse midwives to practice independently without physician supervision. Across the United

States, about 8 percent of births are delivered by certified nurse midwives. However, in three states (Alaska, New Mexico, and Vermont), more than 20 percent of births are attended by certified nurse midwives. To highlight the importance of this profession, the World Health Organization designated 2020 as the Year of the Nurse and Midwife (Martin et al. 2018; Vedam et al. 2018).

NURSES

Nurses are the backbone of healthcare. Nurses can be divided into two categories: *registered nurses (RNs)* and *licensed practical nurses (LPNs)*. Nursing is the biggest and most diverse of the healthcare professions, with more than 3 million RNs and nearly 730,000 LPNs in the United States (BLS 2020). Nurses have responsibility for providing continuous care for the sick and injured in a wide variety of settings. Nurses are also actively involved in health policy, research, quality improvement, patient rights, and management.

Florence Nightingale is undoubtedly the most famous nurse, and she is credited with establishing the tradition of educating and training nurses using scientific principles. In 1854, the British government asked Nightingale and a small group of nurses to visit a military hospital in what is now Turkey. She learned of their practices of sanitizing hospital rooms, providing patients with nourishing food, and efficiently administering medications and treatments. Within weeks of her return to Britain, soldiers there fared much better. Death rates plummeted, and soldiers no longer suffered from infectious diseases associated with poor sanitary conditions.

Until the second half of the twentieth century, most nurses were trained in hospitals, which had their own nursing schools; now, however, most nurses are trained in nursing programs at colleges and universities. Today, nearly 2,000 basic RN programs exist in the United States (National League for Nursing 2018). The training offered in these programs differs. Some programs offer one year of coursework and clinical experience, after which students can take a state-required test and apply for a license. Those individuals can go on to complete a second year of study and clinical practice, take another exam, and become a registered nurse. They typically receive an associate's degree in nursing (ADN). Most states have agreements that allow nurses to practice in a number of states after completing their study and exams. An LPN or RN who receives a license to practice in Utah, for example, may practice in 25 other states (National Council of State Boards of Nursing 2020).

LPNs are known in some states (e.g., California and Texas) as *licensed vocational nurses*. They practice in a number of settings, such as schools, home health care agencies, nursing homes and other long-term care facilities, physician offices and private practices, private hospitals, universities, and other facilities.

Beyond the two-year RN license, a number of schools in the United States offer a bachelor's degree in nursing (BSN), which requires two to three years of additional education after the ADN. Some programs skip the ADN and require students to complete the BSN degree (*Nurse Journal* 2020a). Online education programs are also available for those who have been practicing as an RN for a number of years and want to complete the BSN.

Arguments exist for the necessity of both two-year and the four-year RN degrees. Practically, it comes down to what employers—or, in some cases, states—require. For instance, in 2017, New York State passed a "BSN in 10" law, requiring all nurses to obtain a BSN within ten years of receiving their initial RN license. This law was passed in response to a 2010 recommendation by the Institute of Medicine that 80 percent of the nursing workforce should hold a BSN by 2020 (Mararac 2017). Many US hospitals plan to hire only nurses with at least a BSN, but most healthcare organizations do not distinguish between two-year and four-year degrees in terms of salary and promotion (Coutre 2016).

In 2019, median pay for LPNs was $47,480 per year, and the profession is projected to grow 11 percent between 2018 and 2028. The median pay for RNs was $73,300 per year in 2019, and their job outlook was slightly better, projected to grow 12 percent during the same ten-year period (BLS 2020).

ALLIED HEALTH PROFESSIONALS

The Association of Schools of Allied Health Professions (2020) defines allied health professionals as "concerned with the identification, diagnostic evaluation, and treatment of acute and chronic diseases and disorders; provision of dietary and nutrition services; rehabilitation services; and the management and operation of health systems."

Allied health professionals include, but are not limited to, anesthesia technologists, audiologists, medical and clinical laboratory technologists, dental hygienists, dietitians, emergency medical technicians, exercise physiologists, lactation consultants, nuclear medicine technologists, occupational therapists, providers of orthotics and prosthetics, physical therapists, radiation therapists, radiologists, respiratory therapists, speech-language pathologists, and vocational rehabilitation counselors. Exhibit 2.4 lists some of these allied health professions, their educational requirements, and median pay in the United States.

As indicated in exhibit 2.4, allied health occupations can be categorized, roughly, into those who help diagnose diseases or injuries, those who treat diseases or injuries, and those who support the treatment or prevention of diseases or injuries. Experts in radiology, diagnostic imaging, and medical laboratory sciences, for example, are healthcare "detectives" who work to identify an injury or determine a patient's disease. Occupational, physical, and respiratory therapists, along with speech-language pathologists, often assess and treat diseases and injuries. Dental hygienists and dieticians both treat diseases and help prevent more extensive disease.

Exhibit 2.4
Allied Health
Occupations in the
United States

Occupation	Job Summary	Entry-Level Education	2019 Median Pay
Audiologist	Work on patients' hearing, balance, or ear problems	Doctoral or professional degree	$77,600
Dental hygienist	Clean teeth, look for oral diseases, and provide preventive care	Associate's degree	$76,220
Diagnostic medical sonographer	Operate special imaging equipment to help physicians diagnose problems	Associate's degree	$68,750
Dietitian	Experts in nutrition who advise people on what to eat to promote wellness or cope with medical conditions	Bachelor's degree	$61,270
Emergency medical technician or paramedic	Care for the sick and injured in emergency medical settings	Postsecondary nondegree award	$35,400
Health information technologist	Organize and manage health information data, using classification systems to code and categorize patient information	Postsecondary nondegree award or associate's degree	$42,630
Medical/clinical laboratory technologist	Collect samples and perform tests to analyze body fluids, tissue, and other substances	Associate's or bachelor's degree	$53,120
Nuclear medicine technologist	Prepare radioactive drugs and administer them to patients for imaging	Associate's degree	$77,950
Occupational therapist	Treat injured, ill, or disabled people through the therapeutic use of daily activities	Master's degree	$84,950

(continued)

Exhibit 2.4
Allied Health
Occupations in the
United States
(*continued*)

Occupation	Job Summary	Entry-Level Education	2019 Median Pay
Pharmacist	Dispense prescription medications and offer advice on the safe use of prescriptions	Doctoral or professional degree	$128,090
Physical therapist	Help injured or ill people improve their movement and manage pain	Doctoral or professional degree	$89,440
Radiation therapist	Treat cancer and other diseases in patients with radiation treatments	Associate's degree	$85,560
Respiratory therapist	Care for people with breathing problems, from infants to the elderly	Associate's degree	$61,330
Speech-language pathologist	Assess, diagnose, treat, and help prevent communication and swallowing problems in children and adults	Master's degree	$79,120

Source: BLS (2020).

(✳) DEBATE TIME Changing Practice Requirement for Healthcare Professionals

Entry-to-practice requirements are changing for many health professionals. Registered nurses now need at least a bachelor's degree. Physiotherapists and other types of therapists must have a master's degree. Some professions prefer a doctoral degree for licensing. These greater educational requirements are not always popular with professionals who are already practicing or their employers. Some argue that the higher level of education is not necessary, while others believe that the complexity of healthcare warrants increased education and training.

Form a team and debate the merits and challenges of mandating advanced degrees in healthcare. Consider patient outcomes, cost, time, staff retention, rural health, and other issues.

INTERPROFESSIONAL HEALTHCARE TEAMS

Healthcare is a team sport. As illustrated in the sidebar, collaboration among interdisciplinary teams often is necessary to diagnose and treat complex illnesses or injuries. As early as the 1970s, the Institute of Medicine identified the importance of team-based patient care and its role in patient safety and health outcomes (Institute of Medicine 1972, 2001). *Interprofessional practice and education* is the term that is used to describe two or more professions working and learning together in an educational or clinical setting. These teams include many of the professionals discussed in this chapter. In some grassroots efforts, they also include patients and their communities (Wood 2012).

✱ HEALTHCARE IS A TEAM SPORT

In 1981, Ned traveled abroad with a group of dancers. In a hurry one day, he brushed his teeth using the tap water in his room rather than the bottled water offered by the hotel. By the time the group left two weeks later, Ned's hands and feet hurt so badly that he could hardly move. The trip back to the United States was long and uncomfortable.

Ned lost a significant amount of weight over the next few weeks. After seeing his doctor, he checked into a regional academic medical center for care. Medical students, interns, residents, and Ned's attending physician visited him often during the few days he was there. Nurses cared for him. Lab workers drew blood for diagnostic tests. Housekeepers and dietary workers were also part of Ned's care team.

Only after Ned started feeling better and left the hospital did the answers come back from the labs and physicians—Ned had contracted a water-borne parasite during his trip.

Often, physicians and nurses come to mind when the public thinks about healthcare. Ned's care was provided by a variety of professionals, all of whom are vital to healthcare. In his case, support came in the form of treating symptoms, expressing concern, providing food that tasted good, keeping his room clean and bright, and asking the right questions. To be successful, healthcare involves a team of professionals.

The Affordable Care Act of 2010 created incentives for interprofessional teams to focus on value-based care, as opposed to the traditional fee-for-service model on which healthcare was built. The act created two new types of organizations: accountable care organizations (ACOs) and patient-centered medical homes (PCMHs) (discussed in chapter 3). Both ACOs and PCMHs focus directly on patients and use care coordinators to coach patients and promote communication among healthcare providers during the entire process of care. Care teams have opportunities for consultation and education. ACOs receive financial incentives for teamwork leading to better health outcomes.

Higher education today supports interprofessional education. Schools and health providers are creating opportunities for students in different medical programs to work and learn together. In 2009, the leading health-related associations formed the Interprofessional Education Collaborative (IPEC) to promote learning experiences in team-based care (IPEC 2020). Members of IPEC include the following organizations:

◆ Academy of Nutrition and Dietetics

◆ American Association of Colleges of Nursing

◆ American Association of Colleges of Osteopathic Medicine

◆ American Association of Colleges of Pharmacy

◆ American Association of Colleges of Podiatric Medicine

◆ American Association for Respiratory Care

◆ American Council of Academic Physical Therapy

◆ American Dental Education Association

◆ American Occupational Therapy Association

◆ American Psychological Association

◆ American Speech-Language-Hearing Association

◆ Association of Academic Health Sciences Libraries

◆ Association of American Medical Colleges

◆ Association of American Veterinary Medical Colleges

◆ Association of Chiropractic Colleges

◆ Association of Schools and Colleges of Optometry

◆ Association of Schools and Programs of Public Health

◆ Association of Schools of Allied Health Professions

◆ Council on Social Work Education

◆ National League for Nursing

◆ Physician Assistant Education Association

Developing, implementing, and assessing interprofessional education, however, presents a number of challenges. Traditionally, medical education has been fragmented into many separate disciplines. To create interprofessional education, training in these disciplines must be unified. However, changing curricula is difficult and costly. Although accrediting organizations for a variety of healthcare education programs now recognize the need for interprofessional teamwork, many still insist on course content, experiences, and competencies specific to each field of study. Educators find it difficult to add content to an already full plate.

In addition, universities rarely offer programs that represent the wide variety of healthcare workers and instead create interprofessional experiences that include only a handful of professions. Medical and nursing students, for example, may come together with a few other professions in an academic medical center. However, they may not include respiratory therapy, medical laboratory sciences, the rehabilitation sciences, or even pharmacy. Creating equal representation among disciplines and finding faculty who can teach across disciplines remains difficult (Schapmire et al. 2018).

ADMINISTRATIVE POSITIONS

Healthcare settings, especially large hospitals and healthcare systems, need a variety of support personnel who are not associated with providing clinical care. For example, network personnel maintain complex information systems. Likewise, housekeeping staff are responsible for ensuring that surgical rooms are sterile and free of infectious agents that might harm patients. Engineers design, build, and maintain specialized biomedical equipment. Security personnel keep buildings and the people in them safe. Executives and managers focus on efficiency, patient and staff safety, and strategic planning to ensure the success of the organization.

MANAGEMENT

Although one might not think of management as support staff, healthcare management spans multiple levels, beginning with frontline supervisors—those who work directly with patient and care providers—to mid-level managers, to senior executives at the local or facility level. In bigger systems, management includes regional managers and system-level senior executives. At the most senior level of leadership, both locally and nationally, governing boards of trustees and a medical executive, such as a chief medical officer, often exist. In some cases, the board is advisory, while in others, the board makes management decisions setting policy and selects and retains the hospital's chief executive officer. To become a successful healthcare leader, one must transition from being a doer of things to a motivator of others to achieve (see sidebar).

> ## ✱ BEING A HEALTHCARE LEADER   ·
>
> "When one becomes the senior leader of an organization, there is a big transition from a lifetime of being a 'doer' to accomplishing things through other people—effectively becoming the orchestra conductor. The real challenge is to find the best violinist, the best horn player, and the right people to perform in that orchestra and then give them the tools to do what they need to do and take pride and joy in the music that comes out."
>
> —*Marna P. Borgstrom, FACHE, president and CEO of Yale New Haven Health System and CEO of Yale New Haven Hospital, Connecticut (O' Connor 2014)*

The role of the hospital executive or *chief executive officer (CEO)* requires competencies in interpersonal skills, communication, information management, financial analysis, leadership, critical thinking, knowledge of the healthcare industry, policymaking, decision-making, strategic planning and more (Calhoun et al. 2002). The American College of Healthcare Executives divides these competencies into five key areas (ACHE 2020):

1. *Communication and relationship management* includes skills in relationship management, communication, facilitation, and negotiation.

2. *Leadership competencies* focus on behavior, organizational climate and culture, communicating a vision, and managing change.

3. *Professionalism* involves personal and professional accountability, continued learning, and contributions to the community and profession.

4. *Knowledge of the healthcare environment* suggests an executive would understand health systems and organizations, personnel, the patient's perspective, and the community.

5. *Business skills and knowledge* include general management, financial management, human resource management, organizational dynamics and governance, strategic planning and marketing, information management, risk management, quality improvement, and patient safety.

CEOs create a vision for the organization and promote it to key **stakeholders**, who are "individuals or groups that have some investment in an organization or obtain

stakeholder
An individual or group that has some investment in an organization or obtains some benefit from it.

some benefit from it" (Walston 2018, 119). CEOs work extensively with key stakeholders, including employees, physicians, community leaders, government officials, and board members. The *chief operating officer (COO)* and other mid-level executives have the primary responsibility for interpersonal roles and making sure the activity of the organization matches the strategic plan or vision.

The relationship between the CEO and the *chief medical officer (CMO)* is essential to the success of a healthcare organization. The CMO is the liaison between the administration and the physicians who practice at the medical facility. The director deals with issues of professionalism, quality of care, patient satisfaction, medical teaching, malpractice, equipment and capital, and strategic initiatives. Typically, the CMO is a physician who is recruited for his or her competencies and record of accomplishments. The CMO's primary focus is the welfare of patients and of the doctors, nurses, and other clinicians who care for them (Kossaify, Rasputin, and Lahoud 2013).

Healthcare executives at the senior level most often hold an advanced degree, such as a master of health administration (MHA), a master of business administration (MBA), or another master's degree. Some executives are physicians with a medical degree (MD or DO). Mid-level and frontline managers frequently have bachelor's degrees. Some have a clinical degree, such as a BSN, and may supervise a hospital department or medical clinic.

A 2019 *Business Insider* article reported the median annual salary of a hospital CEO at $242,550 (De Luce, Court, and Hoff 2020). CEOs of large healthcare systems make much more. In 2017, the salaries of the top executives at the leading 82 nonprofit healthcare systems averaged $3.5 million, with the highest-paid CEO making $21.6 million (Paavola 2019). Individuals who earn a bachelor's degree and manage a clinical area or department or even the medical practice of a group of physicians had a median salary of $98,350 in 2017 (BLS 2020).

Filling out the management team are experts in human resource management, health information technology and management, accounting and other financial services, community services, and population health.

SUPPORT SERVICES

Serving alongside the clinical experts and administrators are the many support teams that make up a healthcare system. These include a wide range of departments that are vital to managing the operational and business side of a healthcare organization, such as business and financial services, health information management, supply chain services, housekeeping and maintenance, security, and others.

Business and Finance

Healthcare systems, hospitals, nursing homes, and other large institutions have teams of individuals who work with patient records, determine the care or treatment they received, and submit bills to insurance plans and patients. They collect on accounts due, manage the funds received, and monitor the entire revenue cycle.

These revenue cycle operations are constantly changing, especially as high-deductible insurance plans and value-based reimbursement models become more common (Murphy 2017). Some healthcare organizations outsource such services to companies that have the resources to keep up with these changes. Many hospitals continue to employ such experts.

The business and finance workforce is made up of individuals with a variety of educational backgrounds, from a high school diploma to a graduate or master's degree, and their salaries vary accordingly. Often, business and finance staff members have a bachelor's degree in finance or accounting. Many healthcare administrative careerists get their start in this field.

The person who leads the business and finance area is generally called the *chief financial officer (CFO)* or the (executive) vice president for finance. The CFO manages all the financial and business office functions of a hospital or healthcare system and generally participates as a member of the senior leadership team.

Health Information Management

Once called medical records technology, health information management has evolved with the creation of electronic health records (EHRs). Typically, the *chief information officer (CIO)* or *chief technical officer (CTO)* oversees these and other health information technology (IT) systems within an organization. These individuals are not only technology experts—many of whom have advanced degrees—but also experienced innovators who are responsible for transforming health IT within organizations. Health information management today is moving away from the legacy IT infrastructures of the late twentieth century to what some call the four pillars of digital transformation, known as SMAC: social, mobile, analytics, and cloud computing (Sullivan and Miliard 2018) (see sidebar).

Health Informatics

Many healthcare providers provide health informatics, also known as health information systems support. These personnel use technology to aggregate and analyze data from health records to produce better health outcomes. Healthcare informatics bring together "healthcare sciences, computer science, information science, and cognitive science" to manage healthcare information (Sweeney 2017). Informatics specialists exist in many areas of healthcare, including pharmacy, nutrition, and nursing.

 **THE CLOUD**

IT continues to evolve, and one reason is the move to cloud computing. "Going out to the cloud for analytics, clinical decision support, EHRs, not to mention a raft of mobile apps and social networks, might seem like something everybody does nowadays but it's still a radically different model than IT departments packed with software architects and programmers building proprietary programs or keeping massive databases and enterprise apps up and running" (Sullivan and Miliard 2018).

Other Support Services

The workforce that is employed to keep facilities running varies from organization to organization. The maintenance of buildings and grounds is vital. Services such as waste management, laundry, and nutrition or food services are sometimes provided onsite and sometimes outsourced. The Centers for Disease Control and Prevention notes the important function of these services in infection control and patient safety. Everything from exhaust ventilation to cleaning spills to disinfecting of surgical rooms is vital (CDC 2019). Occupational safety experts work to prevent injuries to healthcare workers from the accidental poke of a contaminated needle or lifting a heavy patient from a bed to a wheelchair. They are responsible for ensuring that the buildings and equipment are safe, which includes adherence to life safety codes and fire protection. Security teams are common in today's hospitals to protect staff and patients from physical harm.

Education and experience in these services produce good leaders who run departments. Workers often receive on-the-job training. Some require professional licensure, as in the case of electricians, plumbers, and similar skilled trades workers.

SUMMARY

A variety of professionals put their skills and passions to work in healthcare. Jobs in healthcare have a wide range of educational requirements: While some occupations require only a high school education, others required many years of highly specialized training. Likewise, salaries range from minimum wage to six- or seven-figure incomes.

Jobs in healthcare can be divided into two categories: clinical care positions and administrative positions. Clinical care positions include physicians, physician extenders (nurse practitioners and physician assistants), nurses, and allied health professionals. These professionals all work directly with patients. Administrative positions include management and administration, business and finance, health information management, health informatics, and other support services, such as housekeeping, maintenance, and dietary services.

A diverse healthcare workforce requires teamwork and communication to provide high-quality patient care and ensure good health outcomes. To reinforce this need for cooperation, many schools and training programs have joined forces to give students interprofessional team experiences before they enter the workforce.

Healthcare occupations are among the fastest-growing jobs in the United States, projected to increase 18 percent from 2016 to 2026, according to the US Bureau of Labor Statistics. The aging of the US population will only increase the demand for healthcare. Clearly, the many professions within the health industry continue to be dynamic and growing, offering opportunities for many different individuals.

QUESTIONS

1. Give three examples of clinical professions and describe the tasks they perform.
2. What are the three types of physician extenders, and what are their roles?
3. Give three examples of allied health professions and describe the tasks they perform.
4. List a few examples of healthcare management positions and the responsibilities of each.
5. Outline the educational requirements for physicians, nurses, five allied health positions of your choice, a hospital CEO, and a chief medical officer.
6. Research current salaries for physicians, nurses, five allied health positions of your choice, and a hospital CEO. What accounts for the differences in their salaries?
7. Why is interprofessional teamwork important in healthcare?
8. What effect will the aging US population have on the demand for healthcare professionals?
9. How do the roles of the chief executive officer (CEO) and chief operating officer (COO) differ?
10. Describe the job of the chief medical officer. How does this position relate to the management of healthcare?

ASSIGNMENTS

1. Research a small hospital located in a rural setting and a larger one located in an urban setting. Compare and contrast the workforces of the two hospitals. Specifically, consider the following:
   a. What types of physicians (specialties) practice in the two facilities?
   b. Which support services are provided in house, and which are outsourced?
   c. How do the management structures of the two hospitals differ? List the top leadership positions and the number of department heads. Does each hospital have a medical director and a board of trustees?
2. Research a physician clinic that provides multiple services. What kinds of professions are employed in that clinic?
3. Describe the healthcare professions that meet the following criteria:
   a. Two years of college or less, takes care of patients
   b. High school education, takes care of patients (you might need to do a little research for this one)
   c. Many years of education, does not give direct patient care
   d. Training in a skilled trade, does not give direct patient care
   e. Works directly with patients and might be part of a team

CASES

OLIVIA'S STAFFING DILEMMA

Olivia is suffering from burnout. Dr. Kritcher has just left her office, complaining loudly that his nurse is gone. She is taking some vacation time, and he does not like "that other nurse" who is now working with him. She is unfamiliar with his way of doing things. He wants his nurse back!

Olivia has been the manager of a large outpatient center for only two years, and during that time, she has had to constantly deal with staffing issues. Hiring and retaining new staff is hard enough. Filling short-term vacancies because of vacations, staff illness, pregnancy or child care needs, and short-term disability is especially difficult. When workers are gone, she receives complaints from physicians and other staff members who are overworked. Overtime, in some cases, has led to high costs. She could use temporary help from float pools or groups of individuals who could fill in as needed, but this option is very expensive.

Olivia has some other options: She could hire extra staff and send them home when the patient load decreases. Another option would be to cross-train staff where possible. For example, a medical assistant could learn the duties of a receptionist or clerk.

Olivia is unsure what to do. She has a meeting scheduled with the clinic's CEO two days from now, and she wants to have a plan ready to present. She needs to show that she can maintain costs and still cover the clinic's patient care needs.

Discussion Questions

1. With a small group of classmates, discuss the staffing options open to Olivia. What are the pros and cons of each option?
2. What information does Olivia need when she meets with her supervisor?
3. How might Olivia reduce some of her job stress?

STAFFING A SKILLED NURSING FACILITY

When Conrad sat in his classes at the local university, he imagined that his job as a nursing home administrator would involve walking the floors and visiting with patients. His grandfather was currently in such a facility, and Conrad liked to visit him. He felt comfortable in that setting, and he was looking forward to his chosen career.

A year later, Conrad was in the middle of his Administrator-in-Training program, which involved 1,000 hours of on-the-job training required by his state for licensure. His training included experience in areas such as patient care, health maintenance, social and psychological needs, food service program, recreational and therapeutic recreational activities, medical records, pharmaceutical programs, personnel management, grievance procedures, personnel policies, and financial management. He learned a great deal about regulation and working with the many government agencies that survey nursing homes to keep them safe.

Conrad began to see that as an administrator, he would spend much of his time working with staff and addressing personnel needs. In particular, he learned that one of the biggest challenges in long-term care is staff turnover.

Discussion Questions

1. What types of healthcare professionals might be found in a skilled nursing facility? (Note: Chapter 5 of this book deals with long-term care.)
2. Why are turnover rates higher for some positions than others?
3. What would you do to decrease turnover rates among these staff members?

Challenge

Visit with a local nursing home administrator and find out what the biggest staffing challenges are. Find out how much time the administrator spends on recruiting new staff and what is done to retain them.

REFERENCES

American Academy of Family Physicians. 2020a. "Primary Care." Accessed March 5. www. aafp.org/about/policies/all/primary-care.html.

———. 2020b. "Training Requirements for Family Physicians." Accessed March 5. www. aafp.org/medical-school-residency/premed/training.html.

American Academy of Physician Assistants. 2020. "What Is a PA?" Accessed March 5. www. aapa.org/what-is-a-pa.

American Association of Colleges of Osteopathic Medicine. 2020. "A Brief History of Osteopathic Medicine." Accessed March 5. www.aacom.org/become-a-doctor/about-om/ history.

American Association of Nurse Practitioners. 2020. "NP Fact Sheet." Updated February. www.aanp.org/all-about-nps/np-fact-sheet.

———. 2018. "State Practice Environment." Updated December 20. www.aanp.org/legislation-regulation/state-legislation/state-practice-environment.

American College of Healthcare Executives (ACHE). 2020. *ACHE Healthcare Executive: 2020 Competencies Assessment Tool.* Accessed March 5. www.ache.org/pdf/nonsecure/careers/competencies_booklet.pdf.

American Midwifery Certification Board. 2020. "Number of Certified Nurse-Midwives by State." Accessed June 1. www.amcbmidwife.org/docs/default-source/reports/number-of-cnm-cm-by-state---february-2019-present.pdf?sfvrsn=bb309d57_10.

American Osteopathic Association. 2018. *Osteopathic Medical Profession Report 2018.* Accessed June 2. https://osteopathic.org/wp-content/uploads/2018-OMP-Report.pdf.

Association of American Medical Colleges. 2020. "About AAMC." Accessed June 8. www.aamc.org/system/files/2019-11/2019_FACTS_Table_B-1.1.pdf.

———. 2019. "2018 Physician Specialty Data Report." Accessed June 26, 2020. www.aamc.org/system/files/2019-08/2018executivesummary.pdf.

———. 2015. "Active Physicians in the Largest Specialties, 2015." Accessed March 5. www.aamc.org/data/workforce/reports/458480/1-1-chart.html.

Association of Schools of Allied Health Professions. 2020. "What Is Allied Health?" Accessed March 5. www.asahp.org/what-is.

Calhoun, J., P. Davidson, M. Sinioris, E. Vincent, and J. Griffith. 2002. "Toward an Understanding of Competency Identification and Assessment in Healthcare Management." *Quality Management in Healthcare* 11 (1): 14–38.

Cawley, J., S. Lane, N. Smith, and E. Bush. 2016. "Physician Assistants in Rural Communities." *Journal of the American Academy of Physician Assistants* 29 (1): 42–45.

Centers for Disease Control and Prevention (CDC). 2019. "TB Infection Control in Health Care Settings." Updated May 14. www.cdc.gov/tb/topic/infectioncontrol/default.htm.

Coutre, L. 2016. "Bachelor's in Nursing Is Becoming a Must." *Modern Healthcare*. Published September 12. www.modernhealthcare.com/article/20160912/NEWS/160919995.

De Luce, I., E. Court, and M. Hoff. 2020. "Today Is National Nurses Day. Here's How Much 30 Types of Hospital Workers on the Front Lines of the Coronavirus Pandemic Are Paid." *Business Insider Australia*. Published May 31. www.businessinsider.com.au/how-much-everyone-makes-in-a-hospital-2019-5?r=US&IR=T.

Harrington, L., and M. Heidkamp. 2013. *The Aging Workforce: Challenges for the Healthcare Industry Workforce*. Issue Brief, National Technical Assistance and Research Leadership Center. Published March. www.heldrich.rutgers.edu/sites/default/files/products/uploads/NTAR_Issue_Brief_Aging_Workforce_Health_Care_Final.pdf.

Institute of Medicine. 2008. *Retooling for an Aging America: Building the Healthcare Workforce*. Washington, DC: National Academies Press.

———. 2001. *Crossing the Quality Chasm: A New Health System for the 21st Century*. Washington, DC: National Academies Press.

———. 1972. *Educating for the Health Team*. Washington, DC: National Academies Press.

Interprofessional Education Collaborative (IPEC). 2020. "Membership." Accessed March 5. www.ipecollaborative.org/membership.html.

Kaiser Family Foundation. 2020. "Professionally Active Primary Care Physicians by Field." Accessed June 8. www.kff.org/other/state-indicator/primary-care-physicians-by-field/?currentTimeframe=0&sortModel=%7B%22colId%22:%22Location%22,%22sort%22:%22asc%22%7D.

———. 2018. "Total Number of Medical School Graduates." Accessed March 5. www.kff.org/other/state-indicator/total-medical-school-graduates/?currentTimeframe=0&sortModel=%7B%22colId%22:%22Location%22,%22sort%22:%22asc%22%7D.

Kavailanz, P. 2018. "The U.S. Can't Keep Up with Demand for Health Aides, Nurses and Doctors." CNN. Published March 4. https://money.cnn.com/2018/05/04/news/economy/health-care-workers-shortage/index.html.

Kossaify, A., B. Rasputin, and J. Lahoud. 2013. "The Function of a Medical Director in Healthcare Institutions: A Master or a Servant." *Health Service Insights* 6: 105–10.

Mann, S. 2017. "Research Shows Shortage of More Than 100,000 Doctors by 2030." Association of American Medical Colleges. Published March 14. https://news.aamc.org/medical-education/article/new-aamc-research-reaffirms-looming-physician-shor/.

Mararac, M. 2017. "New York's 'BSN to 10' Law and the Push for 80 Percent of Nurses to Hold BSN by 2020." Nurse.org. Updated December 30. https://nurse.org/articles/BSN-initiative-80-2020.

Martin, J., B. Hamilton, M. Osterman, A. Driscoll, and P. Drake. 2018. "Births: Final Data for 2016." *National Vital Statistics Reports* 67(1). Published January 31. www.cdc.gov/nchs/data/nvsr/nvsr67/nvsr67_01.pdf.

Mercer. 2018. "Demand for Healthcare Workers Will Outpace Supply by 2025: An Analysis of the US Healthcare Labor Market." Accessed June 1. www.mercer.us/our-thinking/career/demand-for-healthcare-workers-will-outpace-supply-by-2025.html.

Murphy, B. 2017. "How Hospitals Can Protect the Bottom Line, Increase Efficiency by Outsourcing Key Revenue Cycle Functions." *Becker's Hospital CFO Report*. Published March 20. www.beckershospitalreview.com/finance/how-hospitals-can-protect-the-bottom-line-increase-efficiency-by-outsourcing-key-revenue-cycle-functions.html.

National Council of State Boards of Nursing. 2020. "Nurse Licensure Compact." Accessed March 5. www.ncsbn.org/nurse-licensure-compact.htm.

National League for Nursing. 2018. "Nursing Programs, 2013–2014." Accessed March 5. www.nln.org/newsroom/nursing-education-statistics/nursing-programs.

Nurse Journal. 2020a. "BSN Degree vs RN Differences." Accessed March 5. https://nursejournal.org/bsn-degree/bsn-degree-rn-differences.

———. 2020b. "Requirements to Become a Nurse Practitioner." Accessed March 5. https://nursejournal.org/nurse-practitioner/what-to-know-to-become-a-nurse-practitioner.

————. 2020c. "Nurse Midwife Careers and Salary Outlook." Accessed May 11. https:// nursejournal.org/nursing-midwife/nursing-midwife-careers-salary-outlook/.

O'Connor, S. 2014. "Interview with Marna P. Borgstrom, FACHE, President and CEO of Yale New Haven Health System and CEO of Yale-New Haven Hospital, Connecticut." *Journal of Healthcare Management* 59 (2): 85–88.

Paavola, A. 2019. "Top 5 Nonprofit Hospitals for Executive Pay." *Becker's Hospital Review*. Published June 26. www.beckershospitalreview.com/compensation-issues/top-5-nonprofit-hospitals-for-executive-pay.html.

Rappleye, E. 2019. "28 States with Full Practice Authority for NPs." *Becker's Hospital Review*. Published December 23. www.beckershospitalreview.com/hospital-physician-relationships/28-states-with-full-practice-authority-for-nps.html.

Roberson, J. 2020. "*U.S. News & World Report* Updates Description of PAs in 2020 Best Jobs Ranking." Published January 7. www.aapa.org/news-central/2020/01/u-s-news-world-report-updates-description-of-pas-in-2020-best-jobs-rankings/.

Salsberg, E., and C. Erikson. 2017. "Doctor of Osteopathic Medicine: A Growing Share of the Physician Workforce." *Health Affairs Blog*. Published October 23. www.healthaffairs.org/do/10.1377/hblog20171023.624111/full/.

Schapmire, T., B. Head, W. Nash, P. Yankeelov, C. Furman, B. Wright, R. Gopalraj, B. Gordon, K. Black, C. Jones, M. Hall-Faul, and A. Faul. 2018. "Overcoming Barriers to Interprofessional Education in Gerontology." *Advances Medical Education Practice* 9: 109–18.

Sullivan, T., and M. Miliard. 2018. "Meet the Modern Healthcare CIO: A Business Leader That Is Casting Off Their Traditional IT Role." *Healthcare IT News*. Published March 29. www.healthcareitnews.com/news/meet-modern-healthcare-cio-business-leader-casting-their-traditional-it-role.

Sweeney, J. 2017. "Healthcare Informatics." *Online Journal of Nursing Informatics* 21 (1). www.himss.org/library/healthcare-informatics.

US Bureau of Labor Statistics (BLS). 2020. "Occupational Outlook Handbook: Healthcare Occupations." Updated April 10. www.bls.gov/ooh/healthcare/home.htm.

U.S. News & World Report. 2018. "Physician Assistant Salary." Accessed March 5. https://money.usnews.com/careers/best-jobs/physician-assistant/salary.

USA Today. 2018. "U.S.A. Snapshots." April 25.

Van Vleet, A., and J. Paradise. 2015. "Tapping Nurse Practitioners to Meet Rising Demand for Primary Care." Issue Brief, Kaiser Family Foundation. Published January 20. www.kff.org/medicaid/issue-brief/tapping-nurse-practitioners-to-meet-rising-demand-for-primary-care.

Vedam, S., K. Stoll, M. MacDorman, E. Declercq, R. Cramer, M. Cheyney, T. Fisher, E. Butt, T. Yang, and H. Kennedy. 2018. "Mapping Integration of Midwives Across the United States." *PLOS ONE*. Published February 21. https://doi.org/10.1371/journal.pone.0192523.

Walston, S. 2018. *Strategic Healthcare Management: Planning and Execution*. Chicago: Health Administration Press.

Wood, D. 2012. "Collaborative Healthcare Teams a Growing Success Story." AMN Healthcare. Published April 25. www.amnhealthcare.com/latest-healthcare-news/collaborative-healthcare-teams-growing-success-story.

Young, A., H. Chaudhry, X. Pei, K. Arnhart, M. Dugan, and G. Snyder. 2017. "A Census of Actively Licensed Physicians in the United States, 2016." *Journal of Medical Regulation* 103 (2): 7–21.

CHAPTER 3

HOSPITALS AND HEALTHCARE SYSTEMS

The last several decades have seen a major realignment of hospitals and healthcare systems in the United States as a result of factors such as the rising use and costs of healthcare. Health plans and healthcare providers increasingly are competing to control how healthcare is financed and delivered. Health plans are spending aggressively to expand their control over care delivery, while healthcare provider systems are merging, consolidating, and acquiring other practices to protect their hospital franchises and expand their geographic reach. Major mergers, acquisitions, and consolidations in 2018 and 2019 included the following:

◆ CVS Health acquired Aetna, one of the country's largest health insurers, for nearly $70 billion.

◆ Advocate and Aurora Healthcare, major regional health systems in Chicago and Milwaukee, respectively, announced a merger to form a multistate system comprising 27 hospitals.

◆ Dignity Health and Catholic Health Initiatives finalized a $29 billion merger agreement, creating a national Catholic healthcare system, renamed CommonSpirit, with 142 hospitals in 21 states and more than 25,000 physicians and advanced practice clinicians.

◆ New Hampshire health systems Dartmouth-Hitchcock Health and GraniteOne Health agreed to merge. This merger would combine the two systems' eight hospitals and some of the largest employers in New Hampshire.

◆ Highmark Blue Cross Blue Shield announced a partnership with Penn State Hershey Medical Center to invest $1 billion jointly in care delivery in central Pennsylvania, creating a competitive alternative to the UPMC–PinnacleHealth affiliation that was announced in September (Anderson and Morris 2018; O'Brien 2019).

Hospitals and healthcare systems must adapt to keep pace with the continuously changing market for healthcare services. Hospital markets and hospitals' relationships with their patients and with other hospitals are always evolving. This chapter will help you understand hospitals, their components, and some of the challenges they face.

LEARNING OBJECTIVES

After reading this chapter, you will be able to

➤ Compare and contrast the levels of care and the types of care provided by hospitals.

➤ Describe the types of hospitals and what distinguishes them.

➤ Explain why hospital care continues to shift from inpatient services to outpatient services.

➤ Discuss the importance of safety net hospitals.

➤ Understand the effects of hospital concentration.

➤ Contrast the leadership structure of traditional organizations with that of hospitals.

➤ Predict the future of hospitals.

LEVELS OF CARE

primary care
Basic care, usually provided by doctors, nurse practitioners, and physician assistants in an ambulatory care setting.

Healthcare organizations can be categorized by the level of care that they provide. Generally, care is divided into primary, secondary, tertiary, and quaternary care (see exhibit 3.1).

The first level is **primary care**, which involves basic care, usually provided by doctors, nurse practitioners, or physician assistants. As discussed in chapter 2, most primary care physicians are family physicians, internal medicine physicians, or pediatricians; gynecologists and geriatricians may also serve as primary care physicians.

EXHIBIT 3.1
Referral Patterns in Healthcare

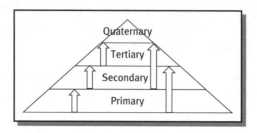

EXHIBIT 3.2
Eight Models of
Ambulatory Care

1. Smartphones, computers, and the internet
2. Mobile care (vehicles take care to the patient)
3. Convenient care and retail clinics
4. Urgent care
5. Freestanding emergency departments
6. Work-based clinics (clinics at work to keep employees healthy)
7. Primary care clinics
8. Specialty care and high-tech centers

Source: Aliber (2016).

Typically, primary care serves as the first contact and continuous care for patients. In addition, primary care providers often have the responsibility to coordinate patient care among healthcare providers and specialists. Primary care providers treat a wide scope of illnesses and conditions across all ages. Thus, they are required to have a breadth of knowledge.

Almost all primary care is provided in an ambulatory care setting. Ambulatory care literally means "walking care," or care that a patient receives on an outpatient basis. The terms *ambulatory care* and *outpatient care* are often used interchangeably. Ambulatory care is broad in scope, encompassing models of care ranging from digital contacts to emergency care to specialty care and surgery. The variety of ambulatory care can be seen in exhibit 3.2, which lists eight models of ambulatory care.

The next level of care is **secondary care**. Secondary care focuses on the prevention, diagnosis, and treatment of more serious illnesses and injuries. Generally, services are provided for a short period of time. Secondary care includes childbirth services, emergency services, and general surgery. Secondary care requires greater specialization and specific expertise. Secondary care usually results from a referral from a primary care provider. Most hospitals provide secondary services.

Tertiary care encompasses even more complicated and sophisticated services. Tertiary services generally result from referrals from primary or secondary providers. Examples include heart surgery, renal dialysis, and neurosurgery. Smaller hospitals often do not provide tertiary services, so patients must go to larger urban facilities.

Quaternary care consists of highly specialized healthcare services offered at large hospitals. This high level of specialized care typically is provided only at academic or research facilities and may involve experimental treatments and procedures.

secondary care
Care that focuses on the prevention, diagnosis, and treatment of more serious illnesses and injuries for short periods of time. Secondary care includes childbirth services, emergency services, and general surgery.

tertiary care
Care that encompasses complicated services and results from referrals from primary or secondary providers.

quaternary care
Highly specialized healthcare services offered at large hospitals; quaternary care may involve experimental treatments and procedures.

TYPES OF CARE

In addition to the level of care provided, healthcare organizations can also be classified according to the types of care that they offer. This section discusses acute care, outpatient or ambulatory care, and long-term care.

ACUTE CARE

Acute care involves short-term treatment for conditions or injuries that are potentially life-threatening or severe enough that they require constant monitoring by a healthcare professional. This could include care for a serious injury or an urgent medical condition (e.g., an accident, heart attack, poisoning, or seizure). Acute care may be provided in an emergency room, ambulatory surgery center, or urgent care facility, or it may involve multiple hospital departments.

As mentioned in chapter 1, the concept of acute care in hospitals emerged in the United States in the nineteenth and early twentieth centuries. The earliest acute care was provided in so-called pesthouses—places where the sick were isolated to protect the general population. Today, acute care **hospitals** are defined as healthcare institutions that provide medical and surgical treatment and nursing care for patients who are sick or injured.

Acute care requiring an overnight stay is called **inpatient care**. Most inpatient care is delivered in a hospital setting.

OUTPATIENT CARE

Outpatient care, also called *ambulatory care*, consists of healthcare services that do not require an overnight stay in a medical facility, such as a hospital. Outpatient care can be provided in medical offices, hospitals, and outpatient surgery centers. Outpatient care may include surgery, laboratory tests, emergency room visits, X-rays, immunizations, and so on. Outpatient services are generally less expensive than inpatient treatments.

Outpatient care services have grown tremendously, as shown in exhibit 3.3, from almost a quarter of total hospital revenues to almost half. Outpatient care is predicted to continue to grow, as new technology allows more healthcare services to be shifted to outpatient settings (Burrill, Gerhardt, and Arora 2020).

LONG-TERM CARE

Long-term care differs from short-term acute care in that services are provided in a setting for patients with chronic illnesses or disabilities who require care for an extended period. Chapter 5 discusses long-term care, its services, and settings in more depth.

---

acute care
Immediate, short-term treatment for conditions or injuries that may be life-threatening or require constant monitoring by healthcare professionals.

hospital
A healthcare facility that provides medical and surgical treatment and nursing care for patients who are sick or injured.

inpatient care
Care that requires at least an overnight stay in a medical facility, usually a hospital.

outpatient care
Care that does not require an overnight stay in a medical facility, such as a hospital; also called *ambulatory care*.

long-term care
Care that is provided for an extended period of time to patients with chronic illness or disability.

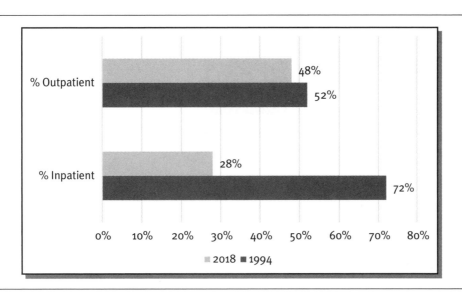

EXHIBIT 3.3
Change in
Hospital Inpatient
and Outpatient
Revenues,
1994–2018

Source: Data from Burrill, Gerhardt, and Arora (2020).

TYPES OF HOSPITALS

Many different types of hospitals exist today. Hospitals can be categorized in a variety of ways. As discussed earlier in this chapter, some hospitals provide acute care, while others offer long-term care. In addition, hospitals can be distinguished as community or noncommunity hospitals. Hospitals can be further subdivided into for-profit and not-for-profit organizations, urban and rural hospitals, independent or system-affiliated facilities, and general or specialty hospitals.

COMMUNITY HOSPITALS

Community hospitals are facilities that are governed locally, accessible to the general public, and not owned by the federal government (e.g., a Department of Veterans Affairs hospital). Community hospitals provide acute, short-term medical or surgical care and serve a local community. In 2018, 5,198 community hospitals were in operation, admitting more than 34 million people and accounting for almost $1 trillion in expenses. Community hospitals provide various levels of care and may offer general or specialized services. As shown in exhibit 3.4, community hospitals can be located in urban or rural settings, and their ownership can be classified as for-profit or not-for-profit.

For-Profit and Not-for-Profit Community Hospitals

Community hospitals can be divided into two categories based on their ownership: not-for-profit hospitals and for-profit hospitals. Exhibit 3.5 presents a breakdown of US community hospitals by ownership type and by geographic location (urban or rural).

Exhibit 3.4
Types of
Community
Hospitals

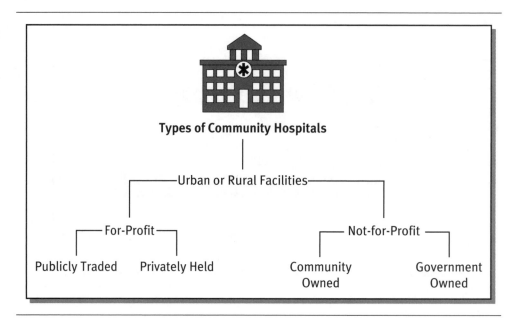

Not-for-profit hospitals are legally organized as nonprofit corporations, and they are obliged to invest all of their profits back into the organization because they provide community benefits. Community benefits include providing charity care to the poor, along with public education and efforts to improve community health (James 2016). Because of the community benefits they provide, not-for-profit hospitals are exempt from paying state and federal income and property tax. A majority of community hospitals—2,937 of 5,198 hospitals, or 56 percent—are nongovernment not-for-profit organizations. These hospitals are often owned by communities or not-for-profit healthcare systems and may be located in urban or rural areas.

For-profit hospitals make up the next-largest category of community hospitals (1,296 of 5,198 hospitals, or 25 percent). For-profit hospitals pay state and federal income and property tax and can distribute profits to their investors and raise money from investors and stock offerings. These hospitals are also referred to as *investor-owned hospitals.* They may be either publicly owned with shareholders or privately held. The largest for-profit, publicly owned hospital group in the United States is HCA Healthcare, headquartered in Nashville, Tennessee. HCA is the 67th-largest publicly traded company in the United States, comprising 184 hospitals and about $50 billion in revenues (Stewart 2019). Anyone can buy shares of HCA Healthcare stock, which sold for about $130 per share in 2019. Steward Health Care, headquartered in Dallas, Texas, comprising 36 hospitals and $8 billion in revenues, is the principal private, for-profit acute care hospital group. It is primarily owned by a surgeon, Dr. Ralph de la Torre (MacDonald 2017). As a private company, Steward Health Care's ownership is restricted, and the public cannot buy its stock.

EXHIBIT 3.5
US Hospital
Statistics, 2018

Total community hospitals	5,198
Staffed beds	792,417
Admissions	34.3 million
Expenses	$1.010 trillion
Ownership	
Nongovernment not-for-profit	2,937
Investor-owned for profit	1,296
Government-owned	
State and local government	965
Federal government	209
Nonfederal psychiatric	616
Other	123
Geographic location	
Urban	1,821
Rural	3,377
Part of a healthcare system	3,491

Source: Data from AHA (2020).

State and Local Government-Owned Community Hospitals

Community not-for-profit hospitals can be owned by state and local governments. These hospitals account for 965 or 18 percent of all community hospitals. They are owned by cities, counties, states, or special districts. The share of government-owned hospitals varies significantly from state to state. For instance, almost 74 percent of hospitals in Wyoming are state or locally owned facilities, while there are no government-owned community hospitals in Vermont, Rhode Island, North Dakota, New Hampshire, or Delaware (Kaiser Family Foundation 2018).

Urban or Rural Hospitals

Community hospitals are also distinguished by their urban or rural settings. More than one-third of all US hospitals are located in rural areas. Rural hospitals, such as Bear River Valley Hospital in Utah, generally are small facilities that offer limited services. These hospitals often struggle financially, as they have low occupancies and treat relatively few patients. Between 2010 and 2020, 120 rural hospitals closed, and another 450 are at risk of closing (Chartis Group 2020).

Hospital and Healthcare Systems

Many community hospitals are part of larger healthcare systems that comprise many facilities. The trend toward large healthcare systems is driven by lower reimbursements, demands for better electronic health records, and greater efficiencies. In 2018, 3,491 (67.2 percent) of the 5,198 community hospitals belonged to a healthcare system (AHA 2020). A hospital system is made up of a network of hospitals that share some level of cooperative services. Systems may consist of many hospitals or a single diversified hospital. Multihospital systems have two or more hospitals that are owned or leased by a central organization or have management and service contracts with other hospitals.

As illustrated in exhibit 3.6, US hospital systems have grown very large. The top five not-for-profit US hospital systems are members of the Catholic Health Association,

Exhibit 3.6
Largest US Not-for-Profit and For-Profit Hospital Systems, 2019

Not-for-Profit Hospital Systems

System	Headquarters	Number of Hospitals	Annual Revenue (billions)
CommonSpirit Health	Englewood, CO	202	$28.4
Ascension	St. Louis, MO	124	$17.1
Providence St. Joseph	Renton, WA	51	$25.0
Trinity Health	Livonia, MI	93	$13.1
Dignity Health	San Francisco, CA	39	$11.8

For-Profit Hospital Systems

System	Headquarters	Number of Hospitals	Annual Revenue (billions)
HCA Healthcare	Nashville, TN	211	$39.8
Tenet Healthcare	Dallas, TX	84	$13.6
Community Health Systems	Franklin, TN	111	$10.9
LifePoint Hospitals	Brentwood, TN	86	$7.3
Prime Healthcare Services	Ontario, CA	45	$3.6

Sources: Definitive Healthcare (2019); Ernst & Young (2019); *Fortune* (2020); Providence (2020).

with each generating more than $11 billion in revenues each year. HCA Healthcare is the dominant for-profit system, producing more than twice the revenue of the next-largest for-profit system.

Community hospitals vary significantly in their size and scope of services (see sidebar). Most community hospitals offer an array of services, including surgery, obstetrics, pediatrics, and emergency care. Other community hospitals specialize and provide more limited services. For example, 220 children's hospitals in the United States focus their care and services on pediatrics (CHA 2020). Other specialty hospitals focus on orthopedics, women's health, cardiology, psychiatry, and cancer care.

✱ THE SIZE AND SCOPE OF COMMUNITY AND SPECIALTY HOSPITALS

Community hospitals that offer general services vary in their size and complexity. Here are three examples:

Bear River Valley Hospital (https://intermountainhealthcare.org/locations/bear-river-valley-hospital/), located in rural northern Utah, offers a basic emergency room and 16 inpatient beds in a 44,000-square-foot facility. An adjoining medical clinic, Bear River Clinic, provides an additional 20,000 square feet. The hospital is a part of Intermountain Healthcare, based in Salt Lake City, Utah, and supported by more than 50 doctors.

Delray Medical Center (delraymedicalctr.com), owned by Tenet Healthcare, a for-profit healthcare organization, is a 536-bed acute care hospital that serves the communities of South Palm Beach County, Florida. The hospital has 1,600 employees, 600 physicians, and numerous community volunteers. It provides the highest level of trauma services, along with sophisticated cardiac, orthopedic, and neurology services.

French Hospital Medical Center (www.dignityhealth.org/central-coast/locations/frenchhospital), part of San Francisco–based Dignity Health, is a 112-bed not-for-profit facility located in San Luis Obispo, California. The hospital is best known for its general cardiac, obstetrics, and emergency services. It has been rated as one of the top 100 hospitals in the United States. The hospital is the home to the Hearst Cancer Resource Center, which offers free education and resources to support cancer patients and their families.

The following are examples of specialized community hospitals:

Wills Eye Hospital (willseye.org), part of Thomas Jefferson Hospitals in Philadelphia, Pennsylvania, focuses only on eye conditions and treats more than 350,000 patients annually. The not-for-profit hospital has 120 inpatient beds and provides some of the

(continued)

most advanced eye research and treatment. It has been recognized as a global leader in eye care and one of the top eye hospitals in the United States.

OrthoIndy Hospital (orthoindy.com/hospital) in Indianapolis, Indiana, is a for-profit hospital with 37 inpatient beds. It is owned primarily by 63 physicians specializing in bone, joint, and spine care and surgery. The hospital's physicians serve as team doctors for 15 sports teams, including professional football, basketball, and racing teams. It admits very few Medicaid and Medicare patients to the hospital.

The University of Texas MD Anderson Cancer Center (mdanderson.org) is recognized as one of the best cancer hospitals in the world. This not-for-profit hospital, owned by the State of Texas as part of the University of Texas System, is located in Houston and focuses exclusively on cancer care, providing cutting-edge research and treatment. Its mission is "to eliminate cancer in Texas, the nation, and the world." Established by the Texas legislature in 1941, MD Anderson generates more than $5 billion in revenues, treats more than 141,000 each year at its 587-bed hospital and facilities, and performs more than 1.4 million outpatient visits annually.

Hospitals may be very small, like Bear River Valley Hospital, with 16 beds, or large, like Delray Medical Center, with 493 beds. They can offer general services, or they may be specialized institutions focused on services such as eye or orthopedic care, such as Wills Eye Hospital and OrthoIndy Hospital.

Hospitals are also frequently classified by the number and types of beds they offer. Surprisingly, determining how many beds a hospital has can be a challenge. There are a number of ways to count beds, which can be broken down into the following categories:

- ◆ *Inpatient beds.* Adult beds, pediatric beds, birthing rooms, and newborn beds maintained in a hospital patient care area for patients needing acute or long-term treatment. Other beds, such as labor, birthing, postoperative, and emergency room beds, are not considered inpatient beds.

- ◆ *Inpatient licensed beds.* The maximum number of inpatient beds for which a hospital holds a state license to operate.

- ◆ *Inpatient physically available beds.* Beds that are licensed, physically set up, and available for use.

◆ *Inpatient staffed beds.* Beds that are licensed and physically available for which staff are on hand to take care of patients who might occupy the bed.

◆ *Inpatient occupied beds.* Beds that are licensed, physically available, staffed, and occupied by a patient. An *average occupied beds* statistic is often used to express the volume of a hospital.

The numbers in these categories can vary greatly even within one hospital. For example, one of the authors was the CEO of a hospital that had 312 licensed beds, 280 physically available beds, and 225 staffed beds but averaged only 185 occupied beds.

Hospital beds also can be categorized according to the types of patients they serve:

◆ *Adult intensive care (ICU).* Beds that support critically ill or injured patients, including ventilator support

◆ *Adult cardiac/coronary care (CCU).* Beds that support critically ill patients with cardiac (heart) symptoms

◆ *General medical/surgical.* Also referred to as "ward" beds that treat recovering medical and surgical patients

◆ *Burn or burn ICU.* Beds set aside to treat burn victims (these beds should not be included in other ICU bed counts)

◆ *Pediatric ICU.* The same as adult ICU, but for patients 17 years and younger

◆ *Pediatrics.* Medical/surgical beds for the treatment of patients 17 and younger

◆ *Psychiatric.* Beds in a closed or locked psychiatric unit used to treat mentally ill patients

◆ *Obstetrics and maternity.* Beds set aside for women who have delivered babies or had surgery

ACADEMIC MEDICAL CENTERS

Another type of hospital that is critical to healthcare in the United States is the **academic medical center (AMC)**. There are about 120 academic medical centers in the United States. AMCs' missions focus on providing care for the poor, training medical students and healthcare professionals, and conducting research. Almost all AMCs are highly sophisticated not-for-profit organizations. Although they represent only 5 percent of hospitals, they provide 37 percent of charity care in the United States (Grover, Slavin, and Willson 2014).

academic medical center (AMC)
An organization whose mission is to provide care for the poor, train medical students and healthcare professionals, and conduct research.

Funding for AMCs has shifted dramatically over the last 50 years. Historically, more than 50 percent of AMCs' costs were covered by federal funding. By 2016, however, this share had declined to less than 20 percent. Conversely, revenues from clinical services provided only about 6 percent of revenues for AMCs in 1966, but by 2016, this share had grown to more than 60 percent (Guadagnolo 2018).

GOVERNMENT HOSPITALS

In 2018, 18.6 percent of US hospitals were owned by a state or local government entity. However, this number varies widely by state. For example, almost 74 percent of hospitals in Wyoming and less than 1 percent of hospitals in Pennsylvania are owned by state or local government (Kaiser Family Foundation 2018).

safety-net hospital
A hospital that is committed by mission or mandate to care for those with limited or no access to healthcare services because they lack financial resources.

State and locally owned hospitals are important to their communities, as they often provide care to the poor and are considered **safety-net hospitals**. Safety-net providers are hospitals that are committed by mission or mandate to care for those with limited or no access to healthcare services because they lack financial resources; more than half of such patients have Medicaid coverage or are uninsured. As a result, safety-net hospitals have very low operating margins and must rely on subsidies to operate (Chokshi, Chang, and Wilson 2017). For example, Jackson Memorial Hospital in Miami, Florida, provides care to many poor patients and is funded mostly from public taxes and bonds (see sidebar).

✳ DEBATE TIME A Closer Look at a Safety-Net Hospital

Public hospitals can be very large. For instance, Jackson Memorial Hospital in Miami, Florida, which is owned by Miami–Dade County, consists of 1,756 beds and is supported by a sales tax. This safety-net hospital provides the only Level 1 trauma center (providing the most sophisticated emergency care) in the county and offers care on three campuses. Traditionally, Jackson Memorial has been the "hospital of last resort" for those living in Miami–Dade County, with a mission to provide care to everyone in the county, regardless of their ability to pay. However, Jackson Memorial has recently begun a renovation and expansion costing more than $1.5 billion, funded primarily by public bonds, to reposition the hospital to attract paying patients (Chang 2018).

Should safety-net hospitals use public funds to compete with other local hospitals, or should they focus only on their mission to serve the poor?

Government hospitals also can be owned and controlled by public hospital districts. Public hospital districts are generally created by state legislative action to establish, fund, and provide healthcare services. Many public hospital districts have been created in rural areas that could not support a hospital without this assistance. For example, in Washington State, almost half of the state's 90 hospitals are part of a public hospital district (UW Medicine 2020).

Orcas Healthcare provides an example of the purpose and importance of public district hospitals in Washington State. In 2018, the residents of Orcas Island approved the creation of a public hospital district to financially support their hospital, which could not survive without outside funds or philanthropic donations. To meet this financial need, the district was authorized to impose a property tax levy on residents (Johnson 2017; McNulty 2018).

The US federal government also provides health services to veterans and active-duty military through a large healthcare system. This system is made up of two components. The first component is the **Veterans Health Administration (VHA)**. The VHA is the largest healthcare system in the United States, consisting of 170 medical centers and more than 1,000 outpatient units that provide traditional hospital and outpatient services to veterans. The VHA serves about 9 million veterans and spends almost $200 billion a year (CNN 2018).

The second component, the **Military Health System (MHS)**, serves active-duty military and their families. The MHS operates 65 military hospitals and 377 military medical clinics for active-duty military personnel across the globe. MHS hospitals admit more than 1 million patients and deliver almost 120,000 babies annually (MHS 2020).

HOSPITAL COMPETITION

Rural areas frequently have only one hospital, and in most urban areas in the United States, competition for hospital services is limited because of hospital mergers and consolidations. By 2016, 90 percent of metropolitan areas in the United States had highly concentrated hospital markets with little competition (Fulton 2017). A lack of competition causes people to pay more for healthcare. A number of studies have shown that healthcare prices rise when price competition decreases (Commonwealth Fund 2017; Dauda 2018; Polyakova et al. 2018).

Exhibit 3.7 illustrates limited hospital competition for the two largest counties in Utah: Salt Lake County, with 1.2 million people, and Utah County, with 620,000 people in 2019. Four hospital systems control all of the community hospital beds in Salt Lake County, with one system having 42 percent of the beds. Only two hospital systems are present in Utah County, with one system, Intermountain Healthcare, having 66 percent of community hospital beds.

Veterans Health Administration (VHA)
A healthcare system run by the US federal government that provides hospital services to current and past military members.

Military Health System (MHS)
A system of military healthcare facilities and providers focused on maintaining the health of active-duty military and reserve personnel.

Exhibit 3.7

Hospital Beds by
Hospital System,
Salt Lake and Utah
Counties, 2017

Salt Lake County	Number of Beds	Share of All Beds in County
HCA Healthcare	293	10%
Intermountain Healthcare	1,194	42%
Steward Health Care	551	20%
University of Utah	777	28%
Total	**2,815**	

Utah County	Number of Beds	Share of All Beds in County
HCA Healthcare	231	34%
Intermountain Healthcare	468	66%
Total	699	

Source: Data from American Hospital Directory (2019).

Limited competition for hospital services has been found to reduce competitive pressure and raise hospital prices. Areas with low competition and high ownership concentration (i.e., many hospitals owned by the same system) have been shown to have healthcare insurance premiums at least 5 percent higher than more competitive markets (Boozary et al. 2019).

ORGANIZATION AND LEADERSHIP OF HOSPITALS

Hospitals are unique in their organizational structure. Rather than having a governing board and management structure, like a traditional business, in most healthcare organizations, the medical staff, which is composed of physicians and other licensed independent healthcare practitioners, plays a significant role in governance. Hospitals have organized medical staffs with officers and committees that provide primary governance of patient care quality and contribute to the overall leadership of the organization.

Although the leadership structure may vary according to a hospital's size, function, and complexity, hospitals tend to have three leadership groups (Schyve 2009):

1. *The governing body.* This body, typically a board of trustees, is the ultimate authority for all decisions made at the hospital. Board members are individuals who have jobs and responsibilities outside the hospital, who come

together to hire and judge the performance of the hospital's chief executive and establish the hospital's vision and path forward.

2. *The chief executive and other senior managers.* This group consists of the executive hospital employees who compose the "C-suite." The chief executive is responsible for ensuring the hospital's compliance with all relevant regulations, laws, and board policies and achieving the organization's financial and strategic goals. The chief executive is responsible for hiring the senior managers.

3. *The leaders of the medical staff.* As medical care is provided by licensed practitioners, whose clinical practice must be supervised by other licensed practitioners, the hospital's organized medical staff provides both clinical supervision and oversight of clinical care and individual practitioner performance.

As shown in exhibit 3.8, these three groups work together to provide governance of hospitals.

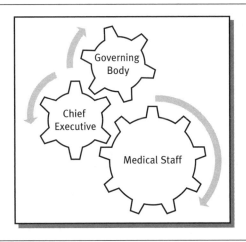

EXHIBIT 3.8
Three Leadership Groups That Make Up Hospital Governance

OUTPATIENT VERSUS INPATIENT CARE
OUTPATIENT CARE

Outpatient care, also called *ambulatory care*, refers to medical services that are provided without an overnight stay in a hospital or other healthcare facility. Today, many surgical procedures are performed on an outpatient basis. Outpatient surgeries are procedures for which patients are expected to remain in the surgical facility for less than 24 hours and are not admitted for inpatient care. As a result of both technological advances and increasing economic pressures, most surgeries have shifted from inpatient to outpatient procedures. As a result, many surgeries that traditionally were performed in hospitals are now performed in outpatient settings. In 1980, only 13 percent of surgeries were done as outpatient procedures; this figure increased to 63 percent by 2002 and 66 percent by 2014 (AHRQ 2003; Steiner et al. 2017).

Outpatient surgeries can be performed in hospitals, physician offices, surgery centers, and other healthcare facilities. As shown in exhibit 3.9, the most common outpatient surgeries dealt with the eye or ear.

The number of outpatient surgeries continues to increase in the United States. In the 50 largest US markets, from 2016 to 2017, overall outpatient surgical volume increased 22.9 percent, to 35.8 million ambulatory procedures. Outpatient surgery is expected to surpass $40 billion by 2020, with significant growth of orthopedic and gynecological surgeries shifting to outpatient settings (Dyrda 2018).

The growth of outpatient surgery is driven by lower costs and reimbursements and by the potential for physicians to earn extra income. For instance, Medicare will pay $3,721 for a pacemaker implant performed in an ambulatory setting but $14,540 for the same procedure in an inpatient setting. Payers and patients seeking lower prices are moving to outpatient locations. On the other hand, doctors can perform many of these procedures in their offices or in facilities in which they may have an ownership stake (Kimmell 2019).

EXHIBIT 3.9

Shares of Procedures Performed in Outpatient Settings

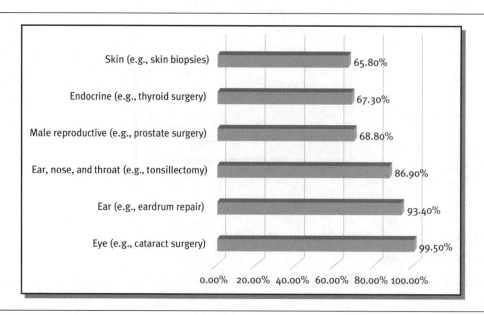

Source: Steiner et al. (2017).

INPATIENT CARE

The volume of inpatient care—generally when patients stay longer than 24 hours in a hospital—has been declining for many years. In 1994, community hospitals totaled more than 207 million **patient days**, the number of overnight stays at a hospital. As can be seen in exhibit 3.10, the total patient days in hospitals has steadily decreased in the past decade and a half. By 2015, this number had decreased to about 180 million, about a 10 percent decline, while the total US population increased by 55 million people (AHA 2018).

A number of factors have influenced this declining trend (Brimmer 2014):

patient day
A unit of measure of the time of one day that a patient remains in a hospital or other overnight facility; also known as an *inpatient day*, *census day*, or *bed occupancy day*.

◆ Higher deductibles and loss of insurance coverage

◆ Pressure to reduce hospital readmissions

◆ Increasing use of observation beds

◆ Increased use of outpatient care

◆ Greater emphasis on prevention and proactive care

◆ Ongoing decline of births

Today, patients typically are admitted to hospitals as inpatients only for serious illnesses or trauma.

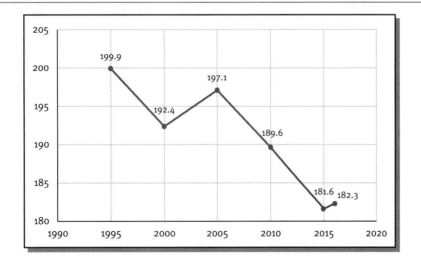

EXHIBIT 3.10
Inpatient Days in Community Hospitals, 1995–2016

Source: AHA (2018).

THE FUTURE OF HOSPITALS

Many experts have questioned the long-term sustainability of hospitals. Some suggest that hospitals require too much capital to fund their large, sprawling structures, pricey machines, and expensive staffs. These capital assets have long been hospitals' strategic advantage. However, as more and more patients are cared for in outpatient settings, these heavy capital costs may become unsustainable as the revenue generated from inpatient care declines (Leaf 2018).

In the last decade, some of the largest US hospitals have experienced significant declines in their revenues, and many have lost money. For example, the Cleveland Clinic saw a 71 percent decline in operating income from 2015 to 2016, and MD Anderson, the nation's most prestigious cancer center, lost $266 million in 2016 alone (Goldsmith 2017).

(✳) DEBATE TIME The Ever-Evolving Hospital

"The days of the hospital as we know it may be numbered. In a shift away from their traditional inpatient facilities, health-care providers are investing in outpatient clinics, same-day surgery centers, free-standing emergency rooms and micro-hospitals, which offer as few as eight beds for overnight stays. They are setting up programs that monitor people 24/7 in their own homes. And they are turning to digital technology to treat and keep tabs on patients remotely from a high-tech hub" (Landro 2018).

Do you think that there is a role still for hospitals? If so, what would this be?

---

micro-hospital
A small hospital with 8 to 50 beds that can provide locally needed services, such as exercise facilities, laboratory testing, imaging services, and pharmacies.

While hospitals will never disappear, many healthcare leaders envision that hospitals in the future will act as coordinators, facilitating and empowering patients to manage their health and well-being and supporting their needs with highly sophisticated, complex care (Dyrda 2017). To accomplish this, some hospital systems have moved to **micro-hospitals**, facilities that have 8 to 50 beds and provide locally needed services such as exercise facilities, laboratory testing, imaging services, and pharmacies. These small hospitals are structured to provide patient-friendly care to improve patient satisfaction and quality of care. Although many hospitals are pursuing this concept, the long-term clinical and economic prospects of these facilities remain uncertain (Greenberg and Pesesky 2018) (see sidebar).

(✱) THE RISE OF MICRO-HOSPITALS

The future of healthcare may be small and digital. Micro-hospitals are emerging to fill a community niche, providing lower-cost and more personalized care. For instance, Saint Luke's Health System opened a 17,000-square-foot micro-hospital in Leawood, Kansas, that is about the size of a CVS store (Lovelace 2018).

A national company, Emerus (emerus.com), has been at the forefront of developing micro-hospitals with partners such as Dignity Health, Baptist Health, and Hospitals of Providence. It now has 28 micro-hospitals across the United States.

A significant factor that will affect the future of the traditional hospital is how fees for patient services are paid. Traditionally, hospitals have been reimbursed through a mix of **fee-for-service** methods. Under fee-for-service reimbursement, hospitals are paid for each individual service that is provided. This payment system creates an incentive to provide more services. In essence, providers have operated on the premise that they receive more money when they provide more services. However, as chapter 7 discusses, if reimbursement shifts to fixed payments made through some form of **capitation** or partial capitation, hospitals will become cost generators, which likely would lead to decreasing numbers of hospitals.

Different from fee-for-service reimbursement, capitation pays a fixed amount of money for each patient for all care across a time period. For example, under fee-for-service payment, if you went to hospital twice within 30 days, you or your insurance would be billed for each visit and for each service you received. However, under capitation, the hospital would receive a fixed payment that would cover any services you received during that time, with no additional billing.

Although hospitals are sure to undergo profound transformations in the future, they are bound to continue to be an important part of the healthcare landscape.

fee-for-service
A payment method in which hospitals, physicians, and other healthcare providers are paid for each service provided.

capitation
A payment method in which hospitals, physicians, and other healthcare providers receive a fixed payment per person for providing services for a fixed time period.

SUMMARY

Acute care organizations can be categorized by the level of care and the types of care that they provide. Primary care is the most basic level of care, and it is almost always provided in an outpatient or ambulatory care setting. Hospitals and healthcare organizations provide both outpatient and inpatient services for secondary, tertiary, and quaternary care. The types of care that are provided include acute or short-term care, outpatient or ambulatory care, and long-term care.

Community hospitals can be divided into three categories based on their ownership: not-for-profit, for-profit, and government-owned entities. Most hospitals in the United States are not-for-profit organizations.

Hospitals may also be classified by how many beds they have and the type of patients they serve. Today, about two-thirds of hospitals belong to a healthcare system. Many hospital systems have grown very large. HCA Healthcare is the largest for-profit healthcare system, with 169 hospitals and $43 billion in annual revenues. CommonSpirit Health is the largest not-for-profit healthcare system with 202 hospitals and $28 billion in annual revenues.

Community hospitals differ substantially in their size and scope. They can be very large or quite small, and they can offer general or specialized services depending on the needs of the community.

Academic medical centers provide crucial services to provide care for the poor, train medical students and healthcare professionals, and conduct healthcare research. Although only 5 percent of US hospitals are academic medical centers, they provide 37 percent of charity care. Clinical revenues are increasingly important for academic medical centers, now accounting for more than 60 percent of their revenues.

Government hospitals make up about 20 percent of total hospitals. They are unevenly distributed across the United States; for example, government-owned hospitals account for 74 percent of the hospitals in Wyoming but less than 1 percent in Pennsylvania. These hospitals are important because they act as safety-net hospitals that provide care to the poor and needy. Public district hospitals are government-owned institutions that are created and funded by state legislative action. Public hospitals could not survive without government assistance.

Two other types of government hospitals serve current and past members of the US military. The Veterans Health Administration delivers care to veterans and accounts for about $200 billion a year. Military Health Services operates 65 military hospitals for active-duty military personnel.

Hospitals operate in concentrated markets with limited competition, leading to higher healthcare prices. About 90 percent of US metropolitan areas have highly concentrated hospital markets.

The organizational structure of hospitals has three power bases, rather than two, as in traditional businesses. Hospitals are governed by three leadership groups: a governing body, the chief executive and senior managers, and the leadership of the medical staff. Physicians are organized into a medical staff that provides primary governance for patient care quality and clinical supervision and contribute to the overall leadership of the hospital.

Many outpatient or ambulatory surgery and ambulatory care centers exist in the United States. Outpatient surgeries are procedures for which patients are expected to remain in the surgical facility for less than 24 hours and are not admitted for inpatient care. The majority of surgeries today are performed in outpatient settings. Outpatient surgeries are projected to show the largest growth.

Inpatient care, conversely, has been declining for many years. From 1994 to 2015, total inpatient volume dropped 10 percent, while the US population continued to increase. Lower inpatient volume has resulted from financial and physician practice changes.

The worsening financial condition and payment systems of hospitals will be key factors in their long-term sustainability. Although hospitals will never disappear, in the future they are expected to act as coordinators, facilitating and empowering patients to manage their health and well-being and supporting their needs with sophisticated, complex care. To accomplish this, some hospital systems are moving to micro-hospitals that have 8 to 50 beds and provide locally needed services. Shifts in the way hospitals are reimbursed for services, toward more capitated and value-based payments, will directly affect the health and presence of hospitals.

QUESTIONS

1. How are primary care and ambulatory care similar?
2. What types of hospitals provide quaternary care?
3. Can a not-for-profit hospital make a profit? If so, who receives it?
4. How do inpatient licensed beds and inpatient occupied beds differ?
5. Why have so many hospitals (about two-thirds) joined healthcare systems?
6. What is a safety-net hospital, and why is this type of hospital important?
7. Why might a high concentration of hospitals in a geographic area be a problem?
8. What role does a hospital's medical staff play in the organization's leadership?
9. Why are most surgeries performed in outpatient or ambulatory care settings rather than inpatient settings?
10. What are the advantages of micro-hospitals?

ASSIGNMENTS

1. Look up information on two of the largest healthcare systems in the United States. Compare the two systems on the following dimensions. What differences did you find?
   a. Dispersion across the United States
   b. Ownership
   c. Revenues
   d. Profitability

2. Pick a hospital of your choice. Contact someone at the hospital and ask them the following questions:
   a. How big is the hospital? In licensed beds? Occupied beds? Revenues? Other?
   b. Is the hospital for-profit or not-for-profit? What does the hospital's status mean to the person?
   c. Does the hospital have any other special designation?
   d. Does the hospital provide more than acute care services? If so, what?
   e. What is the governance structure of the hospital? How does the medical staff participate?

CASES

HOSPITALS WITH TWO VERSIONS OF THE FUTURE OF HEALTHCARE

UPMC and Highmark Health are locked in a battle for patients in western Pennsylvania. UPMC started out as a hospital and expanded into health insurance, eventually becoming a $20 billion business. Highmark originated as an insurance company and later began to acquire hospitals; today, it generates about $18.2 billion in annual revenues. Highmark's move into the hospital market precipitated a clash that forced patients to choose between their doctor and their health plan.

Many experts are not certain that these large merged hospital and insurance systems are helping patients, as they often have contrary incentives. Hospitals generally want to fill their beds, whereas insurers want lower costs.

The market dominated by only two healthcare systems has also reduced competition. Martin Gaynor, a professor at Carnegie Mellon University in Pittsburgh, Pennsylvania, stated that the area does not "have effective competition in this market; we have these two huge entities, circling each other looking for some kind of opening." Rather than lowering costs, Pittsburgh's medical spending between 2012 and 2016 rose 20 percent—5 percent higher than the national average.

However, the two systems' strategies differ. UPMC's leadership sees itself becoming involved in every aspect of healthcare, like the Amazon of healthcare. It plans to invest in cutting-edge research in cancer, vision restoration, and transplants and attract patients from around the world. UPMC aims to invent the next groundbreaking healthcare therapy. To do so, it employs 200 software engineers and others to develop and commercialize new healthcare technologies.

Highmark, in contrast, sees its future rooted in providing health insurance, and it wants to pay for healthcare, not research projects. Highmark perceives that its most important work is to keep people out of hospitals and focus on health and wellness pavilions and smaller-scale neighborhood hospitals (Johnson 2018).

Discussion Questions

1. How does the concentration of hospitals affect the healthcare services available and their costs in Pittsburgh?
2. Why do you think the two systems have such different strategies?
3. Which strategy do you think will be most successful? Why?

RURAL HOSPITAL CHALLENGES

More and more rural hospitals are closing every day. Should rural hospitals fight to retain their hospital presence, or should they provide only primary care for their community? Hospitals tend to be the cornerstones of rural communities and the largest or one of the largest employers. They provide jobs and contribute to a town's economy. For many small towns, losing the local hospital would threaten the livelihood of its residents. Nonetheless, rural hospitals cost money, and it can be difficult to hire and retain qualified workers.

More than 670 rural hospitals are at risk of closing, primarily because they have so few occupied beds. Some 25 licensed bed facilities may average only 4 occupied beds. Because of low inpatient volumes, hospitals have difficulty generating enough revenue to support their facilities (St. Clair 2018).

Discussion Questions

1. Could rural hospitals expand into outpatient services and eliminate inpatient care?
2. In your opinion, why do rural citizens care about having a hospital in their community?

REFERENCES

Agency for Healthcare Research and Quality (AHRQ). 2003. "Ambulatory Surgery in U.S. Hospitals, 2003." Accessed April 2. https://archive.ahrq.gov/data/hcup/factbk9/factbk9a.htm.

Aliber, J. 2016. "Eight Ambulatory Models of Care." *Health Facilities Management*. Published January 6. www.hfmmagazine.com/articles/1852-eight-ambulatory-models-of-care.

American Hospital Association (AHA). 2020. "Fast Facts on U.S. Hospitals." Accessed April 2. www.aha.org/statistics/fast-facts-us-hospitals.

————. 2018. "TrendsWatch Chartbook 2018: Trends Affecting Hospitals and Health Systems." *Trendwatch Chartbook 2018*. Accessed April 2. www.aha.org/system/files/2018-05/2018-chartbook-table-3-1.pdf.

American Hospital Directory. 2019. Accessed July 16. www.ahd.com.

Anderson, D., and D. Morris. 2018. "Market Transformation 2018: Strategic Priorities for Health Systems." *Leadership+*. Published January. www.bdcadvisors.com/wp-content/uploads/2018/02/HFMA-Jan-2018.pdf.

Boozary, A., Y. Feyman, U. Reinhardt, and A. Jha. 2019. "The Association Between Hospital Concentration and Insurance Premiums in ACA Marketplaces." *Health Affairs* 38 (4): 668–74.

Brimmer, K. 2014. "The Future of Hospital Inpatient Volumes." *Healthcare Finance*. Published February 24. www.healthcarefinancenews.com/news/future-hospital-inpatient-volumes.

Burrill, S., W. Gerhardt, and A. Arora. 2020. "Hospital Revenue Trends: Outpatient, Home, Virtual, and Other Care Settings Are Becoming More Common." Deloitte Insights. Published February 21. www2.deloitte.com/us/en/insights/industry/health-care/outpatient-virtual-health-care-trends.html.

Chang, D. 2018. "Your Taxes Are Paying for This $1.5 Billion Makeover to Miami's Public Hospital System." *Miami Herald*. Published May 9. www.miamiherald.com/news/health-care/article210704664.html.

Chartis Group. 2020. *The Rural Health Safety Net Under Pressure: Rural Hospital Vulnerability*. Published February. www.ivantageindex.com/wp-content/uploads/2020/02/CCRH_Vulnerability-Research_FiNAL-02.14.20.pdf.

Children's Hospital Association (CHA). 2020. "About Children's Hospital." Accessed June 2. www.childrenshospitals.org/About-Us/About-Childrens-Hospitals.

Chokshi, D., J. Chang, and R. Wilson. 2017. "Health Reform and the Changing Safety Net in the United States." *New England Journal of Medicine* 375 (18): 1790–96.

CNN. 2018. "Department of Veterans Affairs Fast Facts." Published May 2. cnn.com/ 2014/05/30/us/department-of-veterans-affairs-fast-facts/index.html.

Commonwealth Fund. 2017. "Health Care Market Concentration Trends in the United States: Evidence and Policy Responses." Published September 6. www.commonwealthfund.org/ publications/journal-article/2017/sep/health-care-market-concentration-trends-united-states.

Dauda, S. 2018. "Hospitals and Health Insurance Markets Concentration and Hospital Transaction Prices in the U.S. Healthcare Market." *Health Services Research* 53 (2): 1203–26.

Definitive Healthcare. 2019. "Top 10 Largest Health Systems in the U.S." Updated July. https://blog.definitivehc.com/top-10-largest-health-systems.

Dyrda, L. 2018. "10 Key Trends for ASCs and Outpatient Surgery in the Next 10 Years." *Becker's ASC Review*. Published April 2. www.beckersasc.com/asc-turnarounds-ideas-to-improve-performance/10-key-trends-for-ascs-and-outpatient-surgery-in-the-next-10-years.html.

———. 2017. "45 Hospital and Healthcare Executives Outline the Hospital of the Future." *Becker's Hospital Review*. Published July 17. www.beckershospitalreview.com/hospital-management-administration/45-hospital-and-healthcare-executives-outline-the-hospital-of-the-future.html.

Ernst & Young. 2019. "Consolidated Financial Statements: Prime Healthcare Services." Accessed June 2, 2020. www.smmcnj.com/documents/Prime-Healthcare-Services.pdf.

Fortune. 2020. "Fortune 500." Accessed June 2. https://fortune.com/fortune500/.

Fulton, B. 2017. "Healthcare Market Concentration Trends in the United States: Evidence and Policy Responses." *Health Affairs* 36 (9): 1530–38.

Goldsmith, J. 2017. "How U.S. Hospitals and Health Systems Can Reverse Their Sliding Financial Performance." *Harvard Business Review*. Published October 5. https://hbr.org/2017/10/how-u-s-hospitals-and-health-systems-can-reverse-their-sliding-financial-performance.

Greenberg, B., and M. Pesesky. 2018. "How Micro-Hospitals Impact System Strategy. Advisory Board. Published January. www.advisory.com/research/health-care-industry-committee/the-bridge/2018/01/micro-hospitals.

Grover, A., P. Slavin, and P. Willson. 2014. "The Economics of Academic Medical Centers." *New England Journal of Medicine* 370 (25): 2360–62.

Guadagnolo, G. 2018. "Margin Pressures for Academic Medical Centers." EAB. Published March 30. www.eab.com/research-and-insights/business-affairs-forum/expert-insights/2018/segment-spotlight-academic-medical-centers.

James, J. 2016. "Nonprofit Hospitals' Community Benefit Requirements." Health Policy Brief, Robert Wood Johnson Foundation. Published February 25. www.rwjf.org/en/library/research/2016/02/nonprofit-hospitals--community-benefit-requirements.html.

Johnson, C. 2018. "Two Visions for the Future of Healthcare Are at War in Pittsburgh." *Washington Post*. Published February 13. www.washingtonpost.com/business/economy/two-visions-for-the-future-of-health-care-are-at-war-in-pittsburgh/2018/02/13/d987433c-0157-11e8-9d31-d72cf78dbeee_story.html?utm_term=.8be3a05d7363.

Johnson, M. 2017. "Coalition Presents First Public Hospital District Town Hall." *Islands' Sounder* (Eastsound, WA). Published December 7. www.islandssounder.com/news/coalition-presents-first-public-hospital-district-town-hall/.

Kaiser Family Foundation. 2018. "Hospitals by Ownership Type." Accessed May 25. www.kff.org/other/state-indicator/hospitals-by-ownership/?currentTimeframe=0&selectedDistributions=statelocal-government&sortModel=%7B%22colId%22:%22State%2FLocal%20Government%22,%22sort%22:%22desc%22%7D.

Kimmell, J. 2019. "ASCs Are Growing Even Faster than You Think. How Can Hospitals Respond?" Advisory Board. Published March 5. www.advisory.com/daily-briefing/2019/03/05/asc-shift.

Landro, L. 2018. "What the Hospitals of the Future Look Like." *Wall Street Journal*. Published February 25.

Leaf, C. 2018. "2 Forces That Will Drive the Health Industry. *Fortune*. Published January 3. http://fortune.com/2018/01/03/health-care-industry-2018/.

Lovelace, B. 2018. "No-Frills Micro Hospitals with as Few as 8 Rooms Emerge as a New Way to Cut Healthcare Costs." CNBC. Published March 2. www.cnbc.com/2018/03/02/no-frills-micro-hospitals-emerge-as-a-new-way-to-cut-health-care-costs.html.

MacDonald, I. 2017. "Steward Health Completes Acquisition, Officially Becoming the Nation's Largest Private Hospital Provider." Fierce Healthcare. Published October 2. www.fiercehealthcare.com/finance/steward-health-completes-acquisition-and-officially-becomes-nation-s-largest-private.

McNulty, L. 2018. "We Got Us a Hospital District." *Orcas Issues*. Published April 24. https://orcasissues.com/we-got-us-a-hospital-district/.

Military Health System (MHS). 2020. "Elements of the MHS." Accessed April 2. https://health.mil/About-MHS/MHS-Elements.

O'Brien, J. 2019. "Top 6 Healthcare Mergers of 2019." HealthLeaders. Published December 23. www.healthleadersmedia.com/finance/top-6-healthcare-mergers-2019.

Polyakova, M., K. Bundorf, D. Kessler, and L. Baker. 2018. "ACA Marketplace Premiums and Competition Among Hospitals and Physician Practices." *American Journal of Managed Care* 24 (2): 85–90.

Providence. 2020. "Providence Financial Statements." Accessed June 2. www.providence.org/about/financial-statements.

Schyve, P. 2009. *Leadership in Healthcare Organizations: A Guide to Joint Commission Leadership Standards*. Governance Institute. Published Winter. www.jointcommission.org/assets/1/18/WP_Leadership_Standards.pdf.

St. Clair, A. 2018. "Rethinking Rural Health Solutions to Save Patients and Communities." National Public Radio. Published February 28. www.npr.org/sections/health-shots/2018/02/28/588826085/rethinking-rural-health-solutions-to-save-patients-and-communities.

Steiner, C., Z. Karaca, B. Moore, M. Imshaug, and G. Pickens. 2017. "Surgeries in Hospital-Based Ambulatory Surgery and Hospital Inpatient Settings, 2014." Healthcare Cost and Utilization Project. Published May. www.hcup-us.ahrq.gov/reports/statbriefs/sb223-Ambulatory-Inpatient-Surgeries-2014.jsp.

Stewart, A. 2019. "5 Things to Know About HCA Healthcare." *Becker's ASC Review*. Published October 1. www.beckersasc.com/asc-news/5-things-to-know-about-hca-healthcare.html.

University of Washington (UW) Medicine. 2020. "What's a Public Hospital District?" Accessed April 2. www.valleymed.org/district/.

CHAPTER 4

THE PHARMACEUTICAL AND MEDICAL DEVICE INDUSTRIES

Healthcare involves much more than just doctors and hospitals. The pharmaceutical industry is a large and expanding global business, and prices for prescription drugs are among the fastest-growing healthcare costs. Although the following is not the reason for most high drug prices, it occurs all too frequently: "Old drugs are out of patent, which means any company can make them, and usually the price drops very low because of the competition. But [former Turing Pharmaceuticals CEO Martin] Shkreli was an entrepreneur who saw no reason why selling drugs should be any different from selling cars: corner the market and hike the price. He did it a few times, but the one that caused all the trouble was a very cheap drug called pyrimethamine, trade name Daraprim. Daraprim had been out of patent for a very long time, having been approved by the US Food and Drug Administration in 1953. It is an anti-parasitic drug given to people with toxoplasmosis infection, particularly where they have weak immune systems because of AIDS or pregnancy and cannot easily fight it off. Shkreli bought the drug from another company in August 2015 and hiked the price by 5,000%. It went up overnight from $13.50 per pill to $750" (Boseley 2018).

LEARNING OBJECTIVES

After reading this chapter, you will be able to

➤ Compare the pharmaceutical and medical device industries in terms of their size and role in the healthcare industry.

➤ Understand how the two industries contribute to the rising costs of healthcare.

➤ Understand the importance of research and development to the two industries.

➤ Identify the steps of the clinical trial process and the purpose of each step.

The pharmaceutical and medical device industries encompass many large and important companies and products used by American consumers. Both continue to grow and contribute to the escalating costs of healthcare while also providing new and innovative treatments.

PHARMACEUTICAL INDUSTRY

The pharmaceutical industry is an important component of healthcare, as it is responsible for the discovery, manufacture, and distribution of prescription drugs. Each year in the United States, about 4 billion prescriptions are written for some 18,000 approved prescription drugs, accounting for almost $400 billion in consumer spending (PCG 2018). Worldwide, the pharmaceutical industry exceeds $1.11 trillion in annual revenues.

Pharmaceutical companies spend about $150 billion per year on research. The output of that research—new drugs—must obtain approval from the US Food and Drug Administration (FDA), the federal agency that is the chief regulator of drugs in the United States, before it can be sold. In 2017, pharmaceutical companies obtained approval from the FDA for 46 novel (new) drugs and 1,027 generic drugs. FDA approval is critical to ensure the safety and effectiveness of medications sold in the United States. The FDA also issues drug recalls, when necessary, and provides guidelines for prescribing medications. In effect, the FDA controls whether a prescription drug is available to US consumers. This function is extremely important to the major global pharmaceutical companies, as the US market accounts for 45 percent of the worldwide pharmaceutical business (Ellis 2019).

Pharmaceutical companies are large and have a global presence. Exhibit 4.1 lists the ten largest pharmaceutical companies in the world in 2019, ranked by their annual revenues. Six of these companies are headquartered in the United States. All of them generate billions of dollars of revenues per year.

Pharmaceuticals are the most profitable of any industry, both in the United States and worldwide, earning profit margins of around 20 percent (GAO 2017). Some companies, such as Gilead, have enjoyed profit margins exceeding 50 percent (Speights 2016). Over the past two decades, on average, the profits of the 35 largest pharmaceutical firms have been almost twice that of large nonpharmaceutical companies (13.8 percent versus 7.7 percent) (Ledley, McCoy, and Vaughan 2020).

Discovery remains at the center of the pharmaceutical business. When a drug is approved by the FDA, the company that developed it is granted patent protection, which gives it the exclusive right to manufacture the drug for a limited amount of time. Patent protection for drugs generally lasts 20 years, after which time other pharmaceutical companies can produce generic equivalents of the drug, often at a lower cost. For this reason, drug companies spend massive amounts of money on research and development (R&D).

EXHIBIT 4.1
Ten Largest
Pharmaceutical
Companies, 2019

Company	Headquarters Location	Revenues (2019, billions)
Pfizer	United States (Connecticut)	$51.75
Roche	Switzerland	$50.00
Merck & Co.	United States (New Jersey)	$46.84
Novartis	Switzerland	$44.45
GlaxoSmithKline	United Kingdom	$43.54
Johnson & Johnson	United States (New Jersey)	$42.19
AbbVie	United States (Illinois)	$33.27
Sanofi	France	$27.77
Bristol-Myers Squibb	United State (New York)	$26.15
AstraZeneca	United Kingdom	$23.57

Source: Data from Barton (2020).

The pharmaceutical industry accounts for 21 percent of all R&D conducted in the United States (Speights 2016).

  Patented brand-name drugs are marketed under the brand of the manufacturer and receive patent protection, whereas **generic drugs** are copies of brand-name drugs. Generic drugs copy the formulas of brand-name drugs and have the same dosage, intended use, administration, and strength as the original drug. For example, Valium is a brand-name drug that is commonly prescribed to relieve muscle spasms; its generic name is diazepam. Patent-protected drugs account for more than 70 percent of all drug spending in the United States, even though they represent only 10 percent of the prescriptions written (Kodjak 2016). Although patented drugs are legally protected for 20 years, some drug companies use controversial methods to extend their patent protections and continue sales of patented products (Amin 2018). For instance, drug companies have changed the dosage and frequency of medications to win patent extensions. Abbott Laboratories did this with its decades-old cholesterol drug, TriCor; to extend its patent, Abbot lowered the dosage and changed the drug's form from a tablet to a capsule. Likewise, Forest Laboratories obtained a new patent when it changed the dosage of its Alzheimer's disease drug Namenda from twice a day to once a day (Tribble 2018).

  The use of prescription drugs is increasing in the United States. In 2019, almost 50 percent of the US population used a prescription drug (Hagan 2019). One driver of

patented brand-named drug
A drug that is marketed under the manufacturer's name and protected by a patent, usually for 20 years.

generic drug
A copy of a brand-name drug that has the same dosage, intended use, administration, and strength as the original drug.

Exhibit 4.2

Americans'
Prescription Drug
Use by Age, 2019

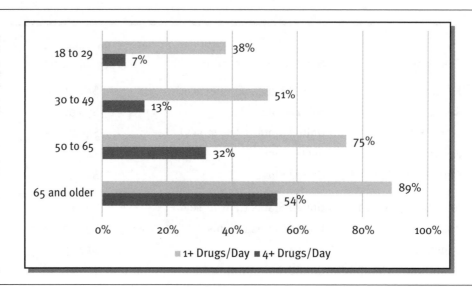

Source: Kirzinger et al. (2019).

the increasing use of prescription drugs is the aging of the population. Older people use prescription drugs more than younger people. As shown in exhibit 4.2, in 2019, 89 percent of Americans over the age of 65 used at least one prescription medication per day, and 54 percent used four or more. By comparison, only 38 percent of 18- to 29-year-olds in the United States took at least one medication per day, and only 7 percent took four or more (Kirzinger et al. 2019). As discussed in chapter 1, the share of older adults in the US population (those 65 and older) is expected to increase from 15 percent to 24 percent by 2060—a continuing boon to prescription drugs sales (Mather, Jacobson, and Pollard 2015).

Pharmaceutical Costs

The United States spends more per person on prescription drugs than other industrialized countries, primarily because of higher drug prices. A 2017 Commonwealth Fund study showed that people in the United States spent more than $1,000 per person per year for prescription drugs, whereas people in Germany and the United Kingdom spent only $686 and $497, respectively. Retail prescription drug prices in these two countries are, on average, 95 percent and 46 percent of prices in the United States (Sarnak, Squires, and Kuzmak 2017). Even though the majority of older Americans have insurance coverage for prescription drugs through Medicare, about three-quarters of those consumers believe the prices of prescription drugs are unreasonable (Kirzinger et al. 2019). Exhibit 4.3 illustrates the disparity in drug prices between the United States and other countries for the brand-name antidepressant Paxil.

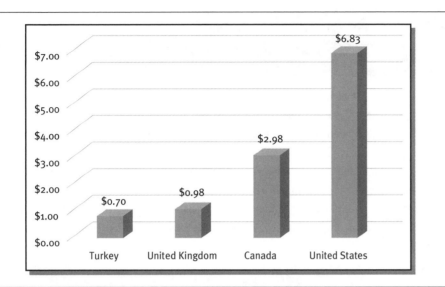

EXHIBIT **4.3**
Prescription Drug
Prices for Paxil
(20 mg tablet)

Source: Data from Boseley (2018).

Drug prices continue to escalate in the United States. From 2008 to 2014, the prices for top brand-name drugs jumped 127 percent, far exceeding the increase in consumer goods, which rose 11 percent (Hirschler 2018). The price of one popular long-lasting brand of insulin (a drug used by people with diabetes), Lantus, rose 54 percent in 2014 alone, even though it had been on the market for decades (Campbell 2019). Although people with diabetes can die without insulin, very few companies produce it in the United States. The lack of competition spurred a price spike. In 2019, a vial of insulin cost $30 in Canada, while in the United States, it cost $340 (Gordon 2019). The rapid increases in drug prices have negatively affected many people. According to one survey, almost 19 percent of people admitted that they had skipped a dose of a drug they needed to save money (AARP 2017). The prices of new drugs in the United States are particularly high, approaching $500,000 for a single treatment in some cases (see sidebar on next page).

Through Medicare Part D, the US federal government pays more than 40 percent of retail prescription drug costs (Brookings Institution 2017). Implemented in 2006, Part D coverage provides prescription drug benefits to those who qualify for Medicare. In 2018, 72 percent of Medicare enrollees (43 million out of 60 million) had Part D coverage. These Medicare beneficiaries pay an average monthly premium of $41, although the actual premiums and prescription drug benefits vary, depending on the plan chosen. For example, about 40 percent of Part D plans require no deductible; for the rest, the annual deductible is $435. About 30 percent of those with Part D coverage also receive low-income subsidies. Total expenses for Medicare Part D in 2020 were expected to reach $88 billion (Kaiser Family Foundation 2019).

(*) DEBATE TIME Are Drug Prices Out of Control?

In 2017, the FDA approved two drugs that provided a radical new treatment for cancer using a patient's own immune system to attack cancer cells. Both treatments were at least partially funded by federal research. The initial prices for these drugs were astonishing: Kymriah, used to treat leukemia, cost $475,000 for a one-time treatment, while Yescarta, for patients with lymphoma, cost $373,000. The high prices of these and other drugs have prompted calls for price controls and complaints that patients are paying for drugs twice: once through their taxes and again at the pharmacy counter (Pear 2018).

Do you think drug prices are out of control? Why do you think prescription drugs cost so much?

---

blockbuster drug
A prescription drug that has annual sales greater than $1 billion.

Pharmaceutical sales in the United States rose to $485 billion in 2018 and are expected to climb to about $655 billion by 2023 (Pharmaceutical Commerce 2019). However, most sales are attributable to a small number of drugs. Although there more than 9,000 drugs on the market that have been approved by the FDA, only 131 drugs have sales greater than $1 billion. These drugs are often referred to as **blockbuster drugs**. As exhibit 4.4

Exhibit 4.4
Top Blockbuster Drugs by Company, 2018

Company	Blockbuster Drugs	Estimated Revenues from Blockbuster Drugs (billions)	Share of Revenues from Blockbuster Drugs
Celgene	Revlimid	$10.9	64%
Bristol-Myers Squibb	Eliquis, Opdivo	$15.2	63%
AbbVie	Humira	$19.6	58%
Merck	Keytruda, Januvia, Janumet	$16.1	36%
Amgen	Enbrel, Neulasta, Neupogen	$8.2	36%
Roche	Rituxan, Herceptin, Avastin	$17.6	30%

Source: Data from Kresge and Lauerman (2019).

shows, many of the largest pharmaceutical companies earn significant portions of their revenues from blockbuster drugs. For example, AbbVie, the seventh-largest pharmaceutical company in the world, earns almost 60 percent of its revenues from just one drug (Humira, used to treat autoimmune disorders), while Roche, the second-largest company, generates 30 percent of its revenues from three drugs (Rituxan, Herceptin, and Avastin, all used to treat cancers) (Campbell 2019; Kresge and Lauerman 2019).

One way that healthcare organizations attempt to save money on prescription drugs is by creating drug formularies. A **formulary**, sometimes called a *drug list*, consists of a list of approved prescription drugs that an insurance plan covers. Organizations, using a panel of experts, generally consider the cost, safety, and effectiveness of a drug when deciding whether to place it on a formulary. This panel of experts, often called a pharmacy and therapeutics committee, meets regularly to discuss new drugs and drug information and to update the formulary.

Formularies are often divided into two or more groups, called **drug tiers**. These tiers represent different drug costs and copays for the consumer. For example, exhibit 4.5 shows a five-tier system that requires higher copays for more expensive brand-name and specialty drugs.

formulary
A list of approved prescription drugs that an insurance plan covers; also called a *drug list*.

drug tiers
Groups of prescription drugs that have different costs and copays for consumers.

EXHIBIT 4.5
Example of a Formulary with Drug Tiers and Copays

Drug Tier	Description	Copay
Tier 1	**Preferred generic.** This tier includes commonly prescribed generic drugs.	$1 to $3
Tier 2	**Generic.** These are also generic drugs, but they cost more than the drugs in Tier 1.	$7 to $11
Tier 3	**Preferred brand.** This tier includes brand-name drugs that do not have a generic equivalent. They are the lowest-cost brand-name drugs on the drug list.	$38 to $42
Tier 4	**Nonpreferred drug.** These are higher-priced brand-name and generic drugs that are not included in a preferred tier.	45% to 50% of the drug cost
Tier 5	**Specialty.** These are the most expensive drugs on the drug list. Specialty drugs are used to treat complex conditions such as cancer or multiple sclerosis. They can be generic or brand-name drugs.	25% to 33% of the retail cost

Source: Blue Care Network of Michigan (2020).

PHARMACEUTICAL DRUG DISCOVERY AND DRUG APPROVAL TRENDS

The drug discovery process has changed substantially in the past few decades, and it is likely to continue to evolve in the future. Pharmaceutical companies spend an average of $2.6 billion over 10 to 20 years to develop a successful new drug, up from $413 million in the 1980s. About 90 percent of drugs that are tested never make it to market. For example, drug companies investigated 123 drugs to treat Alzheimer's disease, but only four obtained market approval from the FDA (Speights 2016). Because of the long and arduous process required to get new drugs approved, the pharmaceutical industry earns almost 90 percent of its revenues from drugs discovered more than five years earlier (Leaf 2018). Some believe that future advances in mobile communications and the introduction of artificial intelligence will greatly facilitate the discovery and approval of new drugs by dramatically reducing the time required for clinical trials through more efficient patient selection and monitoring and communication during trials (Fleming 2018; Harrer et al. 2019; Pisani and Lee 2017).

Some experts suggest that drug companies should consider patient outcomes and focus on *cost-effectiveness* and *comparative clinical effectiveness*. Comparative clinical effectiveness refers to a drug's relative effectiveness in improving health, as measured by health-related outcomes. (For instance, Merck compared the COX-2 inhibitors etoricoxib and diclofenac, which were found to have similar efficacies.) Studies of comparative clinical effectiveness include randomized controlled trials, interventions, database studies, and observational studies. These types of studies compare the risks, benefits, and costs of different treatment options.

Cost-effectiveness refers to a drug's ability to produce better health results at an equal or lower cost compared with existing drugs. Some observers argue that new drugs should only receive FDA approval if they are cost-effective. The federal government could make greater use of comparative effectiveness studies, as other countries do, to establish which drugs produce the most benefits and use this information to negotiate drug prices (Bishop 2018). However, provisions of the Affordable Care Act of 2010 essentially prohibit the use of cost-effectiveness studies (Glick et al. 2015).

By 2019, 14 states had formed a collaborative to perform comparative effectiveness reviews of prescription drugs for their Medicaid populations. This effort has focused on multiple drug studies to compare the benefits and costs of rival drugs, providing states with more information to purchase the least expensive but most effective medicines (NCSL 2019).

external reference pricing
A method that countries use to set and negotiate the prices they will pay for prescription drugs.

Other countries use a method called **external reference pricing** to set and negotiate the prices they pay for prescription drugs. Basically, countries look at what other countries are paying for pharmaceuticals and use that information to establish the prices they are willing to pay. Most industrialized countries now use this method to set drug prices. If the United States used external reference pricing, which has been proposed by the federal government, the Medicare program could save almost $73 billion on prescription drugs (Kang et al. 2019).

EXHIBIT 4.6
Differences
Between Generic
and Biosimilar
Drugs

	Generic	Biosimilar
Development cost (US$)	$2 to $3 million	$100 to $300 million
Time to market	2–3 years	7–8 years
Clinical studies required	Bioequivalence	Through Phase III clinical trials
Patients studied	20–50	100–500

Source: mAbxience (2020).

A growth area in pharmaceuticals is **biosimilars**, which are somewhat different from generic drugs. Generic drugs are chemically identical to the original brand-name drug. Biosimilars have the same clinical effect as a generic drug, but they may differ chemically. Generic drugs are much less expensive and quicker to develop, as biosimilars require more thorough clinical trials with the drug tests on many more people (see exhibit 4.6). Sales of biosimilars are predicted to total $15 billion by 2020 (Chen et al. 2018). The FDA is seeking to develop a low-cost approval process for biosimilars to encourage competition and lower the prices of generic drugs (Campbell 2019).

Today, pharmaceutical companies are challenged to "generate meaningful innovation: not just marginal improvements in drug efficacy or safety, but therapies that really transform healthcare" that can reduce expensive hospitalizations or improve patients' quality of life (Moa 2019).

biosimilar
A drug that has the same clinical effect as a generic drug but a different chemical composition.

PHARMACY BENEFIT MANAGERS

Pharmacy benefit managers (PBMs) are a critical component of the pharmaceutical industry, although they have become quite controversial. As seen in exhibit 4.7, PBMs are go-between companies that work on behalf of insurance companies to manage their drug costs by negotiating with drug makers to determine which drugs will be covered and how much insurance plans will pay for them. They also negotiate with pharmacies over what they are paid for drugs and their dispensing fees. Overall, their role is to manage prescription drug benefits for health plan insurers to lower their drug costs. PBMs help establish formularies, negotiate lower prices with drug manufacturers through rebates and discounts, and directly reimburse individual pharmacies for drugs prescribed to their beneficiaries. PBMs determine which pharmacies are included in an insurance network and how much the pharmacies are paid. Some research has shown that PBMs help lower drug prices and slow the growth of drug spending (Commonwealth Fund 2019) (see sidebar).

pharmacy benefit manager (PBM)
A company that manages prescription drug benefits for health insurers to control drug spending and provide more effective drugs to consumers.

EXHIBIT 4.7
The Role of the
Pharmacy Benefit
Manager

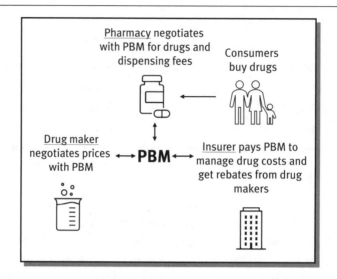

✱ HOW PHARMACY BENEFIT MANAGERS INFLUENCE PRICE

When the antiviral drug sofosbuvir—the first drug shown to cure hepatitis C—was approved by the FDA in 2014, it was very expensive. Initially, each tablet was priced at $1,000, and the total cost to treat one patient exceeded $80,000. However, by 2019, other companies had introduced ten equivalent drugs (Seladi-Schulman 2019). This gave Express Scripts, one of the largest PBMs, with 83 million members and 1.4 billion prescriptions annually, the ability to negotiate better prices by threatening to exclude a drug from its formulary unless the manufacturer lowered the price. As a result, Express Scripts was able to switch to another hepatitis C drug produced by Merck, which lowered the drug's price by 60 percent (Coombs 2014).

However, some accuse PBMs of keeping too much money rather than passing the savings on to patients. In fact, PBMs do receive a share of the rebates that they negotiate with drug manufacturers. PBMs justify this practice by arguing that they are pharmacy experts that obtain more effective and cheaper drugs for their clients. Lobbyists from the pharmaceutical industry, however, claim that PBMs actually cause drug costs to rise (Bluth 2019).

EXHIBIT **4.8**
Largest Pharmacy Benefit Managers in the United States

Company	Owner	Revenues (billions)	Net Income (billions)	Market Share of Prescription Managed Claims
CVS Caremark	Aetna/CVS Health	$257	$12	30%
Express Scripts	Cigna	$100	$4.6	23%
OptumRx	UnitedHealth Group	$74.3	n/a	23%

Note: Data are for 2019 for CVS Caremark and OptumRx and for 2017 for Express Scripts. OptumRx is part of OptumHealth, which is owned by United Health Group.
Sources: Data from *Forbes* (2018); Macrotrends (2020); O'Brien (2020); Paavola (2019).

Although PBMs existed in the 1960s, most were founded after the creation of Medicare Part D in the early 2000s. PBMs in the past were generally small, independent companies, but over the last decade, most have merged, so that three principal companies now control about 75 percent of the US market, and the top six PBMs control more than 95 percent of all prescriptions in the United States (Drug Channels 2019). PBMs have become so big that they manage drugs for more than 180 million people, and some are even bigger than the pharmaceutical companies they work with (Ollove 2019). Exhibit 4.8 provides an overview of the three largest PBMs, which are owned by prominent health insurance companies.

As a result of the consolidation and power of PBMs, even the American Medical Association (AMA) has encouraged regulatory intervention. According to the AMA, "Because of market concentration and lack of transparency, patients and physicians are essentially powerless in the face of PBM pricing and coverage decisions" (O'Reilly 2019). In the future, the role and evolution of PBMs will continue to be decided by market conditions and legislative and regulatory involvement.

CLINICAL TRIALS

Before a drug or pharmaceutical product can be used legally by consumers, it must be tested to make sure it is safe and works for its intended purpose. This is done through **clinical trials**. Clinical trials help researchers answer the following questions:

◆ Does a new treatment work?

◆ Does it work better than other treatments?

◆ Does it have side effects?

clinical trial
A research study in which human subjects are used to evaluate the effects of a medication, medical device, or intervention to determine its effectiveness and safety.

Exhibit 4.9

The Four Phases
of Clinical Trials

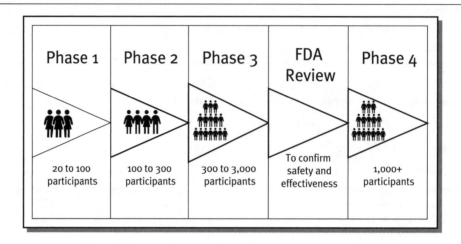

As exhibit 4.9 demonstrates, clinical trials are divided into four phases. Each phase involves research conducted on human subjects. During the first two phases of a clinical trial, researchers determine the safety, appropriate dosage, and side effects of a new drug or treatment. During Phase I, researchers test the new drug or treatment on a small number of people, perhaps 20 to 100. About 70 percent of Phase I trials yield positive results and move to Phase II. Phase II trials involve a larger group of subjects—generally up to several hundred volunteers—and go further in examining the safety and efficiency of different dosages.

If the first two phases are successful—which is the case for about one-third of clinical trials—the trial moves on to Phase III. During this phase, the trial is expanded to an even larger group of subjects, typically between 300 and 3,000 volunteers, depending on the disease and treatment being studied. In addition to studying safety, Phase III trials also seek to determine how the drug or treatment is best prescribed and used by patients. This phase also examines the efficacy and monitoring of adverse reactions to the treatment. About 25 to 30 percent of treatments pass Phase III.

The last phase, Phase IV, takes place only if a treatment has received approval by the government (in the United States, approval is granted by the FDA). Phase IV trials study the long-term effects of the drug or treatment across large populations. Several thousand volunteers are monitored, often for many years (FDA 2018b; Seladi-Schulman 2019).

Clinical trials are very expensive to conduct, with costs ranging from $5 million to $347 million (Moore et al. 2018). At any given time, many, many clinical trials are underway. In 2019, the US government listed 296,665 clinical trials ongoing across the 50 US states and 208 countries, with more than half conducted outside the United States (ClinicalTrials.gov 2020). Each clinical trial may take 12 to 15 years and more than $2.6 billion to take a new drug from the laboratory and to the pharmacy shelf, where it is available to the public (Drugs.com 2020).

Ensuring diversity in clinical trials is a challenge. Too often in the past, clinical trials were conducted mainly on white men. The FDA has now issued a guide to help researchers recruit subjects who better represent populations that are likely to use the drug. Since clinical trials determine whether medical products are safe and effective for people, participants in clinical trials need to represent potential users of the products. This is critical, as people of different ages, races, and genders may react differently to a medical product (FDA 2018a).

OVER-THE-COUNTER DRUGS

Over-the-counter (OTC) drugs are medicines that can be sold directly to a consumer without a prescription from a healthcare professional. More than 80 classes of OTC medications exist, ranging from acne medicines to weight loss products. People often buy OTC drugs at pharmacies, grocery stores, and even gas stations. The FDA has responsibility for approving OTC ingredients and labeling. Once acceptable ingredients, doses, formulas, and labeling are approved, new products can be created and marketed, as long as they conform to FDA guidelines.

Sales of OTC drugs exceed $35 billion in the United States. The top-selling OTC drugs include those for colds, fever, joint pain, heartburn, and antiperspirants. Although OTC medicines are sold like other consumer goods, they still have the potential to cause harm or addiction. Some of the common OTC drugs are Tylenol, Aleve, Robitussin, Listerine, and Alka-Seltzer. Consumers should always read their labels and follow directions for proper use (Anderson 2019: Stone 2019).

over-the-counter (OTC) drug
A drug that can be purchased without a prescription; often sold in pharmacies, grocery stories, and convenience stores.

MEDICAL DEVICE INDUSTRY

The **medical device industry**, which is also regulated by the FDA, encompasses a wide range of equipment and products that are critical to healthcare delivery. These products include equipment required in the delivery of care, such as surgical gloves and sterile tubing; diagnostic equipment, such as magnetic resonance imaging (MRI) machines; medical implants, such as artificial joints and pacemakers; adaptive equipment, such as crutches; and many other types of products and equipment.

The medical device industry can be divided into six sectors (SelectUSA 2020):

1. Dental equipment and supplies, such as drills, cements, sterilizers, and dental chairs

2. Electro-medical devices, such as pacemakers, patient-monitoring systems, MRI machines, and ultrasound devices

3. In-vitro diagnostics, such as chemicals, biological or radioactive substances for diagnostic tests done in test tubes, and machines

medical device industry
An industry that is regulated by the US Food and Drug Administration (FDA) and encompasses a wide range of equipment and products that are critical to healthcare delivery, such as surgical gloves, artificial joints, crutches, and imaging equipment.

4.   Irradiation devices, such as X-ray devices and other diagnostic imaging devices

5.   Surgical and medical instruments, such as anesthesia machines and orthopedic instruments

6.   Surgical appliances and supplies, such as artificial joints and limbs, stents, and surgical gloves

Similar to the pharmaceutical industry, the medical device industry generates considerable revenues and profits, and large medical device companies enjoy high profit margins of 20 to 30 percent. For Medicare patients alone, hospitals spend more than $24 billion per year on medical supplies. The annual market for the medical device industry exceeds $150 billion in the United States and accounts for 4 to 6 percent of all US healthcare spending. More than 5,500 firms make up this industry, employing over 2 million people in the United States. While most medical devices companies are small—80 percent have fewer than 50 employees, and 88 percent have fewer than 100 workers (MedPAC 2017; SelectUSA 2020)—a few large companies make up most of the industry's revenues and employment. As shown in exhibit 4.10, the ten largest medical device firms generate more than $190 billion in global revenues per year.

EXHIBIT 4.10
Ten Largest Medical Device Companies, 2018

Rank	Company	Headquarters	Global Medical Device Revenues (billions)
1	Medtronic	United States	$30.6
2	Johnson & Johnson	United States	$27.0
3	Royal Philips	Netherlands	$21.4
4	GE Healthcare	United States	$19.8
5	Fresenius Medical Care	Germany	$19.6
6	Siemens Healthcare	Germany	$15.9
7	Cardinal Health (medical segment)	United States	$15.6
8	Danaher	United States	$15.6
9	Stryker	United States	$13.6
10	EssilorLuxottica	France	$12.8
	Total		**$191.9**

Source: Data from Popa (2019).

New medical devices are constantly being developed, with more than $2 billion spent each year on R&D. As illustrated in exhibit 4.11, new, innovative medical devices includes such diverse products as heart, eye, and brain devices (Kirsh 2019).

EXHIBIT 4.11
Ten Most Innovative Medical Devices of 2019

Rank	Name	Company	Description
1	Recombinant human platelet-derived growth factor	Lynch Biologics	Assists in blood vessel formation and growth
2	CustomFlex artificial iris	HumanOptics	A prosthetic iris for reconstruction of eyes
3	Gentlewave	Sonendo	An endodontic to provide more efficient fluid delivery for root canal therapy
4	HeartLogic	Boston Scientific	An implantable device to detect heart failure
5	Inspiris Resilia Aortic Valve	Edwards Lifesciences	An implantable aortic valve
6	iStent Inject	Glaukos	Reduces intraocular pressure in patients with glaucoma
7	Magtrace magnetic localization system	Endomagnetics	tissue magnetic tracer system to guide lymph node biopsies
8	Brain Modulation	Medtronic	Stimulates the deep brain to reduce the frequency of seizures
9	Papyrus-covered coronary stent system	Biotronik	Provides greater flexibility for implantable heart stents
10	ProAir Digihaler	Teva Pharmaceutical Industries	A digital inhaler connected to a smartphone to improve monitoring for those with asthma and chronic obstructive pulmonary disease

Source: Kirsh (2019).

Medical devices are extremely costly for hospitals, particularly in the areas of orthopedics, neurosurgery, cardiovascular surgery, and interventional cardiology. In fact, the cost to hospitals for medical devices may equal what a hospital gets paid to perform the procedure using the device. For instance, the cost of a neuro-stimulator implant is 85 percent of the amount that a hospital would be reimbursed for the procedure (Paavola 2019). As illustrated in the sidebar, even procedures with good clinical outcomes might have negative financial consequences for hospitals.

LOW REIMBURSEMENTS FOR SOME MEDICAL DEVICES

Cardiovascular surgeons have found significant clinical benefits from implanting a MitraClip device to reduce heart failure and hospitalizations. Studies have shown a 47 percent reduction in heart failure in patients using this device. Hospitals are reimbursed between $28,398 and $40,176 for these procedures, but the device alone costs about $30,000—resulting in a loss of about $10,000 per procedure. Although these procedures have positive clinic outcomes, hospitals appear to have financial incentives to avoid them (Wendling 2019).

In the future, Medical device companies are predicted to expand more into wearable medical devices. Wearable medical devices are used to diagnose and monitor medical conditions. Some of these products are now used to encourage general wellness. For instance, the Apple Series 4 watch, which has EKG (electrocardiogram) and heart monitoring functions, has been recognized as a Class II medical device by the FDA (Speer 2018). Although these devices are increasingly popular, insurance companies do not generally reimburse patients for them, and many patients and providers are still unaware of their scope and potential. Nevertheless, many industry observers believe that by 2021, sales of wearable medical devices will reach $12 billion (Shepard 2018).

SUMMARY

The pharmaceutical and medical device industries are large and important components of the US healthcare system. The pharmaceutical industry is responsible for the discovery, manufacture, and distribution of prescription drugs. Before drugs can be made available to consumers, they must be approved by the US Food and Drug Administration, the federal agency that regulates drugs in the United States.

The pharmaceutical industry is a global business. Six of the ten largest pharmaceutical companies are headquartered in the United States, although all of the companies sell drugs worldwide. The industry continues to innovate and produce new products, but this innovation comes with a high price tag—estimated at $2.6 billion per new product. Even considering the high research and development (R&D) costs, the pharmaceutical industry remains extraordinarily profitable, with average profit margins of 20 to 30 percent.

The pharmaceutical industry produces both brand-name and generic drugs. Brand-name drugs receive patent protection, which gives the manufacturer exclusive protection to produce and sell the drug for a limited period of time, usually 20 years. After that time, other companies can produce generic versions of brand-name drugs. Generic drugs have the same dosage, intended use, administration, and strength of the original drug, but they often are sold at a lower cost.

The use of prescriptions continue to increase, driven by the aging US population. Older adults use many more drugs per person than younger people. In addition, the United States spends much more than other countries on prescription drugs, primarily because of higher prices. High drug costs are a burden on US government spending, as the federal government pays more than 40 percent of prescription drug costs. The US government's prescription drug costs increased with the implementation of Medicare Part D.

Healthcare organizations seek to control drug costs by using formularies, which are approved drug lists. These lists are created by experts based on drug cost, safety, and effectiveness. Formularies are organized by tiers, which correspond to the amount that consumers pay. Pharmacy benefit managers (PBMs) were established to set formularies and lower prescription drug prices for health insurance companies. Today, the largest three PBMs are owned by insurance companies; some question their commitment to passing savings onto healthcare consumers.

Drug discovery is expensive: Taking a single drug to market may cost billions of dollars in R&D. Most pharmaceutical company revenues (90 percent) come from products that were developed more than five years ago. Some believe that advances in mobile communication and artificial intelligence will facilitate the development of new drugs in the future.

The medical device industry represents a variety of different products and billions of dollars in expenditures. Although many medical device firms operate in the United States, just a few make up most of the industry's revenues and employment. The medical device industry continues to innovate, with significant impacts on consumers' health and healthcare costs.

QUESTIONS

1. What is the difference between a patented brand-name drug and a generic drug?
2. Why does the United States spend more per capita on prescription drugs than other countries?
3. Why does the US federal government spend so much on prescription drugs?
4. What is a formulary, and how does it save money?
5. What are the four phases of clinical trials, and what does phase each focus on?

Assignments

1. Look at Johnson & Johnson's product website at www.jnj.com/healthcare-products. Identify ten types of medical devices that the company produces. Which are expensive, and which are relatively lower in cost?
2. Read the following article: "Why Our Drugs Cost So Much," AARP, May 1, 2017, at www.aarp.org/health/drugs-supplements/info-2017/rx-prescription-drug-pricing. html. Write a one-page paper explaining why prescription drug prices are so high in the United States.

Cases

The Challenge of Increasing Prices

Chuck, an independent truck driver who had diabetes, had to make a tough choice when he was informed that his health insurance plan would no longer cover the brand of insulin, Humalog, that he had used for 17 years to control his type 1 diabetes. The change was precipitated by a spike in the price of Humalog—a 290 percent cost increase over ten years. As a result, Humalog was taken off the insurance company's formulary, causing Chuck's copayment for a 90-day supply of the drug to increase almost threefold, to $500. As he appealed the sudden and costly change in coverage, he decreased his dose of Humalog. Lacking the insulin he needed, Chuck became so sick that he had to go to the emergency room several times with dangerously high blood sugar levels. Being ill made it difficult for Chuck to continue driving, which lowered his income, making it even more difficult for him to buy insulin.

Discussion Questions

1. How do increases in drug costs affect patients?
2. Why does taking a drug off a formulary increase the prices to the consumer?
3. What should Chuck do?

Medical Device Representatives in the Operating Room

Sue works as a medical device salesperson, selling titanium screws designed for orthopedic surgery. She enters the operating room at the invitation of the doctor and provides verbal instructions to surgeons as they operate. At times, she has even has physical contact with patients. Sue sees this interaction as very important, especially for sales of new technology and innovative products. In such cases, she often has more knowledge about the product than the doctors. Since most of her compensation comes from commissions based on her sales, she is willing to help doctors choose her products.

Discussion Questions

1. What problems could arise from having medical device representatives in the operating room? For background, read the following article: "Why Is That Salesman in the Operating Room for Your Knee Replacement," *Washington Post*, November 14, 2016, at www.washingtonpost.com/national/health-science/why-is-that-salesperson-in-the-operating-room-for-your-knee-replacement/2016/11/14/ab8172fa-78e6-11e6-beac-57a4a412e93a_story.html?utm_term=.07e1b96feb23.

2. Should medical device salespeople be banned from the operating room? For background, read the following article: "Will the Sales Representative in the Operating Room Become Extinct?," Strategic Dynamics, February 1, 2016, at https://strategicdynamicsfirm.com/will-the-sales-representative-in-the-operating-room-become-extinct/.

REFERENCES

AARP. 2017. "Why Prescription Drugs Cost So Much." *AARP Bulletin*. Published May. www.aarp.org/health/drugs-supplements/info-2017/rx-prescription-drug-pricing.html.

Amin, T. 2018. "The Problem with High Drug Prices Isn't Foreign Freeloading, It's the Patent System." CNBC. Published June 27. www.cnbc.com/2018/06/25/high-drug-prices-caused-by-us-patent-system.html.

Anderson, L. 2019. "Over the Counter Medications." Drugs.com. Reviewed May 7. www.drugs.com/otc/.

Barton, C. 2020. "Annual Revenue of Top 10 Big Pharma Companies." The Pharma Letter. Published March 3. www.thepharmaletter.com/article/annual-revenue-of-top-10-big-pharma-companies.

Bishop, S. 2018. "Policy Prescriptions for High Drug Costs: Experts Weigh In." Commonwealth Fund. Published April 3. www.commonwealthfund.org/blog/2018/policy-prescriptions-high-drug-costs-experts-weigh.

Blue Care Network of Michigan. 2020. "How Do Drug Tiers Work?" Accessed April 6. www.bcbsm.com/medicare/help/understanding-plans/pharmacy-prescription-drugs/tiers.html.

Bluth, R. 2019. "Can Someone Tell Me What a PBM Does?" Kaiser Health News. Published April 9. https://khn.org/news/senate-hearing-drug-pricing-lesson-on-pharmacy-benefit-managers/.

Boseley, S. 2018. "Why Do New Medicines Cost So Much, and What Can We Do About It?" *The Guardian*. Published April 9. www.theguardian.com/news/2018/apr/09/why-do-new-medicines-cost-so-much-and-what-can-we-do-about-it.

Brookings Institution. 2017. "Ten Challenges in the Prescription Drug Market—and Ten Solutions." Policy Brief. Published May 2. www.brookings.edu/research/ten-challenges-in-the-prescription-drug-market-and-ten-solutions/.

Campbell, K. 2019. "Why Are Prescription Drug Prices Rising?" *U.S. News & World Report*. Published February 6. https://health.usnews.com/health-care/for-better/articles/2019-02-06/why-are-prescription-drug-prices-rising.

Chen, Y., J. Dikan, J. Heller, and J. Santos da Silva. 2018. "Five Things to Know About Biosimilars Right Now." McKinsey & Company. Published July 17. www.mckinsey.com/industries/pharmaceuticals-and-medical-products/our-insights/five-things-to-know-about-biosimilars-right-now.

ClinicalTrials.gov. 2020. "Trends, Charts, and Maps." US National Library of Medicine. Accessed April 6. https://clinicaltrials.gov/ct2/resources/trends.

Commonwealth Fund. 2019. "Pharmacy Benefit Managers and Their Role in Drug Spending." Published April 22. www.commonwealthfund.org/publications/explainer/2019/apr/pharmacy-benefit-managers-and-their-role-drug-spending.

Coombs, B. 2014. "For Sovaldi Patients, Expensive Hepatitis C Cure Is Priceless." CNBC. Published May 23. www.cnbc.com/2014/05/23/for-sovaldi-patients-expensive-hepatitis-c-cure-is-priceless.html.

Drug Channels. 2019. "CVS, Express Scripts, and the Evolution of the PBM Business Model." Published May 29. www.drugchannels.net/2019/05/cvs-express-scripts-and-evolution-of.html.

Drugs.com. 2020. "FDA Approval Process." Accessed June 28. www.drugs.com/fda-approval-process.html.

Ellis, M. 2019. "Who Are the Top 10 Pharmaceutical Companies in the World? (2010)." Proclinical. Published March 20. www.proclinical.com/blogs/2018-3/the-top-10-pharmaceutical-companies-in-the-world-2018.

Fleming, N. 2018. "How Artificial Intelligence Is Changing Drug Discovery." *Nature*. Published May 30. www.nature.com/articles/d41586-018-05267-x.

Forbes. 2018. "Express Scripts" Published June 6. www.forbes.com/companies/express-scripts/#38a2a2c3cc70.

Glick, H. A., S. McElligott, M. V. Pauly, R. J. Willke, H. Bergquist, J. Doshi, L. A. Fleisher, B. Kinosian, E. Perfetto, D. E. Polsky, and J. S. Schwartz. 2015. "Comparative Effectiveness and Cost-Effectiveness Analyses Frequently Agree on Value." *Health Affairs* 34 (5): 805–11.

Gordon, S. 2019. "Why Are Insulin Prices Still So High for Patients in the U.S.?" *U.S. News & World Report*. Published November 6. www.usnews.com/news/health-news/articles/2019-11-07/why-are-insulin-prices-still-so-high-for-us-patients.

Hagan, S. 2019. "Nearly One in Two Americans Takes Prescription Drugs: Survey." Bloomberg News. Published May 7. www.bloomberg.com/news/articles/2019-05-08/nearly-one-in-two-americans-takes-prescription-drugs-survey.

Harrer, S., P. Shah, B. Antony, and J. Hu. 2019. "Artificial Intelligence for Clinical Trial Design." *Trends in Pharmacological Sciences* 40 (8): 577–91.

Hirschler, B. 2018. "How the U.S. Pays 3 Times More for Drugs." *Scientific American*. Published October 13. www.scientificamerican.com/article/how-the-u-s-pays-3-times-more-for-drugs/.

Kang, S., M. DiStefano, M. Socal, and G. Anderson. 2019. "Part D to Reduce Drug Price Differentials with Other Countries." *Health Affairs* 38 (5): 804–11.

Kaiser Family Foundation. 2019. "An Overview of the Medicare Part D Prescription Drug Benefit." Published November 13. www.kff.org/medicare/fact-sheet/an-overview-of-the-medicare-part-d-prescription-drug-benefit/.

Kirsh, D. 2019. "The 17 Most Innovative Medical Devices of 2019." Medical Design & Outsourcing. July 18. www.medicaldesignandoutsourcing.com/17-most-innovative-medical-devices-2019/2/.

Kirzinger, A., T. Neuman, J. Cubanski, and M. Brodie. 2019. "Data Note: Prescription Drugs and Older Adults." Kaiser Family Foundation. Published August 9. www.kff.org/health-reform/issue-brief/data-note-prescription-drugs-and-older-adults/.

Kodjak, A. 2016. "Tighter Patent Rules Could Help Lower Drug Prices, Study Shows." National Public Radio. Published August 23. www.npr.org/sections/health-shots/2016/08/23/491053523/tighter-patent-rules-could-help-lower-drug-prices-study-shows.

Kresge, N., and J. Lauerman. 2019. "Big Pharma Faces the Curse of the Billion-Dollar Block-buster." *Bloomberg Businessweek*. Published January 11. www.bloomberg.com/news/articles/2019-01-11/big-pharma-faces-the-curse-of-the-billion-dollar-blockbuster.

Leaf, C. 2018. "How Stale Is Innovation in Drug Discovery? Think: 5-Year-Old Yogurt." *Fortune*. Published March 6. http://fortune.com/2018/03/06/big-pharma-innovation-rut/.

Ledley, F., S. McCoy, and G. Vaughan. 2020. "Profitability of Large Pharmaceutical Companies Compared with Other Large Public Companies." *Journal of the American Medical Association* 323 (9): 834–43.

mAbxience. 2020. "Generics, Biologics, Biosimilars: Who's Who?" Accessed June 3. www.mabxience.com/products/biosimilar/generics-biologics-biosimilars-whos-who/.

Macrotrends. 2020. "CVS Health Operating Income 2006–2020." www.macrotrends.net/stocks/charts/CVS/cvs-health/operating-income.

Mather, M., L. A. Jacobson, and K. M. Pollard. 2015. "Fact Sheet: Aging in the United States." *Population Bulletin* 70 (2). www.prb.org/wp-content/uploads/2016/01/aging-us-population-bulletin-1.pdf.

Medicare Payments Advisory Commission (MedPAC). 2017. "An Overview of the Medical Device Industry." Report to Congress: Medicare and the Healthcare Delivery System. Published June. http://medpac.gov/docs/default-source/reports/jun17_ch7.pdf?sfvrsn=0.

Moa, A. 2019. "6 Pharma Trends for 2019 That Will Set the Pace for Industry." Tribeca Knowledge. Published January 14. www.tribecaknowledge.com/blog/top-6-pharma-trends-for-2019-that-will-set-the-pace-for-industry.

Moore, T., H. Zhang, G. Anderson, and G. Alexander. 2018. "Estimated Costs of Pivotal Trials for Novel Therapeutic Agents Approved by the U.S. Food and Drug Administration, 2015–2016." *JAMA Internal Medicine* 178 (11): 1451–57.

National Conference of State Legislatures (NCSL). 2019. "Comparative Effectiveness and Academic Detailing to Evaluate Prescription Drugs." Published May 21. www.ncsl.org/research/health/comparative-effectiveness-and-academic-detailing-to-evaluate-prescription-drugs.aspx.

O'Brien, J. 2020. "UnitedHealth Group Ends 2019 with $242 B in Revenues." HealthLeaders. Published January 15. www.healthleadersmedia.com/finance/unitedhealth-group-ends-2019-242b-revenues.

Ollove, M. 2019. "Drug-Price Debate Targets Pharmacy Benefit Managers." Pew Charitable Trusts. Published February 12. www.pewtrusts.org/en/research-and-analysis/blogs/stateline/2019/02/12/drug-price-debate-targets-pharmacy-benefit-managers.

O'Reilly, K. 2019. "Time to Scrutinize PBMs' Outsized Role in Rx Decision-Making." American Medical Association. Published June 10. www.ama-assn.org/delivering-care/public-health/time-scrutinize-pbms-outsized-role-rx-decision-making.

Paavola, A. 2019. "Top PBMs by Market Share." *Becker's Hospital Review*. Published May 30. www.beckershospitalreview.com/pharmacy/top-pbms-by-market-share.html.

PCG. 2018. *Rising Prescription Drug Costs: A Report on State and Federal Efforts to Contain Costs*. Published March. www.publicconsultinggroup.com/media/1594/rising-prescription-drug-costs-state-and-federal-efforts-to-contain-costs.pdf.

Pear, R. 2018. "Paying Twice: A Push for Affordable Prices for Taxpayer-Funded Drugs." *New York Times*. Published May 28. www.nytimes.com/2018/05/28/us/politics/drug-prices.html.

Pharmaceutical Commerce. 2019. "Global Pharma Spending Will Hit $1.5 Trillion in 2023, Says IQVIA." Published January 29. https://pharmaceuticalcommerce.com/business-and-finance/global-pharma-spending-will-hit-1-5-trillion-in-2023-says-iqvia/.

Pisani, J., and M. Lee. 2017. "A Critical Makeover for Pharmaceutical Companies: Overcoming Industry Obstacles with a Cross-Functional Strategy." Strategy&, PwC. Published January 10. www.strategyand.pwc.com/reports/critical-makeover-pharmaceutical-companies.

Popa, R. 2019. "The World's Top 10 Largest Medical Device Companies." *Becker's ASC Review*. Published September 18. www.beckersasc.com/supply-chain/the-world-s-top-10-largest-medical-device-companies.html.

Sarnak, D. O., D. Squires, and G. Kuzmak. 2017. "Paying for Prescription Drugs Around the World: Why Is the U.S. an Outlier?" Commonwealth Fund. Published October 2017. www.commonwealthfund.org/publications/issue-briefs/2017/oct/paying-prescription-drugs-around-world-why-us-outlier.

Seladi-Schulman, J. 2019. "What Happens in a Clinical Trial?" Healthline. Updated June 21. www.healthline.com/health/clinical-trial-phases.

SelectUSA. 2020. "Medical Technology Spotlight." Accessed June 2. www.selectusa.gov/medical-technology-industry-united-states.

Shepard, S. 2018. "Wireless Wearables: Challenges to Tackle." MD+DI. Published November 12. www.mddionline.com/wireless-wearables-challenges-tackle.

Speer, J. 2018. "Predictions for the Medical Device Industry in 2019." *Greenlight Guru*. Published December 9. www.greenlight.guru/blog/medical-device-industry-predictions-2019.

Speights, K. 2016. "12 Big Pharma Stats That Will Blow You Away." The Motley Fool. Published July 31. www.fool.com/investing/2016/07/31/12-big-pharma-stats-that-will-blow-you-away.aspx.

Stone, K. 2019. "List of Best-Selling Over-the-Counter (OTC) Drugs." Verywell Health. Published August 10. www.verywellhealth.com/top-selling-otc-drugs-by-category-2663170.

Tribble, S. 2018. "Drugmakers Play the Patent Game to Ward Off Competitors." NBC News. Published October. www.nbcnews.com/health/health-news/drugmakers-play-patent-game-ward-competitors-n915911.

US Food and Drug Administration (FDA). 2018a. "Minorities in Clinical Trials." Reviewed August 6. www.fda.gov/consumers/minority-health/minorities-clinical-trials.

———. 2018b. "Step 3: Clinical Research." Reviewed January 4. www.fda.gov/ForPatients/Approvals/Drugs/ucm405622.htm.

US Government Accountability Office (GAO). 2017. "Drug Industry: Profits, Research and Development Spending, and Merger and Acquisition Deals." Report No. GAO-1840. Published November 17. www.gao.gov/products/GAO-18-40.

Wendling, P. 2019. "COAPT: MitraClip Adds Years of Life, but at a Steep Price." Medscape. Published October 4. www.medscape.com/viewarticle/919450.

CHAPTER 5

LONG-TERM CARE

An April 2018 episode of the CBS news program *60 Minutes* recounted the story of Mike and Carol Daly. In 2008, Carol was diagnosed with Alzheimer's disease. Every year for ten years, *60 Minutes* correspondents interviewed the couple. Early on, Carol was bright and conversational and concerned about her illness, although she maintained a positive attitude. Her husband, Mike, spoke of his determination to stay by her side and help attend to all her needs. Over the ten years of interviews, Carol began to lose her memory and forget simple words; eventually, she did not even know her husband. By 2018, she was unresponsive. At first, Mike was able to care for Carol on his own. As the disease progressed, however, Mike needed help, and eventually Carol required 24-hour care. Finally, Mike had to admit his wife to a nursing home. Mike spoke about the struggles he faced financially and emotionally—and even confessed that he had considered suicide at one point (CBS News 2018).

The situation that Mike and Carol faced is familiar to many people in the United States. Thousands of seniors experience some sort of dementia or other serious health problem, and their loved ones must shoulder the burden of providing long-term care for them.

By the time the youngest baby boomers turn 65—around 2030—this generation is expected to number about 60 million. For the first time, the US population aged 65 and older will exceed the number of children by 2030, with 77 million over 65 and 76.5 million people under the age of 18. By 2050, the number of seniors is projected to reach 83.7 million (US Census Bureau 2018). The health challenges of seniors and the people who care for them will be enormous.

After reading this chapter, you will be able to

➤ Describe the history of long-term care.

➤ Differentiate among skilled nursing and assisted living facilities, respite care, hospice services, and other long-term care settings.

➤ Value the challenges and demands of informal caregivers.

➤ Comprehend the different educational requirements, skills, and demand for formal long-term care workers.

➤ Analyze the challenges of paying for long-term care.

➤ Evaluate the seriousness of elder abuse.

➤ Analyze the future of long-term care.

A HISTORICAL LOOK AT LONG-TERM CARE

Early American settlers had few choices when it came to survival. They found food by hunting, fishing, and gathering edible plants; they lived off others who supported them; they robbed from others to survive; or they cleared the land and grew crops that they could eat or trade for other goods. Farming families generally relied on their children and extended family members to help with chores (McGurdy 2009). Many of these early families had no neighbors or communities they could rely on.

By the mid-1800s, the Industrial Revolution had displaced many older Americans. Younger people moved to cities to work in factories and supported their elderly parents with their earnings. Those who were childless but wealthy could hire help. Some elderly people were "boarded out"—that is, their children paid other families to provide a place to live and care for their parents. Those who had no money and no children needed help from the community to survive (Social Security Administration 1937). Later, the Civil War ripped families apart, leaving many elderly parents to fend for themselves or seek care from others after losing their adult children to the war.

Before the nineteenth century, public welfare was not a federal obligation. Local government was

"The home of a pioneer family was a little world in itself. Members of the family were their own farm and factory workers, butchers, bakers, and barbers; policemen and firemen; often their own doctors and nurses, and sometimes their own teachers as well" (Social Security Administration 1937).

almshouse

A house originally built by an organization or person to take care of the poor.

poorhouse

A home or residential institution where people were required to live if they could not financially support themselves.

tasked with taking care of those who could not provide for themselves. Cities and counties built **almshouses**, **poorhouses**, poor farms, county infirmaries, asylums, and county homes for the poor and incapacitated. A few states paid individuals to care for the poor. Tennessee actually auctioned paupers to the lowest bidder (Hoyt 2018). Local governments preferred to put the poor and elderly in group housing rather than give handouts of food and clothing.

As is the case today, a common concern among administrators of poorhouses was to prevent people from taking advantage of living at the expense of taxpayers. Individuals had to prove they needed support—that is, they had to show that they had no children or others who could care for them. Life in almshouses was deliberately made tough and unappealing to discourage dependence. Church groups created facilities where only "worthy individuals" of their own religion, ethnic background, or culture could live (Rincon del Rio 2017). In the early twentieth century, nearly 70 percent of the people who lived in the poorhouses were elderly poor. They often lived together in the same rooms with criminals, alcoholics, and the mentally ill.

The 1920 census reported for the first time that more people lived in towns and cities than on farms. More young people were moving to places where they could work in factories and mines. They were helping to make and sell goods. Many found jobs in new occupations such as bookkeepers, accountants, bankers, store clerks, doctors, dentists, and nurses. People needed more education to prepare for these jobs, so new laws were created to protect children from the dangers of working in industry, allowing them to continue their schooling. This left many elderly people alone on farms with no children to care for them as they grew older. For many elderly, the only option was to find someone else or some institution to care for them.

In 1935, the federal government took action to abolish the almshouses and to provide financial support to the elderly. The Social Security Act of that year provided for

---

✳ FEDERAL EMERGENCY RELIEF

President Franklin D. Roosevelt initiated several Federal Emergency Relief Administration (FERA) programs in the mid-1930s as millions of Americans attempted to recover from the Great Depression. An estimated 15 percent of the population was dependent on FERA programs. The elderly, many of whom had lost all of their savings, investments, and retirement funds, could not find work or were not well enough to work.

Even though the elderly were now dependent on their children, many families split up to find jobs. Children were sent to orphanages, and older parents ended up in poorhouses (Hoyt 2018).

older people, the blind, dependent and disabled children, maternal and child welfare, some public health measures, and the administration of unemployment benefits (Social Security Administration 1935). It barred support for those living in poorhouses, as officials hoped to abolish such institutions. Residents of privately funded homes for the elderly were eligible to receive these new federal funds, however. States reacted quickly by transferring some of their county-owned poorhouses to private control. The residents and their supervisors were the same, but they could now enjoy the support of federal funds (Rincon del Rio 2017).

By the 1950s, federal government policy had shifted, barring almshouses from receiving Social Security funds, and they began to shut their doors. In response, policymakers pushed to provide a better alternative. In 1954, amendments to the Hill-Burton Act provided funding for nursing homes built alongside—and modeled after—hospitals. The goal was to construct hospitals in rural and poor areas that did not already have them and to update or modernize some hospitals already existing in cities. The Hill-Burton Act led to a rapid expansion of public and not-for-profit hospitals. An unplanned result of the legislation was the conversion of older buildings such as hotels, homes, and old hospitals into nursing homes (Minnesota Department of Health 2009).

A 1948 report published by the Social Security Advisory Council suggested that the elderly poor needed Old Age Assistance. The report noted that while some elderly people had enough wealth or savings that they may not need protection, others did not have adequate funds to live on as they aged. "Since the interest of the whole Nation is involved," the report pointed out, "the people, using the Government as the agency for their cooperation, should make sure that all members of the community have at least a basic measure of protection against the major hazards of old age and death" (Social Security Administration 1948). The report spurred expanded coverage under Social Security, setting up the program that is in place today.

The creation of Medicare in the 1960s led to greater demand for nursing home care. As soon as new beds became available, they were filled. Inadequate funding for this demand, however, prompted the US Department of Health, Education, and Welfare (now the US Department of Health and Human Services) to discontinue much of the financial coverage initially allowed for long-term care. Concerns about the quality of care and the safety of nursing homes grew along with their expansion. A report of the Special Committee on Aging indicated that 44 percent of nursing home beds did not meet the standards established by the Hill-Burton Act, meaning that they offered limited services, had poorly trained or unlicensed staff, and did not meet fire safety standards. In fact, the adequacy of state licensing standards and the variability of enforcement efforts was in question (Institute of Medicine 1986).

In the face of growing demand for nursing home beds, there was little government oversight and few restrictions on how nursing homes operated. Moreover, a number of nursing homes experienced fatal fires during this time, underscoring the immediate

EXHIBIT 5.1
Major Multi-Fatality
Nursing Home
Fires

Date	Location	Fatalities
October 31, 1952	Hillsboro, MO	20
March 29, 1953	Largo, FL	33
January 30, 1957	Hogham, WA	21
February 17, 1957	Warrenton, MO	72
November 23, 1963	Fitchville, OH	63
December 18, 1964	Fountaintown, IN	20
January 9, 1970	Marietta, OH	31
January 30, 1976	Chicago, IL	23

Source: Data from Hoyt (2018).

need to advance laws related to long-term care. Exhibit 5.1 lists several of the largest and most devastating nursing home fires that occurred between 1952 and 1976 (Hoyt 2018). A standards guide did not become available until 1963.

Elder abuse in nursing homes became a national scandal in the 1970s. Some facilities resembled the almshouses of the past. In 1972, the federal government created specific standards for nursing homes funded by the recently created Medicare and Medicaid programs. New regulations required nursing homes to meet the life safety code of the National Fire Protection Association, and nursing homes called "skilled nursing facilities" were required to have at least one full-time registered nurse on staff. At the same time, reimbursements for many services decreased, creating a demand for new facilities where licensed practical nurses, nurse aides, and others who were not registered nurses could provide assistance with the activities of daily living.

LONG-TERM CARE TODAY

The Centers for Disease Control and Prevention (CDC) reported that more than 4 million Americans are admitted to or reside in nursing homes or skilled nursing facilities each year, and nearly 1 million people live in assisted living facilities (CDC 2019). In 2016, according to the National Center for Health Statistics, 65,500 long-term care providers served 8.3 million people in the United States. Exhibit 5.2 presents the number of long-term care service providers in 2016. Nursing homes alone accounted for 1.7 million licensed beds and 1.3 million residents. Around 69 percent of these nursing homes were for-profit institutions. Most nursing homes and residential care communities were affiliated with a

EXHIBIT 5.2
Long-Term Care
Service Providers,
2016

Type of Facility	Number
Adult day service centers	4,600
Home health agencies	12,200
Hospice providers	4,300
Nursing homes	15,600
Residential care communities	28,900

Source: NCHS (2019).

national postacute care organization or healthcare system, while the majority of adult day service centers were independently or government-owned (NCHS 2019).

The same CDC report indicated that in 2016, clients of adult day service centers were younger than those in skilled nursing facilities, assisted care, and other services, and that they were the most racially and ethnically diverse among long-term care clients: about one-fifth of adult day service users were Hispanic/Latino, and one-fifth were non-Hispanic/Latino Black. Nursing homes had the largest share of clients diagnosed with Alzheimer's disease and other forms of dementia.

About 20 percent of all adults, or 53 million people in the United States, and more than one-third of adults aged 65 or older have a functional disability, such as limited mobility, eyesight, hearing, cognition, or self-care, and need paid or unpaid help with basic daily living skills (CDC 2015). On average, the people with disabilities require such help for three years—3.7 years for women and 2.2 years for men (Kemper, Komisar, and Alecxih 2005–06). During those three years, the average American user will take advantage of these services at home and one-third in either a nursing home or an assisted living facility (HHS 2012).

LONG-TERM CARE SETTINGS

Long-term care providers offer a range of services. These services are provided in a number of settings. This section covers skilled nursing facilities, assisted living facilities, senior centers, continuing care retirement centers, respite care and adult day services, and hospice care.

SKILLED NURSING FACILITIES

Skilled nursing facilities (SNFs), also known as *skilled nursing centers*, are licensed long-term care facilities that provide general nursing care to those who are chronically ill or

skilled nursing facility (SNF)
A licensed facility that provides general nursing care to those who are chronically ill or unable to take care of their daily living needs; also called a *skilled nursing center*.

unable to take care of their daily living needs. Outside of hospitals, SNFs offer the highest level of care. SNFs are most appropriate for certain types of patients (HelpGuide 2019):

◆ Individuals whose medical and personal care needs are too great to be handled at home or in another facility, because of a recent hospitalization or chronic illness.

◆ Individuals who need shorter-term care after a hospitalization until it is safe for them to return home.

SNFs provide what is known as "custodial care," which includes basic services such as bathing, feeding, dressing, and help getting into and out of bed. They also provide medical services that can be delivered only by a registered nurse or doctor. A licensed physician supervises each patient's care, and a nurse is present in the facility. Nurses dispense medication and perform other medical procedures that are not available at other long-term care facilities. Other healthcare professionals, such as occupational or physical therapists, are also available to patients (HelpGuide 2019). Most SNFs have agreements with hospitals or similar providers for emergency care. In fact, many SNFs are located near a hospital (SeniorCaring.com 2016). The US Department of Health and Human Services and the Centers for Medicare & Medicaid Services (CMS) together regulate most aspects of care provided in SNFs.

ASSISTED LIVING FACILITIES

Assisted living facilities, also known as *residential care communities*, are living arrangements that are designed to meet basic personal care needs and to provide assistance with the **activities of daily living (ADLs)**, limited administration of medications, and services such as laundry and housekeeping. Exhibit 5.3 lists some of the most common ADLs. Assisted living facilities offer less intensive services than skilled nursing facilities and vary in size and style. Some are similar to a large home, with a number of client rooms. Others look like apartment complexes. Assisted living facilities offer different levels of care and often provide daily social activities for their residents. They often provide transportation to local events or, in some cases, a personal event. Assisted living facilities are designed to allow residents relative independence.

The National Center for Assisted Living reports that more than half of the residents in assisted living facilities are the "oldest old"—that is, aged 85 and older. Most are female and non-Hispanic/Latino white. Their most common needs are bathing and dressing. Nearly half of assisted living residents have a cardiovascular disease, and four in ten have Alzheimer's disease or another form of dementia. The average stay in an assisted living facility is 22 months; around 60 percent of residents then move to a skilled nursing facility (National Center for Assisted Living 2020).

assisted living facility
A living arrangement designed to provide basic personal care needs, assistance with activities of daily living (ADLs), limited administration of medications, and services such as laundry and housekeeping; also known as a *residential care community*.

activities of daily living (ADLs)
Routine activities that people do every day, such as eating, bathing, getting dressed, toileting, transferring, and continence.

Bathing = 62%   Dressing = 47%   Toileting = 39%   Bed transfer = 30%   Eating = 20%

EXHIBIT 5.3
Common Activities of Daily Living for Assisted Living Residents

Source: National Center for Assisted Living (2020).

SENIOR CENTERS

Senior centers are available to the elderly in many communities. They typically provide services at a community-based center. Some services are available to individuals as young as 50 years old. Programs at senior centers address the individual needs of functionally or cognitively impaired adults as well as those who simply want to socialize with other people their age. These structured, comprehensive programs provide social and support services in a protective setting during any part of a day, but they do not provide 24-hour care (National Council on Aging 2020a). Many adult day service programs include health-related services, meal and nutrition programs, information and assistance, transportation, employment assistance, social and recreational activities, and educational and arts programs.

The National Institute of Senior Centers reports that 11,000 such facilities exist across the United States, serving about 1 million adults. About 70 percent of the visitors at these centers are women and, compared with their peers, participants tend to have higher levels of health, social interaction, and life satisfaction (National Council on Aging 2020a).

senior center
A community-based center that provides services to the elderly. Programs at these centers address the individual needs of functionally or cognitively impaired adults as well as those who simply want to socialize with others their age.

CONTINUING CARE RETIREMENT COMMUNITIES

A **continuing care retirement community (CCRC)** is a retirement complex that offers a range of services and levels of care. Residents may move into a house or an apartment where they take care of themselves. They come and go as they please. CCRCs provide social activities and support in the maintenance and upkeep of the home. If needed, CCRCs may provide an assisted living unit or an on-site or affiliated skilled nursing facility (Administration on Aging 2017b).

CCRCs are the most expensive of all long-term care options. Some may require a high entrance fee as well as monthly charges. Entrance fees can range from $100,000 to $1 million, and monthly charges are typically an additional $3,000 to $5,000. Fees may be higher or lower depending on residents' health, the type of housing needed or chosen, the number of residents living in the facility, and the variety of services requested (AARP 2019).

continuing care retirement community (CCRC)
A retirement complex that offers a range of services and levels of care.

RESPITE CARE

Respite care or *adult day services* offer family and other **caregivers** the opportunity to have someone else take care of their loved one or client for a short time, often just for the day. Adult day services are divided into three areas: the first is social and may include meals, recreation, and some health-related services; the second focuses on basic medical or health needs; and the third includes more complex types of health services or therapeutic needs, such as care for patients with dementia (NADCSA 2020).

Depending on the state in which a client resides, Medicaid sometimes pays for a limited amount of respite care, typically 14 to 21 days per year. However, some caregivers must work and rely on adult day services to watch their loved one daily. Without some form of long-term care insurance, they must incur the costs themselves. Respite care may take place in a private home, a stand-alone center, or even a skilled nursing facility (Administration on Aging 2017b).

The elderly are not the only clients offered respite care. Children with a variety of physical or mental concerns are also clients. Respite care is available, for example, to children with autism or physical disabilities such cerebral palsy or muscular dystrophy, those needing treatment for cancer or other illnesses, children born with alcohol or drug exposure, children or adolescents at risk of abuse, and those with HIV/AIDS (ARCH National Respite Network and Resource Center 2020).

HOSPICE CARE

Hospice care is not long-term care but rather provides short-term supportive and sometimes palliative care for terminally ill patients. These patients typically have life expectancies of six months or less. The goal of hospice care is to reduce the patient's pain and stress. It focuses on emotional, spiritual, and physical support, not only for the patient but also for the family. Many hospice workers come to the patient's home, a long-term care facility, or a hospital, or clients may be admitted to a hospice center (Administration on Aging 2017a). Exhibit 5.4 shows the location of hospice care by the percentage of days of care.

Some hospice caregivers are volunteers. In fact, hospice care was initially provided by volunteers. Hospice caregivers provide support for patients, respite and support for family members, child care assistance, bereavement support, fundraising and administrative support, and a variety of other special skills and interests (Hospice Foundation of America 2020). Most volunteers are 18 years old or older. Hospices that receive payment from Medicare are required to have at least 5 percent of their services provided by volunteers (NHPCO 2019).

UNPAID CAREGIVERS

Not all long-term care is provided in a facility. In 2015, 34.2 million Americans served as unpaid or informal caregivers to someone 50 or older (see sidebar). The majority cared for a relative: 47 percent for a parent and 10 percent for a spouse. Around 60 percent of

Exhibit 5.4
Location of
Hospice Care by
Percentage of Days
of Care, 2015

Location	Percentage of Days of Care
Home	56.0%
Nursing facility*	42.7%
Inpatient hospice facility	0.2%
Acute care hospital	0.1%
Other	1.1%

* Includes skilled nursing facilities, nursing facilities, assisted living facilities, and routine hospice care
  days in a hospice inpatient facility.
Source: Data from NHPCO (2019).

caregivers helped someone aged 50 or older with at least one activity of daily living. The
same percentage assisted with medical or nursing tasks, and 43 percent did so without any
prior training. Almost half of these caregivers (46 percent) cared for the oldest old. The
most common tasks that caregivers performed were transportation (78 percent), grocery
shopping (76 percent), and housework (72 percent) (AARP 2015).

(✱) A SNAPSHOT OF THE UNPAID CAREGIVER

A 2015 AARP report described a typical caregiver for the oldest old. She is a 58-year-old
white unemployed female, currently providing care 23 hours a week along with other
unpaid help. She has been providing care for her 90-year-old mother for 4.6 years. Her
mother has "old age" issues, Alzheimer's disease, or feebleness. The caregiver often
communicates with care professionals to advocate for their loved one or to arrange
outside services (AARP 2015).

Unpaid caregivers are typically not trained health professionals. Even those who
are can become stressed or burned out. Caregivers often do not have the funds they
need to cover the expenses that are required. They often give up family vacations or
time they might otherwise spend with their children. They may feel like they cannot
offer the kind of care the elderly need.

On the other hand, many will benefit from the experiences they have with their
parents or grandparents. They worry less about the type of care they might get away
from home. Even grandchildren gain a perspective on life the others might miss.

Older caregivers tend to care for their spouses. They provide care for many hours and often suffer themselves from stress, physical strain, and financial loss. Those who care for their parents also struggle to balance their own work and family demands with the hours they spend caring for their loved one. They often must learn or get training related to the care they provide. They sometimes use their sick leave or vacation time. Some caregivers receive support themselves. This support might include modifications to their homes related to the care they are giving, financial support, transportation services for the elderly, and respite care (AARP 2015).

In 2017, the estimated economic value of unpaid caregiving totaled $470 billion. This consisted of 41 million family caregivers providing around 34 billion hours of care to an adult with a disability (Reinhard et al. 2019). This amount exceeded Medicaid spending of state and federal contributions combined. For comparison, total out-of-pocket spending on healthcare in 2017 was $366 billion, and the total combined value of the US agriculture, forestry, and mining industries equaled $438 billion. The value of family caregiving equaled about $1,450 per US citizen that year (Reinhard et al. 2019).

THE FORMAL LONG-TERM CARE WORKFORCE

A 2019 report from the National Center for Health Statistics indicated that 1.5 million caregiver employee full-time equivalents (FTEs) worked in long-term care. These were mostly registered nurses, licensed practical or vocational nurses, and nurse aides. In addition, about 35,000 social work employee FTEs supported clients (NCHS 2019). Exhibit 5.5 outlines the staffing levels of long-term care facilities by staff type. (See chapter 2 for more information on occupations in the healthcare industry.)

NURSE AIDES

Certified nurse aides, home health care aides, and home care or personal care workers are referred to as *direct care workers*, as they provide direct, hands-on care to patients. They perform duties such as feeding, bathing, dressing, moving patients, and changing linens. They sometimes transfer or transport patients (BLS 2017). Direct care workers typically have a high school education. Some receive postsecondary training and earn a certificate or are registered by the state in which they work. The median wage for direct care workers in 2019 was $24,060 per year (BLS 2020).

Direct care workers are the backbone of the formal long-term care system, providing eight out of ten hours of paid care. These aides have the most influence over the patient's type of care and quality of life (Stone and Harahan 2010). Direct care positions are also some of the most difficult jobs to fill, especially during times of high employment. Long-term care administrators spend a great deal of time recruiting and retaining nurse aides.

Exhibit 5.5
Staffing Characteristics of US Long-Term Care Service Providers, by Staff Type, 2016

	Adult Day Service Centers	Home Health Agencies	Hospice Care	Skilled Nursing Facilities	Residential Care Communities
Total number of nursing and social work employee FTEs	19,900	145,000	85,600	945,700	298,800
Distribution of Staff by Provider (%)					
Registered nurses	20.6	53.0	48.0	11.9	6.5
Licensed practical nurses or licensed vocational nurses	11.3	19.5	8.8	22.4	9.9
Nurse aides	56.8	25.1	31.8	63.9	83.3
Social workers	11.3	25.1	11.4	1.8	0.8

Source: Data from NCHS (2019).

LICENSED PRACTICAL NURSES

Licensed practical nurses (LPNs), also called licensed vocational nurses (LVNs), attend to the clinical needs of patients and some of the activities of daily living. These professionals also provide education to patients and their caregivers. They counsel clients regarding their treatment plan and work with their superiors to implement that plan. LPNs and LVNs care for patients in a variety of settings, including skilled nursing facilities, extended care facilities, hospitals, residential care facilities, home health agencies, and private homes. Their median wage in 2019 was around $47,500 per year (BLS 2020).

Employment for LPNs and LVNs is projected to grow 12 percent from 2016 to 2026, faster than the average for all occupations (NCHS 2016). Increasing demand for LPNs and LVNs is driven by the aging population in the United States, especially the large number of baby boomers who are now beginning to need long-term care. State nursing boards across the United States license and determine the specific tasks performed by LPNs and LVNs.

REGISTERED NURSES

Some long-term patients with clinically complex needs require ventilator care or tracheostomy care. They may be comatose or need respiratory therapy, dialysis, or radiation therapy.

Some require oxygen, transfusions, chemotherapy, or intravenous medications. All of these functions require the care of a registered nurse (RN).

RNs have at least an associate's degree in nursing (ADN); many have a bachelor of science degree in nursing (BSN). RNs coordinate and provide clinical care to the elderly. They educate patients, their families, and the public about health conditions. RNs often give emotional support to both patients and their families. In 2019, the median wage for RNs was $73,300 per year (BLS 2020).

RNs work in adult day service centers, skilled nursing facilities, and residential care communities. They make up nearly half or more of all nursing positions in both hospice and home health agencies (NCHS 2016).

Effective nursing leadership in long-term care has a number of positive outcomes, including improved quality of care, increased staff retention and job satisfaction, better workplace environment, and reduced costs of care (Harvath et al. 2008).

SOCIAL WORKERS

Social workers may play a variety of long-term care roles, depending on the setting. For example, they may be responsible for admitting new residents and helping them get used to their surroundings. They may deal with the financial aspects of admission to a facility. They may organize recreational activities or attend to the social needs of clients. They may also provide services to residents, their families, long-term care staff, or even the community. Social workers in hospice settings include social work clinicians, bereavement counselors, and coordinators of volunteer services for clients and families (Dhooper 2012).

Some social workers only need a bachelor's degree. Clinical social workers must hold a master of social work degree (MSW), complete postgraduate training, and be licensed in the state in which they practice. The median pay for social workers in 2019 was $50,500 per year (BLS 2020). Demand for social workers is projected to grow as much as 16 percent from 2016 to 2026, much faster than the average for all occupations (BLS 2017).

PAYING FOR LONG-TERM CARE

Long-term care is expensive. According to one study, on average, an American who turned 65 in 2016 will pay $138,000 in long-term care costs. Families will pay half of the costs themselves out of pocket, with public and private payers covering the rest. About 70 percent of those turning 65 will need long-term care at some time during the rest of their lives. On average, women use long-term care for 3.7 years, while men use long-term care for 2.2 years. Many families need these services for many years, at a cost of hundreds of thousands of dollars (Favreault and Dey 2016; Weston 2019). The cost of long-term care depends on a number of factors, including the type and duration of care needed, the provider used, and the location of care. An examination of the costs of long-term care in the

United States indicated that, on average, people pay the following amounts (Administration on Aging 2017b):

◆ $225 per day or $6,844 per month for a semiprivate room in a nursing home

◆ $253 per day or $7,698 per month for a private room in a nursing home

◆ $119 per day or $3,628 per month for care in an assisted living facility (for a one-bedroom unit)

◆ $25.50 per hour for a home health aide

◆ $20 per hour for homemaker services (e.g., meal preparation, cleaning, household tasks)

◆ $68 per day for services in an adult day service center

Most Americans believe that their health insurance will cover the costs of long-term care, but in fact, neither private health insurance nor Medicare covers long-term services and support (Favreault and Dey 2016; Weston 2019). Medicaid covers medical and non-medical services for people with a chronic illness or disability. For those who meet their state's criteria, Medicaid also pays for long-term healthcare services. Typically, however, Medicaid patients have little money or have very high medical bills and little income or assets to pay for them. For example, in many states, people with more than $2,000 in assets, outside of their primary home, cannot qualify for Medicaid long-term care payments (ElderLawAnswers 2020).

In 2016, Medicaid spending on long-term care was approximately $167 billion. Medicaid is the largest payer of long-term care services (Eiken et al. 2018). Exhibit 5.6 illustrates the percent of Medicaid dollars that states spend on home and community-based services (HCBS). Spending patterns vary among the states, ranging from 21 to 78 percent of total Medicaid long-term care dollars in 2013.

Medicare spending on skilled nursing facilities totaled $29.8 billion in 2015 (MedPAC 2017). Medicare covers acute care, such as physicians' visits and hospitalization, and some postacute services, such as recovery in a skilled nursing facility (e.g., after surgery or a hospital stay). Medicare also covers home health care, inpatient rehabilitation, hospice services, and even long-term hospitals that provide beneficiaries care for relatively extended periods. However, a facility that provides skilled nursing care covered by Medicare may often provide long-term care services that are not covered. Medicare does not cover personal care services. Postacute nursing facility care is covered for up to 100 days following a qualified hospital stay (Reaves and Musumeci 2015).

Private long-term care insurance has been around for many years, but typically it is not available to those who have current or near-future needs because the premiums

EXHIBIT 5.6

Proportion of
Medicaid Long-
Term Services and
Supports Spending
for Home and
Community-Based
Services, 2013

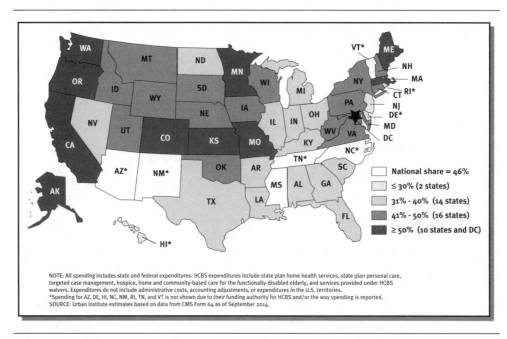

NOTE: All spending includes state and federal expenditures. HCBS expenditures include state plan home health services, state plan personal care, targeted case management, hospice, home and community-based care for the functionally-disabled elderly, and services provided under HCBS walvers. Expenditures do not include administrative costs, accounting adjustments, or expenditures in the U.S. territories.
*Spending for AZ, DE, HI, NC, NM, RI, TN, and VT is not shown due to their funding authority for HCBS and/or the way spending is reported.
SOURCE: Urban Institute estimates based on data from CMS Form 64 as of September 2014.

Source: Reaves and Musumeci (2015).

are very high. Seniors on fixed incomes, for example, would have a tough time paying for long-term care insurance. Seniors of color are especially at risk of living with less income and more health problems after they retire. In 2018, 350,000 Americans bought long-term care insurance policies, paying $2,000 to $3,400 per year for the coverage (AALTCI 2019).

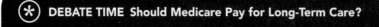

(✳) **DEBATE TIME Should Medicare Pay for Long-Term Care?**

Some are surprised that Medicare does not cover long-term nursing care, assisted living, or adult day services. Medicare also does not the cover the cost of home-based care such as help with activities of daily living.

Form two groups and debate this issue. One group might focus on the need for home-based care and how such care could lessen the overall cost of healthcare. This group could also discuss the benefits of home care for the elderly. Another group could focus on the costs associated with home care and the already heavy financial burden on Medicare (more details on the Medicare program can be found in chapter 7).

A challenge associated with purchasing long-term care insurance is that buyers must estimate when the insurance will go into effect and how long they might need it (Reaves and Musumeci 2015). The decision to buy long-term care insurance is much different from the typical decision to purchase health or life insurance. Age and life expectancy affect the decision to buy long-term care insurance—the longer you live, the more likely you will need long-term care. Women are more likely to need long-term care and to need it for longer than men. Buyers must determine whether their adult children will be able to care for them when they are elderly. Finally, health status and income and assets are important considerations when buying long-term care insurance. A long-term care policy is not a wise

---

(✱) THE DECISION TO BUY LONG-TERM CARE INSURANCE

Paul began smoking when he joined the US Air Force in World War II. He tried to stop many times, but he was not successful until, at age 63, he suffered a panic attack and thought he was going to die. Paul and his family were optimistic that he would enjoy good health for many years to come—then came the news that he had emphysema, a disease that would slowly kill him over the next ten years. By that time, it was too late to purchase long-term care insurance—it was just too expensive.

Toward the end of his life, Paul needed assistance with basic personal tasks, but he did not want to burden his children. The only option was to enter a skilled nursing facility. Medicare covered Paul's stay for the first few weeks, because of his emphysema, but then he would have to pay $4,500 a month. Medicaid would kick in only after Paul had depleted nearly all of his assets. He was spending down the savings he had hoped to pass on to his children. Paul died after staying only two months in the facility.

Paul's sister-in-law, Betty, lived much longer, but she, too, eventually was admitted to a long-term care facility for daily care. Betty's son, who had worked in healthcare his entire life, had purchased long-term care insurance for his mom nearly 40 years earlier. His challenge was to determine how much insurance she would need and at what age she would start using it. He guessed correctly and her care was covered, and her finances were more secure during the time she needed help. If she had been able to live in her home until her death with help from family and friends, she would not have needed the insurance. In the end, paying the premiums for long-term care insurance was a smart choice.

choice for buyers with few assets or limited incomes, as it is likely that Medicaid would cover some of their long-term care costs (NAIC 2020).

Long-term care insurance claims climbed from $8.14 billion in 2015 to $10.3 billion in 2018 and are anticipated to continue increasing. These insurance claims represent only 5 percent of the total expenditures for long-term care in the United States. Most of the costs are paid by government sources or out of patients' own funds (AALTCI 2019; NAIC 2020). (See sidebar on page 125 for an example of the decision to buy long-term care insurance and how it played out in the lives of two elderly individuals.)

QUALITY OF LONG-TERM CARE

Imagine looking for a facility where a loved one will reside, potentially for a long time. You and your family members undoubtedly will be concerned about the quality of care your loved one will receive and who will be providing the hands-on care. Depending on the local resources that are available to you, information about the quality of long-term care services can be difficult to find.

Quality standards for long-term care vary by state, making it difficult to compare standards and quality measures such as the condition of the building, staffing levels, processes such as patient assessment and schedules of activities of daily living, and performance outcomes (Reaves and Musumeci 2015). CMS created the Five-Star Quality Rating System to help families make decisions about long-term care facilities. This system gives nursing homes a rating between one and five stars, with five stars representing above-average quality. A one-star rating signifies lower than average quality. Ratings are given on the basis of health inspections, staffing, and quality measures (CMS 2019).

Nursing homes that are certified to receive payments from Medicare and Medicaid are regulated and subject to national and state quality standards. The Affordable Care Act of 2010 incorporated the Nursing Home Transparency and Improvement Act, the Elder Justice Act, and the Patient Safety and Abuse Prevention Act, requiring CMS and nursing homes "to aim at improving transparency and accountability, enforcement, and resident abuse prevention" (Reaves and Musumeci 2015).

Long-term care quality continues to focus on staffing levels, abuse and neglect, unmet resident needs, quality problems (activities of daily living worsened, pain management, pressure ulcers, use of restraints, infections), worker training and competency, and lack of integration with medical care (Harrington et al. 2017). Exhibit 5.7 illustrates quality-monitoring programs for a variety of long-term services.

About 93 percent of nursing homes received at least one inspection deficiency citation for violations of federal regulations in 2015. The share of nursing homes that received citations for serious violations—causing harm or jeopardy to residents or the potential for harm or jeopardy—was 21 percent, although this percentage is down compared with

Exhibit 5.7

Long-Term Care Quality Monitoring by Provider Type

Provider Type	Survey Entity	Frequency	Dominant Standards	Public Reporting
Nursing homes	State agencies under contract with CMS	Every 9–15 months	Medicare and Medicaid conditions of participation	CMS Nursing Home Compare/Five Star Rating System
Hospices	State agencies under contract with CMS	Every 3 years	Medicare and Medicaid conditions of participation	CMS Hospice Compare
Home health agencies	State agencies under contract with CMS or private accrediting agencies	Every 3 years	Medicare and Medicaid conditions of participation	CMS Home Health Compare/Five State Rating System
Residential Care facilities	State agencies	Varies by state	State licensure and Medicaid requirements	Varies by state
Personal care and other HCBS providers	State agencies	Varies by state	State licensure and Medicaid requirements	Varies by state

Source: Data from Harrington et al. (2017).

previous years. Nursing homes with high concentrations of minority residents tend to have more quality problems (Harrington et al. 2017).

Home health quality has generally improved over time. Fewer clients in 2016 (16 percent) were admitted to hospitals as compared with 2004 (28 percent) and 2009 (22 percent). Clients had less pain, were more compliant in taking their medications, and had better results in walking or moving. Scores on the Home Health Consumer Assessment of Healthcare Providers and Systems ranged from 83 to 88 percent. These scores indicate how patients rated care given in a professional way, providers' communications with the patient, and overall care (CMS 2020).

States regulate residential care facilities and home and community-based services, so nationwide data for the United States are harder to report. CMS continues to focus on quality initiatives, and a 2014 rule for the HCBS waiver program now requires states to identify, respond to, and attempt to prevent abuse, neglect, exploitation of elders, and unexplained death. States must also have an incident management system in place, allowing them to respond to and resolve quality issues (CMS 2014).

Elder Abuse

One in ten Americans aged 60 or older experience elder abuse during a given year, and many experience it in multiple forms (Acierno et al. 2010). Elder abuse can take many different forms, including physical abuse, emotional abuse, neglect, abandonment, sexual abuse, financial abuse, and healthcare fraud (see sidebar). Most victims are women (National Institute on Aging 2016). A 2011 study conducted in New York State found that for every elder abuse case known to programs and agencies, 23.5 were unknown. The authors found that for every case of financial exploitation known to authorities, 44 cases went unreported (Lifespan of Greater Rochester 2011). Elders who experience abuse are at risk for more psychological distress than nonvictims, and they may die sooner (National Center on Elder Abuse 2015).

ABUSE IS MORE THAN PHYSICAL

Although elder abuse is often physical, the results of that abuse go beyond a wound. "Most physical wounds heal in time. But, any type of mistreatment can leave the abused person feeling fearful and depressed. Sometimes, the victim thinks the abuse is his or her fault. Protective services agencies can suggest support groups and counseling that can help the abused person heal the emotional wounds" (National Institute on Aging 2016).

Elder abuse can happen in any long-term care facility. However, in almost 60 percent of elder abuse and neglect cases, a family member is at fault, most often an adult child or spouse (National Council on Aging 2020b). Caregiver stress is a significant factor in abuse and neglect. The load of caring for a loved one, along with personal problems such as stress, mental illness, addictions, job loss, financial difficulties (including financial dependence on the elderly), can result in abuse. Older people may also be abusive themselves; the risk of elder abuse is higher in those instances (APA 2018).

The American Psychological Association recommends education for caregivers about the unique needs and problems of older adults and how to deal with those problems. Respite care to give the caregiver a break for a few hours is important. Social and contact support for older people and their family members can help caregivers share concerns and ideas. Counseling is also an option for those with mental health or substance abuse issues (APA 2018).

THE FUTURE OF LONG-TERM CARE

Retirement looks much different today than it did in the past. People are moving into neighborhoods to support each other, share resources, and foster a sense of community—trends that will persist into the future. As of December 2017, more than 230 such neighborhoods existed, and another 130 were in development (Jaffe 2017). Many of these communities have formed in neighborhoods among the elderly who have lived there for years and want to remain in their homes.

Likewise, long-term care is changing as well, providing more hospitality services and updating technology. Owners and managers of long-term care facilities have learned that seniors are shopping for the best environment in which to live. They want their new living space to feel like home. Many facilities allow residents to bring personal items to decorate their rooms, depending on the level of care needed. They offer a variety of services and activities designed to create an environment that provides as much freedom as possible.

The government has recognized the need for some changes in long-term care as well. CMS, for example, set new regulations for good food and proper nutrition in 2016. Among other guidelines established, facilities must take into consideration residents' food preferences (Richardson 2016). Some facilities offer restaurant-style dining and upscale décor (Lee 2018). Greater emphasis on personal choice, quality of care, payment issues, access to home care, and concerns for staffing and workforce needs are expected in the future (see exhibit 5.8). Nursing homes are embracing a national movement to improve quality of life. In some areas, "Green House" homes have opened, providing care for just a few residents (6–12) who have more privacy for bathing and personal care but share a common kitchen and living area (Sloan, Zimmerman, and D'Souza 2014).

One of the most likely changes in long-term care will be more options and alternatives to living at home. Fewer family members available to care for the aging population will create a need for more home health aides and support for family caregivers.

Financing long-term care continues to be a challenge for the elderly, policymakers, and other stakeholders. Some attention to home and community-based services resulted in the creation of the Money Follows the Person (MFP) Rebalancing Demonstration Grant in 2016. The goals of the MFP program include the following:

◆ Increase the use of HCBS and reduce the use of institutionally based services

◆ Eliminate barriers in state law, state Medicaid plans, and state budgets that restrict the use of Medicaid funds related to long-term care

◆   Improve the ability of Medicaid programs to provide HCBS to people who would like to move out of institutions

◆   Improve quality assurance of HCBS

CMS has awarded similar MFP funding to five states with tribal partners in building services provided to Native Americans (Medicaid.gov 2020).

As the US population ages, state and federal policymakers and other stakeholders will be challenged to find ways to provide diverse long-term care services, both at the home and in resident facilities. The health and well-being of the elderly, along with their rights and preferences, will continue to demand resources and funding (see sidebar).

EXHIBIT 5.8

Key Trends in Long-Term Care for Older Adults

- **Aging of baby boomers.** Experimentation and diversity in forms of care will increase.
- **Emphasis on personal choice and person-centered care.** Choice in all aspects of care will increase.
- **Emphasis on quality improvement.** Publicly available quality ratings will increasingly drive quality improvement.
- **Technological innovation.** Robots, smart homes, electronic health monitoring and communication, and other innovations will reduce dependence on human caregivers.
- **Search for new treatments for dementia.** Development of new treatments for dementia will be a major determinant of the need for and format of long-term care.
- **Funding of care by private payment and Medicaid.** Dependence on private payment and Medicaid is likely to continue; hopes for long-term care insurance have not been realized.
- **Financial pressure to contain public costs.** There will be increased accountability among both home-based and long-term care services, as well as increased copayments and deductibles.
- **Trend toward home care rather than institutional care.** The trend toward home-based service models will continue, especially for those who do not have extensive care needs or dementia.
- **Workforce needs and shortages.** Immigration laws may change to allow an influx of foreign workers to serve as nursing assistants and home health aides.

Source: Sloan, Zimmerman, and D'Souza (2014).

(*) SAVE YOUR MONEY, KIDS

The future of long-term care is certain to be characterized by growth, and it will continue to be expensive. Here is a final story with some advice:

> Marilyn Oliver, 89, a resident who now lives at a senior living "smart home" in Houston, Texas, that has improved and modernized its services and technology, says that many of her friends could not afford to live in such a place. She pays $5,200 a month, which includes meals, transportation, housekeeping, and utilities. She uses all of her savings, her Social Security income, and her late husband's pension to pay for her care. Her advice? "Save your money, kids. It's going to be expensive when you get to be this age" (Lee 2018).

Whether the funds come from the user's pockets, an insurance company, or the government, growth in the number of elderly will demand growth in long-term care. The question is, are Americans prepared?

SUMMARY

The US population is aging, and large numbers of seniors over age 65 will need formal and informal long-term care for many years to come. This challenge puts pressure on families to care for their loved ones and creates increased demand for formal long-term care services, such as skilled nursing and assisted living facilities. Nurses, nurse aides, and other direct care workers will continue to be in demand, as will home-based services. The demand for healthcare workers creates competition with other industries to fill those roles. It is one of the biggest challenges facing long-term care managers.

Most long-term care services are regulated and surveyed regularly at the state and national level to improve quality. Quality is improving, but elder abuse remains still common; in the majority of cases, elder abuse in committed by a family member. Government leaders, facility owners, administrators, and users continue to look closely at quality concerns facing long-term care.

Long-term care is expensive and will continue to be so in the future. While the federal and state governments cover some long-term care costs, mostly through Medicaid, individuals bear much of the cost, using up their savings and retirement funds. Long-term care insurance is available, but it is difficult to understand and costly to purchase.

The good news is that providers of long-term care are updating and improving their services. Many elderly are forming neighborhoods and communities to provide support to one another and services that meet their needs. Policymakers understand the voting power of the elderly. They will not be able to ignore such a large group of constituents. These leaders and other stakeholders continue to look for ways to diversify long-term care services and meet the needs of the elderly.

QUESTIONS

1. How did the shift from agriculture as a way of life to the industrial age affect the elderly? How is that similar to what is happening today?
2. What change in the 1930s initiated the modern system of long-term care?
3. How are skilled nursing facilities and assisted living facilities similar, and how do they differ?
4. Describe the care given by respite care and hospice care providers.
5. Which group provides the most care to the elderly?
6. Which members of the LTC workforce are licensed? Who is certified?
7. How is long-term care funded?
8. Describe the Five-Star Quality Rating System for long-term care facilities.
9. How is long-term care quality monitored?
10. Who is most often a perpetrator of elder abuse?

ASSIGNMENTS

1. Read the following article about long-term care insurance: "Understanding Long-Term Care Insurance," AARP, May 2016, at www.aarp.org/health/health-insurance/info-06-2012/understanding-long-term-care-insurance.html. Why do you think purchasing long-term care insurance is so difficult?
2. List the major types of providers in the long-term care system. Then, describe the characteristics of a typical resident or patient of each type of provider.
3. Interview a friend or relative who is in their 80s—perhaps a grandparent. Ask that person for one piece of advice. What would he or she like to tell you that might help you face the future? Audio or video record your interview. Play the recording for your class or report on what you learned. (You may need written permission, in some cases, to record an individual for your class project.)

CASES

HOW CAN LONG-TERM CARE SURVIVE?

In 2010, 40 million Americans were aged 65 or older. By 2050, that number is expected to jump to nearly 88 million. Seventy percent of seniors are expected to need long-term care, although not all of that care will take place in a formal setting. The "oldest old," those 85 and older, are expected to number 19 million people. The costs of caring for the elderly will be enormous. At the same time, a decreasing number of working adults will be paying taxes into the already struggling Medicare and Medicaid systems (Freundlich 2014).

Discussion Questions

1. How do you think the United States will pay for long-term care in the future—or should it? What services should Medicaid or Medicare cover? How does the shrinking number of taxpayers affect your argument?

2. Should long-term care look different in the future? What services could be offered differently, and how might the workforce change?

ETHAN AND VIRGINIA

Ethan and Virginia celebrated their 75th wedding anniversary a couple of years ago. As they got older, Virginia struggled with arthritis, and Ethan had vision and hearing loss. Both of them had been otherwise healthy in the past. They never considered residing in a long-term care facility. In fact, they had lived with their daughter in another city, but they missed their home so much that they returned. Their other children helped Ethan and Virginia by shopping for groceries and doing household chores for them.

At age 95 and still living at home, Virginia passed away. Ethan attended her funeral and almost immediately started to "go downhill." His children were concerned about how to care for him. They discussed whether he should live with them or be cared for at a local nursing home or assisted care center. They felt guilty for even considering putting their father in a nursing home, but were not sure they could offer appropriate care in their homes.

Discussion Questions

1. What issues must Ethan and his children consider? What goes into the decision about caring for an elderly loved one? Include your thoughts about finances, physical needs, emotional concerns, and stress. What about the safety of the facilities, such as the need to protect against falls?

2. What would you do? If you decided to find a formal care setting for your elderly parent, what might a list of pros and cons include? Create your list and compare it with a classmate's or a group's. Discuss how your lists are similar or different.

References

AARP. 2019. "How Continuing Care Retirement Communities Work." Updated October 24. www.aarp.org/caregiving/basics/info-2017/continuing-care-retirement-communities. html.

——. 2015. "Caregivers of Older Adults: A Focused Look at Caregivers of Adults Age 50+." Published June. www.aarp.org/content/dam/aarp/ppi/2015/caregivers-of-older-adults-focused-look.pdf.

Acierno, R., M. A. Hernandez, A. B. Amstadter, H. S. Resnick, K. Steve, W. Muzzy, and D. G. Kilpatrick. 2010. "Prevalence and Correlates of Emotional, Physical, Sexual, and Financial Abuse and Potential Neglect in the United States: The National Elder Mistreatment Study." *American Journal of Public Health* 100 (2): 202–97.

Administration on Aging. 2017a. "Glossary." Updated October 10. https://longtermcare.acl. gov/the-basics/glossary.html#long-term-care-services.

——. 2017b. "What Long-Term Care Insurance Covers." Updated October 10. https:// longtermcare.acl.gov/costs-how-to-pay/what-is-long-term-care-insurance/what-long-term-care-insurance-covers.html.

American Association for Long-Term Care Insurance (AALTCI). 2019. "Long-Term Care Insurance Facts: 2019 Report." Accessed April 13, 2020. www.aaltci.org/long-term-care-insurance/learning-center/ltcfacts-2019.php#2019costs.

American Psychological Association (APA). 2018. "Elder Abuse and Neglect: In Search of Solutions." Accessed April 13, 2020. www.apa.org/pi/aging/resources/guides/elder-abuse.pdf.

ARCH National Respite Network and Resource Center. 2020. ARCH Factsheets. Accessed June 4. https://archrespite.org/productspublications/arch-fact-sheets#Autism.

CBS News. 2018. "Following a Couple from Diagnosis to the Final Stages of Alzheimer's." CBS News, *60 Minutes*. Published April 22. www.cbsnews.com/news/alzheimers-disease-following-a-couple-from-diagnosis-to-the-final-stages.

Centers for Disease Control and Prevention (CDC). 2019. "Nursing Homes and Assisted Living (Long-Term Care Facilities [LTCFs])." Reviewed February 24. www.cdc.gov/longtermcare.

———. 2015. "Prevalence of Disability and Disability Type Among Adults—United States, 2013." *Morbidity and Mortality Weekly Report*. Published July 15. www.cdc.gov/mmwr/preview/mmwrhtml/mm6429a2.htm?s_cid=mm6429a2_w.

Centers for Medicare & Medicaid Services (CMS). 2020. Home Health Compare datasets. Updated May 21. https://data.medicare.gov/data/home-health-compare.

———. 2019. "Five-Star Quality Rating System." Published October 7. www.cms.gov/medicare/provider-enrollment-and-certification/certificationandcomplianc/fsqrs.html.

———. 2014. "Medicaid Program: State Plan Home and Community-Based Services, Provider Payment Reassignment, and Home and Community-Based Setting Requirements for Community First Choice and Home and Community-Based Services (HCBS) Waivers. Final Rule." *Federal Register* 79 (11): 2947–3039.

Dhooper, S. S. 2012. *Social Work in Healthcare: Its Past and Future*, 2nd ed. Thousand Oaks, CA: Sage.

Eiken, S., K. Sredl, B. Burwell, and A. Amos. 2018. "Medicaid Expenditures for Long-Term Services and Support in FY 2016." Medicaid Innovation Accelerator Program. Published May. www.medicaid.gov/sites/default/files/2019-12/ltssexpenditures2016.pdf.

ElderLawAnswers. 2020. "Five Myths About Medicaid's Long-Term Care Coverage." Published March 11. www.elderlawanswers.com/five-myths-about-medicaids-long-term-care-coverage-12114.

Favreault, M., and J. Dey. 2016. "Long-Term Services and Supports for Older Americans: Risks and Financing Research Brief." US Department of Health and Human Services, Office of the Assistant Secretary for Planning and Evaluation. Revised February. https://aspe.hhs.gov/basic-report/long-term-services-and-supports-older-americans-risks-and-financing-research-brief.

Freundlich, N. 2014. "Long-Term Care: What Are the Issues?" Health Policy Snapshot, Robert Wood Johnson Foundation. Published February 1.

Harrington, C., J. M. Wiener, L. Ross, and M. Musumeci. 2017. "Key Issues in Long-Term Services and Supports Quality." Kaiser Family Foundation. Published October 27. www.kff.org/medicaid/issue-brief/key-issues-in-long-term-services-and-supports-quality/.

Harvath, T., K. Swafford, K. Smith, L. Miller, M. Volpin, K. Sexson, D. White, and H. Young. 2008. "Enhancing Nursing Leadership in Long-Term Care: A Review of the Literature." *Research in Gerontological Nursing* 1 (3): 187–96.

HelpGuide. 2019. "Senior Housing Options." Updated November. www.helpguide.org/articles/alzheimers-dementia-aging/senior-housing.htm.

Hospice Foundation of America. 2020. "Become a Volunteer." Accessed April 16. http://hospicefoundation.org/Volunteer.

Hoyt, J. 2018. "History of Senior Living." SeniorLiving.org. Accessed April 16. www.seniorliving.org/history.

Institute of Medicine. 1986. *Improving the Quality of Care in Nursing Homes*. Washington, DC: National Academies Press.

Jaffe, I. 2017. "'Village Movement' Allows Elderly to Age in Their Homes. National Public Radio. Published December 12. www.npr.org/2017/12/12/570248798/village-movement-allows-elderly-to-age-in-their-homes.

Kemper, P., H. Komisar, and L. Alecxih. 2005–06. "Long-Term Care over an Uncertain Future: What Can Current Retirees Expect?" *Inquiry* 42 (4): 335–50.

Lee, A. 2018. "To Keep Up with an Aging Generation, Experts Say Senior Living Is Being Viewed More as Hospitality." Marketplace. Published April 18. www.marketplace.org/2018/04/18/life/keep-aging-generation-experts-say-senior-living-being-viewed-more-hospitality.

Lifespan of Greater Rochester. 2011. *Under the Radar: New York State Elder Abuse Prevalence Study: Self-Reported Prevalence and Documented Case Surveys, Final Report.* Published May. https://ocfs.ny.gov/main/reports/Under%20the%20Radar%2005%20 12%2011%20final%20report.pdf.

McCurdy, J. G. 2009. *Citizen Bachelors: Manhood and the Creation of the United States.* Ithaca, NY: Cornell University Press.

Medicaid.gov. 2020. "Money Follows the Person." Accessed June 4. www.medicaid.gov/medicaid/ltss/money-follows-the-person/index.html.

Medicare Payment Advisory Commission (MedPAC). 2017. *Report to Congress: Medicare Payment Policy.* Published March. http://medpac.gov/docs/default-source/reports/mar17_entirereport.pdf.

Minnesota Department of Health. 2009. "Hospitals and Long-Term Care Facilities." Accessed April 16, 2020. www.health.state.mn.us/about/history/Chapter6.pdf.

National Adult Day Care Services Association (NADCSA). 2020. "Overview and Facts." www.nadsa.org/consumers/overview-and-facts. Accessed April 13.

National Association of Insurance Commissioners (NAIC). 2020. "Long-Term Care Insurance." Updated February 4. www.naic.org/cipr_topics/topic_long_term_care.htm.

National Center for Assisted Living. 2020. "Facts and Figures." Accessed June 4. www.ahcancal.org/ncal/facts/Pages/default.aspx.

National Center for Health Statistics (NCHS). 2019. *Long-Term Care Providers and Services Users in the United States, 2015–2016.* Vital and Health Statistics Series 3, No. 43. www.cdc.gov/nchs/data/series/sr_03/sr03_43-508.pdf.

————. 2016. "Nursing Home Care." Reviewed March 11. www.cdc.gov/nchs/fastats/nursing-home-care.htm.

National Center on Elder Abuse (NCEA). 2015. "Elder Abuse and Its Impact: What You Must Know." Published February. https://ncea.acl.gov/NCEA/media/Publication/Elder-Abuse-and-Its-Impact-What-You-Must-Know-2013.pdf.

National Council on Aging. 2020a. "Facts and Benefits of Senior Centers You Probably Didn't Know." Accessed April 13. www.ncoa.org/national-institute-of-senior-centers/tips-for-senior-centers/what-you-dont-know-about-your-local-senior-center.

————. 2020b. "What Is Elder Abuse?" Accessed April 13. www.ncoa.org/public-policy-action/elder-justice/elder-abuse-facts/.

National Hospice and Palliative Care Organization (NHPCO). 2019. *NHPCO Facts and Figures: Hospice Care in America, 2018 edition*. Published July 2. www.nhpco.org/wp-content/uploads/2019/07/2018_NHPCO_Facts_Figures.pdf.

National Institute on Aging. 2016. "Elder Abuse." Reviewed December 29. www.nia.nih.gov/health/elder-abuse.

Reaves, E. L., and M. Musumeci. 2015. "Medicaid and Long-Term Services and Supports: A Primer." Kaiser Family Foundation. Published December 15. www.kff.org/medicaid/report/medicaid-and-long-term-services-and-supports-a-primer.

Reinhard, S. C., L. F. Feinberg, R. Choula, and A. Houser. 2019. "Valuing the Invaluable: 2019 Update." AARP Public Policy Institute. Published November. www.aarp.org/content/dam/aarp/ppi/2019/11/valuing-the-invaluable-2019-update-charting-a-path-forward.doi.10.26419-2Fppi.00082.001.pdf.

Richardson, B. 2016. "New CMS Long-Term Care Requirements: Food, Nutrition, and Dining Are Critical Components." *Nutrition and Foodservice Edge*, November–December. www.anfponline.org/docs/default-source/legacy-docs/docs/nc112016.

Rincon del Rio. 2017. "History of Nursing Homes." Published June 18. http://rincondelrio.com/info-for-seniors/the-history-of-nursing-homes-from-almshouses-to-skilled-nursing.

SeniorCaring.com. 2016. "The Difference Between Skilled Nursing Facilities and Nursing Homes." Published May 20. www.seniorcaring.com/resources/the-difference-between-skilled-nursing-facilities-and-nursing-homes.

Sloan, P., S. Zimmerman, and M. D'Souza. 2014. "What Will Long-Term Care Be Like in 2040?" *North Carolina Medical Journal* 75 (5): 326–30.

Social Security Administration. 1948. "Proposed Changes in Old-Age and Survivors' Insurance: Report of the Advisory Council on Social Security to the Senate Finance Committee." *Social Security Bulletin* 11 (5): 21–28. www.ssa.gov/history/reports/48advise1.html.

———. 1937. "Social Security History." Accessed April 16, 2020. www.ssa.gov/history/whybook.html.

———. 1935. "The Social Security Act of 1935." Accessed June 4, 2020. www.ssa.gov/history/35act.html. Accessed April 20, 2020.

Stone, R., and M. Harahan. 2010. "Improving the Long-Term Care Workforce Serving Older Adults." *Health Affairs* 29 (1): 109–15.

US Bureau of Labor Statistics (BLS). 2020. "Occupational Outlook Handbook: Healthcare Occupations." Updated April 10. www.bls.gov/ooh/healthcare/home.htm.

———. 2017. "Occupational Employment Statistics: Occupational Employment and Wages, May 2017, 31-1014 Nursing Assistants." Accessed April 13, 2020. www.bls.gov/oes/2017/may/oes311014.htm.

US Census Bureau. 2018. "Older People Projected to Outnumber Children for First Time in U.S. History." News release, March 13. www.census.gov/newsroom/press-releases/2018/cb18-41-population-projections.html.

US Department of Health and Human Services (HHS). 2012. "Long-Term Care Insurance." Office of the Assistant Secretary for Planning and Evaluation Research Brief. Published June. https://aspe.hhs.gov/basic-report/long-term-care-insurance-research-brief.

Weston, L. 2019. "What Will Long-Term Care Cost You?" NerdWallet. Published June 12. www.nerdwallet.com/article/investing/long-term-care.

CHAPTER 6

MENTAL HEALTH

The treatment of mental illness has become a major challenge for Americans. Symptoms of mental illness may be first seen by a primary care physician. Yet "primary care has woeful rates of diagnosing and treating mental health problems. . . . about 15 percent of people with a serious mental disorder receive what has been called 'minimally adequate treatment'" (Sederer 2015). This failure to identify and treat mental health disorders is not attributable to bad doctors but to ineffective service models. Mental health conditions are more common than heart disease or diabetes—why, then, do primary care physicians not screen for them routinely, as they do for high blood pressure or blood sugar levels? Although mental illness can be diagnosed and often treated in primary care settings, few people who are referred to specialized mental health providers ever go. They may be deterred by the stigma of mental illness, a preference for one-stop healthcare shopping, a shortage of services, or the disproportionate denial of insurance claims for mental health services.

Consider the case of a 14-year-old girl with chronic asthma and post-traumatic stress disorder resulting from early childhood experiences (Sederer 2015). This patient may be seen by her primary care doctor for her asthma, but she might not receive treatment for the mental health disorder. Healthcare professionals and educational institutions recognize that primary care should better address patients' mental health needs (American Academy of Family Physicians 2018).

LEARNING OBJECTIVES

After reading this chapter, you will be able to

➤ Discuss the serious mental health challenges facing Americans.

➤ Illustrate the history of mental health treatment in the United States.

➤ Compare the different types of mental health providers.

➤ Outline the reasons for inequities in mental health treatment in the United States.

➤ Discuss the difficulty of treating of mental health disorders in the United States.

➤ Describe the reasons why it is difficult to recruit mental health providers.

➤ Recognize new, innovative methods for treating mental health.

Mental health is a serious issue in the United States. About 44.7 million adults have some form of mental illness that may severely affect their quality of life or even become life-threatening. People who have a mental illness often have other chronic medical conditions as well, and on average, their life expectancies are 25 years less than those without a mental illness (Levine 2018). Moreover, mental illness is the third leading cause of disability and frequently leads to suicide (NIMH 2017). Suicide is one of the leading causes of death among young people, and more than 90 percent of children who die by suicide have a mental health condition. In addition, approximately 20 percent of those held in jails and prisons exhibit symptoms of mental illness. Mental illness costs the United States around $190 billion annually in lost earnings and more than $110 billion in total healthcare spending. The United States has the highest rate of death from mental illness of any industrialized country (Kamal 2017; NAMI 2019a).

The History of Mental Health Care

For thousands of years, mental illness was misunderstood. Historically, most people believed that mental illness was caused by demons or evil spirits. This belief was reflected in Jewish, Christian, and Islamic literature. As a result, treatments for mental illness included exorcism and the use of religious relics to cast out demons. People with mental health problems were often stigmatized and frequently punished or ostracized.

By the nineteenth and twentieth centuries, most of Western civilization had come to recognize mental illness as a type of medical illness, but unconventional (and, we now know, ineffective) treatments persisted. For instance, some people with mental illness were placed in cages and lowered into water. Others were spun around until they vomited. Cold water was sometimes poured over a patient's head and hot water over their feet. Patients were given chemicals that induced seizures or insulin, which caused coma. Eventually, asylums were established for people with mental illness, with the idea that creating a safe environment would restore their sanity (Malcolm and Blumer 2016).

Asylums provided a means of controlling populations by removing the mentally ill from society. The first mental health asylum in the United States was organized in 1752 by Quakers (members of the Religious Society of Friends) in Philadelphia. The facility housed patients in rooms equipped with shackles in the basement of the Pennsylvania Hospital.

As discussed in chapter 5, for most of the nineteenth century, many people with mental illness either lived in the community or were cared for in public almshouses. During the first half of the twentieth century, patients' length of stay in mental hospitals increased dramatically. Through the late 1800s, around 40 percent of patients eventually left these hospitals. By the twentieth century, however, the proportion of short-term cases decreased and the proportion of long-term patients increased. By 1910, the proportion of short-term patients fell to only 12.7 percent (Grob 1992).

Even as recently as the 1960s, care for the mentally ill remained inadequate; patients were often relegated to crowded and understaffed facilities (see sidebar). Treatments for mental illness frequently were untested folk remedies and often verged on the bizarre.

> ## (✳) ST. ELIZABETHS HOSPITAL
>
> One of the oldest public mental health hospitals, St. Elizabeths Hospital in Washington, DC, provides an example of how such facilities operated in the nineteenth and twentieth centuries. Although St. Elizabeths was established with good intentions, a lack of funding and overwhelming demand resulted in inadequate mental health treatment for many poor people. Opened in 1855 as the first federally operated psychiatric hospital, St. Elizabeths sought to provide a better option for the treatment of the mentally ill. In the 1940s and 1950s, the institution treated as many as 8,000 each year. Eventually, St. Elizabeths became known as the "Government Hospital for the Insane." At the same time, the hospital participated in controversial studies that treated the mentally ill with mind-altering drugs, truth serums, and forced lobotomies (Leshan 2016; Stamberg 2017).

In response to the wide variation in treatments for mental illness and uncertainty surrounding their effectiveness, in 1946 the US federal government passed the National Mental Health Act, which established and provided funds for the National Institute of Mental Health (NIMH). Today, the NIMH "is the lead federal agency for research on mental illnesses, with a mission to transform the understanding and treatment of mental illnesses through basic and clinical research, paving the way for prevention, recovery, and cure." The NIMH was extremely important in establishing proven methods of treating mental illness. With an annual budget of more than $1.6 billion in 2017 (NIMH 2018), the agency's objectives include the following (NIMH 2017):

◆ Define the mechanisms of complex mental disorders

◆ Chart mental illness trajectories to determine when, where, and how to intervene

◆ Strive for prevention and cures

◆ Strengthen the public health impact of NIMH-supported research

During the 1950s, concurrent with the development of antipsychotic drugs and financial pressures to better fund hospital or institutional care, treatment for the mentally ill was moved out of hospital settings to outpatient and community-based settings. The 1960s marked a significant transition from institutional hospital care to community health centers for mental health treatment in the United States. The number of mentally ill patients in hospitals fell from about 560,000 in the 1950s to 70,000 by 1994. In 1963, the Community Mental Health Act established community mental health centers and helped shift the delivery of mental health services even more to outpatient services. Coupled with advances in psychotropic medications, the law allowed many more patients to be treated in their communities (Torrey 1997).

Americans spend more than $186 billion per year on mental health treatment. Most of that money pays for prescription drugs (27 percent) and outpatient treatment (35 percent). Slightly less than 16 percent is spent on inpatient hospital treatment (Franki 2017). The number of mental health inpatient treatment beds in 2016 amounted to only 3 percent of the total number of inpatient hospital beds in the United States (Snook and Torrey 2018). At the same time, serious mental illness, including severe schizophrenia, bipolar disorder, and major depression, occurs at least 50 percent more often among the poor than among the general population. Some experts suggest that our mental health care system is still broken: About 25 percent of adults living in homeless shelters have a serious mental illness, and more than one-third of all adults with a serious mental illness do not obtain needed treatment (Kamal 2017).

An unfortunate side effect of moving so many patients out of hospitals was that by the 1970s, the mentally ill were incarcerated more often. In 2017, according to the Bureau of Justice Statistics (an agency of the US Department of Justice), more than half of all prisoners suffered from a mental illness, and the three largest institutions providing psychiatric care were jails in New York, Los Angeles, and Chicago, where the mentally ill received inadequate treatment for their conditions (American Psychiatric Association 2020; Kozlowska 2015; Roth 2018). By 2014, prisons and jails housed ten times the number of people suffering from severe mental illness than state mental hospitals

---

⊛ DEBATE TIME

Jails are not an appropriate place for the mentally ill. Yet frequently people are arrested for a crime triggered by a mental health crisis, jailed, and found incompetent to stand trial, but then they are kept in jail for long periods of time because of a lack of mental health facilities for prisoners. For example, Elle was arrested for sleeping in someone's car in a garage and had opened the glove box. Bail was set at $50,000, as this was not her first arrest. Six months later, the judged ruled her incompetent to stand trial. Part of the delay was her erratic behavior and delusions. She stayed in jail for another eight months before she was treated at the state mental health hospital. After four months of treatment at the hospital, she was found competent and sent back to the judge, who dropped all charges except trespassing.

Although increased funding for mental health treatment may seem like an simple solution, what can communities do to better care for people with mental illness who are arrested?

(Snook and Torrey 2018). One report indicated that 56 percent of those in state prisons, 45 percent in federal prisons, and 64 percent in local jails had a recent mental health problem (Kamal 2017).

The loss of state psychiatric hospitals may have limited treatment options for the severely mentally ill, who need inpatient care but lack the funds to pay for it. For low-income patients, Medicaid is often the only source of care. However, Medicaid does not pay for long-term mental health treatment. As a result, a high percentage of these patients use the emergency room (ER) as their primary source of healthcare. After these patients are seen in the ER, they are frequently sent back to their communities, and many become homeless (Raphelson 2017).

Community hospitals are not set up to be a solution for mental health treatment. Generally, they are not organized to care for patients needing more than 72 hours of immediate care. The low number of inpatient beds allocated for mental health patients forces people who are acutely mentally ill to wait for extended treatment. This situation often creates a devastating downward spiral effect, as patients' mental health conditions deteriorate while they wait for treatment. People with untreated mental illness may act out, injure themselves, lose their jobs, or commit or be the victim of crimes. These actions lead to additional visits to the ER, homeless shelters, or prison (Snook and Torrey 2018).

Thirteen percent of patients who are admitted to community hospitals for mental illness are readmitted within 30 days (Kamal 2017). Most ER patients receive only temporary or urgent care and fail to obtain coordinated care from a primary care provider. In addition, of the many people with mental illnesses who are incarcerated each year, an estimated 15 percent of men and 30 percent of women have serious mental health concerns (NAMI 2020).

TYPES OF MENTAL HEALTH PROVIDERS

Many different types of providers care for people with mental illness. These providers vary by their level of education, scope of practice, and the services they can offer. The following are most common types of providers focusing almost exclusively on mental health (NAMI 2019b):

◆ A *psychiatrist* is a medical doctor who has completed a residency in psychiatry. Psychiatrists can diagnose mental illnesses, prescribe and monitor medications, and provide therapy. They must be licensed in the state in which they practice and may be board certified by their professional association (e.g., American Board of Psychiatry and Neurology).

◆ A *psychologist* holds a doctoral degree—either a doctor of philosophy (PhD) or a doctor of psychology (PsyD)—in psychology, counseling, or education. Psychologists use clinical interviews, psychological evaluations, and testing to assess and diagnose patients. They must be licensed in the state in which they practice.

◆ A *psychiatric or mental health nurse practitioner* may be a registered nurse (RN) with a master of science (MS) or doctor of philosophy (PhD) in nursing, specializing in psychiatry. Nurse practitioners provide assessment, diagnosis, and therapy. They must be licensed as RNs and may need to be supervised by a psychiatrist.

◆ A *licensed clinical social worker* holds a master's degree in social work (MSW). Social workers are trained to evaluate mental health, use therapeutic techniques, and provide case management and advocacy services. Licensure is required in most states.

◆ A *counselor or therapist* usually holds a master's degree in a mental health discipline (e.g., counseling, marriage and family therapy). Counselors are trained to use therapeutic techniques to evaluate and treat patients. Licensure is required in some states.

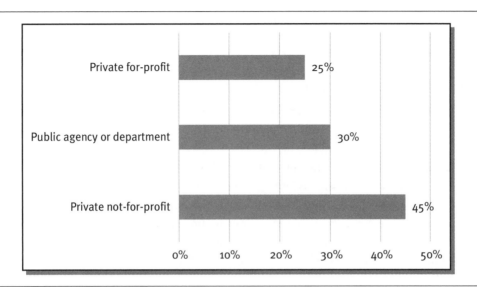

EXHIBIT 6.1
Ownership of Mental Health Hospitals, 2018

Source: Data from Statista (2020).

OWNERSHIP OF MENTAL HEALTH FACILITIES

About three-quarters of mental health hospitals are not-for-profit or public institutions. Private not-for-profit facilities account for almost half of mental health hospitals, while 30 percent are owned by public (government) entities (see exhibit 6.1).

MENTAL HEALTH TREATMENT SETTINGS

Mental health treatment is offered in a variety of settings. More than one-third of treatment facilities provide only outpatient services, although many provide more than one level of care. For instance, many facilities provide a mix of inpatient, residential, and outpatient care. In addition, most facilities (58 percent) restrict the age groups that they treat (SAMHSA 2018).

Psychiatric care for the general public (excluding prisoners) that necessitates overnight treatment is provided in different types of settings, including specialized public and private psychiatric hospitals, psychiatric inpatient care in community hospitals, and licensed residential treatment units. Inpatient treatment is reserved mostly for patients with severe mental illnesses such as schizophrenia, mood disorders, major depression, suicidal ideation, and bipolar disorder (Kamal 2017).

In all, 692 psychiatric hospitals are in operation in the United States. This figure includes 206 public and 486 private facilities (SAMHSA 2018). Approximately 195 state-run psychiatric hospitals are in operation in the United States (NASMHPD 2020). Fourteen states have only one state psychiatric hospital (Parks and Radke 2014). Public psychiatric hospitals average more inpatient beds (182 per facility) than private facilities (73 per facility) (SAMHSA 2018).

STATE MENTAL HEALTH FACILITIES

State mental health facilities primarily serve those who enter the mental health system through the courts. Many state mental hospitals struggle financially as a result of budget cuts, which may affect the quality of care. For instance, when Florida enacted budget cuts of about $100 million to its state mental hospital system, some reported that this "turned state-run mental-health hospitals" into "treacherous warehouses where violence is out of control and patients can't get the care they need" (Snook and Torrey 2018).

States' underfunding of mental health has also led to the closure of many inpatient facilities without adequate increases in funding for alternative services. Since 2005, publicly funded inpatient psychiatric beds have dropped by 40 percent, to about 700 beds (*Boston Globe* 2016).

COMMUNITY HOSPITAL EMERGENCY ROOMS

The lack of psychiatric inpatient beds causes patients to seek treatment through ERs located in community hospitals, which often are not equipped to treat psychiatric emergencies. The psychiatric care that ERs can provide is fairly limited. ERs often do not have the time and expertise to treat those needing psychiatric care; as a result, patients may be kept in the ER for multiple days, until appropriate resources can be located (Kalter 2019). In fact, one survey indicated that 62 percent of ER doctors felt they could not provide appropriate psychiatric services. However, the demand for psychiatric care in ERs has grown significantly. For example, between 2006 and 2013, psychiatric visits to ERs increased more than 50 percent (Kennedy 2018). Most experts agree that the ER is not the best location for psychiatric care, as wait times are long, costs are high, and psychiatric and mental health treatment is often poor (Miller 2015).

COMMUNITY HEALTH CENTERS

community health center
A neighborhood health center that generally serves low-income and uninsured populations.

More than 2,600 **community health centers** in the United States provide care for 27 million patients, many of whom have a need for some type of mental health treatment (Simmons 2018; SAMHSA 2018). Almost half (49 percent) of all community health center patients are covered by Medicaid, and about one-quarter (23 percent) have no insurance. Almost all community health center patients (92 percent) come from low-income families. About 10 percent of all visits to community health centers are for mental health services (Rosenbaum et al. 2018). Some community mental health centers are creating innovative partnerships to improve the health of those suffering from mental health issues (see sidebar).

PRIVATE MENTAL HEALTH HOSPITALS

As a result of the declining numbers of public hospital beds, many for-profit psychiatric treatment facilities have emerged. Private hospitals can provide more services and often more comprehensive care for those who can afford it. These hospitals also may provide scenic, quiet settings for treatments that might include gourmet meals and highly qualified healthcare professionals. Many of these firms, such as Acadia Healthcare (see sidebar), have grown rapidly and now operate across much of the United States.

Investment in private hospitals has increased. For instance, US HealthVest raised almost $100 million in capital to build psychiatric hospitals in New York and Georgia. For-profit psychiatric hospitals tend to provide high profits for their investors. For example, the largest for-profit provider of psychiatric care, Universal Health, recorded operating margins of 23 percent—more than twice that the 11 percent earned by general community hospitals (Sachdev 2016).

ACADIA HEALTHCARE

Some private, for-profit psychiatric companies have expanded rapidly. Acadia Healthcare (www.acadiahealthcare.com), a for-profit psychiatric care provider based in Tennessee, operated 589 behavioral health facilities in 2019, with 18,000 beds in 40 states in the United States and the United Kingdom. Acadia provides services including inpatient psychiatric care, specialty treatment facilities, residential treatment centers, and outpatient clinics, bringing in annual revenues of around $3 billion. Large healthcare chains like Acadia are increasingly influencing the provision of mental health services across the United States. However, these private facilities are generally only available to those who can afford such care or have health insurance that covers these services.

For many people, however, private, for-profit psychiatric care is inaccessible. Most for-profit facilities do not accept Medicaid, and care can cost upwards of $30,000 per month (Raphelson 2017). For example, a residential treatment program at the Gunderson Residence in Cambridge, Massachusetts, costs $1,350 per day, or $81,000 for a 60-day treatment period (Khazan 2018). These high costs allow only the wealthy to have access to these quality programs and exclude those who lack funds. Private, for-profit mental health services are often marketed as luxury facilities. For instance, one private facility describes its hospital as follows:

> The Beach Cottage at Seasons in Malibu is a stand-alone facility that offers life-changing treatment for individuals suffering with mental health disorders. . . . Once admitted, clients are safely ensconced in a warm, beachy ambiance, with close-up ocean views, a private path to the beach, sumptuous meals prepared by our chefs, and 24-hour compassionate care from our staff. A typical day might begin with a beach walk followed by yoga and breakfast, and end around the fire pit with other clients, processing what you have learned and experienced that day. (Seasons in Malibu 2020)

Private facilities may be a good solution for those with the means to pay for them, but they do not provide solutions for many mentally ill patients.

RESIDENTIAL TREATMENT CENTERS

residential treatment center
A mental health facility where psychiatric treatment is provided in a home-like environment with less medical involvement.

Residential treatment centers are another setting for psychiatric care. Residential treatment centers provide care in a less resource-intensive setting than inpatient care. These centers provide a more home-like environment with less medical involvement. Many patients leaving inpatient care may be placed in residential treatment centers. In fact, most recovery programs are residential centers with outpatient treatment options (see sidebar). Residential treatment may continue over long periods of time and often treats those with chronic psychiatric conditions such as schizophrenia, bipolar disorder, or **dual diagnoses** (patients who have both a mental illness and a substance abuse disorder). These centers can be not-for-profit or for-profit.

dual diagnosis
The diagnosis of both a mental illness and a substance abuse disorder.

(✳) DEBATE TIME Healthcare Homes for Mental Illness

Do we need new models of treatment for the mentally ill? Some states, such as Missouri, have begun to experiment with ways to better treat mental health problems. In 2012, Missouri created Community Mental Health Centers (CMHCs) to act as healthcare homes for those with mental illness. The centers combined mental health and primary care to provide more comprehensive treatment for those struggling with mental illness. By 2016, results from these CMHCs were very positive, as mental health patients' overall health indicators improved significantly. For instance, their blood cholesterol levels decreased, diabetes was better controlled, and the use of emergency rooms and hospitalizations plummeted. In just three years, Missouri saved $98 million in healthcare costs (Levine 2018). Perhaps a more comprehensive effort like Missouri's could be used across the United States to address the struggles of so many mentally ill patients. Why do you think more states do not use this approach and focus only on psychiatric care?

psychiatric unit
A unit (department) within a community hospital that is dedicated to the inpatient treatment of mental illness.

COMMUNITY HOSPITAL PSYCHIATRIC UNITS

A patient requiring hospitalization can use a facility dedicated only to psychiatric care or obtain care from community hospitals that offer psychiatric services. A number of community hospitals have dedicated **psychiatric units** dedicated to mental health, but many general hospitals that lack specialized mental health units also provide inpatient treatment for individuals with mental illnesses in "scatter beds" (inpatient beds outside a specialized psychiatric unit) and in their emergency departments (Lutterman, Shaw, and Fisher 2017).

About 25 to 30 percent of community hospitals have dedicated psychiatric units. These units provide the majority of inpatient hospital psychiatric care in the United States, measured by the number of admissions. The quality of care may vary, as psychiatric patients in community hospitals may not be treated by psychiatrists but by internal medicine specialists and other medical staff with limited training in psychiatry (Mark et al. 2010).

OUTPATIENT PSYCHIATRIC TREATMENT

Outpatient services are those services that do not require a continuous stay of 24 hours or longer in a treatment facility. As with general hospital care, most psychiatric care has shifted to outpatient settings. More than 4 million people received some type of **outpatient psychiatric treatment** in 2016 (SAMHSA 2018). Outpatient treatments include a variety of services, such as those listed in exhibit 6.2.

outpatient psychiatric treatment
Psychiatric services offered on an ambulatory basis that do not require a continuous stay of 24 hours or longer in a treatment facility.

- Depression screenings
- Individual or group psychotherapy
- Family counseling
- Psychiatric evaluations
- Medication management visits
- Injections of some types of drugs
- Diagnostic tests

EXHIBIT 6.2
Types of Mental Health Outpatient Treatments

Source: Medicare.gov (2020).

SUBSTANCE ABUSE AND MENTAL ILLNESS

There is a strong connection between substance abuse and mental illness. About half of those with mental illness experience substance abuse problems. The use of illegal drugs during childhood and adolescence has also been shown to enhance the risk for mental illness; at the same time, mental health problems in young people increase their risk for later substance abuse. As a result, better treatment occurs when substance abuse and mental health are addressed simultaneously (National Institute on Drug Abuse 2020). As shown in exhibit 6.3, people with mental illness consume a large share of addictive substances when one considers that only about 24 percent of the US population in any given year has a diagnosable mental illness.

EXHIBIT 6.3

Share of Additive
Substances Used
by People with
Mental Illness

Coexisting with Mental Illness	Mental Illness During Lifetime
Alcohol—38%	Alcohol—43%
Cocaine—44%	Cocaine—84%
Cigarettes—40%	Cigarettes—68%

Source: Data from NBER (2018).

Some drug use directly exacerbates mental health problems. For example, depression commonly occurs when crystal meth and alcohol begin to wear off (Foundations Recovery Network 2020). As a result of the connection between substance and abuse and mental illness, it is important to treat them jointly.

CHALLENGES IN MENTAL HEALTH CARE

SUPPLY OF PROVIDERS

The United States has a shortage of mental health providers. Decreasing availability of psychiatric medical residencies and low job satisfaction often deter people from entering the psychiatric professions. Because so few physicians are training in psychiatry, it is an aging profession: About 70 percent of practicing psychiatrists are over age 50, and 60 percent are 55 or older. At the same time, demand for mental health services is increasing (Japsen 2018). Almost every county in the United States has reported an unmet need for psychiatrists. Even in urban areas, people needing mental health treatment have difficulty getting an appointment for care. According to one study, only 12 percent of callers to a mental health facility in Boston were able to obtain an appointment with an initial call, and 23 percent never received an appointment even after calling twice (Davio 2018). By 2025, a significant shortage of psychiatrists, psychologists, social workers, mental health counselors, and marriage and family therapists is predicted across the United States (NCHWA 2016).

Accessing psychiatric care is even more challenging in rural areas. Most mental health providers reside in urban areas, and few live in rural areas (Butryn et al. 2017). Individuals with mental illness who reside in rural areas experience greater difficulty finding care. Most rural areas (65 percent) lack a psychiatrist, and almost half (47 percent) do not have any psychologists. This shortage has a direct impact on rates of drug abuse and suicide. As the Centers for Disease Control and Prevention (CDC) states, "Suicide, drug abuse and addiction are certainly problems that affect all populations and all parts of the

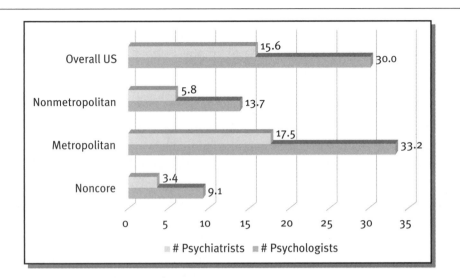

Exhibit 6.4
Behavioral Health
Practitioners by
County Type
(providers per
100,000 people)

Note: Noncore counties are those counties where the major cities or clusters of cities have a population
of less than 10,000 or there is no substantial population center.

Source: Data from Willingham and Elkin (2018).

country, but both drug deaths and suicide deaths disproportionately affect rural America"
(Willingham and Elkin 2018).

As shown in exhibit 6.4, smaller communities (referred to as "noncore" communities) and areas outside of metropolitan areas have almost one-third the number of key
mental health providers. Even if there is a psychologist or psychiatrist available, given their
low income levels and lack of transportation, people in rural areas still may not be able to
access care (Willingham and Elkin 2018).

COST AND FUNDING OF MENTAL HEALTH SERVICES

States have cut more than $4 billion from their public mental health funding since 2008.
Today, many people cannot afford to receive mental health services. According to one estimate, only 20 percent of youth and children who need mental health care receive it, and
payments for psychiatric services are so low that many providers lose money on many of
their services (Davio 2018). Because mental health providers feel that insurance companies
do not reimburse them adequately, only 55 percent of psychiatrists accept insurance, and
many require cash payments, which can amount to hundreds of dollars per session.

According to a study conducted by federal researchers, about half of patients who
did not receive treatment for a mental health problem cited cost as a significant barrier to
care. They indicated that they lacked insurance covering mental health treatment or could

not afford the cost of treatment (GAO 2019). However, lowering the cost of mental health care to increase its use could decrease suicide rates in the United States (Garfield and Brueck 2018). Sadly, suicide rates for youth jumped 56 percent from 2007 to 2017, from 6.8 to 10.6 deaths per 100,000 people (Santhanam 2019).

STIGMA

Many people still feel threatened by and uncomfortable with those with mental illness. These feelings can foster discrimination and exclusion, creating a mental health stigma. This stigma can come from social or self-perceptions that lead to feelings of shame, prevent treatment, and result in poor mental health outcomes (Davey 2013). People often are reluctant to discuss their mental health issues because they fear embarrassing their family or even losing their job (Seervai and Lewis 2018). To obtain appropriate care, people with mental illness need to be able to discuss their illness openly without fear of social judgment. As one person who lost her mentally ill brother to suicide commented, "Fear of social rejection, ridicule, discrimination and judgment often keep people from sharing their struggle" (Warrell 2018).

Some efforts are being made to reduce the stigma. Professional athletes, for example, have been outspoken about their own struggles with mental illness in the hope of opening lines of communication and encouraging earlier treatment (Gabriel 2018). Likewise, Catholic bishops published a pastoral letter encouraging empathy and condemning the "unjust social stigma of mental illness," which "is neither a moral failure nor character defect" (White 2018). In addition, some healthcare groups and primary care physicians are working together to integrate mental health care with primary care and to reduce stigma (AIMS Center 2020).

RACIAL AND ETHNIC DISPARITIES

The use of mental health services is much lower among African Americans, Asians, and Hispanics/Latinos than among whites (Kamal 2017). For example, more than 70 percent of African American youth with major depression do not receive treatment, and minority groups are less likely to receive a diagnosis and treatment for mental illness. In addition, they are much more likely to use the emergency room for mental health services than community mental health services (HHS 2019). Minorities often lack convenient access to quality mental health care, have higher levels of stigma against mental health treatment, have fewer financial resources and less health insurance coverage, and may have language barriers, all of which lower the use of mental health services among these populations. As a result, minorities receive lower-quality care and experience poorer outcomes related to mental illness (St. John 2016).

SUMMARY

The diagnosis and treatment of mental health has a profound impact on a wide swath of Americans. Historically, mental illness was misunderstood, and those suffering from it were often punished or shunned. By the nineteenth and twentieth centuries, most Western civilizations recognized mental disorders as medical illnesses, but ineffective and sometimes bizarre treatments persisted. Concentrating the mentally ill in asylums and public almshouses isolated them from their community.

Change came slowly to US institutions treating the mentally ill. As late as the 1960s, care for the mentally ill was inadequate, often provided in crowded and understaffed facilities. The creation of the National Institute of Mental Health in 1946, the development of antipsychotic drugs, and financial pressures prompted a shift from inpatient care to outpatient and community-based treatment. Today, the vast majority of expenditures on mental health care go toward prescription drugs and outpatient treatment.

An unfortunate side effect of the move to outpatient treatment and inadequate funding has been the imprisonment of many people with mental illness. About half of all prisoners in the United States have a psychiatric disorder. The three largest institutions providing psychiatric care are jails in New York, Los Angeles, and Chicago.

A variety of mental health providers exist. Most provide therapy, assessment, and diagnosis. The most commonly used mental health providers are psychiatrists and psychologists, but many others provide care, such as psychiatric nurse practitioners, social workers, and counselors and therapists.

Most organizations that provide mental health services are not-for-profit facilities; slightly less than 20 percent are for-profit institutions. A majority of mental health providers offer a mix of inpatient and outpatient care. Inpatient care can be provided in a variety of settings. It is used mostly for those suffering from schizophrenia, mood disorders, major depression, and bipolar disorder.

All states have at least one state mental health hospital. State psychiatric hospitals primarily serve those coming from the court system. Underfunding has led to long waits for care and increased use of emergency rooms for the mentally ill. Community health centers have also filled a need for many.

The wealthy have many options for mental health treatment. Many for-profit companies offer luxury facilities with extensive treatment options, but at very high costs.

Community hospitals offer psychiatric services in dedicated units, in scattered beds, and in their emergency rooms. A majority of inpatient admissions to psychiatric units take place in community hospitals.

Many individuals struggle with both substance abuse and mental illness, and there is a direct correlation between them. Both issues need to be treated jointly.

The United States faces a lack of mental health providers as a result of the decreasing number of psychiatric residencies, low job satisfaction, and lower earning potential. A majority of psychiatrists today are over the age of 55. Almost all counties in the United States report a need for more mental health services, although people in rural areas experience greater difficulty accessing services.

The lack of public funding and the high costs of care create significant barriers to mental healthcare and treatment. Many mental health providers do not accept insurance and require individuals to pay for services out of pocket. In addition to cost, some people feel threatened by and uncomfortable with others with mental illness. This often results in discrimination and exclusion, creating a stigma toward mental illness.

QUESTIONS

1. What were some of the treatments given to the mentally ill during the nineteenth and early twentieth centuries? How do we regard those treatments today?
2. What was the original function of asylums?
3. When was the National Institute of Mental Health created, and why?
4. Why did the number of people hospitalized for mental illness decline in the 1960s?
5. What are the side effects of people with mental illness leaving hospitals?
6. What is the difference between a psychiatrist and a psychologist?
7. What is the ownership structure of most mental health treatment providers in the United States?
8. Why are state mental health facilities struggling financially?
9. If people cannot obtain care from mental health providers as a result of lack of funds or limited services, where do they go for care?
10. What factors contribute to the declining number of psychiatrists in the United States?

ASSIGNMENTS

1. Locate the website of a private not-for-profit mental health provider, a private for-profit mental health provider, and a state mental health agency. Describe the differences among them.
2. Read the following article about differences in funding for mental health treatment by state: "Funds for Treating Individuals with Mental Illness: Is Your State Naughty or Nice?," Mental Illness Policy Org, December 17, 2017, at https://mentalillnesspolicy.org/national-studies/funds-for-mental-illness-is-your-state-generous-or-stingy-press-release.html. Prepare to speak to your group about the following questions:
   a. Why are there such large funding differences among states?

b. What impacts on physical and mental health would you predict in the states that spend the most? The least?

c. Can you find any evidence to show that greater funding decreases opioid use and incarceration?

CASES

STRUGGLING WITH MENTAL HEALTH

My name is Tim and I am 30 years old. I was diagnosed with depression and anxiety when I turned 21, but it seems like I have been struggling with anxiety my whole life. At times, my depression and anxiety overwhelm me and make me feel hopeless. In the past decade, I have tried 16 different psychiatric medications and currently take four. I have also had four long-term individual therapists. I would have liked to have maintained my relationships with them, but I ran out of insurance coverage and had to seek alternatives. A couple of times, things got too challenging and I was hospitalized, once for three weeks. I am afraid that I have few insurance benefits left, which makes me very anxious. I also want to say that I have a mental illness, but I am afraid of the stigma that comes with it.

Discussion Questions

1. What are the major challenges that Tim faces?
2. What steps could Tim take to improve his mental health?
3. What do you think American society could do to improve mental health treatment?

JAIL FOR THE MENTALLY ILL

Travis was jailed on charges that he broke into his father's home to steal food. His family often found him delusional: he said that he could hear voices, and he believed that tiny robots had been implanted under his skin. One day, his father returned home to find the front door broken, and he called the police. Even though his father did not want his son to be arrested, the police took him to jail and charged him with a class B felony. Travis languished in jail for 18 months until a judge found him incompetent to face trial. During his incarceration, Travis refused to comply with many of the rules, and once he threw his plate of food at a guard, earning him time in solitary confinement. During the year and a half that he was incarcerated, his delusions increased, and he received very little mental health treatment.

Discussion Questions

1. What problems result from incarcerating people with mental illness?
2. What could governments do to provide better treatment for people with mental illness in jails?

REFERENCES

Advancing Integrated Mental Health Solutions (AIMS) Center. 2020. "Collaborative Care." Accessed April 20. https://aims.uw.edu/collaborative-care.

American Academy of Family Physicians. 2018. "Mental Health Care Services by Family Physicians." Position Paper. Accessed April 20, 2020. www.aafp.org/about/policies/all/mental-services.html.

American Psychiatric Association. 2020. "Criminal Justice." Accessed June 5. www.psychiatry.org/psychiatrists/advocacy/federal-affairs/criminal-justice.

Boston Globe. 2016. "State Must Deal with the Grim Aftermath of Psychiatric Hospital Closings." Published July 7. www.bostonglobe.com/opinion/editorials/2016/07/06/state-must-deal-with-grim-aftermath-psychiatric-hospital-closings/FloBRFjZaY84Q-idgjHfODP/story.html.

Butryn, T., L. Bryant, C. Marchionni, and F. Sholevar. 2017. "The Shortage of Psychiatrists and Other Mental Health Providers: Causes, Current State, and Potential Solutions." *International Journal of Academic Medicine* 3 (1): 5–9.

Davey, G. 2013. "Mental Health & Stigma." *Psychology Today*. Published August 20. www.psychologytoday.com/us/blog/why-we-worry/201308/mental-health-stigma.

Davio, K. 2018. "Single-Payer System Is the Solution for Mental Healthcare, Panelists Say." *American Journal of Managed Care*. Published May 7. www.ajmc.com/conferences/apa-2018/singlepayer-system-is-the-solution-for-mental-health-care-panelists-say.

Foundations Recovery Network. 2020. "The Connection Between Mental Illness and Substance Abuse." Accessed April 20. www.dualdiagnosis.org/mental-health-and-addiction/the-connection/.

Franki, R. 2017. "Outpatient Care 35% of Mental Health Costs and Growing." Clinical Psychiatry News/MDedge. Published July 7. www.mdedge.com/psychiatry/article/142102/business-medicine/outpatient-care-35-mental-health-costs-and-growing.

Gabriel, E. 2018. "NBA Stars Join Fight Against Stigma Surrounding Mental Illness." CNN. Published March 28. www.cnn.com/2018/03/02/health/nba-mental-health-stigma/index.html.

Garfield, L., and H. Brueck. 2018. "There May Be One Big Reason Suicide Rates Keep Climbing in the U.S., According to Mental-Health Experts." *Business Insider*. Published June 9. www.businessinsider.com/anthony-bourdain-kate-spade-suicide-rate-mental-healthcare-costs-2018-6.

Grob, G. 1992. "Mental Health Policy in America: Myths and Realities." *Health Affairs* 11 (3): 7–22.

Japsen, B. 2018. "Psychiatrist Shortage Escalates as U.S. Mental Health Needs Grow." *Forbes*. Published February 25. www.forbes.com/sites/brucejapsen/2018/02/25/psychiatrist-shortage-escalates-as-u-s-mental-health-needs-grow/#36b702c51255.

Kalter, L. 2019. "Treating Mental Illness in the ED." Association of American Medical Colleges. Published September 3. www.aamc.org/news-insights/treating-mental-illness-ed.

Kamal, R. 2017. "What Are the Current Costs and Outcomes Related to Mental Health and Substance Abuse Disorders?" Peterson-KFF Health System Tracker. Published July 31. www.healthsystemtracker.org/chart-collection/current-costs-outcomes-related-mental-health-substance-abuse-disorders/#item-start.

Kennedy, M. 2018. "'Failing Patients': Baltimore Video Highlights Crisis of Emergency Psychiatric Care." National Public Radio, April 29. www.npr.org/sections/health-shots/2018/04/29/599892160/failing-patients-baltimore-video-highlights-crisis-of-emergency-psychiatric-care.

Khazan, O. 2018. "Trump's Call for Mental Institutions Could Be Good." *The Atlantic*. Published February 23. www.theatlantic.com/health/archive/2018/02/mental-institutions/554015/.

Kozlowska, H. 2015. "Should the U.S. Bring Back Psychiatric Asylums?" *The Atlantic*. Published January 27. www.theatlantic.com/health/archive/2015/01/should-the-us-bring-back-psychiatric-asylums/384838/.

Leshan, B. 2016. "The Lobotomist: Ghosts of St. Elizabeths Hospital." WUSA. Published May 19. www.wusa9.com/article/news/local/the-lobotomist-ghosts-of-st-elizabeths-hospital/204464983.

Levine, D. 2018. "What Are the Advantages of Health Homes for Mental Healthcare?" *U.S. News & World Report*. Published February 23. https://health.usnews.com/health-care/patient-advice/articles/2018-02-23/what-are-the-advantages-of-health-homes-for-mental-health-care.

Lutterman, T., R. Shaw, and W. Fisher. 2017. "Trend in Psychiatric Inpatient Capacity, United States and Each State, 1970 to 2014." National Association of State Mental Health Program Directors, Assessment No. 10. Published August. www.nri-inc.org/media/1319/tac-paper-10-psychiatric-inpatient-capacity-final-09-05-2017.pdf.

Malcolm, L., and C. Blumer. 2016. "Madness and Insanity: A History of Mental Illness from Evil Spirits to Modern Medicine." ABC Health. Published August 2. www.abc.net.au/news/health/2016-08-02/mental-illness-and-insanity-a-short-cultural-history/7677906.

Mark, T., R. Vandivort-Warren, P. Owens, J. Buck, K. Levit, R. Coffey, and C. Stocks. 2010. "Patient Discharges in Community Hospitals With and Without Psychiatric Units: How Many and for Whom?" *Psychiatric Services* 61 (6): 562–68.

Medicare.gov. 2020. "Your Medicare Coverage: Mental Health Care (Outpatient)." Accessed April 20. www.medicare.gov/coverage/outpatient-mental-health-care.html.

Miller, A. 2015. "What to Do During a Mental Health Crisis." *U.S. News & World Report*. Published July 21. https://health.usnews.com/health-news/best-hospitals/articles/2015/07/21/what-to-do-during-a-mental-health-crisis.

National Alliance on Mental Illness (NAMI). 2020. "Jailing People with Mental Illness." Accessed April 20. www.nami.org/learn-more/public-policy/jailing-people-with-mental-illness.

———. 2019a. "Mental Health by the Numbers." Updated September. www.nami.org/learn-more/mental-health-by-the-numbers.

————. 2019b. "Types of Mental Health Professionals." Updated April. www.nami.org/ Learn-More/Treatment/Types-of-Mental-Health-Professionals.

National Association of State Mental Health Program Directors (NASMHPD). 2020. "State Hospital Organizations." Accessed April 20. www.nasmhpd.org/content/ state-hospital-organizations.

National Bureau of Economic Research (NBER). 2018. "Mental Illness and Substance Abuse." www.nber.org/digest/apr02/w8699.html.

National Center for Health Workforce Analysis (NCHWA). 2016. "National Projections of Supply and Demand for Selected Behavioral Health Practitioners: 2013–2025." Published November. https://bhw.hrsa.gov/sites/default/files/bhw/health-workforce-analysis/ research/projections/behavioral-health2013-2025.pdf.

National Institute of Mental Health (NIMH). 2018. "FY 2019 Budget." Accessed April 20, 2020. www.nimh.nih.gov/about/budget/cj2019_156766.pdf.

National Institute on Drug Abuse. 2020. "Common Comorbidities with Substance Use Disorders." Updated April. www.drugabuse.gov/publications/research-reports/ common-comorbidities-substance-use-disorders/part-1-connection-between- substance-use-disorders-mental-illness.

————. 2017. "The NIH Almanac." Reviewed February 17. www.nih.gov/about-nih/ what-we-do/nih-almanac/national-institute-mental-health-nimh.

Parks, J., and A. Radke, eds. 2014. "The Vital Role of State Psychiatric Hospitals." National Association of State Mental Health Program Directors, Technical Report. Published July. www.nasmhpd.org/sites/default/files/The%20Vital%20Role%20of%20State%20 Psychiatric%20HospitalsTechnical%20Report_July_2014.pdf.

Raphelson, S. 2017. "How the Loss of U.S. Psychiatric Hospitals Led to a Mental Health Crisis." National Public Radio. Published November 30. www.npr.org/2017/11/30/567477160/ how-the-loss-of-u-s-psychiatric-hospitals-led-to-a-mental-health-crisis.

Rosenbaum, S., J. Tolbert, J. Sharac, P. Shin, R. Gunsalus, and J. Zur. 2018. "Community Health Centers: Growing Importance in a Changing Healthcare System." Kaiser Family Foundation. Published March 9. www.kff.org/medicaid/issue-brief/community-health-centers-growing-importance-in-a-changing-health-care-system/.

Roth, A. 2018. *Insane: America's Criminal Treatment of Mental Illness*. New York: Basic Books.

Sachdev, A. 2016. "For-Profit Psychiatric Care Firm Says It's Filling Gap in the Chicago Area." *Chicago Tribune*. Published July 1. www.chicagotribune.com/business/ct-psychiatric-hospital-northbrook-0703-biz-20160701-story.html.

Santhanam, L. 2019. "Youth Suicide Rates Are on the Rise in the US." *PBS NewsHour*. Published October 18. www.pbs.org/newshour/health/youth-suicide-rates-are-on-the-rise-in-the-u-s.

Seasons in Malibu. 2020. "Seasons in Malibu Mental Health Treatment Center." Accessed June 5. https://seasonsmalibu.com/treatment-programs/mental-health-treatment-facilities/.

Sederer, L. 2015. "Tinkering Can't Fix the Mental Healthcare System." *U.S. News & World Report*. Published March 20. www.usnews.com/opinion/blogs/opinion-blog/2015/03/20/fixing-the-mental-health-system-requires-disruptive-innovation.

Seervai, S., and C. Lewis. 2018. "Listening to Low-Income Patients: Mental Health Stigma Is a Barrier to Care." Commonwealth Fund. Published May 20. www.commonwealthfund.org/publications/publication/2018/mar/listening-low-income-patients-mental-health-stigma-barrier-care.

Simmons, A. 2018. "NACHC Statement on the FY 2018 Omnibus Appropriations." National Association of Community Health Centers. Published March 23. www.nachc.org/news/nachc-statement-on-the-2018-omnibus-legislation-passed-by-congress/.

Snook, J., and E. F. Torrey. 2018. "America Badly Needs More Psychiatric-Treatment Beds." *National Review*. Published February 23. www.nationalreview.com/2018/02/america-badly-needs-more-psychiatric-treatment-beds/.

Stamberg, S. 2017. "Architecture of an Asylum Tracks History of U.S. Treatment of Mental Illness." National Public Radio. Published July 6. www.npr.org/sections/health-shots/2017/07/06/535608442/architecture-of-an-asylum-tracks-history-of-u-s-treatment-of-mental-illness.

Statista. 2020. "Number of Psychiatric Hospitals in the U.S. in 2018 by Operation Type." Accessed June 5. www.statista.com/statistics/712645/psychiatric-hospitals-number-in-the-us-by-operation-type/.

St. John, T. 2016. "8 Reasons Racial and Ethnic Minorities Receive Less Mental Health Treatment." Arundel Lodge Behavioral Health. Published August 2. www.arundellodge.org/8-reasons-cultural-and-ethnic-minorities-receive-less-mental-health-treatment/.

Substance Abuse and Mental Services Administration (SAMHSA). 2018. "National Mental Health Services Survey: 2018, Data on Mental Health Treatment Facilities." Published October. www.samhsa.gov/data/sites/default/files/cbhsq-reports/NMHSS-2018.pdf.

Torrey, E. F. 1997. *Out of the Shadows: Confronting America's Mental Illness Crisis*. New York: John Wiley & Sons.

US Department of Health and Human Services (HHS). 2019. "Minority Mental Health Awareness Month—July." Office of Minority Health. Published July 1. www.minorityhealth.hhs.gov/omh/content.aspx?ID=9447.

US Government Accountability Office (GAO). 2019. "Behavioral Health: Research on Health Care Costs of Untreated Conditions Is Limited." Report to Congressional Requesters. Published February. www.gao.gov/assets/700/697178.pdf.

Warrell, M. 2018. "The Rise and Rise of Suicide: We Must Remove the Stigma of Mental Illness." *Forbes*. Published June 9. www.forbes.com/sites/margiewarrell/2018/06/09/the-rise-and-rise-of-suicide-we-must-remove-the-stigma-of-mental-illness/#42ebf9b77526.

White, C. 2018. "California Bishops Call for End to Social Stigma Around Mental Illness." *Crux*. Published May 2. cruxnow.com/church-in-the-usa/2018/05/02/california-bishops-call-for-end-to-social-stigma-around-mental-illness/.

Willingham, A., and E. Elkin. 2018. "There's a Severe Shortage of Mental Health Professionals in Rural Areas: Here's Why That's a Serious Problem." CNN. Published June 20. www.cnn.com/2018/06/20/health/mental-health-rural-areas-issues-trnd/index.html.

CHAPTER 7

GOVERNMENT INVOLVEMENT IN US HEALTHCARE

What role should government play in our healthcare system? This question has been debated, without resolution, for decades. Americans are divided on the appropriate level of government involvement in healthcare. A poll conducted by the Kaiser Family Foundation found that a majority of people (74 percent) believe the federal government should do more to provide health insurance for Americans. This percentage has been relatively stable since 2008. However, there is a partisan divide on this issue: According to the survey, 94 percent of Democrats are strongly in favor of more government intervention, compared with only 40 percent of Republicans. Support from Democrats has been stable since 2008, whereas Republican support dropped from 49 percent in 2008 to 40 percent in 2019. Yet many of those who oppose government involvement in healthcare still believe that the Medicare and Medicaid programs should continue. Far from any easy resolution, this debate will certainly continue for many years to come (Kaiser Family Foundation 2020).

LEARNING OBJECTIVES

After reading this chapter you will be able to

➤ Discuss the ways in which governments influence healthcare in the United States.

➤ Describe why governments in the United States make regulations.

➤ Comprehend the purpose of licensure and what it accomplishes and lacks.

➤ Talk about the major agencies that regulate healthcare in the United States.

➤ Discuss the main ways that healthcare is purchased in the United States.

➤ List and describe the two largest healthcare systems owned and operated by the US government.

➤ Outline the costs of providing healthcare to people who are incarcerated.

➤ Describe the types of government-sponsored programs for health services research and training and the rationale for them.

➤ Talk about your personal opinion regarding the role of government in healthcare.

Like governments around the world, governments in the United States—at the federal, state, and local levels—are actively involved in the regulation, provision, and funding of healthcare. Today, more and more citizens believe that government has a primary responsibility to ensure that Americans have access to healthcare coverage.

Federal and state governments' involvement in healthcare expanded dramatically in the mid-1960s as a result of the enactment of Medicare and Medicaid. By 2016, the federal and state governments paid for 45.2 percent of total healthcare costs in the United States (CMS 2020a). Today, governments are involved in healthcare through regulation, subsidies for research and education, tax policy, payments, and the provision of healthcare. Government involvement in healthcare has grown as healthcare costs have continued to rise, and government entities have intervened to try to solve the problems of quality, cost, and access. Over time, more Americans support government intervention and involvement in healthcare.

REGULATION

Because the decisions made by providers, facilities, and insurance companies affect Americans' lives and health, healthcare is one of the most regulated industries in the United States (Rubenfire 2017). Regulation of healthcare occurs through a patchwork of federal and state laws. Almost every aspect of healthcare is regulated. For example, regulations dictate minimal healthcare standards to protect consumers from unsafe environments; from incompetent, impaired, or poorly trained providers; and from services that could cause harm. Regulatory efforts often focus on structural requirements, such as having sinks in all patient rooms, and ensuring minimum competency levels for healthcare providers through educational or licensure requirements. For example, to practice medicine, a physician must take a number of steps that are regulated by different government and nongovernment entities (see sidebar).

> (✱) **DEBATE TIME** Regulatory Hurdles to Practice Medicine
>
> The path to practicing medicine is paved with regulatory hurdles implemented by an assortment of bureaucracies. An individual who wants to become a physician first must attend a medical school that is accredited by a private body, then take a national examination administered by another nongovernmental organization, obtain licensure from a state medical board, complete a hospital residency that is funded and governed by the federal Medicare program, receive certification from a private specialty board, and, finally, obtain clinical privileges at a hospital that may operate as either a private or public entity (Field 2008).
>
> Why do we require such regulation before we allow doctors to practice? Is there any negative aspect of this regulation?

Regulations usually are developed as a result of legislation. Laws are passed, and then regulations must be put in place to ensure compliance with the law. As the laws change, regulations proliferate. In 2016, for instance, the federal government alone added 23,531 pages of regulations affecting hospitals and health systems (Rubenfire 2017).

The responsibility for crafting, implementing, and enforcing regulations falls to government departments and agencies. The largest federal healthcare agency is the US Department of Health and Human Services (HHS). In 2020, the HHS had a budget of more than $1.29 trillion and employed more than 79,000 people (HHS 2020). As illustrated in exhibit 7.1, the HHS is composed of many agencies that have responsibilities for specific areas of healthcare. By far the largest HHS agency is the Centers for Medicare & Medicaid Services (CMS), which spends more than $1 trillion per year.

The federal government provides standards and rules for almost all healthcare settings, including long-term care facilities, home health care agencies, hospitals, and ambulatory care centers, but it leaves regulation and inspections primarily to state governments and accreditation agencies.

LICENSURE

Almost all licenses for healthcare professionals are granted by state or local authorities. Licenses are awarded by a government licensing agency and give an individual the legal authority to work in a profession. The requirements for licenses depend on the occupation

Exhibit 7.1

Agencies of the
US Department of
Health and Human
Services

Agency	Function	2020 Budget
Centers for Medicare & Medicaid Services	Administers the two largest federal health-care programs, Medicare and Medicaid. CMS also administers other major programs such as the State Children's Health Insurance Program; the Medicare Prescription Drug, Improvement, and Modernization Act; and the Health Insurance Portability and Accountability Act	$1.2 trillion
Administration for Children and Families	Provides services to improve the economic and social well-being of children, families, individuals and communities	$52 billion
National Institutes of Health	Conducts biomedical and public health research; composed of 27 institutes and centers	$41.7 billion
Health Resources and Services Administration	Directs national health programs that improve Americans' health by ensuring equitable access to comprehensive, quality healthcare	$10.7 billion
Centers for Disease Control and Prevention	Promotes health and quality of life by preventing and controlling disease, injury, and disability; monitors health, detects and investigates health problems, conducts research to enhance prevention, develops and advocates sound public health policies	$6.6 billion
Food and Drug Administration	Ensures the safety of foods and cosmetics and the safety and efficacy of pharmaceuticals, biological products, and medical devices	$6.2 billion
Indian Health Service	Provides direct medical and public health services to members of federally recognized Native American tribes and Alaska Native people	$6.0 billion
Substance Abuse and Mental Health Services Administration	Works to improve the quality and availability of prevention, treatment, and rehabilitative services to reduce illness, death, disability, and cost to society resulting from substance abuse and mental illness	$5.5 billion

Source: HHS (2020).

and state regulations, but all licenses have predetermined criteria, such as a specific college degree or a passing grade on a state-administered exam.

Almost three-quarters of all healthcare practitioners and technical personnel hold a license. Physicians, dentists, nurses, pharmacists, dental hygienists, occupational therapists, physical therapists, audiologists, and dental assistants, among many others, are healthcare professions that most often require a license (Torpey 2016). As seen in exhibit 7.2, the requirements even for a nurse aide certification can be lengthy.

Licensure serves the following purposes (NCSBN 2009):

◆ Protect the public from unscrupulous, incompetent, and unethical practitioners

◆ Assure the public of a minimum level of competence from healthcare providers

◆ Provide a mechanism to discipline providers who fail to comply with professional standards

However, some claim that licensing laws increase the costs of and diminish access to healthcare. License requirements may unreasonably restrict the scope of many healthcare professionals. This may be especially true for physician assistants, nurses, and nurse practitioners, as some states, such as California, Texas, and Florida, restrict the ability to prescribe medications, while others grant full practice authority. These restrictions may increase costs and limit access (Timmons 2016).

EXHIBIT 7.2
Washington State Home Care Aide License Requirements

- **Education.** Complete 75 hours of training through a program approved by the Department of Social and Health Services
- **Examination.** Successfully pass the home care aide certification examination
- **State license verification.** Submit all states where the applicant holds or did hold credentials
- **Personal data.** Each applicant must answer personal data questions and must explain any convictions or legal proceedings
- **Background check.** Successfully pass a background check
- **Annual renewal requirements.** Credentials expire on the credential holder's birthday
- **Continuing education.** Twelve hours of continuing education approved by the Department of Social and Health Services is due each year with renewal of the certification.

Source: Washington State Department of Health (2020).

The COVID-19 pandemic highlighted the problem of state-level licensure. During the pandemic, many states with high rates of the virus had difficulty bringing in nurses and doctors who were licensed in other states, prompting calls to facilitate multistate licensing (Mitchell and Thierer 2020).

GOVERNMENT AS A PURCHASER OF HEALTHCARE

Governments in the United States have also become major purchasers of healthcare. In fact, government's share of US health spending amounts to almost half of total healthcare expenditures (Himmelstein and Woolhandler 2016). As discussed in chapter 1, Medicare and Medicaid are major healthcare programs that are paid for by the US federal government and the states. Medicare is a national program that is paid for by the federal government, while Medicaid is a state-based program that is paid for jointly by state and federal governments.

The federal government is the largest purchaser of healthcare in the United States, spending more than $750 billion in 2018 for services provided to nearly 60 million citizens, primarily for hospital, physician, prescription drugs, and dialysis services (CMS 2020a; Cubanski, Neuman, and Freed 2019). Medicare payments account for more than 21 percent of all US healthcare expenses. Medicaid covers about 44 million people, and its expenditures account for about 16 percent of US healthcare costs, totaling $597 billion in 2018 (CMS 2020b; HHS 2018; Rosenbaum et al. 2018).

As shown in exhibit 7.3, the largest expenditures for Medicare are payments for Medicare Parts A, B, and C, which are the traditional ways in which Medicare has covered hospital and outpatient medical services (see the next section for an explanation of these components of Medicare). However, Parts A and B payments have decreased, from 68 percent of total Medicare expenditures in 2008 to 55 percent in 2018. This shift can be primarily attributed to the growth of Medicare Part C, the managed care Medicare programs, which in 2018 accounted for 32 percent of spending.

MEDICARE

As shown in exhibit 7.4, most people receiving Medicare are over the age of 65. People with disabilities who are younger than 65 and individuals who have end-stage renal disease and require dialysis or a kidney transplant are also eligible for Medicare. In 2019, the latter groups accounted for only 8.5 million (13.9 percent) of the 61.3 million people with Medicare coverage. Medicare is a national program that provides standardized benefits to those who are eligible. Medicare benefits comprise four parts, A through D:

◆   *Part A* pays for inpatient hospital, skilled nursing facility, some home health, and hospice care costs. Medicare patients pay an annual deductible for Part

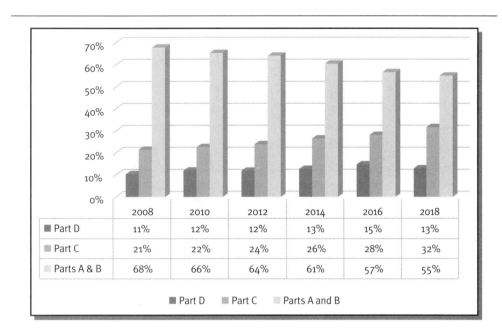

EXHIBIT 7.3
Share of Medicare Payments, 2008–2018

	2008	2010	2012	2014	2016	2018
■ Part D	11%	12%	12%	13%	15%	13%
■ Part C	21%	22%	24%	26%	28%	32%
▨ Parts A & B	68%	66%	64%	61%	57%	55%

■ Part D   ■ Part C   ▨ Parts A and B

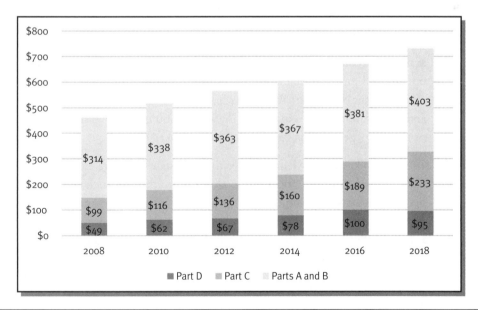

■ Part D   ■ Part C   ▨ Parts A and B

Source: Data from Cubanski, Neuman, and Freed (2019).

A benefits, which was $1,364 in 2019. Part A also includes coinsurance for extended inpatient hospital stays and skilled nursing facility admissions. Everyone who is eligible for Medicare can enroll in Part A, and most pay no monthly premium. Part A is funded primarily through a payroll tax.

EXHIBIT 7.4
Medicare
Beneficiaries
by Type, 2019
(millions)

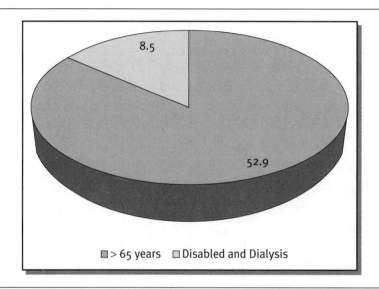

Source: CMS (2020a).

◆ *Part B* pays for physician, outpatient, preventive, and some home health services. Many services have an annual deductible, which was $198 in 2020, and usually coinsurance of 20 percent. Coinsurance and deductibles are not charged for most wellness or preventive services. Medicare enrollees can choose to opt out of Part B. Those who want coverage must enroll in Part B and pay a monthly premium, which was $144.60 in 2020. Part B is funded primarily by general taxes and Part B premiums.

◆ *Part C*, also known as Medicare Advantage, allows Medicare enrollees to join a private managed care organization (MCO) health plan, such as a health maintenance organization (HMO) or preferred provider organization (PPO). Enrollees receive all Medicare-covered Part A and Part B services and usually Part D benefits. Those who enroll in Part C pay a monthly premium; the average across private plans was $28 in 2019.

◆ *Part D* pays for prescription drugs through private plans that contract with Medicare. Part D helps pay for enrollees' drug costs. Enrollees pay monthly premiums, which in 2019 averaged $41 per month. Enrollment in Part D is voluntary. Part D is funded through general taxes, monthly premiums, and state payments (Kaiser Family Foundation 2019; Medicare Advantage 2019).

Medicare primarily pays providers on a fee-for-service basis. As seen in exhibit 7.5, under this payment method, providers are paid for each service that they provide. For

Exhibit 7.5
Fee-for-Service
Reimbursement

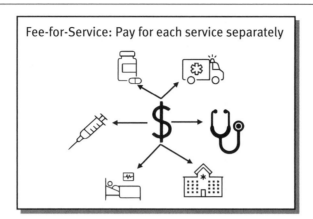

Fee-for-Service: Pay for each service separately

instance, hospital payments are based on predetermined rates for each visit or treatment and can be adjusted for the severity of a patient's illness and other factors. Base payments are set for each of more than 700 categories of diagnoses (called diagnosis-related groups or DRGs). Under fee-for service payment, providers are paid more when they see more patients and deliver more services. About 70 percent of Medicare reimbursements are fee-for-service payments. The remaining 30 percent of payments are made through *Medicare Part C*. These plans are provided by private companies, which are paid a flat amount per person per month (capitation, as mentioned in chapter 3) for hospital and physician care (RevCycle Intelligence 2018).

The fee-for-service payment system, referred to as a prospective payment system, has been in place since the mid-1980s (Cubanski et al. 2015). However, many people believe that this payment system is outdated. In its place, a variety of **value-based payment** models have been proposed, which, it is argued, would be more effective at holding providers accountable for the cost and quality of the healthcare that they provide. To move toward value-based payment, the system of paying for healthcare must change (Horner et al. 2019).

To move toward value-based care, many argue that full or partial capitation is needed to control costs and improve quality (James and Poulsen 2016). As seen in exhibit 7.6, capitation differs from fee-for-service in that it pays for a package of services, rather than for each service individually. **Full capitation** involves paying a fixed amount to an organization to provide a comprehensive set of healthcare services for a set period of time; **partial capitation** pays a fixed amount for a narrower set of healthcare services. For instance, a fixed payment for only physician or hospital services would be considered partial capitation.

Others think that **bundled payments** are the best way to improve patient satisfaction and control costs (Maddox and Epstein 2018). Bundled payments provide a set payment

value-based payment
A payment system in which provider payments are linked to the cost and quality of care.

full capitation
A payment method in which a fixed amount is paid to an organization to provide a comprehensive package of healthcare services for a set period of time.

partial capitation
A payment method in which an organization is paid a fixed amount to provide a select set of healthcare services for a set period of time.

bundled payments
A payment method in which healthcare providers are paid a set amount for an episode or cycle of care (e.g., hip surgery).

Exhibit 7.6
Capitated
Reimbursement

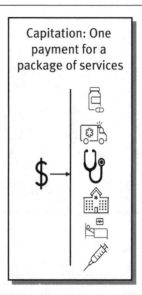

for an episode or cycle of care. For example, some insurers make fixed payments for hip and knee replacements that include all the costs of the procedure for hospital, physicians, and tests.

MEDICAID AND CHILDREN'S HEALTH INSURANCE PROGRAM (CHIP)

Two major health insurance partnerships between the US government and the states are Medicaid and the Children's Health Insurance Program (CHIP). In January 2020, Medicaid covered 63.9 million Americans, and CHIP provided care to 9.6 million children (Medicaid.gov 2020).

Medicaid provides health insurance for about 20 percent of Americans and is administered jointly by the federal and state governments. Therefore, eligibility requirements and payment systems for Medicaid vary according to state laws. Medicaid eligibility generally is based on individuals' income in relation to the federal poverty level (FPL). Almost all states provide Medicaid to children who live in families with incomes up to 200 percent of the FPL, which in 2019 was $42,660 for a family of three. Eligibility for parents varies much more across states: In 11 states, only parents earning less than 50 percent of the FPL, $10,665 in 2019, are eligible for Medicaid; 6 states cover those earning up to 138 percent of the FPL, and 33 states provide Medicaid coverage for those with incomes greater than 138 percent of the FPL. Coverage for adults who are not parents typically is lower. In 13 states, adults without children at any income level are ineligible for Medicaid (Brooks et al. 2020).

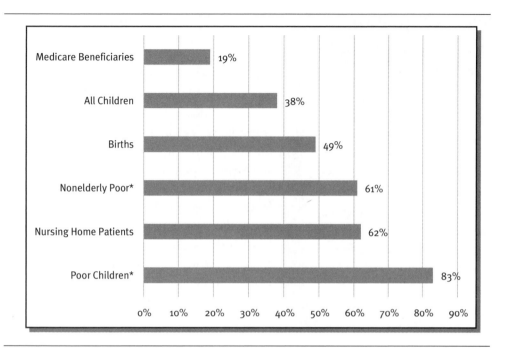

EXHIBIT 7.7
Share of the
Population
Covered by
Medicaid, 2017

* Income below the federal poverty line.

Source: Kaiser Family Foundation (2019).

Medicaid provides health insurance for a wide swath of Americans. Exhibit 7.7 shows that 83 percent of poor children and 61 percent of the nonelderly poor, along with 62 percent of nursing home patients, are covered by Medicaid. In addition, almost half of births are paid for through Medicaid.

Only about one-third of Medicaid payments are made on a fee-for-service basis. Instead, many states have shifted to capitated payments. Many states now pay providers through managed cared organizations (MCOs) under alternative payment methods (capitation, partial capitation, or bundled payments). In 2019, 33 states paid for Medicaid services through MCOs, with more proposing this form of payment. At that time, more than half the states reported that their top priority was better aligning Medicaid payments with health outcomes (Gifford et al. 2019).

MCOs are organizations that "manage" the patients' healthcare by establishing preferred (or restrictive) networks and by setting policies to reduce costs (see chapter 8 for further discussion of MCOs). Some MCOs may go beyond managing traditional healthcare services to address issues of housing, mental health, substance abuse, and transportation (RevCycle Intelligence 2018; Rosenbaum et al. 2018). Some states, such as Oregon, call their MCOs "coordinated care organizations," which set capitation rates that cover Medicaid patients and many of their citizens (see sidebar on next page).

Many states are setting capitated rates to cover their Medicaid populations. For example, Oregon pays capitated rates for their coordinated care organizations (CCOs). The state pays a per-member-per-month amount to the CCOs "to coordinate healthcare for nearly 1 million Oregonians on the Oregon Health Plan (Medicaid)." In 2018 Oregon paid an average net payment of $427.70 per month for each member. The state does pay CCOs more per member for people with disabilities, as they generally have higher healthcare costs (Sawyers 2018). Such rates are often adjusted annually to reflect cost and use changes.

CHIP, signed into law in 1997, was designed to provide health insurance to children living with families whose incomes are too high to qualify for Medicaid. The program gives federal matching funds to states to provide this health insurance. Most states extend CHIP to children whose families earn up to at least 200 percent of the FPL. Many states have combined their CHIP and Medicaid programs. In 2019, 16 states administered their CHIP programs as extensions of their Medicaid programs. However, in 2020, 35 states operated separate CHIP programs. Like Medicaid, CHIP benefits, coverage, enrollment requirements, and cost-sharing requirements vary from state to state. For instance, 30 states charge a premium or enrollment fee for some children, and 21 states charge copayments (Brooks et al. 2020).

Both Medicaid and CHIP provide healthcare for a sizeable share of Americans. As shown in exhibit 7.8, these two government health programs provide health insurance for more than half of Americans under the age of 21 and for almost 20 percent of people aged 27 to 45.

EXHIBIT 7.8
Share of the US Population Covered by Medicaid and CHIP by Age, 2017

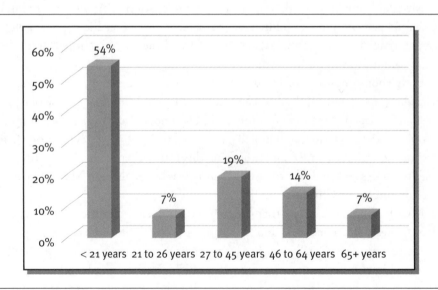

Source: Medicaid.gov (2020).

OTHER FEDERAL GOVERNMENT HEALTH SUPPORT

As a result of the passage of the Affordable Care Act (ACA) in 2010, the federal government has also begun to provide large subsidies for lower-income individuals to purchase health insurance. The Congressional Budget Office estimates that between 2019 and 2028, these subsidies will cost $800 million, while Medicaid and associated benefits will cost about $4 trillion (CBO 2018).

The federal government also helps pay for prescription drugs. Since 2003, with the passage of the Medicare Prescription Drug, Improvement, and Modernization Act, the federal government dramatically increased the amount it pays for prescriptions. This law, often referred to as the Medicare Part D Prescription Drug Benefit, is a voluntary benefit requiring a moderate premium that Medicare recipients pay. In 2019, the average monthly premium was $33.19 (National Council on Aging 2019). Medicare now spends more than $174 billion annually for prescription medications, and the costs continue to escalate (Luhby 2018).

GOVERNMENT AS A PROVIDER OF HEALTHCARE

Governments in the United States also own and operate healthcare services. Many of these services are targeted to improve the lives and take care of the poor or particular groups of citizens. For example, the federal government operates the Veterans Health

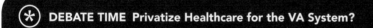

⊛ DEBATE TIME Privatize Healthcare for the VA System?

Should the VA privatize and pay private healthcare providers to take care of veterans? The US Department of Veterans Affairs has proposed to take billions of dollars used to operate government-run veterans' hospitals to instead pay private providers. If this plan is approved, veterans could more easily obtain care in private hospitals. Many veterans experience long wait times to access hospitals and veterans' clinics. Proposed solutions to these delays have fractured by political party, with Republicans pushing privatization and Democrats favoring an increase in the number of VA doctors and hospital space. Proponents of privatization point to shorter wait times and more choices. Opponents note that monies would come from existing VA operations; this could cause existing VA hospitals to close and private costs to skyrocket, as experts predict that the cost of allowing veterans to use private services could exceed $100 billion per year (Steinhauer and Philipps 2019). What do you think the VA should do?

Administration (VHA); the Military Health System (MHS), which includes military hospitals and clinics; and the Indian Health Service. In addition, states and counties provide many healthcare services, including hospitals, public health departments, and healthcare for the incarcerated.

The Veterans Health Administration is both the largest government-owned healthcare system and the largest healthcare system in the United States overall, providing care at more than 1,200 facilities, including 170 hospitals and 1,074 outpatient sites. The VHA serves about 9 million military veterans per year and has a budget of nearly $200 billion per year. As a large-scale organization, the VHA also has large-scale problems. For instance, it for decades has struggled with an antiquated medical record-keeping system, long wait times for some services, frequent leadership turnover, and challenges attracting personnel (Steinhauer 2020; Wax-Thibodeaux 2018).

The federal government also owns and generally operates healthcare facilities for active and retired military personnel and their dependents through the MHS, which is part of the US Department of Defense. The MHS serves more than 9.5 million beneficiaries. It has an annual budget of about $50 billion and comprises 723 military treatment facilities, 109 of which are located outside the United States (CRS 2019). The mission of the MHS focuses on keeping military personnel and their families healthy so that they are able to carry out their military national security and wartime functions (MHS 2020).

> **Indian Health Service**
> The federal government health system that provides healthcare services to Native Americans.

The federal government also provides healthcare services through programs of the **Indian Health Service (IHS)**. Through the IHS, the US government operates health services for Native Americans or contracts with tribes to provide their own healthcare services. The IHS serves members from 573 federally recognized tribes, totaling 2.3 million people. An annual budget of more than $5 billion funds 45 hospitals, 335 health centers, and 217 clinics and health stations (IHS 2019). However, many of the facilities struggle to maintain their buildings and update their technology. Many IHS facilities lack the necessary organization and structure to meet patients' health needs and improve their health (see sidebar).

States and local governments also own and provide services through state and county facilities, such as state mental health hospitals, county hospitals, public health departments, and healthcare facilities in jails and prisons. As seen in exhibit 7.9,

✳ STRUGGLING IHS FACILITIES

A government evaluation of the IHS found major underlying problems, such as a lack of clear structure and roles, that may keep the troubled agency from fixing long-standing quality issues. The agency lacked formal structures, policies, and definitions of roles to correct problems. Accountability was lacking. In addition, hospital performance and problems were not understood by the system's leadership, which has led to a lack of confidence in the leadership's ability to achieve the necessary changes. One employee told the survey team that making change was very difficult: "It feels like we are trudging in the mud. Things are more difficult bureaucratically than they should be" (Murrin 2019).

Year	Percentage
2005	27.60%
2015	30.70%
2025 estimated	38.30%

EXHIBIT 7.9

Share of State and Local Budgets Spent on Healthcare and Social Services

Source: Data from Court (2018).

state and local governments spend almost one-third of their annual budgets on healthcare; that share is projected to continue to increase substantially over the coming years.

Counties provide healthcare services in many ways. There are more than 900 county-supported hospitals, 800 county-owned long-term care facilities, and almost 2,000 county public health departments across the United States. The majority of these facilities are located in rural or small counties and may be the only provider available in the area (National Association of Counties 2018).

Public health department services are organized and supported financially at the state and local levels. State health departments have the primary functions of providing health surveillance, promoting health, setting and enforcing standards, and providing health services.

Public health is provided by a mix of state and local governments. Some states, such as New Mexico, South Carolina, and Vermont, have centralized state public health organizations, whereas others, such as Florida and Georgia, share the responsibilities with local public health agencies. Still other states, such as California and New York, have decentralized local public health entities. More than 2,800 local health departments exist in the United States; their services vary widely according to the populations they serve (ASTHO 2012; CDC 2020; Leider et al. 2018).

Public health agencies also play a major role in emergency preparedness and responses to disasters (e.g., floods, hurricanes). Public health agencies provide critical training, communication, coordination with other government agencies, and infectious disease and injury prevention before, during, and after disasters (Trust for America's Health 2018).

Perhaps surprisingly, the United States spends relatively little on public health—only about $12 billion a year. For comparison, the food stamp program spends more than $100 billion annually (Carroll and Frakt 2018). Many experts believe that public health expenditures should be increased dramatically, arguing that as much as 30 percent of total healthcare spending is dedicated to low-value services that could be shifted to higher-value public health activities (Tran, Zimmerman, and Fielding 2017).

HIGH HEALTH COSTS FOR THE INCARCERATED

State and local governments allocate large amounts of money to healthcare provided in prisons; these amounts sometimes overshadow governments' other public health expenditures. For instance, in Cook County, Illinois (where Chicago is located), the Health and Hospitals System spent nearly $100 million providing healthcare in correctional institutions in fiscal year 2016—more than seven times the amount that the county spent on traditional public health services. Likewise, in Cumberland County, North Carolina, healthcare for the incarcerated receives more local funding than any other health program (Pew Charitable Trusts 2018).

Governments also run healthcare facilities for those who are incarcerated. Prisoners are one of the few populations that are constitutionally guaranteed medical treatment. The United States has the largest prison population among industrialized countries, with 2.3 million incarcerated in 1,833 state prisons, 110 federal prisons, 1,772 juvenile correction facilities, 3,134 local jails, 218 immigration detention facilities, and 80 Indian county jails. The majority of prisoners (1.3 million) are incarcerated in state prisons and 631,000 in local jails (Sawyer and Wagner 2020). Federal, state, and local governments pay for prisons and jails and their associated healthcare costs. Correctional facilities in many states have become part of the healthcare safety net for the poor.

Healthcare in correctional institutions may be provided directly by employees of the government that operates them, or, as in many states, care may be contracted out to private companies. However care is provided, healthcare costs for the incarcerated are high and increasing (see sidebar).

GOVERNMENT-SPONSORED HEALTH SERVICES RESEARCH AND TRAINING

State and federal governments also sponsor and fund health services research. The US federal government in particular provides significant support for health services research, contributing almost $36 billion—around 23 percent of all healthcare research dollars spent in the United States. Responsibility for health services research is spread across a number of federal agencies. These sponsors include the National Institutes of Health, the US Department of Defense, the Centers for Medicare & Medicaid Services, the US Food and Drug Administration, the National Science Foundation, the Centers for Disease Control and Prevention, the US Department of Veterans Affairs, and the Agency for Healthcare Research and Quality. As exhibit 7.10 shows, the National Institutes of Health controls and allocates the vast majority, more than 82 percent, of federal government's annual research investment (Research America 2020).

The federal government also provides significant funding for training of healthcare professionals. The US federal government spends about $15 billion, about two-thirds through Medicare payments, on training new doctors each year through its Graduate

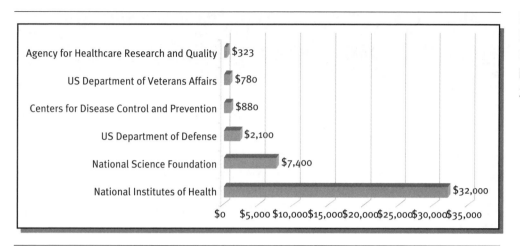

EXHIBIT 7.10
Medical and Health
Research Spending
by Federal Agency,
2017 (millions)

Source: Data from Research America (2020).

Medical Education program (Millman 2014). In addition, the Health Resources and Services Administration (HRSA), part of the HHS, provides almost $10 billion to programs to assist medically underserved areas, including about $775 million for workforce programs. As exhibit 7.11 illustrates, the HRSA sponsors many programs to train healthcare professionals. The largest expenditures are for the National Health Service Corps and Nursing Workforce Development (HRSA 2019). The National Health Service Corps gives

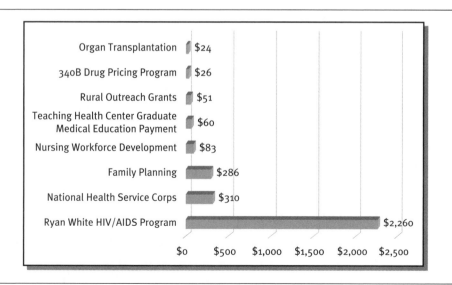

EXHIBIT 7.11
HRSA Training
Programs (millions)

Source: Data from HRSA (2019).

NATIONAL HEALTH SERVICE CORPS SCHOLARSHIPS

Meeting the need for primary care providers, especially in rural areas, remains a challenge. One way the government is seeking to address these shortages is by providing scholarships for those studying in needed healthcare professions. One federal agency, the National Health Service Corps, provides scholarships to health professions students in primary care disciplines, including physicians, dentists, nurse practitioners, certified nurse-midwives, and physician assistants. The scholarships cover tuition, fees, and educational costs and provide a monthly stipend for a minimum of two years and up to four years. For every year of scholarship funding, one year of service commitment is required, generally in low-income areas that have chronic healthcare service needs.

Since the program's inception, more than 50,000 healthcare professionals have taken advantage of the scholarships and served in one of more than 5,000 approved sites. Many of these locations would not have had these healthcare services available in their area without this program (see https://bhw.hrsa.gov/loansscholarships/nhsc).

scholarships to a wide array of healthcare professionals in exchange for a commitment to work in low-income areas of the country after graduation (see sidebar).

Government also extends its involvement in healthcare by allowing the costs of employer-sponsored healthcare to be exempt from taxes. This exemption is the largest federal tax break, amounting to about $250 billion per year. Tax-exempt employer-paid health insurance encourages the purchase of more health insurance than employees might otherwise purchase; most of this subsidy goes to those who are employed and generally more well-off (Butler 2015). Some have suggested that this popular exemption is unfair and inefficient, as it lowers employees' take-home pay and fuels the rapid increase in healthcare costs (Antos 2016).

Major Legislation

The US government has passed many laws influencing the practice of and access to healthcare. Many of these laws were enacted to protect patients or to expand patients' access to healthcare services. Some of the major acts that were passed in the last three decades are highlighted here.

The **Emergency Medical Treatment and Labor Act** was passed in 1986 to prevent "patient dumping," the practice of emergency rooms refusing to treat people who lack the financial resources to pay for their care. Because of this law, emergency rooms must minimally screen patients with appropriate diagnostic tests and examinations to determine whether an emergency medical condition is present. If such a condition exists, the hospital must treat and stabilize the patient without regard to their finances (Sawyer 2017).

The **Health Insurance Portability and Accountability Act (HIPAA)** was enacted in 1996. This law set national standards to protect the privacy and security of patients' health information. Privacy and security concerns became especially important with the widespread introduction of electronic health records and health information systems (HHS 2013). Penalties for HIPAA violations can be severe. For example, in 2018, the University of Texas's MD Anderson Cancer Center was fined $4,348,000 for HIPAA violations (Cohen 2018). In addition, HIPAA protected health insurance coverage for people changing jobs, restricted the use of preexisting conditions to deny medical claims, and set guidelines for medical savings accounts, among other things (Edemekong, Annamaraju, and Haydel 2020).

The **Balanced Budget Act of 1997** authorized Medicare Part C, expanding managed care programs under Medicare. The law also expanded the State Children's Health Insurance Program, which pays for health insurance for children whose families earn less than 200 percent of the federal poverty level. The legislation also reduced Medicare spending (Moon 1997).

The ACA, enacted in 2010, spurred major healthcare reform and increased government involvement in healthcare. The law provided subsidies to allow lower-income people (those earning between 100 and 400 percent of the federal poverty level) to buy health insurance, expanded the Medicaid program, prohibited insurance companies from refusing coverage for preexisting conditions, allowed parents to keep children on their insurance coverage until age 26, and defined ten required essential health benefits that must be included in health insurance plans (HealthCare.gov 2020).

THE CONTESTED ROLE OF GOVERNMENT IN HEALTHCARE

The role of government in healthcare continues to be a bitterly contested political issue: Up to two-thirds of Americans believe that universal health coverage should be provided to all Americans, while one-third oppose government involvement. Fifty-four percent of Americans favor a national Medicare-for-all health plan, and 41 percent oppose such a plan. This issue marks a significant political divide, with 71 percent of Republicans wanting the government to stay out of healthcare, insisting on Medicaid cuts and a repeal of the ACA, while 79 percent of Democrats are in favor of promoting greater government involvement in healthcare and expansion of existing programs to provide greater access to care (Kaiser Family Foundation 2020; Levin and Ponnuru 2018).

Emergency Medical Treatment and Labor Act
A federal law passed in 1986 to prevent "patient dumping," the practice of emergency rooms refusing to treat people who lack the financial resources to pay for their care.

Health Insurance Portability and Accountability Act (HIPAA)
A federal law passed in 1996 that set national standards to protect the privacy and security of patients' health information.

Balanced Budget Act of 1997
A federal law that authorized Medicare Part C, expanding managed care Medicare programs and the State Children's Health Insurance Program.

Some have long called for greater government intervention in healthcare to resolve the cost inequities and quality problems that vex the US healthcare system (Schoenbaum, Audet, and Davis 2003). This debate regarding the role of government in healthcare began long ago and will certainly continue. Given the amount that the United States spends on healthcare and continuously increasing costs, health costs have become a top healthcare concern for many Americans. Nevertheless, most Democrats (84 percent) and independents (64 percent) oppose major restrictions on Medicaid; a slight majority (51 percent) of Republicans do (Kirzinger, Wu, and Brodie 2018). Many Democrats see healthcare access as a moral imperative. To be sure, the extent of future government involvement in healthcare will be a major topic of discussion in future elections and legislative debates (Krieg and Wright 2018).

SUMMARY

The federal, state, and local governments in the United States are actively involved in the regulation, provision, and funding of healthcare. Healthcare is one of the most regulated industries in the United States. Regulations usually are developed as a result of legislation and seek to establish minimum standards to protect healthcare consumers. Regulation occurs at both the state and federal levels. States generally have responsibility for regulating healthcare providers and insurance companies, while the federal government oversees almost all aspects of healthcare.

The largest federal healthcare agency is the US Department of Health and Human Services (HHS), which has a budget of more than $1.15 trillion and employs more than 79,000 people. The HHS is composed of agencies that have responsibilities for specific areas of healthcare; the HHS agency with the largest annual budget is the Centers for Medicare & Medicaid Services.

Most healthcare professionals require licenses to practice, which are issued by state and local governments. Licenses are necessary to protect the public, assure a level of competence from healthcare providers, and provide a mechanism to discipline providers who fail to meet professional standards.

Governments influence healthcare by being major purchasers of care. The US federal government spends more than $700 billion on care for about 60 million Medicare recipients and almost $600 billion for about 75 million Medicaid recipients. Since the passage of the Affordable Care Act in 2010, the federal government also subsidizes the purchase of health insurance for lower-income people.

Governments also own and operate healthcare services. The federal government provides healthcare through the Veterans Health Administration, the Military Health Service, and the Indian Health Service. States operate hospitals, public health departments, and healthcare facilities in prisons and jails. Healthcare expenses for state and local governments account for almost one-third of their budgets.

Many health services research and training programs are sponsored by the federal government. The US government contributes about $36 billion for healthcare research through many different agencies. In addition, billions are spent annually to support the training of healthcare professionals.

The government is indirectly involved in healthcare by providing tax exemptions for employers' cost of employer-sponsored healthcare. This costs the federal government about $250 billion a year in lost taxes.

In the past three decades, several important healthcare laws have had significant impacts on healthcare in the United States. These include the Emergency Medical Treatment and Labor Act, which requires emergency treatment to be provided regardless of ability to pay; the Health Insurance Portability and Accountability Act, which protects the privacy and security of patients' health information; the Balanced Budget Act of 1997, which expanded Medicare programs and children's health insurance; and the Affordable Care Act, which increased subsidies for the poor and standardized health insurance offerings, among many other provisions.

The role of government in healthcare continues to evolve, as Americans see the cost of healthcare as a major issue. The future of government involvement is complicated by the polarized positions taken by the major political parties in the United States. The extent of future government involvement in healthcare will be a major topic of discussion in future elections and legislative debates.

QUESTIONS

1. What caused the escalation of healthcare costs and government involvement in healthcare during the mid-1960s?
2. What type of standards do regulations seek to set?
3. What level of government regulates physicians and insurance companies?
4. What does the Food and Drug Administration do?
5. What percentage of healthcare practitioners and technical personnel have licenses?
6. How does government involvement provide a mechanism to discipline healthcare providers who fail to comply with professional standards?
7. How many people have Medicare or Medicaid coverage?
8. What does Medicare Part D cover?
9. What is the largest government-owned healthcare system, and who does it serve?
10. In your opinion, why does the United States spend relatively little on public health?
11. What percentage of research is funded by government?
12. What obligations do those who accept scholarships from the National Health Service Corps make?

ASSIGNMENTS

1. Public health services are organized differently depending on the state. Go to the CDC's Health Department Governance page at www.cdc.gov/stltpublichealth/sitesgovernance. Choose two states: one that has a centralized health department and one that has a decentralized health system. Compare the organizations and the services they offer. Write a one-page paper explaining why you think the structures of the organizations and their services differ.

2. Read about the many activities performed by the Health Resources and Services Administration at www.hrsa.gov/sites/default/files/hrsa/about/budget/budget-justification-2018.pdf. Write a one-page paper discussing (1) why the US federal government should be involved in these programs or (2) why the US federal government should not be involved in these programs.

CASES

GETTING A PHYSICIAN LICENSE IN COLORADO

Rebecca has worked as a physician for ten years in Virginia, but she has always dreamed of practicing medicine in Colorado. She has finally decided to move, but she knows that each state medical board has different requirements and takes a different amount of time to process medical licenses. In a few states, such as Texas and Arkansas, the medical licensure process takes six months or more. Some states offer reciprocal licensing agreements, meaning that they accept medical licenses from other states. However, Colorado does not. To get a medical license, Rebecca wonders what she will need to do and why.

Discussion Questions

1. Why are most physicians and healthcare professionals licensed by states and not the national government?
2. What steps does Rebecca need to take to get licensed in Colorado? See the state's licensing requirements at www.colorado.gov/pacific/dora/Physician_Licensing_Requirements.

VETERANS ADMINISTRATION SYSTEM OR CONTRACT

Some people advocate retaining the healthcare system administered and operated by the US Department of Veterans Affairs (VA), which is made up of 172 hospitals and more than 1,000 outpatient sites. However, others are now pushing to expand the VA Choice program, which was set up in 2014. This proposal would make the VA system more like Medicare by allow it to contract with outside, independent private healthcare providers. However, the implementation of such a system remains contentious. Many worry that contracting with outside providers will change the nature and role of the VA. Others believe that contracting will improve access and response time.

Discussion Questions

1. In your opinion, what are the advantages and disadvantages of owning, funding, and providing care in the same healthcare system versus contracting for services?
2. Search the internet and find two articles that discuss the VA Choice program and the problems it has had. What are these problems, and how could they be fixed?

REFERENCES

Antos, J. 2016. "End the Exemption for Employer-Provided Healthcare." *New York Times*. Published December 6. www.nytimes.com/roomfordebate/2015/04/14/the-worst-tax-breaks/end-the-exemption-for-employer-provided-health-care.

Association of State and Territorial Health Officials (ASTHO). 2012. "State Public Health Agency Classification: Understanding the Relationship Between State and Local Public Health." Accessed April 23, 2020. www.astho.org/Research/Major-Publications/ASTHO-NORC-Governance-Classification-Report/.

Brooks, T., L. Roygardner, S. Artiga, O. Pham, and R. Dolan. 2020. "Medicaid and CHIP Eligibility, Enrollment, and Cost Sharing Policies as of January 2020: Findings from a 50-State Survey." Kaiser Family Foundation. Published March 26. www.kff.org/report-section/medicaid-and-chip-eligibility-enrollment-and-cost-sharing-policies-as-of-january-2020-findings-from-a-50-state-survey-looking-ahead/.

Butler, S. M. 2015. "Will Employer-Sponsored Health Insurance Fade Away?" Brookings Institution. Published March 31. www.brookings.edu/opinions/will-employer-sponsored-health-insurance-fade-away/.

Carroll, A., and A. Frakt. 2018. "It Saves Lives. It Can Save Money. So Why Aren't We Spending More on Public Health?" *New York Times*. Published May 28. www.nytimes.com/2018/05/28/upshot/it-saves-lives-it-can-save-money-so-why-arent-we-spending-more-on-public-health.html.

Centers for Disease Control and Prevention (CDC). 2020. "Public Health Professionals Gateway." Accessed April 24. www.cdc.gov/stltpublichealth/sitesgovernance/.

Centers for Medicare & Medicaid Services (CMS). 2020a. "CMS Fast Facts." Updated April 16. www.cms.gov/Research-Statistics-Data-and-Systems/Statistics-Trends-and-Reports/CMS-Fast-Facts.

———. 2020b. "NHE Fact Sheet." Updated March 24. www.cms.gov/research-statistics-data-and-systems/statistics-trends-and-reports/nationalhealthexpenddata/nhe-fact-sheet.html.

Cohen, J. 2018. "3 Major HIPAA Fines So Far in 2018." *Becker's Hospital Review*. Published July 3. www.beckershospitalreview.com/cybersecurity/3-major-hipaa-fines-thus-far-in-2018.html.

Congressional Budget Office (CBO). 2018. *Federal Subsidies for Health Insurance Coverage for People Under Age 65: 2018 to 2028*. Published May 23. www.cbo.gov/publication/53826.

Congressional Research Service (CRS). 2019. "Defense Primer: Military Health System." Updated December 18. https://fas.org/sgp/crs/natsec/IF10530.pdf.

Court, E. 2018. "These 7 States Are Most at Risk from Rising Health-Care Costs." MarketWatch. Published June 14. www.marketwatch.com/story/these-7-states-are-most-at-risk-from-rising-health-care-costs-2018-06-13.

Cubanski, J., T. Neuman, and M. Freed. 2019. "The Facts on Medicare Spending and Financing." Kaiser Family Foundation. Published August 20. www.kff.org/medicare/issue-brief/the-facts-on-medicare-spending-and-financing/.

Cubanski, J., C. Swoope, C. Boccuti, G. Jacobson, G. Casillas, S. Griffin, and T. Neuman. 2015. "A Primer on Medicare: Key Facts About the Medicare Program and the People It Covers." Kaiser Family Foundation. Published March 20. www.kff.org/report-section/a-primer-on-medicare-how-does-medicare-pay-providers-in-traditional-medicare/.

Edemekong, P., P. Annamaraju, and M. Haydel. 2020. "Health Insurance Portability and Accountability Act (HIPAA)." Published March 29. www.ncbi.nlm.nih.gov/books/NBK500019/.

Field, R. 2008. "Why Is Healthcare Regulation So Complex?" *Pharmacy & Therapeutics* 33 (10): 607–8.

Gifford, K., E. Ellis, A. Lashbrook, M. Nardone, E. Hinton, R. Rudowitz, M. Diaz, and M. Tan. 2019. "A View from the States: Key Medicaid Policy Changes." Kaiser Family Foundation. Published October 18. www.kff.org/report-section/a-view-from-the-states-key-medicaid-policy-changes-delivery-systems/.

HealthCare.gov. 2020. "Affordable Care Act (ACA)." Accessed April 23. www.healthcare.gov/glossary/affordable-care-act/.

Health Resources and Services Administration (HRSA). 2019. "Fiscal Year 2019: Budget in Brief." Accessed June 8, 2020. www.hrsa.gov/sites/default/files/hrsa/about/budget/HRSA-fy-2019-budget-in-brief.pdf.

Himmelstein, D., and S. Woolhandler. 2016. "The Current and Projected Taxpayer Shares of U.S. Health Costs." *American Journal of Public Health* 106 (3): 449–52.

Horner, B., W. van Leeuwen, M. Larkin, J. Baker, and S. Larsson. 2019. "Paying for Value in Health Care." Boston Consulting Group. Published September 3. www.bcg.com/en-us/publications/2019/paying-value-health-care.aspx.

Indian Health Service (IHS). 2019. "IHS Profile." Published June. www.ihs.gov/newsroom/factsheets/ihsprofile/.

James, B., and G. Poulsen. 2016. "The Case for Capitation." *Harvard Business Review* 94 (7–8): 102–11.

Kaiser Family Foundation. 2020. "Public Opinion on Single-Payer, National Health Plans and Expanding Access to Medicare Coverage." Published April 3. www.kff.org/

slideshow/public-opinion-on-single-payer-national-health-plans-and-expanding-access-to-medicare-coverage/.

———. 2019. "An Overview of Medicare." Kaiser Family Foundation. Published February 13. www.kff.org/medicare/issue-brief/an-overview-of-medicare/.

Kirzinger, A., B. Wu, and M. Brodie. 2018. "Kaiser Health Tracking Poll—February 2018: Health Care and the 2018 Midterms, Attitudes Towards Proposed Changes to Medicaid." Kaiser Family Foundation. Published March 1. www.kff.org/health-reform/poll-finding/kaiser-health-tracking-poll-february-2018-health-care-2018-midterms-proposed-changes-to-medicaid/.

Krieg, G., and D. Wright. 2018. "It's Healthcare, Stupid! Democrats Dig In as Midterms Ramp Up." CNN. Published May 31. www.cnn.com/2018/05/31/politics/democrats-health-care-2018/index.html.

Leider, J., B. Resnick, D. Bishai, and D. Scutchfield. 2018. "How Much Do We Spend?" *Annual Review of Public Health* 39: 471–87.

Levin, Y., and R. Ponnuru. 2018. "A New Healthcare Debate." *National Review*. Published March 29. www.nationalreview.com/magazine/2018/04/16/a-new-health-care-debate/.

Luhby, T. 2018. "Check Out How Much Medicare Spends on Drugs." CNN. Published May 15. https://money.cnn.com/2018/05/15/news/economy/medicare-drug-spending/index.html.

Maddox, K., and A. Epstein. 2018. "Using Bundled Payments to Improve the Patient Experience." *Harvard Business Review*. Published October 29. https://hbr.org/2018/10/using-bundled-payments-to-improve-the-patient-experience.

Medicaid.gov. 2020. "January 2020 Medicaid & CHIP Enrollment Data Highlights" Accessed May 6. www.medicaid.gov/medicaid/program-information/medicaid-and-chip-enrollment-data/report-highlights/index.html.

Medicare Advantage. 2019. "2019 Medicare Premiums at a Glance." Accessed April 23, 2020. www.medicareadvantage.com/resources/2019-medicare-premiums.

Military Health System (MHS). 2020. "About the Military Health System." Accessed April 24. www.health.mil/About-MHS.

Millman, J. 2014. "The U.S. Spends $15B a Year to Train Doctors, but We Don't Know What We Get in Return." *Washington Post*. Published July 29. www.washingtonpost.com/news/wonk/wp/2014/07/29/the-u-s-spends-15b-a-year-to-train-doctors-but-we-dont-know-what-we-get-in-return/?utm_term=.4c1424c02da5.

Mitchell, T., and A. Thierer. 2020. "Licensing Restrictions for Health Care Workers Need to Be Flexible to Fight Coronavirus." *Dallas News*. Published March 23. www.dallasnews.com/opinion/commentary/2020/03/23/licensing-restrictions-for-healthcare-workers-need-to-flexible-to-fight-coronavirus/.

Moon, M. 1997. "An Examination of Key Medicare Provisions in the Balanced Budget Act of 1997." Commonwealth Fund. Published September 1. www.commonwealthfund.org/publications/fund-reports/1997/sep/examination-key-medicare-provisions-balanced-budget-act-1997.

Murrin, S. 2019. "Organizational Challenges to Improving Quality of Care in Indian Health Services Hospitals." US Department of Health and Human Services, Office of the Inspector General. Published August. https://oig.hhs.gov/oei/reports/oei-06-16-00390.pdf.

National Association of Counties. 2018. *Medicaid and Counties: Understanding the Program and Why It Matters to Counties*. Published February. www.naco.org/resources/medicaid-and-counties-understanding-program-and-why-it-matters-counties-0.

National Council of State Boards of Nursing (NCSBN). 2009. *Changes in Healthcare Professions' Scope of Practice: Legislative Considerations*. Accessed April 23, 2020. www.ncsbn.org/ScopeofPractice_09.pdf.

National Council on Aging. 2019. "How Much Does Medicare Part D Cost?" My Medicare Matters. Accessed April 23, 2020. www.mymedicarematters.org/costs/part-d/.

Pew Charitable Trusts. 2018. *Jails: Inadvertent Healthcare Providers*. Published January. www.pewtrusts.org/-/media/assets/2018/01/sfh_jails_inadvertent_health_care_providers.pdf.

Research America. 2020. *U.S. Investments in Medical and Health Research and Development, 2013–2019.* Published Fall. www.researchamerica.org/sites/default/files/Publications/InvestmentReport2019_Fnl.pdf.

RevCycle Intelligence. 2018. "The Difference Between Medicare and Medicaid Reimbursement." Published June 9. https://revcycleintelligence.com/features/the-difference-between-medicare-and-medicaid-reimbursement.

Rosenbaum, S., R. Gunsalus, M. Velasquez, S. Hones, S. Rothenberg, and J. Beckerman. 2018. "Medicaid Payment and Delivery Reform: Insights from Managed Care Plan Leaders in Medicaid Expansion States." Commonwealth Fund. Published March 7. www.commonwealthfund.org/publications/issue-briefs/2018/mar/medicaid-payment-and-delivery-reform-insights-managed-care-plan.

Rubenfire, A. 2017. "Trump Wants to Thin Federal Regulations, and the Healthcare Industry Would Love to Help." *Modern Healthcare*, February. www.modernhealthcare.com/article/20170204/MAGAZINE/302049968.

Sawyer, N. T. 2017. "Why the EMTALA Mandate for Emergency Care Does Not Equal Healthcare 'Coverage.'" *Western Journal of Emergency Medicine* 18 (4): 551–52.

Sawyer, W., and P. Wagner. 2020. "Mass Incarceration: The Whole Pie 2020." Prison Policy Initiative. Published March 24. www.prisonpolicy.org/reports/pie2020.html.

Sawyers, M. 2018. "OHA Amends 2018 CCO Capitation Rates." State of Reform. Published April 24. https://stateofreform.com/featured/2018/04/oha-amends-2018-cco-capitation-rates/.

Schoenbaum, S., A. Audet, and K. Davis. 2003. "Obtaining Greater Value from Healthcare: The Roles of the U.S. Government." *Health Affairs* 22 (6): 183–90.

Steinhauer, J. 2020. "Veterans Affairs, a Trump Signature Issue, Is Facing Turmoil Again." *New York Times*. Published February 13. www.nytimes.com/2020/02/13/us/politics/veterans-affairs-trump.html.

Steinhauer, J., and D. Philipps. 2019. "V.A. Seeks to Redirect Billions of Dollars into Private Care." *New York Times*. Published January 12. www.nytimes.com/2019/01/12/us/politics/veterans-administration-health-care-privatization.html.

Timmons, E. 2016. "Medicine Is Not a Turf War." *U.S. News & World Report*. Published January 26. www.usnews.com/opinion/blogs/policy-dose/articles/2016-01-26/medical-licensing-laws-stand-in-the-way-of-affordable-health-care.

Torpey, E. 2016. "Will I Need a License or Certification for My Job?" Career Outlook, US Bureau of Labor Statistics. Published September. www.bls.gov/careeroutlook/2016/article/will-i-need-a-license-or-certification.htm.

Tran, L., F. Zimmerman, and J. Fielding. 2017. "Public Health and the Economy Could Be Served by Reallocating Medical Expenditures to Social Programs." *Population Health* 3: 185–91.

Trust for America's Health. 2018. "The Critical Role of Public Health Programs in Responding to Natural Disasters." Published September 12. www.tfah.org/wp-content/uploads/2018/09/Public_Health_In_Disasters_Fact_Sheet_091318.pdf.

US Department of Health and Human Services (HHS). 2020. "HHS (2020) FY 2020 President's Budget for HHS." Accessed June 8. www.hhs.gov/sites/default/files/fy-2020-budget-in-brief.pdf.

———. 2018. "Fiscal Year 2018: Health Resources and Services Administration: Justification of Estimates for Appropriations Committees." Accessed April 23, 2020. www.hrsa.gov/sites/default/files/hrsa/about/budget/budget-justification-2018.pdf.

———. 2013. "Summary of the HIPAA Security Rule." Reviewed July 26. www.hhs.gov/hipaa/for-professionals/security/laws-regulations/index.html.

Washington State Department of Health. 2020. "Home Care Aide License Requirements." Accessed June 28. www.doh.wa.gov/LicensesPermitsandCertificates/ProfessionsNewReneworUpdate/HomeCareAide/LicenseRequirements.

Wax-Thibodeaux, E. 2018. "Here Are 5 Urgent Problems a New VA Secretary Would Need to Tackle." *Washington Post*. Published April 25. www.washingtonpost.com/news/checkpoint/wp/2018/04/25/here-are-5-urgent-problems-a-new-va-secretary-would-need-to-tackle/?utm_term=.b1b5328e2292.

CHAPTER 8

THE ECONOMICS OF HEALTHCARE

W hat is the value of economics in healthcare? Healthcare is complicated, and economics provides a lens through which to see and understand the complexities. "Economics does not allow us to predict the future, but it does allow us to see the world more clearly. It is a good pair of glasses, not a crystal ball." Economics also helps us weigh the trade-offs that are inherent in healthcare decisions. "Everything has a cost. . . . 'There ain't no such thing as a free lunch.' Economics taught me that time has a cost. Even if I am attending a "free" lecture, watching a "free" movie online, or enjoying someone else's "free" food, I am paying a cost, whatever else I could have done. . . . Economics taught me to consider all available alternatives. Every decision is about the best choice given the proper understanding of cost, not just price. Viewing time, price, and countless other subjects under one idea, cost, helps improve decision-making. Dollars and cents can be an easy approximation, but life isn't about easy" (Albrecht 2014). This chapter provides some basic economic principles to help you understand decision-making in healthcare.

LEARNING OBJECTIVES

After reading this chapter you will be able to

➤ Discuss the principles of health economics.

➤ Describe how the allocation of scarce resources affects the production function and the output of products and services.

➤ Compare the concepts of diminishing returns and opportunity costs.

➤ Evaluate the impact of adverse selection on risk pools.

➤ Appraise the issue of preexisting conditions and its effects on insurance costs and access.

➤ Formulate examples of externalities in healthcare.

➤ Explain how asymmetric information and third-party payment systems increase the use and price of healthcare.

The healthcare industry is large and complex, accounting for almost 20 percent of US gross domestic product. It is important to understand the principles and dynamics of healthcare economics before we can understand the ramifications of the decisions we face in healthcare today. The principles of economics can help explain, for example, why access to care and quality of care vary across the country and why people choose the types of healthcare they do.

Healthcare economics relates to the efficiency, effectiveness, value, and behavior of those who produce and consume healthcare. Although the healthcare industry's resources are vast, they are not infinite; therefore, not all demands can be met. In economic terms, insufficient resources such as healthcare are known as **scarce resources**. Resources that are scarce must be managed and allocated among those seeking products and services.

THE HEALTHCARE PRODUCTION PROCESS

Healthcare is considered an economic good, and healthcare economics helps explain how and why individuals, healthcare providers, and governments make decisions about health and healthcare (Morris et al. 2012). As seen in exhibit 8.1, healthcare is made up of a number of resources that are combined to create products and services.

Resources, also referred to as **inputs**, include things such as people (e.g., doctors, nurses, laboratory technicians), equipment, buildings, land, and supplies. These resources are combined in settings such as physician offices, hospitals, clinics, surgery centers, and dentist offices. Healthcare goods and services—referred to as **outputs**—are produced in these settings. The conversion of inputs into outputs is called a **production function** (Scott, Solomon, and McGowan 2001).

scarce resources
Resources that are limited and may not be sufficient to meet demand.

inputs
Resources that are combined to produce outputs; in healthcare, inputs include personnel, equipment, buildings, land, and supplies.

outputs
Goods and services that are produced from a combination of inputs (resources).

production function
The conversion of inputs into outputs.

EXHIBIT 8.1
The Healthcare Production Process

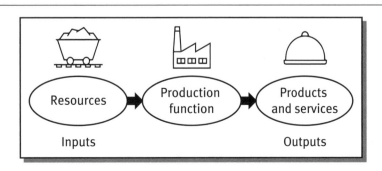

| Resources → Production function → Products and services |
| Inputs   Outputs |

Healthcare economics focuses on two key issues. The first is the *allocation of resources*—that is, how to allocate limited resources when demand is unlimited. The second is the *efficient use of resources*—in other words, how to get the most value from the resources that are available. There are never enough resources to satisfy all stakeholders. Therefore, choices have to be made about which goods and services should be produced, how they will be produced, and who will consume the goods and services. Because resources are limited, trade-offs must be made in deciding what is produced and what is not. This trade-off is universal: No country in the world allocates enough resources (money, taxes, etc.) to meet all of its citizens' wants.

Some suggest that to improve health, we only need to add more resources. Although adding resources will work, up to a point, as with most products, continuing to add resources becomes less efficient over time and, ultimately, has little or no effect on the health of a population. Exhibit 8.2 illustrates how adding health inputs (from 0 to 400) rapidly increases the health status of a population. However, at a certain point (about 800 in this graph), the increases in health status become progressively smaller with each incremental increase in healthcare inputs. In economics, this is called a **diminishing return**. For instance, administering one vaccination for whooping cough may result in a large improvement in health among children, but administering a second or third shot in subsequent years may have little or no additional effect on health. Likewise, giving one drug may provide significant benefit. Giving two may still add improvements, but adding a third, fourth, or fifth drug might provide almost no extra value and may actually have a negative impact on the patient.

diminishing return
A progressively smaller increase in outputs with each incremental increase in inputs.

EXHIBIT 8.2
Production of Health

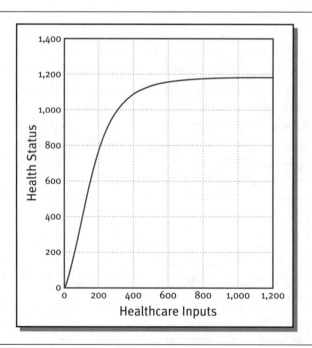

SUPPLY AND DEMAND

Opportunity cost is an economic principle that relates to the choices that must be made in allocating scarce resources. Opportunity cost represents the benefits that are given up by choosing an alternative. In other words, opportunity cost is the value of a resource when it is employed in its next-best use. For example, in healthcare, resources could be used to open a primary care clinic, or the same resources could be used to investigate a new drug. If the primary care clinic is chosen, the opportunity cost would be the forgone benefits of the choice that is not taken—investigating a new drug.

opportunity cost
The benefits that are given up by choosing an alternative; in other words, the value of a resource when it is employed in its next-best use.

(✳) DEBATE TIME

Suppose you are given $1 million to expand healthcare services in your community. Here are a few examples of how you might spend that money:

- 25,000 flu shots at $40 per flu shot

- 500 LASIK eye surgeries at $2,000 per eye surgery

- 83 treatments for infertility at $12,000 per unit

- 50 surgeries for obesity (bariatric surgery) at $20,000 per surgery

How would you spend your money? How would you propose to choose among these options? Is there opportunity cost involved? Why or why not?

Markets play a central role in economics. Markets consist of settings in which buyers and consumers, or sellers and suppliers, interact. Within markets, the supply and demand for goods and services can be observed and measured. For most products, the amount of buying and selling depends on the price of the good or service. Consumers will buy more at a lower price, but suppliers want to sell more at a higher price. When demand exceeds supply, prices will rise; conversely, when supply exceeds demand, prices will fall. Over time, higher demand encourages suppliers to produce more goods and services, which causes prices to decrease.

Again, for most products, supply and demand will rise and fall until an equilibrium is reached, at the point where demand matches the supply for the given price (see exhibit 8.3). When demand for a product increases, as from D1 to D2, the equilibrium (denoted by the dashed lines) shifts higher. That shift causes an increase in the quantity produced and, subsequently, higher prices.

Exhibit 8.3

Supply, Demand, and Equilibrium

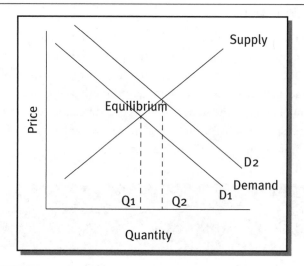

A change in government policy or insurance coverage might increase quantity or prices. For instance, before 1965, only 24 percent of healthcare costs were covered by health insurance. After Medicare and Medicaid were instituted, demand for healthcare increased among senior and low-income populations. As a result, health spending rose almost 12 percent per year for the next decade. In 1960, the average annual cost of healthcare per person in the United States was just $146; by 2017, that number had skyrocketed to $10,739 (Amadeo and Boyle 2020).

Another factor that affects the consumption of healthcare, in economic terms, is the **elasticity of demand** for healthcare. Elasticity of demand refers to how much the demand for or quality of a product or service changes in response to an increase or decrease in price. For most products, as shown in exhibit 8.3, consumption of a product changes when prices increase or decrease.

The demand for healthcare, however, does not change very much when prices change. For instance, if your child were injured in a bicycle accident, you would not call around to check on the cost of emergency care—you would seek the most immediate care possible. The consumption of most healthcare products and services changes very little when prices increase or decrease. Economists call this **inelastic demand**.

Exhibit 8.4 shows the difference between inelastic and elastic demand. Demand for a product or service such as healthcare is inelastic, which means that when prices go up (P1 to P2), the demand for the product does not change much (Q1 to Q2). With elastic demand—for example, soft drinks—if price goes up (P1 to P2), the demand and quantity consumed drop dramatically (Q1 to Q2).

elasticity of demand
The change in the demand for or quality of a product or service in response to an increase or decrease in price.

inelastic demand
Little change in the consumption of a product or service when prices increase or decrease.

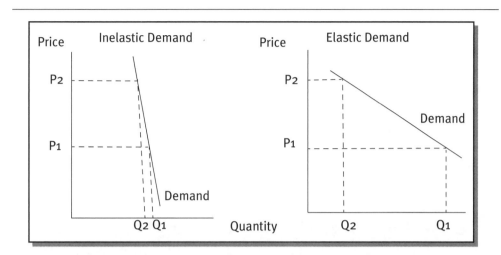

EXHIBIT 8.4
Difference
Between Elastic
and Inelastic
Demand

Alternatively, some healthcare services are more elastic, or price sensitive, and their utilization does decrease when prices increase. These elastic services include plastic surgery, dental work, pharmaceuticals, and preventive care; for these services, consumption declines when prices rise (Ellis, Martins, and Zhu 2017).

UNIQUE QUALITIES OF THE HEALTHCARE MARKET

Generally, when people make a large purchase, they take the time to research the available options, determine their preferences, and find the best price. For instance, someone who is planning to buy a car would narrow down the make and model, features, and maybe even the color before making the purchase.

Healthcare is a different kind of market. People typically do not plan to get sick. They generally do not review all of their treatment options in advance of their illness, save up money, and make a purchase, as with larger expenses such as buying a car. When people are diagnosed with an illness or injury, an urgent demand is created. They may face a lot of uncertainty, because they do not know whether the treatment will work. Patients might ask questions and compare a few options, but still they are faced with uncertain outcomes. It is not so much the demand for healthcare but the unplanned response to illness or injury that makes the economics of healthcare and healthcare markets unique.

The concept of supply and demand in healthcare is different from that in other industries. People have almost an insatiable demand for health. Consider an individual who exercises daily—perhaps a runner who is preparing for her next half marathon. As this individual gets healthier, often she wants to achieve even better health. She might purchase protein powder, better running shoes, a new pair of running shorts, or a watch that tells her how fast and how far she runs—all for just a small return in better health or faster time.

At the other end of the spectrum, a 90-year-old man may undergo a knee replacement, even at the risk of severe complications from surgery, to achieve a minimal improvement in his quality of life for a few years (Miric et al. 2014). In many cases, patients' choices are influenced by the amount that their health insurance will pay for services (see sidebar).

Patients want the best physician, the best hospital, and the best equipment, all for the best outcomes. A shopper in a local market will look for opportunities to buy more for less; this is not the case in medicine. In many cases, patients are willing to spend more for higher perceived quality (Getzen 2010).

✴ DEBATE TIME   A Trade-Off Between Treatments

Older people often face trade-offs between treatments that might extend their lives. For instance, at age 85, Bill was diagnosed with an incurable form of cancer. Bill's options are to undergo chemotherapy, which is uncomfortable and will extend his life two to three years, or to take a new cancer agent that is much more comfortable than chemotherapy and may give him five or more additional years of life. However, the new cancer agent costs about $400,000 a year and must be taken monthly to remain effective. Chemotherapy costs much less, estimated at $100,000 per year.

Bill may choose the new cancer agent if his insurance will pay for it, but if not, he will probably choose the chemotherapy. Bill wants to live, but he is worried about his quality of life. Yet, if he sold all of his assets, he would only have enough money to pay for the first year of the new treatment. Treating him with chemotherapy for three years would cost only $300,000, whereas the new cancer agent could cost $2 million to extend his life for five years. What do you think Bill should do?

RISK SHARING

risk pool
A cluster of people whose medical costs are combined to determine health premiums.

Healthcare differs from other consumer goods and services in a number of ways. Because healthcare spending is unexpected and often expensive, people are willing to come together and jointly purchase health insurance. In this way, they share the financial risk. The pooling of risk is the basis of insurance. **Risk pools** are clusters of people whose medical costs are combined to determine health premiums. By pooling risk, the higher healthcare costs of sick people are subsidized by the lower healthcare costs of healthier

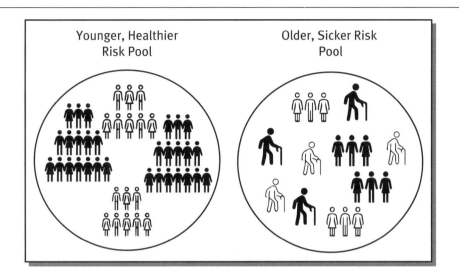

EXHIBIT 8.5
Risk Pools

people, as the premium that individuals pay is based on the *average* healthcare cost of everyone in the risk pool.

As shown in exhibit 8.5, the average costs depend on who is included in the risk pool. If only young, healthy people are included, their average costs will be much lower than a risk pool of older, sicker people. Because illness is generally unplanned, joining a risk pool allows individuals to share the risk of the high cost of sickness with others.

Adverse selection can destroy a risk pool. Adverse selection occurs when insurance customers choose coverage according to their individual health and needs. Individuals with a lot of healthcare needs will enroll in health plans with many benefits, while healthy people with limited healthcare needs might even choose not to have health insurance. When only the sick sign up for health insurance, the average cost of the risk pool can skyrocket, making health insurance unaffordable and causing even more people drop their insurance. Thus, a risk pool of only the very sick remains, further driving up costs.

Which customers to put in risk pools and which to exclude is a contentious policy argument. For example, the Affordable Care Act (ACA) of 2010 prohibited health insurance companies from excluding people with **preexisting conditions** from their health insurance plans. Before passage of the ACA, an estimated 50 million people had preexisting conditions. A preexisting condition is an illness or condition that an individual has prior to enrollment in a health plan. People with preexisting conditions often have illnesses that tend to be costly to treat (Amadeo 2019). Exhibit 8.6 lists some of the most common preexisting conditions in the United States.

adverse selection
A situation in healthcare that occurs when sicker (or potentially sicker) people buy health insurance, while healthier people do not, thus increasing the overall risk of the pool.

preexisting condition
An illness or condition that an individual has prior to enrollment in health insurance coverage.

EXHIBIT 8.6

Most Common
Preexisting
Conditions in the
United States

Condition	Number (millions)
AIDS	1.1
Alzheimer's disease	5
Alcoholism	17.6
Cancer	1.6
Diabetes	20.9
Drug addiction	20
Liver disease	20
Heart attack	7.9
Inflammatory bowel disease	1.3
Kidney failure	20
Rheumatoid arthritis	1.5

Source: Data from Amadeo (2019).

Before passage of the ACA, insurance companies could refuse to insure people with preexisting conditions. Doing so lowered the cost for those accepted by the insurance companies into their plans who did not have such conditions. People with preexisting conditions often had difficulty finding a health insurance plan that would accept them, and if they could find one, they paid very high premiums. The ACA forced insurance companies to add people with preexisting conditions to their risk pools and provide them with health insurance. However, some have sought to reverse this provision of the ACA and allow people with preexisting conditions to again be excluded from health insurance coverage (Rovner 2018).

externality
A side effect or an involuntary cost or benefit imposed on a third party.

Externalities arise frequently in healthcare, most notably in the context of infectious diseases, such as measles. An externality is a side effect or an involuntary cost or benefit imposed on a third party. For example, the decision of parents to refuse to have their children vaccinated against measles has significant effects on other children, not just the child who does not receive the vaccine. This externality has detrimental effects on other children's health (see sidebar). Likewise, secondary smoke from a person who is smoking near others may pollute the air that others breathe, which, according to the Centers for Disease Control and Prevention (CDC 2020), has led to the deaths of 2.5 million people since 1964.

(✱) DEBATE TIME Vaccination and Externalities

Parents' refusal to immunize their children can lead to the externality of other children contracting a disease. For example, measles was thought to have been eliminated from the United States by 2000. However, in 2019, 1,250 individual cases occurred in 31 states. Many of these cases were linked to visits to Disneyland. Parents brought their unimmunized children, who were infected with measles, to Disneyland and unknowingly spread the disease. The measles virus can live on surfaces for hours, and a person can catch it just by being in the room two hours after an infected person is gone. Should people be required to be vaccinated because of the externality of the potential to spread this disease? (Ellis, Levs, and Hamasaki 2015; Hassan 2019).

INFORMATION ASYMMETRY

Healthcare is complex, and best practices are constantly changing. It is no wonder, then, that people often lack the knowledge to make good decisions about healthcare services. Patients rely on their doctor to recommend what kinds of healthcare services they need, as frequently they do not even know what their options are. For example, a patient with terrible stomach pain does not know whether surgery is required and has little knowledge about the skill and quality of the surgeons who could perform it. The knowledge gap that exists between two parties (e.g., between a physician and a patient) is called **asymmetric information**. It creates an advantage for the party with greater knowledge.

asymmetric information
The knowledge gap that exists between two parties.

There are many examples of asymmetric information in healthcare. Information asymmetry occurs between physicians and patients, but also between insurers and the insured and between buyers and sellers of new medical technology. When one party has greater information, economic markets do not perform efficiently. One party ends up with too much or too little of the needed healthcare service (Culyer 2014).

Healthcare demand originates from the desire to improve health or diminish pain. Health and healthcare are not items that can be stored and pulled from a store shelf. Services must be available when they are needed. In addition, the outputs of healthcare can be difficult to understand, and the results of treatments can be unpredictable and hard to measure. In addition, consumers of healthcare almost always have less information than the suppliers of healthcare regarding risks and benefits.

THIRD-PARTY PAYMENT

third-party payer
An entity (a company or individual) that pays for medical services on behalf of a patient.

The US healthcare system's third-party payment system also makes it different from other industries. A **third-party payer** is an entity (a company or individual other than the patient) that pays for medical services on behalf of a patient. The most common types of third-party payers are private insurance companies, such as Blue Cross Blue Shield, or government programs, such as Medicare or Medicaid. Rather than patients paying for their care, a third party takes responsibility for payment and decides which claims to pay for and how much to pay.

Third-party payments through health insurance companies increase the utilization and cost of health services. This occurs because patients do not pay the full cost of healthcare services; often, patients only pay a fraction of the real cost. On average, patients only pay about 11 cents for every dollar charged for healthcare (Buff and Terrell 2014).

✱ THIRD-PARTY PAYMENTS LOWER COSTS TO THE INDIVIDUAL

Insurance companies, which receive money primarily from employers and individuals, pay for most of the healthcare that is provided in the United States. After insurance pays a claim, the individual generally owes much less than the full price charged. After paying their deductible, patients may only have to pay coinsurance. For this reason, individual patients may only pay a fraction of the cost of care. For example, a person may have an MRI that costs $2,000 but only has to pay a $200 copay. If the insurance plan has, say, an annual out-of-pocket limit of $4,000, after that amount is reached, the patient will not have to pay for any additional tests or services.

In a real sense, after the deductibles and maximum out-of-pocket costs are met, all further tests are "free" to patients. Often, at the end of each year, when these costs have been met, people rush to have services or procedures performed before the end of the calendar (or insurance plan) year. Doctors call this the "deductible rush" as patients hurry to have procedures done before the next plan year starts (Snowbeck 2016).

---

marginal benefit
The gain or benefit that a patient receives from consuming an additional unit of service; also referred to as *marginal utility*.

marginal cost
The cost of consuming the next unit of service.

This occurs because people will continue to consume a product as long as the **marginal benefit** exceeds the **marginal cost**. The marginal benefit, also referred to as the *marginal utility*, is the gain or benefit that a patient receives from consuming an additional unit of service. The marginal cost is the cost of consuming the next unit of service. Often, the marginal cost to patients is far below the actual cost of a service, which leads them to consume more services than is efficient (Kaufman 2012).

Most overconsumption of healthcare occurs because of the design of fee-for-service health insurance products, which have copays, deductibles, and maximum out-of-pocket costs. Thus, patients are shielded from the actual costs of care. Researchers believe that up to 34 percent of all US healthcare spending is unnecessary. This unnecessary spending costs up to $1 trillion annually (O'Neill and Scheinker 2018).

THE VALUE OF LIFE

Economics often attempts to assign value or benefits to an action or behavior. One such measure attempts to determine the value of living an extra year with pain or illness versus living an extra year free of any symptoms. Medical technology or treatments are measured in terms of that extra year. Experts use survey data, **econometrics**, and their own experience to place a value on the burden of disability or **morbidity**. This health metric is called the **quality-adjusted life year (QALY)**. QALYs represent a scale ranging from "perfect health," which is assigned 1 QALY, and death, at 0 QALY (Neumann and Cohen 2018).

For example, consider an individual who is diagnosed with kidney disease at age 75 and dies at age 78. If the weighted value or health utility rate for a typical healthy individual in her 70s is 0.95 and the health utility weight for hospital dialysis is 0.65, then after age 70, she accrues (5 years × 0.95) + (3 years × 0.65) = 6.7 QALYs. In other words, living as an older individual who eventually suffers from kidney disease is worth 6.7 years compared with 8 years of symptom-free life (Getzen 2010).

QALYs are used to calculate the cost versus the effectiveness of a medical treatment. If we take the example in the previous paragraph and estimate that the cost of dialysis for three years, without which the patient would have died, is $75,000, the cost-effectiveness ratio is 3 years × 0.65 at a cost of $75,000, or $75,000/1.95 QALY = $38,462 per QALY. Using similar calculations, a variety of treatments for different diseases or disabilities can be compared to determine the most cost-effective response.

Survey research, however, indicates that the public does not always agree with the cost per QALY rankings. Some respondents, for example, favor caring for individuals who are most in need of healthcare, regardless of whether the treatment is most efficient from a QALY standpoint. Some would say that QALYs are not "patient-centric" or that they discriminate on the basis of age and

econometrics
The branch of economics focused on using statistics to describe economic systems.

morbidity
The rate of disease or injury in a population.

quality-adjusted life year (QALY)
A measure of the burden of disability or morbidity; ranges from 1, perfect health, to 0, death.

✳ THE USE OF QALYs

Judging which treatments and services should be given can be difficult. "Because healthcare resources are limited, society needs a way to assess the value of health interventions. By reflecting both longevity and quality of life, QALYs provide a useful, although imperfect, measurement standard. QALYs can help guide health decisions while fostering consistency and transparency and provide a way to represent the output of healthcare and public health systems" (Neumann and Cohen 2018). Although imperfect, QALYs can provide comparative data that can serve as a starting point for informed discussions.

disability. They argue that QALY tables favor those who have more potential QALYs to gain (Neumann and Cohen 2018). Indeed, QALYs are a useful but imperfect measure.

Nevertheless, society needs a way to allocate resources. While no single measurement can define life and the value of symptom-free years, QALYs provide one tool to make significant decisions related to health.

MACROECONOMICS OF HEALTHCARE

Macroeconomics provides a big-picture view of healthcare in the United States. Macroeconomics is concerned with spending, employment, and other aspects of medical care as they affect the economy and the health of the population as a whole. The aging of the US population and the resulting demand for long-term care, durable goods, pharmaceuticals, healthcare workforce, and all of the other market demands related to aging are part of the macroeconomic picture.

Exhibit 8.7 illustrates the increase in personal income in the United States and the subsequent increase in health expenditures. National health expenditures have increased

EXHIBIT 8.7

Per Capita Personal Income and National Health Expenditures in the United States, 1960–2018

Year	Personal Income	Increase	National Health Expenditures	Increase
1960	$2,335		$146	
1965	2,936	26%	209	43%
1970	4,218	44%	355	70%
1975	6,340	50%	605	70%
1980	10,204	61%	1,108	83%
1985	14,779	45%	1,833	65%
1990	19,641	33%	2,571	40%
1995	23,600	20%	3,806	48%
2000	30,640	30%	4,855	28%
2005	35,806	17%	6,854	41%
2010	40,516	13%	8,411	23%
2015	48,921	21%	10,006	19%
2018	54,446	11%	11,172	12%

Sources: Data from CMS (2019); US Bureau of Economic Analysis (2018, 2019).

much more than income every five years, except in the periods 1995–2000 and 2010–2015. The growth of healthcare expenditures clearly exceeds the growth of income per capita (per person).

Income inequality has increased over time in the United States. Family income across the country roughly doubled from the 1940s to 1970. The growth rate was similar for the richest citizens compared with the poor. Beginning in the 1970s, however, income gains for the top 5 percent of the richest Americans have increased more sharply than the increase in income among the bottom half (poorer) of the families in the country. Concurrently, the number of middle-income households has shrunk. In 1971, 61 percent of US households were considered middle class, but by 2019, this figure had decreased to 51 percent. From 2001 to 2016, the wealthiest Americans saw income gains, so that by 2016, they had 7.4 times more wealth than middle-income families and 75 times more than lower-income families. That same year, the median net worth of the top 5 percent of families grew to $4.8 million, while the net worth of poorer families in the second quintile of wealth fell to $19,500. Income inequality continues to grow, and today it is much worse in the United States than any of the major industrialized countries (Horowitz, Igielnik, and Kochhar 2020).

This means that the wealthiest Americans can more easily afford healthcare, while those with lower incomes, who may not have health insurance or cannot afford copays and deductibles, are not getting the help they need. As discussed in more detail in chapter 14, comparisons of global health among industrialized nations show that although the United States spends much more on healthcare than other countries, US health outcomes do not appear to match those of countries in Europe, Japan, and elsewhere. This is the case, in part, because in the United States so many people lack health insurance and adequate financial resources to pay for their healthcare. Research suggests that the United States has done little to improve health equity in the past 25 years (Horowitz, Igielnik, and Kochhar 2020; Zimmerman and Anderson 2019).

Studies indicate that US healthcare prices are higher across the board, including pharmaceuticals and administrative costs, than in other countries. The quality of care in the United States is not as low as some would report, but access to healthcare is. An estimated 22 percent of the US population has missed a medical appointment because they could not afford it. Americans also have the lowest rate of insurance coverage compared with other countries (Papanicolas, Woskie, and Jha 2018).

Income, or the lack of it, is one of the causes of **health disparities** in the United States, as poorer populations frequently lack health insurance and the financial ability to access appropriate healthcare. Health disparities and inequalities continue across a wide range of diseases, behavioral risk factors, environmental exposures, social factors, and access to healthcare by sex, race and ethnicity, income, education, disability status, and other social characteristics. For instance, African American, American Indian, and Alaska Native adults have higher rates of asthma, diabetes, heart disease, and obesity than whites. As a result, these populations are at greater risk of complications and death from

health disparities
Differences in health outcomes and their causes among groups of people.

COVID-19, and they have experienced much higher hospitalization and death rates. For instance, by April 2020 in Louisiana, African Americans made up 32 percent of the state's total population but accounted for 70 percent of COVID-19 deaths (Artiga, Garfield, and Orgera 2020).

Education is another factor associated with health. Those with lower educational attainment tend to have poorer health. For instance, the CDC reports that American Indian and Alaska Natives, along with Hispanics/Latinos, have higher rates of noncompletion of high school and poorer health (CDC 2013). People with more education have lower rates of diabetes, heart disease, and asthma and exhibit less anxiety and depression. Each additional year of education is expected to extend one's life expectancy (Frakt 2019).

Exhibit 8.8 shows the percentage of people without insurance by income and race/ethnicity. As can be seen, about 17 percent of the poor and near poor lack health insurance, compared with only 7.5 percent of the nonpoor. About 19 percent of Hispanics/Latinos lack health insurance compared with 7 percent of whites.

Obesity rates have continued to rise. As shown in exhibit 8.9, obesity rates in the United States have steadily increased but continue to be significantly higher among African American and Hispanic/Latino populations (Vasquez 2020).

Other studies have also found disparities based on socioeconomic divisions. Along with similar data on racial/ethnic disparities, some studies include data related to the lesbian, gay, bisexual, transgender, and questioning/queer (LGBTQ) population. LGBTQ disparities occur across the lifetime, but LGBTQ youth are more likely than their non-LGBTQ peers to be bullied, commit suicide, engage in risky sexual behaviors, and run away or be forced to leave home (Robinson and Espelage 2013). The social challenges that accompany their

EXHIBIT 8.8

Adults Aged 18–64 Without Health Insurance, by Income and Race/Ethnicity, 2017

Poverty status	
Poor	17.2%
Near poor	17.3%
Nonpoor	7.5%
Race/ethnicity	
Hispanic/Latino	18.9%
White, non-Hispanic/Latino	7.3%
American Indian/Alaska Native	22.0%
Asian/Pacific Islander	7.2%

Source: Data from Kaiser Family Foundation (2018).

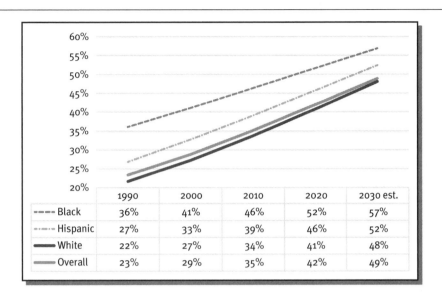

EXHIBIT 8.9
Obesity Rates by
Race, 1990–2030

	1990	2000	2010	2020	2030 est.
Black	36%	41%	46%	52%	57%
Hispanic	27%	33%	39%	46%	52%
White	22%	27%	34%	41%	48%
Overall	23%	29%	35%	42%	49%

Source: Vasquez (2020).

high rates of homelessness include mental health issues, violence, HIV and other sexually transmitted diseases, poverty, substance abuse, and food insecurity (Garofalo and Bush 2008).

Clearly, much work needs to be done to remedy health disparities in the United States. Both the Healthy People 2020 initiative (HHS 2020) and the National Partnership for Action to End Health Disparities (Office of Minority Health 2020) have set goals to address and improve these disparities.

SUMMARY

A basic understanding of healthcare economics helps us understand the ramifications of the decisions we face in healthcare today. The principles of economics can help explain, for example, how and why people make decisions about health and healthcare. Healthcare economics relates to the efficiency, effectiveness, value, and behavior of those who produce and consume healthcare. Although the healthcare industry's resources are vast, they are not infinite; therefore, not all demands can be met. Insufficient resources such as healthcare are known as scarce resources.

Healthcare is made up of a number of resources that are combined to create products and services. Resources, or inputs, can include personnel, equipment, buildings, land, and supplies. These are joined together in settings such as physician offices, hospitals, clinics, surgery centers, and dentist offices to create products and services, referred to as outputs. The conversion of inputs into outputs is called the production function.

Healthcare economics primarily considers the allocation of resources and the efficient use of resources. Some suggest that to improve health, we only need to add more resources. This works up to a point, but past a certain level, the addition of more resources produces smaller and smaller returns. This result is called a diminishing return.

Another economic principle related to the allocation of choices is opportunity cost, which refers to the benefits given up when an alternative is chosen. Opportunity cost refers to the value of a resource when it is employed in its next-best use.

Markets are central to economics. Markets consist of interactions of buyers and sellers. People buy more when prices are lower, and producers want to sell more when prices are higher. Supply and demand rise and fall until equilibrium is achieved—the points at which demand matches supply for a given price.

Healthcare differs from normal economics in that healthcare spending is unexpected and expensive. Individuals want the best in healthcare. As a result, people come together to share the risk of illness by forming risk pools. Risk pools allow health insurance companies to charge premiums that reflect the average cost of everyone in the risk pool.

Adverse selection, however, can destroy risk pools. Sick people will seek more extensive, expensive health insurance, while healthy people either will not pay for health insurance or will buy very limited health insurance. If the sick end up in a separate risk pool from the healthy, their average cost for health insurance will skyrocket and become unaffordable.

Prior to the Affordable Care Act (ACA), people with preexisting conditions were often excluded from risk pools because they increased costs. The ACA prevented such exclusions.

Healthcare is also different from other industries in that it consists of services that cannot be stored and must be available when needed. In addition, understanding healthcare's outputs can be difficult. Healthcare frequently produces externalities, which are secondary impacts on others, such as the effects of smoking on those who breathe the air of smokers but do not smoke themselves.

Asymmetric information also occurs frequently in healthcare. This happens when one party has more knowledge than the other, as when providers of care have much more information than patients. As a result, the patient might not receive the services they might choose if they had all the facts.

Much of healthcare is paid for through third-party payers, such as insurance companies. Third-party payments increase the utilization and cost of healthcare services. Patients only pay a fraction of what is charged, leading to overuse. The overuse of healthcare is a result of fee-for-service payment arrangements.

Furthermore, the demand for healthcare does not change much when prices change. A change in demand in response to a price change is called the *elasticity of demand*. Healthcare demand, however, is mostly inelastic.

Healthcare economics attempts to place a value on the burden of disability or morbidity. It is measured by the quality-adjusted life year (QALY). QALYs are used to calculate the cost-effectiveness of medical treatment.

Macroeconomics provides a big-picture view of healthcare. It is concerned with spending, employment, and other aspects of medical care as they affect the economy and the health of the population as a whole. Per capita income and spending have increased together over time, but healthcare spending has outpaced income for several decades. The wealthiest Americans are often insured and can afford to pay for healthcare. However, the poorest struggle, and most have no insurance. Without insurance, many Americans cannot afford the out-of-pocket cost of healthcare. The gap between the very rich and the poor in the United States is a contributor to inferior health outcomes in the United States compared with other countries.

The Centers for Disease Control and Prevention reports on health disparities and inequalities across a wide range of diseases, behavior risk facts, environmental exposures, social determinants, and access to healthcare by sex, race/ethnicity, income, education, disability status, gender, and other social characteristics. The Healthy People 2020 initiative and the National Partnership for Action to End Health Disparities are among the groups that are working to respond to health disparities.

QUESTIONS

1. Why is allocation of resources important to understanding healthcare economics?
2. What is a diminishing return? How does it impact healthcare?
3. Suppose that you have chosen to attend a university to obtain a degree. What is an example of an opportunity cost in this situation?
4. Why does quantity go up when demand for a product goes up?
5. Why is it bad to only have sick people in a health insurance risk pool?
6. What would happen to a health insurance risk pool if people with preexisting conditions were excluded?
7. Suppose that you catch a disease because your neighbor refused to get a vaccine that would prevent the spread of this disease. What is this called?
8. People generally consume a product until the _____ they receive equals the _____ they spend on the product.
9. What does it mean that healthcare is mostly an inelastic good?

ASSIGNMENTS

1. Read the following article: "High-Risk Pools for Uninsurable Individuals," Kaiser Family Foundation, February 22, 2017, at www.kff.org/health-reform/issue-brief/high-risk-pools-for-uninsurable-individuals. Examine Figure 1 in the article, "Concentration of Healthcare Spending in U.S. Population," which shows that 1 percent of the

US population accounts for 23 percent of total healthcare spending, and 50 percent of the population accounts for just 3 percent of healthcare spending. In terms of creating risk pools, what is the effect on health insurance premiums of creating a risk pool for the top 1 percent? For the lower 50 percent? Or for the all the US population?

2. Search the internet for examples of externalities in healthcare. List three and explain why the externalities occur.

CASES

DIMINISHING RETURNS

Dr. Good wants to help his patients be healthy. In the past, he has allowed them to come into the office for free healthcare screenings and tests. He now has the opportunity to provide free full-body CT scans and full gene mapping. The CT scan would normally cost about $4,000 and the gene mapping about $10,000. He is not certain whether he should offer these new services. Most of the preventive tests and immunizations that he administered in the past were inexpensive but produced significant benefits. He thinks many of his patients would take advantage of the new tests, but is it the right thing to do?

Discussion Questions

1. How is this an example of diminishing returns in healthcare?
2. Would you recommend that Dr. Good offer the new tests? Why or why not?

ADVERSE SELECTION

Somet Health Insurance Company wants to sell a health insurance product for $700 per month. There is no requirement for healthy people to have insurance coverage. The company conducts a survey to see how different populations respond to the proposed cost. People with no illnesses and disabilities, generally the young and healthy, respond that they do not spend $700 on healthcare in an entire year, and most feel they would not waste so much money on premiums when the chance of needing surgery or expensive healthcare treatments is so small. However, older, sicker people think that $700 per month is a great deal, as most of them spend far in excess of this amount on healthcare. It seems like a great deal for them.

Discussion Questions

1. If the company offers this product, how will adverse selection affect it?
2. What will happen to the costs of the health insurance if only the older, sicker people enroll?

REFERENCES

Albrecht, B. C. 2014. "5 Life Lessons Economics Taught Me." *Econ Point of View* (blog), May 1. https://econpointofview.com/blog/5-life-lessons/.

Amadeo, K. 2019. "Obamacare Pre-existing Conditions." The Balance. Published August 29. www.thebalance.com/obamacare-pre-existing-conditions-3306072.

Amadeo, K., and M. Boyle. 2020. "The Rising Cost of Healthcare by Year and Its Causes." The Balance. Updated May 28. www.thebalance.com/causes-of-rising-healthcare-costs-4064878.

Artiga, S., R. Garfield, and K. Orgera. 2020. "Communities of Color at Higher Risk for Health and Economic Challenges due to COVID-19." Kaiser Family Foundation. Published April 7. www.kff.org/disparities-policy/issue-brief/communities-of-color-at-higher-risk-for-health-and-economic-challenges-due-to-covid-19/.

Buff, M., and T. Terrell. 2014. "The Role of Third-Party Payers in Medical Cost Increases." *Journal of American Physicians and Surgeons* 19 (2): 75–79.

Centers for Disease Control and Prevention (CDC). 2020. "Health Effects of Secondhand Smoke." Reviewed February 27. www.cdc.gov/tobacco/data_statistics/fact_sheets/secondhand_smoke/health_effects/index.htm.

———. 2013. "CDC Health Disparities and Inequalities Report—United States, 2013." *Morbidity and Mortality Weekly Report* 62 (3 Suppl.). Published November 23. www.cdc.gov/mmwr/pdf/other/su6203.pdf.

Centers for Medicare & Medicaid Services (CMS). 2019. "National Health Expenditures by Type of Service and Source of Funds, CY 1960–2018." Updated December 17. www.cms.gov/research-statistics-data-and-systems/statistics-trends-and-reports/nationalhealthexpenddata/nationalhealthaccountshistorical.html.

Culyer, A. 2014. *The Encyclopedia of Health Economics*. New York: Elsevier.

Ellis, R., J. Levs, and S. Hamasaki. 2015. "Outbreak of 51 Measles Cases Linked to Disneyland." CNN. Published January 23. www.cnn.com/2015/01/21/health/disneyland-measles/index.html.

Ellis, R., B. Martins, and W. Zhu. 2017. "Healthcare Demand Elasticities by Type of Service." *Journal of Health Economics* 55: 232–43.

Frakt, A. 2019. "Does Your Education Level Affect Your Health?" *New York Times*. Published June 3. www.nytimes.com/2019/06/03/upshot/education-impact-health-longevity.html.

Garofalo, R., and S. Bush. 2008. "Addressing LGBTQ Youth in the Clinical Setting." In *The Fenway Guide to Lesbian, Gay, Bisexual, and Transgender Health*, edited by H. Makadon, K. H. Mayer, J. Potter, and H. Goldhammer, 75–99. Philadelphia: American College of Physicians.

Getzen, T. E. 2010. *Health Economics and Financing*. Hoboken: John Wiley & Sons.

Hassan, A. 2019. "Disneyland Visitor with Measles May Have Exposed Hundreds to Infection." *New York Times*. Published October 23. www.nytimes.com/2019/10/23/us/disneyland-measles.html.

Horowitz, J., R. Igielnik, and R. Kochhar. 2020. "Trends in Income and Wealth Inequality." Pew Research Center. Published January 9. www.pewsocialtrends.org/2020/01/09/trends-in-income-and-wealth-inequality/.

Kaiser Family Foundation. 2018. "Key Facts About the Uninsured Population." Published December 7. www.kff.org/uninsured/fact-sheet/key-facts-about-the-uninsured-population/.

Kaufman, K. 2012. "Bending the Healthcare Cost Curve: More than Meets the Eye?" *Health Affairs Blog*. Published April 13. www.healthaffairs.org/do/10.1377/hblog20120413.018506/full/.

Miric, A., M. Inacio, M. Kelly, and R. Namba. 2014. "Can Total Knee Arthroplasty Be Safely Performed Among Nonagenarians? Evaluation of Morbidity and Mortality Within a Total Joint Replacement Registry." *Journal of Arthroplasty* 29 (8): 1635–38.

Morris, S., N. Devlin, D. Parkin, and A. Spencer. 2012. *Economic Analysis in Healthcare*, 2nd ed. London: John Wiley & Sons.

Neumann, P., and J. Cohen. 2018. "QALYs in 2018—Advantages and Concerns." *JAMA* 319 (24): 2473–74.

Office of Minority Health. 2020. "National Partnership for Action to End Health Disparities." Accessed April 28. https://minorityhealth.hhs.gov/npa.

O'Neill, D., and D. Scheinker. 2018. "Wasted Health Spending: Who's Picking Up the Tab? *Health Affairs Blog*. Published May 31. www.healthaffairs.org/do/10.1377/hblog20180530.245587/full/.

Papanicolas, I., L. Woskie, and A. Jha. 2018. "Healthcare Spending in the United States and Other High-Income Countries." *JAMA* 319 (10): 1024–39.

Robinson, J., and D. Espelage. 2013. "Peer Victimization and Sexual Risk Differences Between Lesbian, Gay, Bisexual, Transgender, or Questioning and Nontransgender Heterosexual Youths in Grades 7–12." *American Journal of Public Health* 103 (10): 1810–19.

Rovner, J. 2018. "Fact Check: Who's Right About Protections for Pre-existing Conditions?" National Public Radio. Published October 11. www.npr.org/sections/health-shots/2018/10/11/656503264/fact-check-whos-right-about-protections-for-pre-existing-conditions.

Scott, R. D., S. Solomon, and J. McGowan. 2001. "Applying Economic Principles to Healthcare." *Emerging Infectious Diseases* 7 (2). Published April. wwwnc.cdc.gov/eid/article/7/2/70-0282_article.

Snowbeck, C. 2016. "Big Deductibles Can Mean Big Stakes in the Timing of a Baby Delivery." *Star Tribune* (Minneapolis, MN). Published January 9. www.startribune.com/big-deductibles-can-mean-big-stakes-in-the-timing-of-a-baby-delivery/364688561/.

US Bureau of Economic Analysis. 2019. "Local Area Personal Income, 2018." Published November 14. www.bea.gov/system/files/2019-11/lapi1119.pdf.

———. 2018. "Personal Income Per Capita (Dollars, Not Seasonally Adjusted)." Retrieved from Federal Reserve Bank of St. Louis. Accessed April 28, 2020. https://fred.stlouisfed.org/series/A792RC0A052NBEA.

US Department of Health and Human Services (HHS). 2020. "Healthy People 2020." www.healthypeople.gov/2020/data-search.

Vasquez, J. 2020. "Obesity in America, in 6 Charts." Advisory Board. Published January 6. www.advisory.com/daily-briefing/2020/01/06/obesity-charts.

Zimmerman, F., and N. Anderson. 2019. "Trends in Health Equity in the United States by Race/Ethnicity, Sex and Income, 1993–2017." *JAMA Network Open* 2 (6): e196386. https://jamanetwork.com/journals/jamanetworkopen/fullarticle/2736934.

CHAPTER 9

HEALTH INSURANCE

Health insurance is very important to Americans. However, the increasing cost of health insurance makes it unaffordable for many people. Insurance premiums are now almost as high as some mortgage payments, exceeding $1,000 a month. Deductibles have risen as well, reaching $6,000 per year for some plans. Although employers are the main source of health insurance for people in the United States, sometimes the cost is so high that individuals are quitting their jobs to qualify for Medicaid. Here is an example:

> Jessie McCormick quit her job to afford health care. Ms. McCormick, 27, who has a heart condition, had an opportunity to move from part time to full time in her job at a small nonprofit in Washington. Working full time would qualify her for the firm's health plan. But she calculated that her out-of-pocket costs would be at least $1,200 per month, about double the money she had left after paying her rent and utilities. Instead, she quit her job last summer so her income would be low enough to enroll in Medicaid, which will cover all her medical expenses. (Abelson 2019)

The rapid increase in healthcare premiums is partly attributable to the fact that many younger and healthier people have chosen not to enroll in health insurance plans, as required by the Affordable Care Act (ACA) of 2010. This resulted in large increases to individual insurance premiums—averaging 25 percent in 2017—which then prompted other relatively healthy people to drop their insurance. This, in turn, led to further premium increases for those who remained enrolled (Alonso-Zaldivar 2017).

After reading this chapter, you will be able to

➤ Explain the basic terminology used to discuss health insurance.

➤ Perceive the advantages and disadvantages of different forms of health insurance networks.

➤ Recognize the risk involved in health insurance and how insurance changes who assumes the risk.

➤ Comprehend the importance of selecting the correct risk pool and its effect on health insurance.

➤ Differentiate among deductibles, coinsurance, and copays and their effects on health insurance premiums.

➤ Describe the reasons why companies shift to self-insured healthcare coverage.

➤ Describe how adverse selection can negatively impact health insurance and why.

➤ Predict options for the future of health insurance in the United States.

For many years, healthcare was paid for directly by individuals. It was common to pay cash, barter with goods or labor, or even prepay for future healthcare services. For most of the seventeenth through the nineteenth centuries, healthcare costs and payments were arranged privately between providers and patients or their families. Access to care was dependent on a patient's ability to pay (Allen 2016).

Health insurance in the United States has become exceedingly complex since it was introduced in the early twentieth century. Americans now have a dizzying array of choices of health insurance companies, plans, coverage, and deductibles. Millions of people still buy individual healthcare plans (i.e., plans that are not provided through an employer), whose costs have skyrocketed. Others receive healthcare coverage as a benefit of employment. Employers often give health insurance coverage to employees as a tax-deductible cost of doing business, and employees usually receive these benefits tax-free.

Businesses see providing health benefits as an important tool for attracting and retaining workers. However, firms can select from a wide range of health insurance plans to offer their employees, which may have high or low deductibles and coinsurance. Sometimes, the health benefits offered to employees are nearly as valuable as their salary. For employees with dependents, these benefits might be even more valuable than their salary.

However, the cost of providing health insurance benefits is becoming increasingly unaffordable for many employers. Healthcare coverage is the largest employee-related expense for US employers. The cost of insurance benefits for private employers in 2015 averaged $2.59 per hour worked, or 8 percent of total employee compensation. By 2018, employers spent an average of $12,666 per employee per year on healthcare coverage (Miller 2018; SHRM 2017).

As explained in chapter 8, health insurance is a way to share the risk of healthcare expenses. Healthcare costs a lot, and few people can afford to pay the full costs of healthcare services by themselves. This chapter provides an overview of the concept of insurance, how it works, why it is important, and who provides it in the United States.

THE CONCEPT OF HEALTH INSURANCE

Insurance is all about sharing risk among groups of people. The risk of and financial catastrophic loss caused by things such as fire, floods, car accidents, or illness cause people to seek protection through insurance. As discussed in chapter 8, groups called *risk pools* contribute money to protect one another from certain types of risk. An example of a risk pool is AARP's auto insurance program, which is available only to people over the age of 50. Those who buy auto insurance through AARP pay a **premium** and share the risk of auto accidents. Insurance is something you need but hope you will never have to use. As a past president of the American College of Physicians stated, "Like auto insurance, health insurance is a service you pay for but hope you will never need. It's there for the unpredictable, unexpected and fundamentally uncontrollable problems that come up in people's lives" (Olivero 2016).

Exhibit 9.1 presents a simple illustration of how insurance premiums are determined. First, a group is selected to share a risk. This population defines the risk pool. Once the risk pool is established, the overall expenses for the risk for this population can be determined. Then a charge, such as a monthly premium or payroll tax, can be established to provide the money to pay for the estimated risk for the overall risk pool.

Many people know little about how health insurance works. According to a Kaiser Family Foundation (2019) quiz, only 76 percent of Americans could define a healthcare premium as a monthly fee that enrollees pay to obtain health insurance coverage.

insurance
The pooling of financial resources by groups of people (called risk pools) to share risk.

premium
The amount that is paid (typically monthly or annually) for an insurance policy.

EXHIBIT 9.1
Simple Insurance Premium Setting

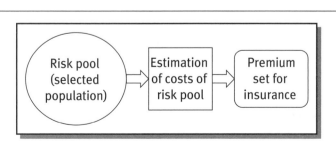

HEALTHCARE ACTUARIES

Estimating the cost of providing healthcare for any risk pool is a challenge. This task generally falls to actuaries. An **actuary** is a professional with advanced training in mathematics and statistics who analyzes the risks and costs associated with different populations, levels of healthcare access, quality, delivery, and financing. Healthcare actuaries analyze potential risks, profits, and trends to set premiums. To become a certified actuary and to practice as one, actuaries must pass a series of examinations, which may take six to ten years to complete (Society of Actuaries 2020).

THE HISTORY OF HEALTH INSURANCE IN THE UNITED STATES

Health insurance was first offered in the United States in the 1920s. Before then, as you learned in chapter 1, healthcare was inexpensive and few people used hospitals. In 1900, the average American spent just $5 on healthcare (Blumberg and Davidson 2009). As more sophisticated hospitals and skilled medical personnel became available, healthcare costs escalated, and doctors sought better ways to get paid for more costly bills.

In the 1920s, Baylor Hospital in Texas was a pioneer in health insurance. The hospital had empty beds and was struggling financially. At the same time, patients had difficulty paying for healthcare services. Baylor sought to address both problems by establishing a health insurance plan that initially was offered to schoolteachers in Dallas. Those who enrolled paid $6 per year for up to 21 days of care a year in the hospital. Baylor's plan became hugely popular: In its first year, more than 1,300 teachers signed up for coverage, and within five years, more than 400 employee groups comprising 23,000 members had enrolled. By 1931, Baylor had expanded its plan to New Jersey. In the 1930s, the American Hospital Association began to build on Baylor's concept, creating a network of nonprofit health insurance plans. These plans soon spread across the United States, becoming known as "Blue Cross" insurance companies (Blumberg and Davidson 2009; Consumer Reports 2019).

In 1962, Blue Cross merged with its counterpart in the Pacific Northwest, Blue Shield. Blue Cross and Blue Shield (BCBS) operated as a nonprofit organization and quickly expanded across the country, becoming the most prominent health insurer for many decades. Today, BCBS companies are a mix of nonprofit and for-profit entities that operate in every US state. Approximately one-third of Americans receive their health insurance through BCBS. The largest BCBS firm is Anthem, a publicly traded company that operates in 14 states (Rappleye 2015).

Health insurance became more popular during the Great Depression and then World War II. However, by 1939, only 3 million Americans out of a total population of 131 million belonged to a health insurance plan. The growth in health insurance enrollment was largely attributable to government regulations. In 1940s, the government mandated a wage freeze during World War II, prompting workers to ask for health insurance as a benefit from their employers. In 1943, the Internal Revenue Service made the health insurance costs provided by companies tax exempt, which spurred even greater growth. The number of Americans who had health insurance increased rapidly during this time. In 1940, only 9 percent of the US population had health insurance, but by 1953, about 63 percent had coverage. By 2018, 91.5 percent of the nation had some type of health insurance coverage (Blumberg and Davidson 2009; Keith 2019; Rosenthal 2017).

The US federal government continued to have a major influence in promoting health insurance. The passage of the Social Security Amendments of 1965 introduced the Medicare and Medicaid programs, significantly expanding health insurance for older and low-income Americans. Today, these two programs together cover more than 100 million people in the United States.

Another major change in health insurance in the United States occurred in 2010, when the ACA was signed into law. The ACA made dramatic changes to the health insurance system and expanded access to health insurance in several ways:

◆ Expanding Medicaid

◆ Setting up health insurance exchanges through which individuals could buy health insurance

◆ Preventing insurers from denying coverage and charging higher premiums for people with preexisting conditions

◆ Requiring all individuals to obtain health insurance (called the "individual mandate")

◆ Penalizing employers who do not offer health insurance coverage to employees

The ACA has been controversial since its passage, and many proposals have been put forth to overturn portions of the law, including the individual mandate (Kaiser Family Foundation 2017; Kenen 2017). Americans hold mixed views about the ACA and its provisions. About half of Americans (52 percent) have a favorable opinion of the ACA, while about 41 percent view it unfavorably. However, most people feel that it is important to retain certain provisions of the ACA. Almost three-quarters (72 percent) of Americans believe that it is important to keep the provision prohibiting insurance companies from denying coverage for preexisting conditions. More than 60 percent believe that it is important to cover preventive services, to prohibit lifetime limits, and to bar insurance companies from charging higher premiums for people with preexisting conditions (Kaiser Family Foundation 2020; Kirzinger, Muñana, and Brodie 2019).

COMMUNITY RATING VERSUS EXPERIENCE RATING

community rating
A method of setting insurance premiums that uses the general community population (e.g., a metropolitan area) as the risk pool.

Health insurance companies generally set premiums using one of two methods: community rating or experience rating (exhibit 9.2). **Community rating** uses the general community population (e.g., a metropolitan area) to set premiums. Under this method, everyone pays the same rate, regardless of age, gender, or health status. The ACA required businesses with more than 50 employees to use community rating.

In contrast, **experience rating** clusters people into smaller risk pools determined by their health history, age, gender, and other factors to set premiums. Under experience rating, healthier populations gain an advantage and pay lower premiums, but those with greater healthcare needs tend to pay more—sometimes much more (Kaiser Family Foundation 2012; Lawley Insurance 2015).

experience rating
A method of setting insurance premiums that clusters people into smaller risk pools determined by their health history, age, gender, and other factors to set premiums.

INDEMNITY VERSUS MANAGED CARE MODEL

Health insurance traditionally was based on an indemnified "fee-for-service" model. An **indemnity healthcare plan** allows individuals to choose their own doctors and hospitals, and the insurance company pays for the services that are used. With indemnity coverage, patients have a great deal of freedom in choosing their providers and can obtain treatment directly from specialists without first having to see a primary care physician. In this environment, healthcare providers are mostly paid on a fee-for-service basis, meaning that providers are paid each time they provide a service to a patient.

indemnity healthcare plan
A health insurance plan that allows individuals to choose their own healthcare providers, providing the greatest amount of flexibility for users. These plans generally use fee-for-service payment.

The indemnity healthcare model creates an incentive to order more tests and perform more services than are necessary, which leads to *physician-induced demand*. Physician-induced demand occurs when unnecessary or inappropriate services are provided to serve the economic self-interest of the physician. Simply, the physician orders more tests and services than are needed to increase his or her income (Mohamadloo et al. 2019). Researchers have long suggested that physician-induced demand has a significant impact on healthcare demand and costs (Wilensky and Rossiter 1983).

Insurance companies found that indemnity insurance provided too much freedom to patients and hampered their ability to control costs. As a result, most health insurance products have moved to some form of **managed care**. Managed care is a type of healthcare delivery system that is organized to manage cost, use, and quality. Managed care serves four key functions:

managed care
A system used by health insurance companies to reduce the costs and improve the quality of healthcare.

1. Establishes standards for selecting providers that are part of the insurance network

2. Sets programs for continuing quality improvement and utilization review

3. Focuses on keeping enrollees healthy and reducing the use of healthcare services

4. Provides financial incentives for enrollees to use in-network providers

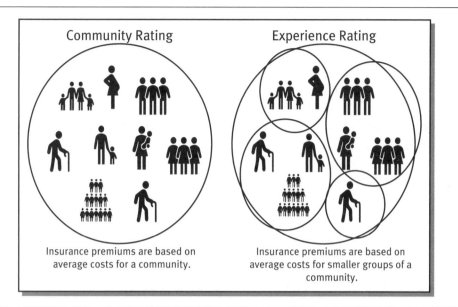

EXHIBIT 9.2
Difference
Between
Community and
Experience Ratings

✳ FEE-FOR-SERVICE MEDICINE

Although many people believe that fee-for-service medicine drives up the cost of healthcare, it remains the primary way most health providers are paid for the services they provide. Physicians recommend and order tests for their patients and get paid for each test ordered and service delivered. Fee-for-service payments in medicine can be compared with payments to your local car mechanic. When you take your car in for preventive maintenance or for a problem, the mechanic recommends and provides services. However, many consumers are unsure whether the mechanic has identified the real problem or has recommended unnecessary services. Frequently, people lack the knowledge they need to decide whether car repairs really need to be done, or if they have been recommended to increase the profits of the mechanic. Fee-for-service healthcare works the same way: A patient obtains a service, trusting the doctor to order the right tests and services but not knowing whether too many tests are being ordered to increase the doctor's profits.

Managed care plans typically restrict enrollees' ability to choose healthcare providers by establishing networks of preferred providers. Some plans, such as health maintenance organizations (HMOs), pay only for care within their network. Other managed care organizations, such as preferred provider organizations (PPOs) and point-of-service (POS) plans, generally pay a portion of the cost for care obtained from a provider outside the network.

Most states have moved to managed care organizations (MCOs) to administer their Medicaid plans. States enlist MCOs and generally pay them a fixed annual fee per Medicaid patient. The MCO oversees the patients' care and has financial incentives to keep patients healthy. For instance, MCOs may offer nonmandated services such as transportation, education, and equipment that, although not required, may increase access to care and lower overall healthcare costs. Managed care organizations may also set other policies to lower costs by implementing utilization management systems to reduce low-value care and improve patients' health (Goldsmith, Mosley, and Jacobs 2018).

HEALTHCARE COSTS BEYOND INSURANCE PREMIUMS

Most people pay additional amounts for healthcare beyond the cost of their health insurance premiums. These costs vary depending on the health insurance plan. Most plans require enrollees to pay some out-of-pocket costs, coinsurance, copayments, and deductibles, and they may impose lifetime or annual limits.

♦ *Out-of-pocket costs.* The amounts that individuals pay from their own resources are known as "out-of-pocket" costs. Out-of-pocket costs are expenses that exceed the amount that insurance pays. For example, for those who do not have health insurance, all healthcare expenses are out-of-pocket costs. In 2017, national out-of-pocket costs for healthcare exceeded $375 billion, or 10 percent of all healthcare spending (CMS 2020). People with Medicare coverage each spent $5,460 annually out-of-pocket costs (Cubanski et al. 2019; Orszag and Emanuel 2018).

♦ *Coinsurance.* Coinsurance is part of many health insurance plans. Coinsurance requires individuals to pay a percentage of the cost for a healthcare service. The amount varies, but most insurance plans pay for about 80 percent of the costs, while the insured must pay the remaining 20 percent.

♦ *Copays.* Although the term "copay" is often used synonymously with coinsurance, unlike coinsurance, copays are a set, flat amounts that individuals pay for a healthcare service. For example, a plan may have a $25 copay for a physician visit or $150 for an emergency room visit.

♦ *Deductibles.* Deductibles are the annual amount of healthcare expenses the insured must pay before the insurance starts covering medical costs. The annual amount of the deductible can vary dramatically, and sometimes reaches as much as $6,000 per year. Many healthcare providers require deductibles to be paid prior to service (see sidebar). Higher deductibles are a financial burden for many people. By 2019, more than a quarter of people working for large companies and half of those working for small businesses had annual deductibles of $2,000 or more (Abelson 2019).

◆ *Lifetime or annual limits.* Lifetime or annual limits set a maximum amount that an insurance company will pay for an individual's healthcare, either in their lifetime or in a year. When this limit is reached, the individual is responsible for any additional medical costs. Following the passage of the ACA, federal law prohibited lifetime or annual limits on most healthcare coverage.

(✱) **DEBATE TIME Pay Your Deductible!**

Many hospitals require up-front payments of deductibles and coinsurance. For many people, these costs are difficult to pay. For example, Aminatou Sow, a popular millennial podcaster, was scheduled for surgery in 2018. Twenty-four hours before her surgery, a hospital representative called to demand payment of her $4,000 deductible before the surgery could take place. Sow tweeted, "Surgery is in ~18 hours and this woman is telling me that I have to pay my entire deductible before surgery. [She tells me] 'Please use a credit card.' How polite. I am stunned. There is a long silence and she says, 'You at least have to pay half to get this surgery.'" When Sow protested, the hospital staff member threatened to cancel the surgery. Ultimately, Sow paid the deductible using her credit card so she could go ahead with the surgery (Olen 2018). Why would a hospital require a deductible to be paid before surgery? Should hospitals do this?

REASONS FOR HIGHER PREMIUMS

People who have chronic health conditions often seek more extensive healthcare coverage. However, younger, healthier people often do not see the value of having health insurance and prefer less coverage. Even with the ACA's individual mandate, many of those in the 18–34 age group chose not to sign up for health insurance after the law was implemented (Herman 2016). Therefore, as more people with chronic health conditions signed up for health insurance, premiums were much higher than expected. This situation illustrates the concept of *adverse selection* (discussed in chapter 8): Those who anticipate having higher

Exhibit 9.3
Adverse Selection

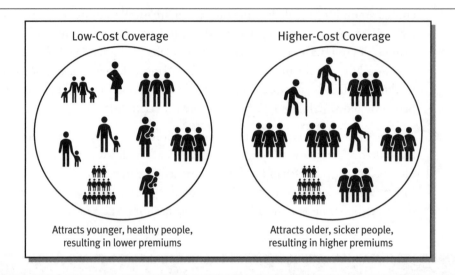

healthcare expenses are more likely to obtain health insurance, while those who anticipate lower expenses do not (exhibit 9.3).

If a risk pool includes only those with chronic health conditions, premiums can become very high, as a small percentage of the population accounts for a significant share of healthcare expenditures (see sidebar) (Mankiw 2017).

✳ A FEW COST SO MUCH

A small share of people account for much of the cost of healthcare. At Arches Health Plan, a now-defunct co-op insurer in Utah, just 200 people—or 0.3 percent of its 63,000 members—accounted for 50 percent of its claims (Herman 2016). This phenomenon is true across the United States as well: Just 5 percent of Americans are responsible for about 50 percent of healthcare spending, and 1 percent of the population incurred almost 22 percent of all healthcare expenses (Sawyer and Claxton 2019).

---

moral hazard
A situation in which people have an incentive to increase their risk when they do not bear the full cost of the risk.

Another problem that may increase the cost of insurance coverage is **moral hazard**. Moral hazard is the tendency for people to increase their use of healthcare, regardless of whether doing so is necessary, because they have health insurance. Insurance companies frequently try to minimize moral hazard in settings outside of healthcare by adding preventive requirements—for example, smoke detectors, sprinklers in buildings, and inspections to identify fire hazards. In healthcare, high copays and deductibles not only help offset the costs of healthcare but also reduce moral hazard.

MEDICAL LOSS RATIOS

One way to gauge how much an insurance company spends on healthcare services is the **medical loss ratio**, which is the percentage of total health insurance premium revenues (not including taxes and fees) that is spent on medical claims and healthcare quality improvement activities (as opposed to administrative and marketing expenses and profits).

$$\text{Medical Loss Ratio} = \frac{\text{Provider Payments \& Quality Costs}}{\text{Health Insurance Premiums}}$$

medical loss ratio
The percentage of health premium dollars that a health insurance plan spends on provider payments (e.g., medical and surgical costs) as opposed to administrative costs.

There is no optimal medical loss ratio. It can exceed 100 percent when an insurance company loses money and spends more than it collects. Normally, the medical loss ratio is less than 100 percent, as insurance companies need to pay for their expenses and make a profit. For instance, in 2015, as exhibit 9.4 shows, the medical loss ratio exceeded 100 percent (103 percent), which means that insurance companies lost 3 percent more than their revenues from premiums. However, in 2018, the medical loss ratio dropped to 70 percent, indicating that insurance companies retained 30 percent of revenues after paying

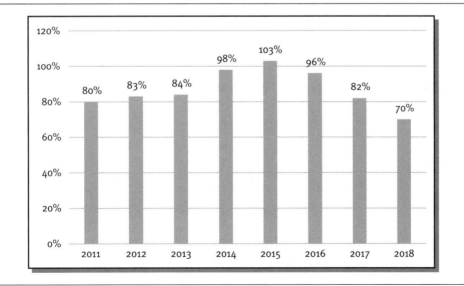

EXHIBIT 9.4
Health Insurance Medical Loss Ratio, 2011–2018

Source: Data from Cox, Fehr, and Levitt (2019).

✱ INSURANCE REBATES

In the past, some major insurance companies had medical loss ratios as low as 68 percent, which many regard as excessive (Haberkorn 2010). Under the ACA, health insurers now must maintain medical loss ratios of 80 percent or higher. If the ratio falls below 80 percent, the company is required to refund the difference to policyholders in the form of a rebate.

Since 2012, millions of Americans have received rebates from their health insurance companies as a result of the ACA. From 2012 to 2018, health insurers issued rebates of $3.24 billion to policyholders. In 2017 alone, rebates totaled almost $447 million to about 3.95 million people. California saw the highest average rebates, at $559 per family (Norris 2018). In 2019, these numbers jumped substantially, as insurers paid rebates of $1.37 billion to 8.9 million Americans. Kansas had the highest per household rebate at $1,081 (HealthInsurance.org 2020).

for medical care (Cox, Fehr, and Levitt 2019). Of note, Medicare maintains a medical loss ratio of 97 to 98 percent (Haberkorn 2010).

The ACA required insurers to maintain a medical loss ratio of no less than 80 percent in the individual market and 85 percent in the large-group market. If insurance companies have lower medical loss ratios than those mandated by the ACA, they must refund money to policyholders (Klinger 2017) (see sidebar).

CHALLENGES OF THIRD-PARTY PAYMENT

Most healthcare costs are not paid by patients but rather by some intermediary, such as a private insurance company or a government program, after services are rendered. Patients may pay their deductible or coinsurance at the time of service, but the bulk of payments are received later from the insurance company or government program. Third-party payers often serve as intermediaries between patients and providers by monitoring the cost and quality of services (see exhibit 9.5). However, third-party payers also add much more complexity to the healthcare system (Kordonowy 2019; Santerre and Neun 2012).

Since healthcare is mostly paid by third parties, users may consume more healthcare services than they would if they were paying the full cost themselves. Without appropriate cost sharing, patients may have an incentive to consume more services than are necessary.

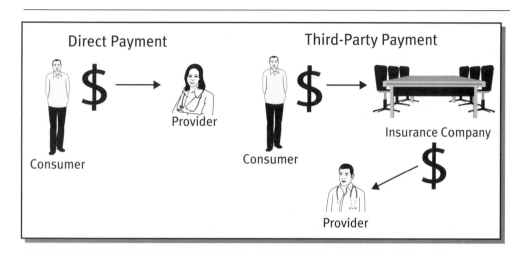

EXHIBIT 9.5
Direct Payment
Versus Third-Party
Payment

The third-party payment system also creates challenges and costs for providers to collect their billings. During the twentieth century, most physicians were able to bill for the amounts that they felt were reasonable and to collect most of those payments. However, insurance companies today negotiate significant discounts and frequently delay or deny payments. Billings may be denied for a variety of reasons. A patient may not be eligible for the service provided, some demographic or identifying information may be missing or incorrect, or the diagnosis codes or modifiers on the claims may not match the requirements of the patient's insurance. Following up on denied billings accounts for about one-third of a physician's billing staff time (Medscape 2019).

HOW HEALTH INSURANCE PREMIUMS ARE SPENT

On average, insurance companies that collect premiums from businesses and individuals spend about 80 cents of each premium dollar on medical expenses. Of this amount, 22 cents are spent on prescription drugs and another 22 cents on physician services. Insurance companies apply 18 cents to their operating costs and retain 3 cents of each dollar as profit (see exhibit 9.6).

WHY HAVE HEALTH INSURANCE?

Having health insurance provides many benefits (HealthCare.gov 2020a):

◆   Provides essential health benefits that are critical to maintaining health and treating acute health conditions and injuries

◆   Protects against unexpected medical costs

EXHIBIT 9.6
Where Do
Health Insurance
Premiums Go?

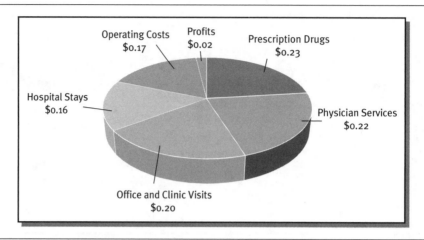

Operating Costs
$0.17

Profits
$0.02

Prescription Drugs
$0.23

Hospital Stays
$0.16

Physician Services
$0.22

Office and Clinic Visits
$0.20

Source: Data from AHIP (2018).

- ◆ Lowers the cost of healthcare
- ◆ Provides access to preventive care

In the United States, whether people receive the quantity and quality of healthcare they need often depends on whether they have insurance and what kind of coverage they have (Teitelbaum and Wilensky 2013). Having health insurance allows patients to receive medical treatments that result in better health. One study showed that obtaining health insurance decreases the likelihood of dying by cardiac arrest by 17 percent (Cedars-Sinai 2017). Other studies have shown that those with health insurance are three times more likely to see a doctor, receive screening tests, and go to the emergency room when they are seriously ill. Having insurance coverage also has been shown to reduce depression and improve overall health (Foutz et al. 2017).

ESSENTIAL HEALTH BENEFITS

Under the ACA, insurers are required to provide coverage for annual checkups, preventive care, and ten essential health services:

1. Preventive and wellness services

2. Ambulatory (outpatient) care services

3. Emergency care

4. Hospitalization

5. Maternity and newborn care

6. Pediatric care

7. Laboratory services

8. Mental health and substance use disorder services

9. Prescription drugs

10. Rehabilitative and long-term disability services

The Donald Trump administration sought to reduce or eliminate the essential benefit requirement (Amadeo 2018), and in 2018 changes to federal rules gave states the ability to allow insurance plans with scaled-back essential benefits (see sidebar).

✳ STATES ALLOW INSURANCE WITHOUT ESSENTIAL BENEFITS

In 2018, the Iowa Farm Bureau started selling unregulated plans in partnership with Wellmark Blue Cross and Blue Shield. The Iowa plans are permitted to deny coverage to individuals with preexisting conditions. In addition, the state of Kansas passed a law to allow similar "skimpy" health insurance plans to begin to be sold in 2019. Kansas claimed that its plans would be 30 to 50 percent cheaper than those offered on the ACA exchanges. Kansas regulators estimate that 11,000 to 42,000 Kansans will be covered by the new plans.

To get around the requirements of the ACA, these states explicitly declare that the plans are not licensed or regulated as health insurance. However, some people are concerned that these scaled-back plans could destabilize the ACA market and drive up premiums (Meyer 2019).

WHO PROVIDES HEALTH INSURANCE?

Broadly speaking, there are two types of health insurance: private health insurance and public or government-provided health insurance, such as Medicare, Medicaid, or TRICARE for active-duty military personnel and their dependents. The US government's policy regarding health insurance remains at odds with almost all other advanced countries. Most other industrialized countries offer some form of universal health coverage to their citizens. However, the US government provides health insurance for only segments of the population and allows private health insurance to cover most of the remaining people.

Exhibit 9.7

Healthcare Coverage by Type of Insurance, 2013–2016 (thousands)

Coverage Type	2013		2014		2015		2016		2017	
	Number	Rate	Number	Rate	Number	Rate	Number	Rate	Number	Rate
Total	313,401		316,168		318,868		320,372		323,156	
Any health plan	271,606	86.7%	283,200	89.6%	289,903	90.9%	292,320	91.2%	294,613	91.2%
Any private plan	201,038	64.1%	208,600	66.0%	214,238	67.2%	216,203	67.5%	217,007	67.2%
Employment based	174,418	55.7%	175,027	55.4%	177,540	55.7%	178,465	55.7%	181,036	56.0%
Direct purchase	35,755	11.4%	46,165	14.6%	52,057	16.3%	51,961	16.2%	51,821	16.0%
Any government plan	108,287	34.6%	115,470	36.5%	118,395	37.1%	119,361	37.3%	121,965	37.7%
Medicare	49,020	15.6%	50,546	16.0%	51,865	16.3%	53,372	16.7%	55,623	17.2%
Medicaid	54,919	17.5%	61,650	19.5%	62,384	19.6%	62,303	19.4%	1,007	19.3%
Military	14,016	4.5%	14,143	4.5%	14,849	4.7%	14,638	4.6%	15,532	4.8%
Uninsured	41,795	13.3%	32,968	10.4%	28,966	9.1%	28,052	8.8%	28,543	8.8%

Source: Data from US Census Bureau (2018).

Exhibit 9.7 shows that a majority of Americans, 56 percent, get their insurance from their employers, while the government covers more than 37 percent of the population.

MAJOR PRIVATE INSURANCE COMPANIES

The private insurance market is dominated by big companies. Exhibit 9.8 shows that in 2018, the five largest US health insurance companies brought in about $453 billion of revenues and enrolled more than 138 million people. The largest health insurance company, United Health Group, has almost 50 million enrolled members.

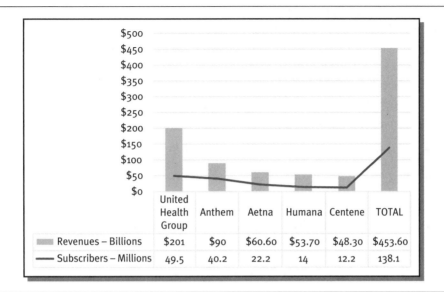

Exhibit 9.8
Largest US Health Insurance Companies by Revenues and Subscribers, 2018

	United Health Group	Anthem	Aetna	Humana	Centene	TOTAL
Revenues – Billions	$201	$90	$60.60	$53.70	$48.30	$453.60
Subscribers – Millions	49.5	40.2	22.2	14	12.2	138.1

Source: Data from Haefner (2019).

The health insurance business continues to be profitable. In the second quarter of 2019, even amid a continued uncertainty about the future of healthcare, the top five companies had more than $11 billion in net earnings (Minemyer 2019).

THE FINANCIAL BURDEN OF HEALTHCARE COSTS

High medical bills are one of the most common reasons Americans file for personal bankruptcy (Olivero 2016). Although even people with health insurance can struggle with the high costs of healthcare, those without insurance experience greater hardship. In fact, the uninsured often pay substantially more than those with insurance for the same services. Hospitals often charge uninsured patients two to four times the amount that private insurance and government programs pay (Foutz et al. 2017). Individual hospitals, however, dictate how much the uninsured are charged. Many hospitals offer standard discounts for low-income patients, but almost half (45 percent) of not-for-profit hospitals routinely bill such patients, whose incomes are often low enough to qualify them for charity care. These hospitals collected $2.7 billion from patients who should have qualified for financial assistance (Rau 2019).

Uninsured patients are charged much more than the actual cost of care. Hospitals deeply discount their prices for insurance companies, but those without insurance often have to pay closer to the listed price. Therefore, the uninsured can pay dramatically more than the insured. For example, a John Hopkins University study of emergency room charges

Healthcare in the United States

showed that an insured person typically pays a $50 to $100 copay, but a person without insurance could pay $150 to $3,000 for the same visit (Hunt 2019).

A study by the Kaiser Family Foundation (Garfield, Orgera, and Damico 2019) found that those without health insurance

- are charged two to four times what health insurers and public programs actually pay for services,

- are often asked to pay the full cost of care before they can see a doctor,

- have fewer overall medical costs but pay a greater percentage of those costs out of pocket, and

- have greater difficulty paying their medical bills and have little savings.

PAYING FOR DEDUCTIBLES AND COINSURANCE

To help employees pay for out-of-pocket costs, coinsurance, copays, deductibles, and other approved healthcare expenses, employers and the federal government established health reimbursement accounts (HRAs), health savings accounts (HSAs), and flexible spending accounts (FSAs). Employees can use the money in these accounts to pay for qualified medical, prescription, dental, and vision expenses. Contributions to these accounts typically are tax exempt.

- *HRAs* are accounts that are funded solely by the employer. The employer determines the amount that will be contributed to the account and retains any unused dollars. The employer decides whether the HRA will pay directly for healthcare expenses not covered by the employee's health insurance plan or whether it will reimburse employees for payments made after a certain amount is reached.

- *HSAs* allow employees to set aside tax-free dollars to pay for medical expenses. HSAs are available only to employees enrolled in high-deductible healthcare plans—typically, plans with deductibles of at least $1,350 for individuals and $2,700 for families. In 2017, employees could contribute $3,400 for individuals and $6,750 for families. Some advantages of HSAs are that unused funds typically roll over from year to year and employees retain ownership of the accounts even if they change jobs (HealthCare.gov 2020b).

- *FSAs* are accounts to which both the employee and the employer can contribute tax-free dollars to up to a federally set maximum. In 2018, the contribution maximum for employees was $2,650 (Miller 2017). These monies can be used to pay deductible, coinsurance, and other qualified healthcare expenses. However, the monies must be used each fiscal year or they are generally returned to the employer.

FULLY INSURED AND SELF-INSURED COMPANIES

Companies can choose to be fully insured or self-insured (self-funded). A **fully insured company** provides a traditional health insurance plan in which the company pays a fixed premium to an insurance firm for coverage of its employees for a one-year period. The premium rate is fixed for the year, and total amount paid depends on the number of enrolled employees. The insurance company is then responsible for paying healthcare claims based on the coverage provided. The insurance company keeps any monies remaining or takes a loss if more money is paid for healthcare expenses (Merhar 2016).

Self-insured companies, conversely, provide their own healthcare plan, which allows them to save the profits and high overhead of some insurance companies. Rather than pay an insurance firm a premium, the company retains financial responsibility for all employee healthcare costs. Companies can reduce their risk by buying **stop-loss insurance**. A stop-loss policy does not directly insure employees or pay healthcare bills, but rather pays the company when it experiences very high medical costs. For instance, a company may absorb

fully insured company
A company that pays a set annual premium to a health insurance firm to provide healthcare coverage to its employees; in this arrangement, the health insurance company assumes the financial risk.

self-insured company
A company that offers its own healthcare coverage and retains financial responsibility for all employee healthcare costs; in this arrangement, the company assumes the financial risk.

stop-loss insurance
An insurance policy that provides protection against large losses for companies that self-fund their employee benefit plans; the policy pays out after a certain threshold of healthcare costs is reached.

✳ XYZ COMPANY SELF-INSURES

XYZ Company employs 1,000 people. Traditionally the company was fully insured, purchasing a healthcare plan from Blue Cross. Its rates began rising rapidly, however, and by 2016, the company was paying about $5,500 per employee, or payments of $5.5 million. In the hope of saving money, XYZ decided to become self-insured. The company calculated that if it could keep employees' healthcare costs below $5.5 million, it would save money. Becoming self-insured allowed XYZ to drop some of its coverage and increase employees' deductibles. The company also hired a third-party administrator that would work with XYZ to directly negotiate rates with local hospitals, audit its bills, reduce administrative costs, and increase their cash flow.

To moderate the risk of high healthcare costs, XYZ bought a stop-loss insurance policy that would pay for any individual claim over $120,000 and for all claims once the company's aggregate claims exceeded $10 million. Although the cost of the stop-loss policy was high, the company expected that it would easily pay for itself.

the first $3 million in healthcare costs, but stop-loss insurance pays for costs over $3 million. This way, companies are protected from large claims and their associated costs. A survey conducted in 2019 makes clear the importance of stop-loss insurance: Almost two-thirds of companies had individual healthcare claims over $500,000, and one-third had single claims in excess of $1 million (Wooldridge 2019).

Companies can pay for their healthcare costs directly or hire a **third-party administrator (TPA)**. A TPA is an entity that performs administrative services such as claims processing for a self-insured employer. For example, Pennsylvania State University in 2018 selected Aetna to be its TPA for medical benefits and CVS Caremark to administer its prescription drug benefits (Pennsylvania State University 2017).

third-party
administrator (TPA)
A company that provides claims processing and employee benefits management without assuming any financial risk.

How Companies Can Lower Healthcare Costs

Almost everyone is affected by the escalating costs of healthcare. Companies continue to take a variety of actions to blunt the costs. Businesses have suggested that the following actions can help control the costs of healthcare (SHRM 2017):

◆ Create an organizational culture that promotes health and wellness.

◆ Offer a variety of PPO plans, including those with high and low deductibles and copays.

◆ Increase employees' share of the total costs of healthcare.

◆ Offer an HMO health plan.

◆ Provide incentives or rewards to promote health and wellness.

◆ Place limits on or increase cost sharing for spousal healthcare coverage.

◆ Increase employees' share of brand-name prescription drug costs.

Others suggest that more systemic changes need to be made, including streamlining the convoluted and expensive healthcare billing systems present in the United States. Some estimate that simplifying the medical billing system could save up to 20 percent of healthcare costs. Cost savings could also be realized by lowering the cost of prescription drugs and by allowing younger and healthier people to enroll in Medicare (Lee 2017).

How Patients Can Lower Healthcare Costs

Patients should review their medical bills for errors, which are common. One study suggests that almost 80 percent of medical bills contain errors, resulting in significant overpayments (*Modern Healthcare* 2019). Patients can ask for an itemized bill that lists all supplies, medications, and procedures for which they are being charged. To manage large bills, patients may hire a billing advocate, who is paid based on the savings realized (Thimou 2017).

Patients can also consider asking for a discount on the amount they owe. Hospitals tend to collect only about 30 percent of charges billed. As a result, around 70 percent of billed charges are "written off" as **contractual allowances** or contractual adjustments, which are the discounts that hospitals give to insurance companies, or **bad debt**, which is money that people owe but do not pay. These adjustments occur because Medicare, Medicaid, and private insurance companies negotiate agreements and contracts to pay much less than the billed amounts. For example, health insurance companies generally pay 30 to 37 percent of what hospitals bill them (Belk 2017; Gee 2019). When patients show they are making an effort to pay their bills, providers and their billing departments often will negotiate the amount that is owed.

BALANCE BILLING

Healthcare costs to patients can also become extremely expensive if **balance billing** is used. Balance billing is the practice of billing patients for the difference between what their health insurance pays and what the healthcare provider charges. Balance billing is sometimes referred to as "surprise billing." This often occurs when the provider or hospital is not part of the patient's insurance network. For instance, a patient who had a bicycle accident and was taken to a hospital in San Francisco was billed $24,074.50 for the emergency room treatment. However, since the hospital was not part of her insurance company's network, the insurance company paid only $3,830.79, leaving her with a bill of $20,243.71 (Kliff 2019).

Balance billing imposes a heavy financial burden on patients. In fact, six states—California, Connecticut, Florida, Illinois, Maryland, and New York—have banned balance billing, and other states are considering restricting it (Hoadley, Lucia, and Kona 2019). Federal legislation has also been introduced to address balance billing, as it has become part of the national debate on healthcare costs (Bluth 2019).

COMMON TYPES OF HEALTH INSURANCE NETWORKS

Most health insurance companies use some type of network to control cost while maintaining quality. Network providers are employed by the network or agree to accept lower fees and other restrictions to belong to the network. The most common types of networks are as follows:

♦ A *health maintenance organization (HMO)* is a type of insurance plan that generally requires all enrollees to have a primary care physician (PCP) who serves as a gatekeeper, meaning that the PCP must provide the patient with a referral to see a specialist. Out-of-network care is generally not covered.

contractual allowances
The difference between the amount that healthcare providers bill for services and the amount they are paid, based on their contracts with third-party insurers and government programs such as Medicare and Medicaid; also called *contractual adjustments*.

bad debt
Charges for services that are billed but uncollectible and are not charity care.

balance billing
The practice of billing patients for the difference between what their health insurance pays and what the healthcare provider charges; also known as *surprise billing*.

◆ A *preferred provider organization (PPO)* is a group of providers that contract with an insurer or third-party administrator to deliver coverage to those insured. Enrollees generally receive substantial discounts when they use the PPO providers.

◆ A *point-of-service (POS) plan* has qualities of both an HMO and a PPO. Enrollees may be required to have a PCP who makes referrals to specialists. These plans allow patients to receive care from out-of-network providers with a higher deductible or copay.

◆ An *exclusive provider organization (EPO)* is an insurance plan that only covers healthcare services provided by providers within the plan's network.

As exhibit 9.9 shows, HMOs tend to be the most restrictive plans but also have lower deductibles. PPOs provide greater flexibility for patients to choose providers, but they also have higher deductibles.

Employees in the United States receive coverage from all four network types. As shown in exhibit 9.10, most companies (81 percent) offer a PPO, and more than half of all employees (52 percent) choose the PPO option. HMOs are the next most popular type of plan, with 29 percent of companies offering an HMO and 13 percent of employees choosing this type of plan. POS and EPO plans are least popular, with 13 percent and 7 percent of companies offering them and 6 percent and 3 percent of employees enrolling, respectively (SHRM 2017).

Exhibit 9.9

Comparison of HMO, PPO, POS, and EPO Plans

Plan Type	PPO	EPO	POS	HMO
Out-of-network benefits	Yes	No	Yes	No
Primary care physician required	No	Sometimes	Yes	Yes
Referral required to see a specialist	No	No	Sometimes	Yes
Flexibility	Highest	High	Medium	Low
Cost	Highest	High	Medium	Low
Preauthorization required	Usually	Usually	No	No
2015 median annual in-network deductible	$1,000	$1,000	$1,000	$300
2015 median annual out-of-network deductible	$2,000	$700	$2,000	$0

Source: Data from SHRM (2017).

EXHIBIT 9.10
Shares of Network
Types Offered
by Employers
and Used by
Employees

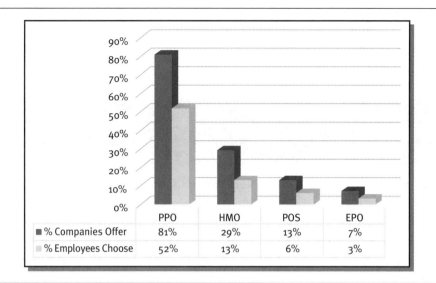

	PPO	HMO	POS	EPO
■ % Companies Offer	81%	29%	13%	7%
% Employees Choose	52%	13%	6%	3%

Source: SHRM (2017).

THE FUTURE OF HEALTH INSURANCE

The future of health insurance remains anyone's guess. The nation's political leaders espouse radically different solutions to address the problems inherent in our current system of health insurance. Among the many proposals for reforming healthcare, three options stand out: (1) businesses taking more responsibility for health insurance; (2) healthcare providers and insurance companies working together to create new health insurance options; and (3) government-provided health insurance for all.

A number of companies are taking action to address burgeoning healthcare costs. In early 2018, three of the biggest companies in the United States employing more than 1 million people—Amazon, Berkshire Hathaway, and JPMorgan—announced that they were forming an alliance to "create a company free from profit-making incentives and constraints . . . that will provide US employees and their families with simplified, high-quality and transparent healthcare at a reasonable cost." This effort could take out the middleman and may lead to the launch of new insurance company (Bomey and Weise 2018). Others call for businesses to eliminate insurance companies as intermediaries and contract directly with healthcare providers (Miller 2019).

Healthcare providers and others are also taking actions to change existing insurance relationships. These might involve providers, pharmacies, and insurers merging or providers building their own insurance companies and providing specialized offerings such as concierge medicine or direct primary care.

A number of healthcare systems have gone into the insurance business, and many more may do so. In 2017, more than 100 health systems operated insurance plans, more are considering this option (Keckley 2017). Other healthcare companies, such as CVS, are partnering with insurance companies such as Aetna to seek efficiencies and to provide more effective healthcare (see sidebar).

 CVS MERGES WITH AETNA

> Will the merger of insurance companies and pharmacy companies help solve our health-care crisis? In November 2018, CVS, with its 9,700 pharmacies and 1,100 walk-in clinics, merged with Aetna, the nation's third-largest health insurance company. The merger proposed to lower drug prices and make care more effective by establishing primary care clinics at pharmacies. This merger was unique in that it crossed industry sectors and realigned previously competing business incentives. Some felt that the merger was a defensive strategy to head off new Amazon ventures in healthcare. However, analysts feel that CVS's knowledge of consumer behavior will help the company meet healthcare consumers' needs and achieve its mission of "helping people on their path to better health" (Binder 2018; CVS 2018).

concierge medicine
A model of healthcare in which patients pay an annual fee or retainer to be a part of a primary care physician's practice. Patients receive greater physician access and enhanced services. The physician may bill the patient's health insurance.

Specialized Healthcare Options

Two specialized options mentioned earlier include **concierge medicine** and **direct primary care (DPC)**. In concierge medicine, physician practices charge patients a flat fee (monthly or annually) for "enhanced" services and greater access to healthcare. These enhanced services may include same-day access to a doctor, online consultations, unlimited office visits with no copay, free prescription refills, house calls, and preventive care services. Most concierge medicine services also bill patients' insurance.

Concierge practices generally charge fees beginning at $175 a month, but some charge upwards of $5,000 per year. Most practices that move to concierge medicine keep only 15 to 35 percent of their existing patients, about 300 to 600 patients. The rest of their patients, up to 3,500 people, must find care with another physician (Colwell 2016; Schwartz 2017).

direct primary care (DPC)
A model of healthcare in which patients pay a flat membership fee for a package of primary care services. The physician does not bill the patient's health insurance.

Direct primary care is similar to concierge medicine in that patients pay a monthly or annual fee for enhanced services and access. DPC differs from concierge medicine, however, as practices do not bill insurance for medical visits, and generally no third party (i.e., insurance company) is involved. Therefore, all of the work associated with billing, claims, and coding is eliminated. DPC services generally include basic lab tests, vaccinations, and generic drugs at near cost. Practices using both of these models derive most of their revenues from membership fees and generally experience an increase in profitability (Qamar 2014). DPC practices tend to charge a bit less, with monthly fees around $100. DPC practices have larger patient panels of 600 to 800 per physician (Colwell 2016).

Some studies suggest that these models provide better care. A study of concierge medicine showed that patients using this model of care decreased hospital use, with 56 percent fewer nonelective admissions and more than 90 percent fewer readmissions (Goodman 2014). Another study indicated that patients in a DPC model had 27 percent fewer emergency room visits and 60 percent fewer hospital days, and their healthcare cost their employers 20 percent less (Beck 2017).

VALUE-BASED PAYMENTS

Most insurance products (private and government provided) are shifting from fee-for-service payment arrangements to value-based payments for healthcare services. *Value-based payment* seeks to improve quality while promoting cost-efficient care. This is done by altering incentives to focus on value by rewarding better health outcomes and lower spending. Often coinsurance is lower for high-value services such as preventive care, medications for chronic diseases, and emergency care. Providers are reimbursed at higher rates for improved quality of care and better patient health outcomes. Some insurance companies, such as Humana, have noted a 20 percent decrease in spending as a result of implementing value-based models (Gruessner 2017; Sanicola 2017).

(✴) VALUE-BASED PAYMENT SYSTEMS CONTINUE TO GROW

Are value-based payment systems the way of the future? By 2014, about 40 percent of private insurance payments to physicians and hospitals included a quality component as a factor in the provider's compensation, compared with less than 3 percent in 2010. Insurance companies are now holding providers accountable for their patients' health and moving away from traditional fee-for-service medicine. The Centers for Medicare & Medicaid Services is also committed to moving healthcare to value-based payments (Zimlich 2017). Value-based payment systems provide incentives for greater collaboration among healthcare providers and encourage more efficient, effective care. Yet changing healthcare's structures and professional relationships remains a challenge.

SINGLE-PAYER SYSTEM

Many people in the United States believe that the country should move toward a **single-payer system** for healthcare, which effectively could eliminate most health insurance companies and establish a single entity to coordinate health insurance (Fuchs 2018). Single-payer systems exist in countries such as South Korea and Canada. A large portion of the US population and some physician and nursing groups support single-payer plans, which is also referred to as "Medicare for all." A single-payer system is projected to reduce healthcare spending by about $600 billion by reducing administrative and pharmaceutical costs. However, political pressures and opposition from affected businesses, coupled with large potential tax increases, may prevent the implementation of such a system in the United States (Adamczyk 2017; Physicians for a National Health Program 2018).

SUMMARY

Health insurance in the United States is complex and increasingly expensive. Health insurance exists to help people pay for their medical expenses. Any type of insurance transfers risk from an individual to a group of people, called a risk pool. Everyone in the risk pool contributes money (in the form of premiums) that covers all of the members for a given risk. Health insurance was first offered in the United States in the 1920s and became common in the 1950s and 1960s. Initially, most companies offering health insurance were not-for-profit companies. Since the 1990s, most insurance companies are for-profit firms.

Health insurance traditionally was based on an indemnity, fee-for-service model. This model allows patients to choose their own providers, and the insurance company pays for the services that are used. Today, however, almost all insurance products are based on a managed care model that directs patients to networks of providers and reviews and manages cost and use.

Premiums for health insurance are set by one of two methods: community rating or experience rating. Community rating uses the general community population as the risk pool to establish premiums. Everyone in the community pays the same premium. Experience rating, however, clusters people by their health history, age, gender, and other factors. Those with greater healthcare needs pay higher premiums than those who are healthier.

Most health insurance plans require enrollees to pay some out-of-pocket costs, coinsurance, copays, and deductibles. Out-of-pocket expenses are costs that individuals pay above and beyond their insurance premiums. Coinsurance and copayments require individuals to pay a share of the cost for health services. Deductibles are the annual amount of healthcare expenses the insured must pay before the insurance starts covering medical costs. In addition, some health plans impose lifetime or annual limits.

Economic concepts that affect the provision of health insurance include adverse selection, moral hazard, medical loss ratios, and third-party payments. Each of these factors influences the use or misuse of healthcare services and insurance.

Almost half (44 percent) of health insurance premiums go toward prescription drugs and physician services. The average health insurance company spends about 21 percent of premiums on overhead operating costs and profits.

There are two types of health insurance: private health insurance and public or government-provided health insurance. More than half of Americans are covered by employer-provided health insurance; government insurance covers more than one-third of the population. The largest health insurance company in the United States is United Health Group, which earns revenues of $180 billion and covers more than 70 million enrollees. In total, the top five US insurers generate more than $430 billion a year in revenues and cover more than 160 million people.

People in the United States struggle with the high costs of healthcare. High medical bills are the most common reason for personal bankruptcy. The uninsured tend to pay much more for healthcare services than the insured.

Health reimbursement accounts (HRAs), health savings accounts (HSAs), and flexible spending accounts (FSAs) exist to help individuals pay for out-of-pocket costs, coinsurance, copays, deductibles, and other approved healthcare expenses. Contributions to these accounts typically are tax exempt.

Businesses can either be fully insured or self-insured. A company that is fully insured provides a traditional health insurance plan in which the company pays a fixed premium to an insurance firm for coverage of its employees; the insurance company assumes the risk for medical costs. Self-insured companies provide their own healthcare plan and retain financial responsibility for all employee healthcare costs. To minimize the risk of large losses, self-insured companies may buy stop-loss insurance. Some self-insured companies employ a third-party administrator to perform administrative services such as claims processing.

Most health insurance plans use some type of network, such as a health maintenance organization (HMO), preferred provider organization (PPO), point-of-service (POS) plan, or exclusive provider organization (EPO). These networks are formed to control costs and monitor quality. HMOs tend to be the most restrictive networks but have lower deductibles. More than half of employees in the United States are insured through a PPO.

The future of health insurance remains uncertain. Businesses are creating new models to address the problems inherent in our current system of health insurance. Likewise, healthcare providers and insurance companies are evolving to streamline care. Specialty care options such as concierge medicine and direct primary care have emerged. Most insurance companies are shifting from fee-for-service payment arrangements to value-based payment. Finally, some recommend the introduction of a single-payer system to coordinate health insurance.

QUESTIONS

1. Why is it important to know the risk pool for health insurance?
2. What is the purpose of health insurance?
3. What are the downsides of traditional indemnified health insurance plans? Why have most insurers shifted to managed care?
4. What are the advantages and disadvantages of community rating and experience rating to set health insurance premiums?
5. What causes adverse selection in health insurance?
6. Does moral hazard exist in healthcare?
7. How is a medical loss ratio determined?
8. How does having health insurance improve a person's health?
9. What are the differences between health reimbursement accounts, health savings accounts, and flexible spending accounts?
10. Why would a business want to be self-insured rather than fully insured?

ASSIGNMENTS

1. Take the Kaiser Family Foundation's Health Insurance Quiz at www.kff.org/quiz/health-insurance-quiz/.
   a. How did you score?
   b. What questions did you get wrong?
2. Kristi has a high annual deductible of $3,000. She falls from a loft and breaks her hip and arm. She visits an emergency room and has surgery, both at a hospital that is part of her insurance plan's network. The total costs are $13,000. Her plan also has a 20 percent coinsurance and a $10,000 annual out-of-pocket limit.

   Trevor is insured through his father's university healthcare plan, which requires no coinsurance or deductible. He pays a $25 copay per physician visit if services are provided in the network, but 25 percent coinsurance and a $350 deductible for services provided out of the network. Trevor has surgery on his wrist that is billed at $12,000 for the hospital and doctor. Trevor used in-network services and had three doctor visits.
   a. What out-of-pocket expenses do Kristi and Trevor incur?
   b. How much would Trevor have paid out of pocket if he had chosen to use an out-of-network service?

ANTHEM'S AVOIDABLE EMERGENCY ROOM POLICY

Anthem, one of the largest healthcare insurers in the United States, implemented an "avoidable ER" policy to help manage the care of its enrollees. The policy stated that Anthem would not pay for emergency room visits if the company determined that the visit was not necessary. The policy, which was instituted in six states beginning in 2015, was meant to encourage patients to seek care in appropriate settings. However, providers feel that this policy might cause patients to avoid emergency treatment, even when it is necessary. In response to customer and provider complaints, Anthem created several exceptions: Claims will be covered if a healthcare provider tells a patient to go to the emergency room, if the patient is under 15 years of age, if the patient is outside his or her state of residence, and if the patient had a CT scan or MRI or underwent surgery. Still, providers are unhappy with the policy (Livingston 2018).

Discussion Questions

1. Why did Anthem implement this policy?
2. How is this policy an example of managed care?
3. What other solutions could be used to minimize costs but ensure access and quality?

THE CONFUSION OF MARKETPLACE HEALTHCARE COVERAGE

Cyndee has been on five insurance plans in five years. Her job does not offer health insurance. Each year, after finally figuring out her plan's deductibles, network, and covered drugs, she has gotten a cancellation notice. Although the Affordable Care Act (ACA) has helped by setting up a market-based system, plans continue to drop out and eliminate preferred doctors and hospitals from their networks. Even when insurers stay in a market, they frequently redesign their plans to raise out-of-pocket costs and lower drug coverage.

Fewer than half of those who purchased individual coverage in 2014 kept the same plan the following year. In 2018, the situation was complicated by large premium increases and a mistaken belief that the federal government had fully or partially repealed the ACA. In addition, the average number of insurance companies selling on the individual marketplace fell from 5.0 to 3.5.

About one-quarter of low-income adults report that they switched health insurance coverage in the previous 12 months. Half of them had gaps in coverage, leading to skipped medications and poorer health outcomes. This is opposite of what the ACA intended; the law aimed to stabilize healthcare coverage and promote continuous preventive care and better health.

After Cyndee's primary care physician left her plan's network this year, she has struggled to find a new one. Although she continues to take some of her medications, she worries that if she goes to a new doctor, she might have to change her medications, or her medications may not be covered (Hancock 2017).

Discussion Questions

1. Why do you think Cyndee has had to change her health insurance plan so many times?
2. Why have premiums increased so much?
3. What would you recommend Cyndee do?

REFERENCES

Abelson, R. 2019. "Employer Health Insurance Is Increasingly Unaffordable, Study Finds." *New York Times*. Published September 25. www.nytimes.com/2019/09/25/health/employer-health-insurance-cost.html.

Adamczyk, A. 2017. "What Is Single-Payer Healthcare and Why Is It So Popular?" *Time*. Published April 13. time.com/money/4733018/what-is-single-payer-healthcare-system/.

Allen, E. 2016. "Paying the Doctor in 18th-Century Philadelphia." *Library of Congress Blog*. Published April 28. https://blogs.loc.gov/loc/2016/04/paying-the-doctor-in-18th-century-philadelphia/.

Alonso-Zaldivar, R. 2017. "Frustration Mounts over Premiums for Affordable Care Act Individual Health Plans." *Denver Post*. Published September 3. www.denverpost.com/2017/09/03/obamacare-individual-health-plan-premium-increases/.

Amadeo, K. 2018. "Donald Trump on Healthcare: How Trump Is Dismantling Obamacare." The Balance. Published January 11. www.thebalance.com/how-could-trump-change-health-care-in-america-4111422.

America's Health Insurance Plans (AHIP). 2018. "Where Does Your Premium Dollar Go?" Published March 2. www.ahip.org/wp-content/uploads/2017/03/HealthCareDollar_FINAL.pdf.

Beck, M. 2017. "With Direct Primary Care, It's Just Doctor and Patient." *Wall Street Journal*, February 27.

Belk, D. 2017. "Hidden Costs: A View of Healthcare Costs from the Inside." The True Cost of Healthcare. Accessed June 9, 2020. http://truecostofhealthcare.org/introduction/.

Binder, L. 2018. "After Another Merger Monday in Healthcare, CVS Is Still the Company to Watch in 2018." *Forbes*. Published January 23. www.forbes.com/sites/leahbinder/2018/01/23/after-another-merger-monday-in-health-care-cvs-is-still-the-company-to-watch-in-2018/#3dc0be14d7cb.

Blumberg, A., and A. Davidson. 2009. "Accidents of History Created U.S. Health System." National Public Radio. Published October 22. www.npr.org/templates/story/story.php?storyId=114045132.

Bluth, R. 2019. "Surprise Medical Bills Are Driving People into Debt: Will Congress Act to Stop Them?" National Public Radio. Published May 22. www.npr.org/sections/health-shots/2019/05/22/725796114/surprise-medical-bills-are-driving-people-into-debt-will-congress-act-to-stop-th.

Bomey, N., and E. Weise. 2018. "4 Ways Amazon-Berkshire-JP Morgan Deal Could Shake Up Healthcare." *USA Today*. Published January 30. www.usatoday.com/story/money/2018/01/30/amazon-berkshire-hathaway-jpmorgan-health-care-deal-could-shake-up-health-care/1078823001/.

Cedars-Sinai. 2017. "Study: Health Insurance Could Be a Matter of Life and Death." *Cedars-Sinai Blog*. Published June 27. https://blog.cedars-sinai.edu/study-health-insurance-matter-life-death/.

Centers for Medicare & Medicaid Services (CMS). 2020. "NHE Fact Sheet." Updated March 24. www.cms.gov/Research-Statistics-Data-and-Systems/Statistics-Trends-and-Reports/ NationalHealthExpendData/NHE-Fact-Sheet.

Colwell, J. 2016. "Concierge Medicine Becomes an Option in Reform Era." Medical Economics. Published August 10. www.medicaleconomics.com/medical-economics-blog/ concierge-medicine-becomes-option-reform-era.

Consumer Reports. 2019. "Blue Cross and Blue Shield: A Historical Compilation." Accessed June 9, 2020. https://advocacy.consumerreports.org/wp-content/uploads/2013/03/ yourhealthdollar.org_blue-cross-history-compilation.pdf.

Cox, C., R. Fehr, and L. Levitt. 2019. "Individual Market Performance in 2018." Kaiser Family Foundation. Published May 7. www.kff.org/private-insurance/issue-brief/ individual-insurance-market-performance-in-2018/.

Cubanski, J., W. Koma, A. Damico, and T. Neuman. 2019. "How Much Do Medicare Beneficiaries Spend Out of Pocket on Health Care?" Kaiser Family Foundation. Published November 4. www.kff.org/medicare/issue-brief/how-much-do-medicare-beneficiaries-spend-out-of-pocket-on-health-care/.

CVS. 2018. "CVS Health Completes Acquisition of Aetna, Marking the Start of Transforming the Consumer Health Experience." Published November 28. https://cvshealth.com/ newsroom/press-releases/cvs-health-completes-acquisition-of-aetna-marking-the-start-of-transforming-the-consumer-health-experience.

Foutz, J., E. Squires, R. Garfield, and A. Damico. 2017. *The Uninsured: A Primer*. Kaiser Family Foundation. Published December. http://files.kff.org/attachment/Report-The-Uninsured-A-Primer-Key-Facts-about-Health-Insurance-and-the-Uninsured-Under-the-Affordable-Care-Act.

Fuchs, V. 2018. "Is Single Payer the Answer for the U.S. Healthcare System?" *JAMA* 319(1): 15–16.

Garfield, R., K. Orgera, and A. Damico. 2019. "The Uninsured and the ACA." Kaiser Family Foundation. Published January 25. www.kff.org/report-section/the-uninsured-and-the-aca-a-primer-key-facts-about-health-insurance-and-the-uninsured-amidst-changes-to-the-affordable-care-act-what-are-the-financial-implications-of-lacking-insu/.

Gee, E. 2019. "The High Price of Hospital Care." Center for American Progress. Published June 26. www.americanprogress.org/issues/healthcare/reports/2019/06/26/471464/high-price-hospital-care/.

Goldsmith, J., D. Mosley, and A. Jacobs. 2018. "Medicaid Managed Care: Lots of Unanswered Questions." *Health Affairs Blog*. Published May 3. www.healthaffairs.org/do/10.1377/hblog20180430.387981/full/.

Goodman, J. 2014. "Everyone Should Have a Concierge Doctor." *Forbes*. Published August 28. www.forbes.com/sites/johngoodman/2014/08/28/everyone-should-have-a-concierge-doctor/#612cba3b6323 .

Gruessner, V. 2017. "Humana, Aetna, Cigna Invest in Value-Based Care Payment Models." HealthPayer Intelligence. Published January 6. https://healthpayerintelligence.com/news/humana-aetna-cigna-invest-in-value-based-care-payment-models.

Haberkorn, J. 2010. "Medical Loss Ratios." Health Policy Brief. Published November 12. www.healthaffairs.org/do/10.1377/hpb20101112.449011/full/healthpolicybrief_30.pdf.

Haefner, M. 2019. "America's Largest Health Insurers in 2018." Becker's Healthcare. Published January 10. www.beckershospitalreview.com/payer-issues/america-s-largest-health-insurers-in-2018.html.

Hancock, J. 2017. "Churning, Confusion and Disruption—The Dark Side of Marketplace Coverage." Kaiser Health News. Published December 7. https://khn.org/news/churning-confusion-and-disruption-the-dark-side-of-marketplace-coverage.

HealthCare.gov. 2020a. "Health Insurance: How It Protects You from Health and Financial Risks." Accessed June 9. www.healthcare.gov/why-coverage-is-important/coverage-protects-you/.

———. 2020b. "Health Savings Account (HSA)." Accessed June 9. www.healthcare.gov/glossary/health-savings-account-hsa/.

HealthInsurance.org. 2020. "ACA's 2019 Medical Loss Ratio Debates." Published April 20. www.healthinsurance.org/obamacare/acas-2019-medical-loss-ratio-rebates/.

Herman, B. 2016. "What, Me Buy Insurance? How the Slow Uptake by 'Young Invincibles' Is Driving the ACA's Exchange Rates Higher." *Modern Healthcare*. Published May 14. www.modernhealthcare.com/article/20160514/MAGAZINE/305149980.

Hoadley, J., K. Lucia, and M. Kona. 2019. "State Efforts to Protect Consumers from Balance Billing." Commonwealth Fund. Published January 19. www.commonwealthfund.org/blog/2019/state-efforts-protect-consumers-balance-billing.

Hunt, J. 2019. "Average Cost of an ER Visit." The Balance. Published March 12. www.thebalance.com/average-cost-of-an-er-visit-4176166.

Kaiser Family Foundation. 2020. "KFF Health Tracking Poll: The Public's Views on the ACA." Published May 27. www.kff.org/interactive/kff-health-tracking-poll-the-publics-views-on-the-aca/#?response=Favorable—Unfavorable&aRange=twoYear.

———. 2019. "Health Insurance Quiz." Accessed June 9, 2020. www.kff.org/quiz/health-insurance-quiz/.

———. 2017. "Summary of the Affordable Care Act." Published March. http://files.kff.org/attachment/Summary-of-the-Affordable-Care-Act.

———. 2012. "Focus on Health Reform: Health Insurance Market Reforms: Rate Restrictions." Kaiser Family Foundation. Published June. www.kff.org/wp-content/uploads/2013/01/8328.pdf.

Keckley, P. 2017. "The Healthcare System in 2018: Combat Zones to Watch." *The Healthcare Blog*. Published December 29. http://thehealthcareblog.com/blog/2017/12/29/the-health-care-system-in-2018-combat-zones-to-watch/.

Keith, K. 2019. "Uninsured Rate Rose in 2018, Says Census Bureau Report." *Health Affairs Blog*. Published September 11. www.healthaffairs.org/do/10.1377/hblog20190911.805983/full/.

Kenen, J. 2017. "The Stealth Repeal of Obamacare." Politico. Published December 19. www. politico.com/story/2017/12/19/obamacare-repeal-tax-bill-trump-243912.

Kirzinger, A., C. Muñana, and M. Brodie. 2019. "KFF Health Tracking Poll—July 2019: The Future of the ACA and Possible Changes to the Current System, Preview of Priorities Heading into 2nd Democratic Debate." Kaiser Family Foundation. Published July 30. www.kff. org/health-reform/poll-finding/kff-health-tracking-poll-july-2019/.

Kliff, S. 2019. "A $20,243 Bike Crash: Zuckerberg Hospital's Aggressive Tactics Leave Patients with Big Bills." Vox. Published January 7. www.vox.com/policy-and-politics/ 2019/1/7/18137967/er-bills-zuckerberg-san-francisco-general-hospital.

Klinger, L. 2017. "MLR Rebates 2017." Leavitt Group. Published October 10. https://news. leavitt.com/health-care-reform/medical-loss-ratio-and-rebates/mlr-rebates-2017/.

Kordonowy, R. 2019. "Reduce Senior Healthcare Costs by Reducing Third-Party Payers." *Sunshine State News*. Published July 24. www.sunshinestatenews.com/story/reduce-senior-healthcare-costs-reducing-third-party-payers.

Lawley Insurance. 2015. "Community Rated Versus Experience Rated? What It Means to Your Business' Employee Benefits." Published September 1. www.lawleyinsurance.com/ employee-benefits/community-rated-versus-experience-rated-what-it-means-to-your-businesss-employee-benefits/.

Lee, K. J. 2017. "Here's How to Reduce Healthcare Costs." Medical Economics. Published May 9. www.medicaleconomics.com/medical-economics-blog/heres-how-reduce-healthcare-costs.

Livingston, S. 2018. "Anthem Makes Changes to Controversial ED Program." *Modern Healthcare*. Published February 15. www.modernhealthcare.com/article/20180215/ NEWS/180219946/anthem-makes-changes-to-controversial-ed-program.

Mankiw, G. 2017. "Why Healthcare Policy Is So Hard." *New York Times*. Published July 28. www.nytimes.com/2017/07/28/upshot/why-health-care-policy-is-so-hard.html.

Medscape. 2019. "Collecting Effectively from Third-Party Payers and Patients." Accessed October 7. www.medscape.com/courses/section/870036.

Merhar, C. 2016. "Fully-Insured vs. Self-Insured (Self-Funded) Health Plans." PeopleKeep. Published February 4. www.zanebenefits.com/blog/fully-insured-vs-self-insured-self-funded-health-plans.

Meyer, H. 2019. "Kansas Bypasses Obamacare; Will Other States Follow?" *Modern Health-care*. Published April 23. www.modernhealthcare.com/insurance/kansas-bypasses-obamacare-will-other-states-follow.

Miller, S. 2019. "Small and Midsize Employers Can Contract with Health Providers." Society for Human Resource Management. Published May 9. www.shrm.org/resourcesandtools/hr-topics/benefits/pages/small-midsize-employers-contract-with-health-providers.aspx.

———. 2018. "Employers Hold Down Health Plan Cost for 2019." Society for Human Resource Management. Published September 20. www.shrm.org/resourcesandtools/hr-topics/benefits/pages/employers-hold-down-health-plan-costs-for-2019.aspx.

———. 2017. "2018 FSA Contribution Cap Rises to $2,650." Society for Human Resource Management. Published October 23. www.shrm.org/resourcesandtools/hr-topics/benefits/pages/2018-fsa-contribution-limits.aspx.

Minemyer, P. 2019. "Here's How the Top Insurers Performed in the 2nd Quarter of 2019." Fierce Healthcare. Published August 23. www.fiercehealthcare.com/payer/big-8-health-insurers-q3-results.

Modern Healthcare. 2019. "Identifying and Addressing Common Medical Billing Errors Pre- and Post-Payment." Published August 29. www.modernhealthcare.com/finance/identifying-addressing-common-medical-billing-errors-pre-post-payment.

Mohamadloo, A., S. Zarein-Dolab, A. Ramezankhani, and J. Jamshid. 2019. "The Main Fac-tors of Induced Demand for Medicine Prescription: A Qualitative Study." *Iranian Journal of Pharmaceutical Research* 18 (1): 479–87.

Norris, L. 2018. "Billions in ACA Rebates Show 80/20 Rule's Impact." HealthInsurance. org. Published January 15. www.healthinsurance.org/obamacare/billions-in-aca-rebates-show-80-20-rules-impact/.

Olen, H. 2018. "Our Healthcare System Is Still a Mess. Trump Isn't Doing Anything Serious About It." *Washington Post*. Published January 29. www.washingtonpost.com/blogs/plum-line/wp/2018/01/29/our-health-care-system-is-still-a-mess-trump-isnt-doing-anything-serious-about-it/?utm_term=.0695f7353ef6.

Olivero, M. 2016. "Why Do You Need Health Insurance?" *U.S. News & World Report*. Published November 1. https://health.usnews.com/health-care/health-insurance/articles/2016-11-01/why-do-you-need-health-insurance.

Orszag, P., and E. Emanuel. 2018. "Out-of-Pocket Health Costs Are Rising, but Not That Much." Bloomberg News. Published January 4. www.bloomberg.com/view/articles/2018-01-04/out-of-pocket-health-costs-are-rising-but-not-that-much.

Pennsylvania State University. 2017. "Penn State Selects New Third-Party Administrators for Healthcare Benefits." Published August 17. http://news.psu.edu/story/478022/2017/08/17/administration/penn-state-selects-new-third-party-administrators-health-care.

Physicians for a National Health Program. 2018. "Beyond the Affordable Care Act: A Physicians' Proposal for Single-Payer Healthcare Reform." Accessed June 11, 2020. www.pnhp.org/nhi.

Qamar, S. 2014. "Direct Primary Care and Concierge Medicine: They're Not the Same." KevinMD.com. Published August 24. www.kevinmd.com/blog/2014/08/direct-primary-care-concierge-medicine-theyre.html.

Rappleye, E. 2015. "25 Things to Know About Blue Cross Blue Shield." *Becker's Hospital Review*. Published June 10. www.beckershospitalreview.com/payer-issues/25-things-to-know-about-blue-cross-blue-shield.html.

Rau, J. 2019. "Nearly Half of Nonprofit Hospital Owners Charge Poor Patients Who Qualify for Charity Care." ABC News. Published October 14. https://abcnews.go.com/Health/half-nonprofit-hospital-owners-charge-poor-patients-qualify/story?id=66261823.

Rosenthal, E. 2017. *An American Sickness*. New York: Penguin.

Sanicola, L. 2017. "What Is Value-Based Care?" Huffington Post. Published February 2. www.huffingtonpost.com/entry/what-is-value-based-care_us_58939f9de4b02bbb1816b892.

Santerre, R., and S. Neun. 2012. *Health Economics: Theory, Insights, and Industry Analysis*, 6th ed. Mason, OH: South-Western/Cengage Learning.

Sawyer, B., and G. Claxton. 2019. "How Do Expenditures Vary Across Populations?" Peterson-KFF Health System Tracker. Published January 16. www.healthsystemtracker.org/chart-collection/health-expenditures-vary-across-population/#item-start.

Schwartz, N. 2017. "The Doctor Is In. Co-Pay? $40,000." *New York Times*. Published June 3. www.nytimes.com/2017/06/03/business/economy/high-end-medical-care.html.

Society for Human Resource Management (SHRM). 2017. 2016 Healthcare Benchmarking Report. Published November. www.shrm.org/hr-today/trends-and-forecasting/research-and-surveys/Documents/2016-Health-Care-Report—All-Industries-All-FTEs.pdf.

Society of Actuaries. 2020. "Be an Actuary." Accessed June 11. www.beanactuary.org/what/?fa=fast-facts-about-actuaries.

Teitelbaum, J., and S. Wilensky. 2013. *Essentials of Health Policy and Law*, 2nd ed. Sudbury, MA: Jones & Bartlett.

Thimou, T. 2017. "How a Medical Billing Advocate Can Significantly Reduce Your Costs." Clark. Published January 31. https://clark.com/insurance/hire-medical-billing-specialist-advocate/.

US Census Bureau. 2018. *Health Insurance Coverage in the United States: 2017*. Published September. www.census.gov/content/dam/Census/library/publications/2018/demo/p60-264.pdf.

Wilensky, G., and L. Rossiter. 1983. "The Relative Importance of Physician-Induced Demand in the Demand for Medical Care." *Milbank Quarterly* 61 (2): 252–77.

Wooldridge, S. 2019. "Stop-Loss Catastrophic Claims Are on the Rise." Benefits Pro. Published October 21. www.benefitspro.com/2019/10/21/stop-loss-catastrophic-claims-are-on-the-rise/?slreturn=20191102170951.

Zimlich, R. 2017. "Value-Based Payment Update: Where We Are and Who Is Most Successful." *Managed Healthcare Executive*. November 16. www.managedhealthcareexecutive.com/benefit-design-and-pricing/value-based-payment-update-where-we-are-and-who-most-successful.

CHAPTER 10

THE QUALITY OF US HEALTHCARE

Walter went to the doctor to find out why he sometimes had a burning sensation in his lips and mouth after eating. His doctor recommended some tests to help diagnose the problem. One involved endoscopy, a procedure used to examine the upper gastrointestinal tract with a small camera attached to a flexible scope that goes down the throat. However, the physician used a scope that was too large and tore a small hole in Walter's esophagus, which was already constricted. Walter ended up in intensive care for ten days until his wound healed. During his stay, Walter's physicians discovered that the cause of the burning sensation was oral allergy syndrome, caused by allergies to foods or even pollen. Although he received the right diagnosis in the end, his endoscopy and certainly the hole in his esophagus could have been avoided.

Walter's story is not more or less important than any of the many stories related to patient safety and quality healthcare. Although Walter recovered from his torn esophagus, others are not so lucky. It is not uncommon for medical or surgical errors to cause death or significant impairment.

LEARNING OBJECTIVES

After reading this chapter, you will be able to

➤ Define healthcare quality from several perspectives.

➤ Be familiar with current healthcare quality initiatives.

➤ List the different types of sentinel events.

➤ Recognize key quality improvement tools.

➤ Understand how power relationships effect healthcare quality.

DEFINING QUALITY

Healthcare quality is a broad concept that encompasses factors such as value, efficacy, reliability, and outcomes (Godfrey 2012). The Institute of Medicine defined healthcare quality three decades ago as "the degree to which health services for individuals and populations increase the likelihood of desired health outcomes and are consistent with current professional knowledge" (Lohr 1990). This definition, however, does not explain how the different stakeholders in the healthcare industry view quality.

Some see quality as clinical outcomes, and others view it as service outcomes. For example, healthcare managers and policy experts might use data, metrics, and benchmarks to analyze clinical quality. They might ask, for instance, how many children have been vaccinated, or they might compare surgeons based on their surgical successes and failures, along with their techniques or equipment used. Another quality measure used by government is the number of patients who are readmitted to a hospital for care within a certain number of days or weeks.

Patients perceive healthcare quality as the quality of the services and facilities. Patients can easily judge the cleanliness of the hospital rooms, the friendliness of the nurses, the tastiness of the food, the availability of parking, how well their care is coordinated, the length of wait times, inclusion in decision-making, and whether their needs were met. These and other factors contribute to patients' perceptions of their experience and the quality of their care. Patients believe that they have received quality care when the following expectations are met (Flavin 2018):

- They feel understood.

- Their appointments are convenient.

- Their care is integrated.

- The facility maintains a calm atmosphere.

- Wait times are short.

- They understand what is happening and receive clear instructions.

- They feel sense of relationship with their providers.

CLINICAL QUALITY

Clinical quality refers to the quality of the treatment that a patient receives. The Institute of Medicine defines six domains or properties of healthcare quality (AHRQ 2018):

1. *Effectiveness* suggests the use of scientific evidence in the use of certain procedures and in achieving positive outcomes.

2.   *Efficiency* is the right amount of care for the best outcomes.

3.   *Equity* is providing equal care to all individuals.

4.   *Patient centeredness* means involving patients in decisions, meeting their needs, and educating them on the processes taking place.

5.   *Safety* is the idea of doing no harm or reducing potential harm.

6.   *Timeliness* means that individuals receive care as they need it.

However, physicians do not always agree on how policy experts should define and measure clinical quality. Some physicians argue that patients' outcomes are hard to compare, as individuals are very different from one another (Godfrey 2012). Some patients have more severe conditions. Some comply with the instructions they are given by their physicians or other healthcare providers, while others do not. Moreover, those with insurance or higher incomes may have access to better care than those who lack insurance or have lower incomes.

One way to measure clinical quality is to compare the expected health benefits of a particular intervention or procedure to its expected health risks. Some argue that poor clinical quality may occur when patients receive too much care (e.g., unnecessary testing, too many different drugs, risky procedures), too little care, or the wrong kinds of care (Schuster, McGlynn, and Brook 2005).

A number of data sources seek to demonstrate healthcare quality. For example, the Healthcare Effectiveness Data and Information Set (HEDIS) reports survey results from a sample of 184 million individuals enrolled in health insurance plans. These data provide measures across six domains: effectiveness of care, access to and availability of care, experience of care, utilization, health plan descriptive information, and measures collected using electronic clinical data systems. Results of the HEDIS survey are used to create "report cards" for health plans, healthcare providers, and healthcare organizations (NCQA 2020).

Another report of healthcare quality comes from the Centers for Medicare & Medicaid Services (CMS) in the form of clinical quality measures (CQMs), which include patient and family engagement, patient safety, care coordination, population/public health, efficient use of healthcare resources, and clinical process/effectiveness (CMS 2020a). The CQM process is an ongoing system for measuring a variety of factors related to quality. Experts or "contractors" define the topics of measurement, gather data, create panels of experts, obtain public comments, test hypotheses, and report results. The reported results relate to all phases of healthcare, including postacute care, home health, hospital quality, nursing homes, physicians, and even specific diseases (CMS 2019b).

(✱) SIDE EFFECTS CAUSE QUALITY FAILURE

Lewis Blackman was born with pectus excavatum—a crease in his chest cavity—a condition that occurs in 1 in 500 people. For many years, experts considered pectus excavatum merely a cosmetic issue, but more recent studies have suggested that it could cause respiratory problems. When Lewis was 15 years old, he and his parents were told that surgery could correct the condition, so they decided to move forward with it.

Following the surgery, Lewis showed signs of distress: He was not producing urine, his temperature dropped significantly, his pulse was rapid, his skin grew pale, and he was in tremendous pain. Nurses and inexperienced physicians failed to recognize the signs that he was having an adverse reaction to a painkiller. They also failed to respond to his mother's request that he be seen by a senior or attending physician.

Within four days of his surgery, Lewis died. The painkiller given to him had caused a perforated ulcer. His abdomen filled with three liters of blood and fluid—most of the blood in Lewis's body. Those who reviewed his case suggested that a routine blood test would have shown that Lewis was bleeding internally.

In the end, Lewis's parents tried to speak with the clinicians and administrators of the hospital where the surgery had been performed to share their ideas about how better communication with patients' families might prevent similar events. Their requests were not granted. The hospital reported that physicians, nurses, and other hospital officials were working together to make changes to procedures and protocols so that such a case does not happen again (Monk 2002).

The surgeon and Lewis's parents had different views of the quality issue that caused Lewis's death. From the parents' point of view, if the nurse or resident physician simply would have responded to their request to consult with a senior physician, Lewis's death may have been prevented. From the surgeon's point of view, this was a "one in a zillion case" (Monk 2002), because the blood from a bleeding ulcer like Lewis's normally passes into the gastrointestinal tract, where it is vomited or passed through the colon. Blood pooling in the abdomen was something the surgeon had never seen in another patient.

PATIENT PERCEPTIONS OF QUALITY

Patients and their families have a different perspective on healthcare quality. Patients often forgive disappointing clinical outcomes if they have had a positive clinical experience or received excellent service (Godfrey 2012). The Institute of Medicine recommends considering the consumer perspective by measuring key aspects of quality such as staying healthy, getting better, living with an illness or disability, and coping with the end of life (AHRQ 2018).

One patient-focused report card on quality is the Consumer Assessment of Healthcare Providers and Systems (CAHPS), which was first compiled in 1995. Healthcare providers today pay close attention to the results of this national report. CAHPS surveys focus on healthcare consumers' views of their healthcare experiences. Consumers rate areas such as the communication skills of their providers and the ease of accessing healthcare services (AHRQ 2020).

Another quality report that is specific to hospitals is the Hospital Consumer Assessment of Healthcare Providers and Systems (HCAHPS). Exhibit 10.1 lists some of the questions that this survey asks. As can be seen, the survey questions deal almost exclusively with service quality and patient satisfaction.

EXHIBIT 10.1

Selected Questions from the Hospital Consumer Assessment of Healthcare Providers and Systems

Survey Topic	Survey Question
How often did nurses communicate well with patients?	During this hospital stay . . . How often did nurses treat you with courtesy and respect? How often did nurses listen carefully to you? How often did nurses explain things in a way you could understand?
How often did doctors communicate well with patients?	During this hospital stay . . . How often did doctors treat you with courtesy and respect? How often did doctors listen carefully to you? How often did doctors explain things in a way you could understand?
How often did patients receive help quickly from hospital staff?	During this hospital stay . . . How often did you get help as soon as you wanted after you pressed the call button? How often did you get help in getting to the bathroom or in using a bedpan as soon as you wanted?
How often did staff explain about medicines before giving them to patients?	Before giving you any new medicine . . . How often did hospital staff tell you what the medicine was for? How often did hospital staff describe possible side effects in a way you could understand?
How often were the patients' rooms and bathrooms kept clean	During this hospital stay . . . How often were your room and bathroom kept clean?
How often was the area around patients' rooms kept quiet at night?	During this hospital stay . . . How often was the area around your room quiet at night?

(continued)

Exhibit 10.1

Selected Questions from the Hospital Consumer Assessment of Healthcare Providers and Systems *(continued)*

Survey Topic	Survey Question
Were patients given information about what to do during their recovery at home?	During this hospital stay . . . Did hospital staff talk with you about whether you would have the help you needed when you left the hospital? Did you get information in writing about what symptoms or health problems to look out for after you left the hospital?
How well did patients understand the type of care they would need after leaving the hospital?	During this hospital stay . . . Did hospital staff consider your healthcare options and wishes when deciding what kind of care you would need after leaving the hospital? Did you and/or your caregivers understand what you would have to do to take care of yourself after leaving the hospital? Did you know what medications you would be taking and why you would be taking them after leaving the hospital?
How do patients rate the hospital?	What number would you use to rate this hospital during your stay?
Would patients recommend the hospital to friends and family?	Would you recommend this hospital to your friends and family?

Source: Medicare.gov (2020).

Doctors and patients often have different perspectives on healthcare quality. Even a decade ago, researchers found that patients believed treatment to be the most important aspect of quality healthcare, but their views on the key components of treatment differed from those of physicians. Patients indicated that inclusion in the decision-making process, discussion of treatment options, and instruction and education on the chosen treatment were even more important than speed and outcomes (Regula et al. 2007).

Few studies, however, report on healthcare quality improvements made as a result of patient satisfaction surveys. However, it is clear that patients appreciate good interpersonal skills such as courtesy, respect, and clear explanations and information from their healthcare provider. These skills appear to be more essential to patients than clinical skills and high-tech hospital settings (Al-Abri and Al-Balushi 2014).

THE IRON TRIANGLE

Introduced by physician William Kissick in 1994, the "Iron Triangle" of Healthcare (discussed at length in chapter 1 and depicted again in exhibit 10.2) illustrates the competing priorities of access, cost, and quality. According to Kissick, these three factors necessarily

EXHIBIT 10.2

The Iron Triangle
of Healthcare

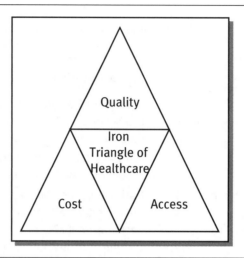

compete with one another—that is, a change in one factor must have an impact on the other two. For instance, the increased use of medical technology from World War II to the present has improved the quality of patient care, but it has also dramatically increased costs. Similarly, the Affordable Care Act (ACA), passed in 2010, has increased access to care for many people, but it has also contributed to increased costs for taxpayers.

Tom Godfrey (2012) compares the Iron Triangle to a tripod, suggesting that when one leg moves, the other two must be adjusted to keep the system balanced. This argument suggests that to get better-quality care and allow everyone to access it, costs must increase.

Access refers to the ability to obtain care when it is needed. Having health insurance or the means to pay for care dramatically increases access. However, where one lives also affects access to care. Those living in rural areas of the United States often struggle to access even primary care and likely have difficulty accessing specialist health professionals.

Not everyone agrees with Kissick's theory. Some argue that the best systems look for ways to displace existing markets, services, and alliances with a better model and that new technology should decrease cost, improve quality, and make services more accessible (Christensen, Bohmer, and Kenagy 2000). Ultrasound, for example, replaced X-ray technology in some cases, making such procedures easier and cheaper. Subsequently, existing X-ray companies did not participate in ultrasound until they saw its success and then acquired the technology (Christensen and Raynor 2003).

Some healthcare technology, such as telemedicine, is designed to increase access while potentially lowering costs and improving the quality of care. Telemedicine connects physicians and patients remotely through telecommunications and information technology. Telemedicine has been found to increase patients' access to care, and it also lowers hospital length of stay and costs (Castro, Miller, and Nager 2014).

Balancing access, cost, and quality remains a challenge for most healthcare organizations. Some believe that the shift to value-based care will require healthcare organizations to make the following changes (Aluko 2017):

1. Deliver transparent, quality outcomes for consumers and patients

2. Exercise cost management and cost transparency

3. Provide superior patient experiences with high patient satisfaction

The Institute for Healthcare Improvement's Triple Aim (discussed in chapter 1) seeks to address all three issues simultaneously.

INITIATIVES TO IMPROVE HEALTHCARE QUALITY

One of the most important initiatives to improve healthcare quality began with the Institute of Medicine's release of its report *America's Health in Transition: Protecting and Improving Quality* in 1996. The Institute concluded that a terrible quality problem existed—that "the burden of harm conveyed by the collective impact of all of our healthcare quality problems is staggering" (Chassin and Galvin 1998).

The publication of this report ignited work on assessing and improving the quality of healthcare across the United States. Subsequent efforts by the Institute of Medicine resulted in two widely read publications, *To Err is Human: Building a Safer Health System* (1999) and *Crossing the Quality Chasm: A New Health System for the 21st Century* (2001). These reports focused on needed change to healthcare policy and practice in the United States. From *To Err is Human*, many learned of the significant amount of medical errors occurring nationally. The publication reported on tens of thousands of Americans who were dying each year as a result of medical errors. The second report defined six aims and ten rules for how care should be delivered to improve quality of care.

Other national efforts have also attempted to improve healthcare quality. A few years prior to the first Institute of Medicine report, other experts founded the Institute for Healthcare Improvement (IHI), a national healthcare organization that is focused on improving healthcare in the United States. The IHI has published extensive research of exchanging knowledge and training physicians on best practices in healthcare quality improvement. The IHI's work has helped clinicians and other healthcare professionals form effective interprofessional teams to focus on improving healthcare delivery.

In the early 2000s, the IHI worked to change mainstream practice standards, launching what it called the "Triple Aim" (depicted in exhibit 10.3). The Triple Aim differs slightly from the Iron Triangle, as it focuses on the interdependencies of access, cost, and quality. The Triple Aim encourages healthcare organizations to focus concurrently on improving the patient experience of care, improving the health of populations, and reducing the per capita cost of healthcare.

Exhibit 10.3

The IHI Triple Aim

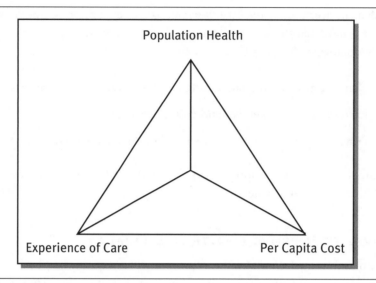

Exhibit 10.3

The IHI Triple Aim

✱ QUALITY IMPROVEMENT EFFORTS ARE ONGOING

Although quality improvement efforts helped decrease the number of hospital stays caused by adverse drug event (ADEs) in hospitals by 27.2 percent from 2010 to 2014, 465,000 ADEs still occurred each year during this period. Reactions to antibiotics and anti-infectives, systemic agents, and hormones were the most common causes of ADE-related hospital stays (Weiss et al. 2018).

The good news, according to the federal Office of Disease Prevention and Health Promotion, is that the large majority of ADEs are preventable. This office, together with other organizations, is working to reduce ADEs through a variety of measures. Surveillance, or tracking, ADEs is key. Prevention measures include provider and patient education and identification of high-priority risks. Incentives and oversight are efforts to provide quality measures, policies, and reward models. Finally, research continues to identify the patients who are at highest risk of ADEs and the most effective prevention strategies (ODPHP 2014).

The IHI pilot-tested the Triple Aim in more than 100 organizations around the world. These efforts promoted a quality process that includes identifying target populations, defining system aims and measures, developing projects strong enough to effect system-level results, then rapid testing and scale-up based on local needs and conditions (IHI 2020b).

Between 2010 and 2014, the IHI continued to focus on improving the health of populations and reducing per capita healthcare costs. In 2017, the IHI merged with the National Patient Safety Foundation and has accelerated its pace of healthcare improvement (IHI 2020a).

MEDICAL AND SURGICAL ERRORS

Supporting the Institute of Medicine's research, a Johns Hopkins University study showed that deaths attributable to medical errors in the United States exceed 250,000 per year. In 2016, that number would have been the third-leading cause of death in the United States (Johns Hopkins Medicine 2016).

The most common medical errors in hospitals are surgical errors. Errors in surgery can be catastrophic. The most common surgical errors include surgery on the wrong site or the wrong patient, the use of unsanitary equipment that causes infection, and improper surgery that damages a patient's organs and nerves (Rogers et al. 2006). Misdiagnosis or failure to diagnose a problem are the most frequent medical errors in outpatient settings (Wallace et al. 2013).

A leading contributor to medical errors is the interaction of communication and power. Studies indicate that one major reason for malpractice lawsuits is the breakdown of communication between the physician and the patient (Huntington and Kuhn 2003). Because patient satisfaction is crucial to healthcare quality, good communication is essential. Patients who have doctors who take the time to communicate about their care are satisfied patients; satisfied patients rarely file lawsuits (Carroll 2015).

The concept of **coproduction of healthcare** suggests that patients, families, and healthcare professionals need to work interdependently to co-create and co-deliver care. This means that patients should be well informed and educated. They should be actively involved in decisions related to their care and its assessment. Patients and families should work proactively with the care team to determine postacute care. Clear communication throughout the process is essential (Batalden et al. 2015): "Co-production is like a new lens on patient-centered care, because it can help providers more clearly see the potential of working with patients to create better healthcare" (Kaplan 2016).

The abuse of power creates conditions in which medical errors are more likely to occur. Power differences exist in all work settings, but in healthcare, physicians in particular

coproduction of healthcare
Collaboration between patients, families, and healthcare providers to co-create and co-deliver care.

are used to being the "captains of their ship." Clinicians who use their power appropriately can produce effective, positive healthcare outcomes. However, if this power is used inappropriately, communication and collaboration can break down within and across care teams, resulting in poor care. Power differences among healthcare providers, conflicting roles or role ambiguity, and interpersonal power conflicts are key sources of communication failures (Sutcliffe, Lewton, and Rosenthal 2004). Providers, staff, and patients may withhold or distort communication because of power differences. One person may perceive the other to be incompetent and therefore fail to communicate. Another might believe that a higher-status person is closed-minded (O'Daniel and Rosenstein 2008).

Research shows that effective communication results in better patient outcomes, greater patient satisfaction, and increased employee satisfaction (O'Daniel and Rosenstein 2008). Two techniques have been shown to be particularly effective in communication and quality care: SBAR and AIDET. The situation-background-assessment-recommendation, or SBAR, technique is a systematic framework for clinics to gather, assess, and share information. It allows nurses, for example, to assess and record changes in a patient's status and communicate key clinical information to the physician.

AIDET is a communication technique that is used directly with patients. In this process, the patient is *acknowledged* by his or her full name, as are family members and visitors in the room. The healthcare professionals then *identify* themselves and indicate their role. They make clear the steps of the procedure taking place and the *duration* of the procedure. The next step is to answer any questions and clearly *explain*. Finally, the healthcare worker *thanks* the individual for choosing the facility and summarizes the patient's visit (Burgener 2017).

✳ DEBATE TIME Rural Health and the Triple Aim

Hospitals in rural America are especially dependent on revenues from elective and non-emergency procedures. However, patients often have difficulty paying for this care. For some, such procedures must be paid for out of pocket because they are not covered by insurance. Transportation is a problem for some individuals, as is finding available appointments. Recruiting healthcare professionals is also tough in rural locations.

Considering the Triple Aim, discuss the provision of healthcare in rural America from three perspectives. First, what are the needs of the population? Consider, for example, maternal and other basic types of care. Second, with limited revenues, how does a small hospital cover costs? Third, how do hospital staff maintain or improve quality, especially when there is a limited workforce?

ACCREDITING ORGANIZATIONS

Healthcare organizations are inspected and accredited by a variety of accrediting bodies. Accreditation teams visit a healthcare organization to identify areas of improvement. Organizations that meet the set of standards established by the accrediting body are accredited. Accreditation is "a symbol of quality that reflects an organization's commitment to meeting certain performance standards" (The Joint Commission 2020a). The purpose of accreditation is to help providers to improve healthcare quality and to signal to the public that they meet the standards and regulations of a recognized external body.

The largest accrediting organization in the United States is **The Joint Commission**, which accredits around 88 percent of US hospitals (Jha 2018). Many healthcare organizations are required to have some form of external accreditation. For instance, the CMS requires hospitals receive accreditation from a recognized accrediting body or pass a state inspection to receive Medicare payments. In 2019, CMS had approved 11 different accrediting organizations (see exhibit 10.4).

The Joint Commission
The largest accrediting organization in the United States, which accredits about 88 percent of all US hospitals.

EXHIBIT 10.4
Accrediting Organizations Approved by the Centers for Medicare & Medicaid Services

Organization	Accredits	Website
Accreditation Association for Ambulatory Health Care	Ambulatory surgery centers	www.aaahc.org
Accreditation Commission for Health Care, Inc.	Home health, hospice	www.achc.org
American Association for Accreditation of Ambulatory Surgery Facilities	Ambulatory surgery centers, outpatient clinics	www.aaaasf.org
American Osteopathic Association/ Healthcare Facilities Accreditation Program	Ambulatory surgery centers, hospitals, clinical laboratories	www.hfap.org
Center for Improvement in Healthcare Quality	Hospitals	www.cihq.org
Community Health Accreditation Partner	Home health, hospice	www.chapinc.org
DNV GL – Healthcare	Hospitals	www.dnvglhealthcare.com
Institute for Medical Quality	Ambulatory surgery centers	www.img.org
National Dialysis Accreditation Commission	Dialysis facilities	www.ndacommission.com
The Compliance Team	Rural health clinics	www.thecomplianceteam.org
The Joint Commission	Ambulatory surgery centers, home health, hospice, hospitals	www.jointcommission.org

Source: CMS (2019a).

EXHIBIT 10.5
Ten Most Common
Sentinel Events
Reported to The
Joint Commission,
2018

Sentinel Event	Number Reported
Unintended retention of a foreign body	111
Falls	111
Wrong patient, wrong site, or wrong procedure	94
Suicide	50
Delays in treatment	43
Other unanticipated events*	59
Criminal events	28
Medication errors	24
Product or device events	29

* Includes asphyxiation, burns, choking, drowning, and being found unresponsive.
Source: The Joint Commission (2019a).

SENTINEL EVENTS

sentinel event
An event that
results in death or
serious physical or
psychological injury to
a patient.

The Joint Commission uses the term **sentinel event** to refer to occurrences that lead to a patient's death or serious injury, including psychological injury. Sentinel events also include the loss of a limb or function (The Joint Commission 2013). The Joint Commission collects data and reports on the most common sentinel events occurring each year. Hospitals voluntarily report these events, so the data may represent only a fraction of the events that actually take place. Exhibit 10.5 lists the ten most common sentinel events reported in 2018.

The Joint Commission determines the highest-priority patient safety issues and develops the National Patient Safety Goals to reduce or eliminate those concerns in hospitals, behavioral health facilities, home health care agencies, ambulatory healthcare settings, and critical access hospitals. The Joint Commission set the following goals for 2019 (The Joint Commission 2019b).

- *Identify patients correctly.* Use two identifiers, such as the patient's name and date of birth, to make sure the right patient gets the correct medicine and treatment.

- *Improve the effectiveness of communication among caregivers.* Get test and diagnostics results to the right people on a timely basis.

- *Improve the safety of using medications.* Label all medications and medication containers.

◆ *Use alarms safely.* Manage alarms to make sure they are heard and responded to on time.

◆ *Prevent infection.* Use hand-washing guidelines provided by the Centers for Disease Control and Prevention and the World Health Organization.

◆ *Identify patient safety risks.* Identify patients who are at risk for suicide.

◆ *Prevent mistakes in surgery.* Make certain that the correct surgery is done on the correct patient and at the correct place on the patient's body.

Hospitals bear the responsibility for eliminating sentinel events and improving patient safety. Hospitals should identify safety risks inherent in their patient populations (see sidebar).

(✱) THE CASE OF JOAN MORRIS

Joan Morris, a 67-year-old woman, was admitted to a teaching hospital for the treatment of two brain aneurysms. One was successfully treated with angiography; the other was to be treated surgically on an upcoming day. After the first procedure, Joan was taken to the wrong unit, rather than to the room she had been assigned. Then, Joan was mistaken for a woman with a similar name. On day two, Joan was given an invasive heart study—not the woman who should have received it. This happened even after Joan told the clinicians she did not want any further procedures to be done. About and hour into the study, it became clear to the clinicians that Joan was the wrong patient, and the study was stopped. The patient who actually needed the heart study was eventually treated. The entire event was replete with communication errors, and it was clearly a serious reportable event (Chassin and Becher 2002).

This is an example of a serious mistake that could have resulted in a deadly outcome. Had Joan's aneurysms not been treated, she could have had a stroke or even died. If the error had not been discovered, the other patient would not have received the heart study she needed.

Similar to The Joint Commission's sentinel events and National Patient Safety Goals is the list of preventable clinical events published by the National Quality Forum (NQF). This nonprofit group uses evidence-based measures and standards of care to develop a list of *serious reportable events* (also known as *never events*) to assess and report on the performance

Exhibit **10.6**
Serious Reportable
Event Categories
According to the
National Quality
Forum

1. Surgical or invasive procedure events such as surgery on the wrong site or performed on the wrong patient. Foreign objects left in the patient would also be included.
2. Product or device events include death associated with contaminated devices or drugs, germs or disease in the surgery rooms, and medical equipment that malfunctions.
3. If a patient is not capable of making decisions but is released to someone other than an authorized person that is included on the NQF list. So is death or injury associated with the patient disappearing. Suicide or attempted suicide while in a healthcare setting is included in this category.
4. Care management events include medication errors, death from unsafe blood products, maternal death from labor and delivery, artificial insemination with the wrong donor sperm or wrong egg, or death/serious injury from not communicating lab, pathology or diagnostic exam results.
5. Electrocution or electric shock, giving oxygen or the wrong gas, death or injury from burns, or injury from restraints are identified as environmental events.
6. Death or serious injury from MRI accidents is a category of its own.
7. Potential criminal events include care ordered by someone impersonating a clinician, abduction of a patient, sexual abuse or assault, and physical assault or battery at a healthcare setting.

Source: NQF (2020).

of healthcare organizations related to safe patient care. Exhibit 10.6 presents examples of serious reported events.

QUALITY IMPROVEMENT TOOLS

A number of well-established quality improvement tools exist. One prominent tool used by the IHI is called the Model for Improvement. This model asks questions such as "What are we trying to accomplish?" "How will we know that a change is an improvement?" and "What change can we make that will result in improvement?" (IHI 2020c). These questions serve as a starting point for other quality improvement tools.

Plan-Do-Study-Act
A four-step quality improvement process; also known as the *Deming Wheel.*

PLAN-DO-STUDY-ACT

The **Plan-Do-Study-Act** cycle (see exhibit 10.7), also known as the "Deming Wheel," was introduced to the management thinker W. Edwards Deming by his mentor, Walter Shewhart of Bell Laboratories in New York (W. Edwards Deming Institute 2020). The

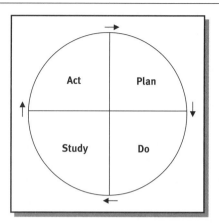

EXHIBIT 10.7
Plan-Do-Study-Act
Cycle

first step in the cycle, *Plan*, begins by answering the initial questions in the IHI's Model for Improvement. A goal or purpose is established, along with a method of defining and measuring success. The *Do* step puts the plan into action. During the *Study* step, data are gathered to gauge progress or success. The final step, *Act*, allows for the entrenchment of a successful result or a change in the goal, methods, or the entire process.

CAUSE-AND-EFFECT DIAGRAM

A **cause-and-effect diagram** graphically depicts the strategy for achieving a specific outcome (effect) and the factors that influence that outcome (causes). It is often referred to as a "fishbone diagram," because it resembles a fish skeleton (see exhibit 10.8 for an example). The first step is to identify a problem statement, shown in the box on the right-hand side of the diagram. Major causes of the problem, given generic headings, are then added as

*cause-and-effect
diagram*
A graphical depiction
of the strategy for
achieving a specific
outcome (effect)
and the factors that
influence that outcome
(causes); also known
as a *fishbone diagram*.

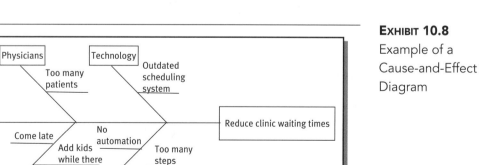

EXHIBIT 10.8
Example of a
Cause-and-Effect
Diagram

shown in the boxes. These causes can be anything, but in a classical design, they include materials, methods, equipment, environment, and people. Finally, causes are listed related to each category. Finally, all of the possible causes of the problem are added to the branches connected to the boxes (IHI 2017).

FLOWCHART

flowchart
A graphical depiction of a process that allows for the identification of problems and bottlenecks.

A **flowchart** is sometimes used to map out a process or a group of processes, clearly identifying each step. As shown in exhibit 10.9, ovals indicate the beginning and end of a process, and a box represents each activity or task. A diamond-shaped box is used to identify a decision point (yes or no). The visual presentation helps teams identify problems or bottlenecks and focus on areas of improvement (IHI 2017).

EXHIBIT 10.9
Example of a Simple Flowchart

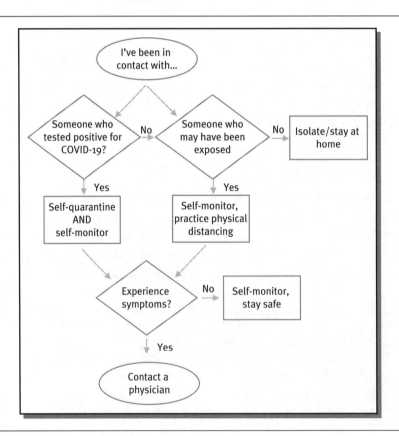

Pareto chart
A bar or line graph that allows for the identification of the causes that contribute to an overall effect.

PARETO CHART

The "Pareto principle" holds that for most events, 80 percent of the effects are caused by 20 percent of the causes; for this reason, it is also called the "80/20 rule" (IHI 2017). A **Pareto chart** allows for the identification of the causes that contribute to an overall effect.

EXHIBIT 10.10
Sources of
Medication Errors

Source of Error	Frequency	Percent	Cumulative Percent
Label/packaging	23	33.3	33.3
Medication dose	15	21.7	55.0
Medication preparation	12	17.5	72.5
Physician's prescription	8	11.6	84.1
Difficulties in using infusion devices	6	8.7	92.8
Nurse's physical exhaustion	5	7.2	100
Total	69		

EXHIBIT 10.11
Pareto Chart of
Medication Errors

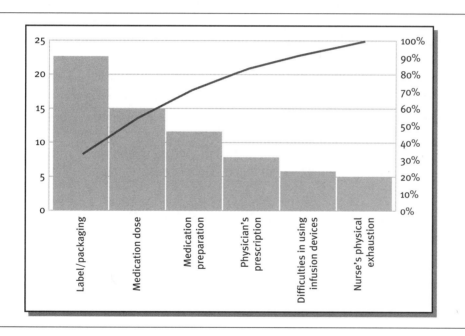

Teams use the information to address the factors causing the majority of the effect. A Pareto chart helps teams concentrate on matters of greatest impact. Exhibit 10.10 presents hypothetical data on sources of medication errors, and exhibit 10.11 uses those data to create a Pareto chart.

OTHER TOOLS

Many other quality improvement models and methodologies exist, such as root cause analysis, Six Sigma, Lean (Hughes 2008), and the change acceleration process, in addition to the many tools used within these methodologies, such as driver diagrams, failure modes and effects analysis, histograms, run and control charts, and scatter diagrams (IHI 2017). Many of the tools introduced in this chapter were created in other industries and adapted for use in healthcare to improve systems and processes, which typically are the causes of most medical errors rather than the behaviors of individual physicians or staff members. Many of these tools can be used together as part of a process improvement project. For instance, a fishbone diagram or Pareto chart might be used to identify some aspect of a process that needs improvement, and then PDSA can be employed to test improvement processes.

Such tools help identify the root causes of error, provide an understanding of the significance of error, track and monitor performance, and standardize successful protocols. Quality improvement tools can be used to make positive changes to faulty processes and enable organizations to implement effective solutions. These solutions might be as simple as a surgical time-out checklist to prevent surgical errors, or they may use sophisticated technology such as an automated pharmacy system. Process improvement tools provide constructive feedback, allowing organizations to accurately identify process issues and more effectively address quality and patient safety concerns (Hughes 2008).

Six Sigma approaches business processes improvement with qualitative and quantitative techniques to increase performance and reduce variation. These tools include statistical control charts, failure modes and effects analysis, and process mapping:

- *Statistical control charts.* Graphs used to study how a process changes over time. Graphs contain a central line for the average and upper and lower control limits.

- *Failure modes and effects analysis.* Analysis of the ways or modes that something might fail. Failures include errors and defects that can potentially impact a consumer.

- *Process mapping.* A tool that visually shows the flow of work and the series of events that produces a desired result.

Lean, which is often merged with Six Sigma to become Lean Six Sigma, seeks to reduce waste and increase value to the consumer. It identifies what adds value, enhances this, and seeks to reduce other actions and processes that do not add value. Lean focuses on areas such as transportation, inventory, motion, waiting, overproduction, overprocessing, and defects (Kanbanize 2019).

Benchmarking to both internal and external standards is another quality improvement tool. Benchmarking involves continual comparison to best performers (Gift and Mosel 1994). Internal benchmarking looks at the best outcomes internally and the processes involved in achieving them. External benchmarking allows for new ideas or practices that

Six Sigma
A business processes improvement method that uses qualitative and quantitative techniques to increase performance and reduce variation.

Lean
A method used to reduce waste and to increase value to the consumer by identifying what adds value, enhancing this, and seeking to reduce other actions and processes that do not add value.

benchmarking
A quality improvement tool in which an organization compares itself to some standard, often industry best practices.

have not yet been incorporated by a healthcare organization. It uses comparative data to judge performance and identify possible improvements (Hughes 2008).

   With all of these tools, surveys, and approaches to improved quality, some would say there is little evidence to suggest that many of the quality measures have led to significantly improved health outcomes. They would argue that to truly improve healthcare quality a greater focus on patient-centered outcomes needs to occur (Saver et al. 2015).

✴ HIGH-RELIABILITY ORGANIZATIONS

The US healthcare system has long been funded through a fee-for-service payment model that reimburses providers based on the amount of business they generate. This model encourages high-cost services that result in a high profit margin for the hospitals and physicians who offer them. With rising healthcare costs in mind, an effort is underway to promote better quality, reduced errors, and less business in the form of readmissions to hospitals or unnecessary care in settings like the emergency department.

   High-reliability organizations (HROs) are touted as a model to provide consistent quality in healthcare. Leadership of HROs is committed to the goal of zero harm. HROs create a culture in which all staff are empowered to speak up. HROs provide tools to address improvement opportunities and create lasting change (The Joint Commission 2020b). HROs focus on six fundamental elements:

1. Sensitivity to operations or recognizing potential error
2. Avoiding simple explanations of failure; asking a number of questions to find all of the causes of problems
3. Predicting and eliminating problems before they happen
4. Deference to expertise—those with the most knowledge relevant to an issue deal with it
5. Dealing quickly with difficulties so that systems are resilient and function effectively
6. Collective mindfulness that allows for continuous learning and making critical adjustments to meet challenges

Increasing numbers of providers have joined this movement over the past 20 years (Deloitte 2017).

VALUE-BASED CARE

As discussed in chapter 9, in an effort to improve quality and reduce healthcare spending, the federal government and some insurance companies have changed the way they pay for care to reward positive quality outcomes. The federal government has been experimenting with this payment method for many years. Medicare's value-based purchasing refers to a set of performance-based payment strategies that the federal government has been testing and reviewing since the 1990s. Value-based payment is also known as pay-for-performance reimbursement. CMS has implemented value-based programs for end-stage renal disease, hospital purchasing, hospital readmission rates, physician services, hospital acquired conditions, skilled nursing facilities, and home health care (CMS 2020b).

Evidence suggests that value-based payment methods have achieved only modest success in improving performance, but public and private payers continue to try new models, including some directed by the ACA (Damberg et al. 2014) (see sidebar). National studies suggest that value-based payment methods are becoming more popular, as about 40 percent of commercial payments to physicians and hospitals now include a quality component, compared with 11 percent in 2013 and only 1 to 3 percent in 2010 (Zimlich 2017).

 VALUE-BASED PAYMENT PROGRAMS

The concept of payment based on quality of care has been around for many years, but the passage of the ACA in 2010 put new emphasis on value-based payment. CMS (2020b) operates seven value-based programs that have been linked to better care for individuals, better health for populations, and lower costs of healthcare.

1. End-Stage Renal Disease Quality Incentive Program

2. Hospital Value-Based Purchasing Program

3. Hospital Readmission Reduction Program

4. Value Modifier Program (also called the Physician Value-Based Modifier)

5. Hospital-Acquired Condition Reduction Program

6. Skilled Nursing Facility Value-Based Program

7. Home Health Value-Based Program

The American Academy of Family Physicians (AAFP) recognizes that many value-based payment models will directly affect its members. It has suggested a number of necessary principles for policymakers in designing these models:

◆   Being responsive to community needs preferences and resources

◆   Being responsive to individual patient preferences

◆   Focusing on tangible improvements in clinical outcomes

Family physicians want to see value-based care reduce the per person cost of healthcare and standardize payment models and performance measures among payers, providers, purchasers, and patients. Balancing the administrative burden and costs to physicians with the proposed improvements of value-based payment may be difficult (AAFP 2016). Value-based care may be the future of healthcare, but most recognize that it still needs continued design improvement.

INEQUALITIES AND QUALITY

Compared with ten other high-income countries, including Germany, Sweden, and France, the United States has the highest healthcare costs and the worst outcomes. The United States ranks at the bottom of the group in terms of equity, access, and healthcare outcomes. Costs impede access to healthcare in the United States more than in other countries. Americans also have significant difficulty paying medical bills and waiting for appointments. In addition, fewer Americans have a regular doctor. The United Kingdom, the Netherlands, and Sweden rank highest on measures related to equity. These three countries also show small differences between lower- and higher-income adults on 11 measures (Schneider et al. 2017).

Economic inequality between the rich and the poor is widening in the United States. Americans with incomes below the federal poverty level have worse access to care than wealthy Americans. Many low-income people remain uninsured, as wages have not kept pace with rapidly rising insurance premiums and patient cost-sharing plans. The life expectancy of the wealthiest Americans now exceeds that of lower-income Americans by 10 to 15 years (Dickman, Himmelstein, and Woolhandler 2017). Health differences between higher- and lower-income groups have changed dramatically, with the low-income Americans having life expectancies equal to those of people living in Sudan or Pakistan, while the richest Americans outlive people in all other countries (Neilson 2019).

The ACA improved coverage for lower-income Americans, women, and minorities, but its overall impact was limited by the choice of many states not to expand their Medicaid programs, which left many people without health insurance. As of 2017, 29 million Americans remained uninsured. Substantial inequalities still exist along economic, gender, and racial lines (Gaffney and McCormick 2017).

The term *structural racism* refers to the variety of ways in which societies are organized to perpetuate racial discrimination in housing, education, media, healthcare, criminal justice, and other areas (Bailey et al. 2017). Negative policies and practices reinforce discrimination, beliefs, values, and the distribution of resources. A focus on structural racism offers a promising approach to improving healthcare equity.

There is also evidence that hospitals vary in the quality of care they deliver to patients according to the type of insurance they have—or the lack thereof. People with private insurance typically have better outcomes and lower death rates than Medicare enrollees. Given this, hospitals might want to measure the quality of care given to different insurance groups to better understand quality outcomes (Spencer, Gaskins, and Roberts 2013).

SUMMARY

The Institute of Medicine defined healthcare quality decades ago; however, clinicians, patients, and administrators may have different perspectives on quality, viewing it through the lenses of their education, training, and experience. Patients, for example, may forgive disappointing clinical outcomes if they receive excellent service. Many different measures of quality exist. One quality report specific to hospitals is the Hospital Consumer Assessment of Healthcare Providers and Systems (HCAHPS), which asks patients about their experiences and is used by hospitals to improve the healthcare experience. This survey is created by the Centers for Medicare & Medicaid Services, which publishes HCAHPS results quarterly.

William Kissick introduced the concept of the "Iron Triangle" of Healthcare in 1994. The Iron Triangle captures three dimensions of healthcare: access, cost, and quality. Many have argued that to get better quality and access, costs must increase. Not everyone agrees with this argument. The Institute of Medicine wrote as early as the 1990s of the need to improve both healthcare policy and practice. The Institute for Healthcare Improvement (IHI) developed the "Triple Aim," which focuses on improving the patient care experience, improving the health of populations, while simultaneously reducing the per capita cost of health.

Medical errors are a significant problem in the United States. Studies show that hundreds of thousands of errors occur each year in US healthcare organizations. The concept of coproduction of healthcare suggests that patients, families, and healthcare professionals must work interdependently to reduce error. Better communication and an understanding of power dynamics in these relationships is vital. Hierarchies among healthcare providers, conflicting roles and role ambiguity, and interpersonal power conflicts are sources of communication failures that contribute to medical errors.

Research shows that effective communication results in better patient outcomes, greater patient satisfaction, and increased employee satisfaction. Ongoing efforts have been made to improve communication within and between healthcare teams to reduce medical and surgical errors. Two techniques have been shown to be particularly effective in improving communication and the quality of care are SBAR (situation-background-assessment-recommendation) and AIDET (acknowledge-identify-duration-explain-thank).

Sentinel events are significant failures that lead to a patient's death or serious injury. The Joint Commission identifies unintended retention of a foreign body; falls; wrong patient, wrong site, or wrong procedure errors; suicide; and delays in treatment among the top occurrences in the United States. The National Quality Forum also tracks medical errors by maintaining a list of "serious reportable events."

Healthcare professionals and other business leaders use a variety of tools to monitor, assess, and improve quality. Common among them are the Plan-Do-Study-Act cycle, cause-and-effect diagrams, flow charts, and Pareto charts.

CMS is using the evidence it gathers to develop performance-based payment strategies called value-based purchasing. This method reimburses hospitals and physicians based on a set of patient outcomes and other quality components related to end-stage renal disease, hospital purchasing, hospital readmission rates, physician services, hospital-acquired conditions, skilled nursing facilities, and home health care. While this concept has been around for some time, the passage of the ACA provided incentives to implement value-based payment.

All of these initiatives have yet to solve the inequalities between the rich and poor in the United States. Structural racism is also a cause of health inequalities. Increased focus on structural racism and on providing access to healthcare for the poor who are uninsured is needed.

QUESTIONS

1. How would you define healthcare quality?
2. What does the HCAHPS survey purport to do?
3. William Kissick's "Iron Triangle" attempted to define the relationship between three dimensions of healthcare. What are the three dimensions?
4. What are the goals of the Institute for Healthcare Improvement's "Triple Aim"?
5. A 2016 Johns Hopkins University study suggested that deaths attributable to medical errors exceed 250,000 a year. Where would this cause of death rank in the CDC's leading causes of death if it were included as such? (You may have to do a quick search of the CDC's leading causes of death.)
6. What aspects of power among providers, patients, and family members affect healthcare outcomes? What is a sentinel event?
7. According to The Joint Commission, what were the top three sentinel events in 2017?
8. What are "never events"?
9. What percentage of commercial payments to hospitals include a quality component?
10. As of 2017, how many Americans were uninsured?

ASSIGNMENTS

1. Compare and contrast three types of quality improvement tools. Suggest situations in which each of the three tools might be most useful.

2. The Joint Commission reported that unintended retention of a foreign body and falls were the top two sentinel events in 2018. Develop and write about steps that might be taken to reduce each of those problems.

3. Consider the following conversation between a physician and a patient. What opportunities for misunderstanding or miscommunication can you identify?

   Doctor: "I have the results from your test we did on your prostate gland. It came back positive."

   Patient: "Wow, that is great!"

   Doctor: "I don't think it is great, but we haven't made a diagnosis yet."

   Patient: "What is so hard about diagnosing a positive result?"

   Doctor: "Well, we will need you to stay in the hospital today for observation."

   Patient: "Is there something in particular that you want me to observe?"

   Identify what the physician is trying to say and how the patient is interpreting the message. What needs to be done for proper communication to take place?

CASES

WAITING, WAITING, WAITING ...

Tim manages a medical clinic with 135 physicians serving a county with a population of 250,000. The clinicians specialize in everything from primary care to urology. The clinic is home to a laboratory, X-ray facility, and outpatient surgery. Patients call to make appointments, and in most cases, they have to wait several days or longer to get in. Once they make it to their appointment, some patients have to wait to get into a room. In making rounds one day, Tim found one patient who had been waiting for 45 minutes and had not even had contact with a receptionist. No one noticed she had been sitting there all that time.

The clinic uses several criteria to slot the patients into appointment times. Some physicians, for example, see a patient and then require an X-ray during the appointment. Other visits are more straightforward and require little time. Most physicians want to see four patients per hour. They definitely do not want any empty appointment slots.

Some patients want to be seen for what they consider urgent needs but in fact are often mild fevers or sore throats. These patients are invited to fill the appointment slots that are left. Some doctors will fit patients in even though they have a full schedule. Some parents bring more than one child to a single appointment. Every day, emergencies occur, ranging from serious medical problems that take extra time to particularly harsh weather that slows or stops patients and staff from coming in.

All of the scheduling is done centrally by staff who are not clinically trained. Some longtime staff know many of the physicians. Some of the scheduling staff are relatively new. They receive on-the-job training and follow written protocols as they schedule appointments. However, most of the staff doing the scheduling are not familiar with the many procedures that take place in the clinic.

Discussion Questions

1. Using a cause-and-effect diagram, identify the problems you see in the clinic's scheduling process.
2. Choose one of the key issues listed on the cause-and-effect diagram and use the Plan-Do-Study-Act cycle to show how you would attempt to improve the process.
3. Consult the Institute for Healthcare Improvement's Quality Improvement Essential Toolkit at www.ihi.org/resources/Pages/Tools/Quality-Improvement-Essentials-Toolkit.aspx, or do some research on your own to find another quality improvement tool. Explain how you might use that tool to tackle this case.

A MOTHER'S INSTINCT

An 18-month-old child was admitted to the hospital after falling into a hot bath. Two weeks later, she was doing well and set to return home. Her mother noticed that the little girl asked for a drink every time she saw one, and she often sucked on a wet washcloth. When the child's mother asked about this behavior, the nurses told her it was normal—they would not ask a physician for permission to give the girl a drink. The nurses told the mother that her child was doing well and that she should go home and get some sleep.

When the mother returned early the next morning, she knew that something was very wrong with her child. The medical team was notified. They administered naloxone, a drug used to block the effects of opioids. They finally allowed the girl to have a drink, and she swallowed a liter of juice. The medical team determined that the girl should not be given any more narcotics. They gave verbal orders.

A nurse entered the girl's room that afternoon with a syringe of methadone. The mother reminded her that no narcotics were to be given. The nurse said that the orders had been changed and gave the little girl the drug. It was not long before her heart stopped. The girl died in her mother's arms two days later. Along with the narcotics, she had a hospital-acquired infection and was severely dehydrated.

Discussion Questions

1. What factors contributed to the girl's death?
2. Consider the power structures in this case. What power did the nurse have? How about the girl's mother? What could the physicians and nurses have done to give the mother more power to affect her daughter's care?
3. How could the girl's death have been prevented? What measures would you put in place to make sure this did not happen to another patient?

REFERENCES

Agency for Healthcare Research and Quality (AHRQ). 2020. "About CAHPS." Reviewed March. www.ahrq.gov/cahps/about-cahps/index.html.

———. 2018. "Understanding Quality Measurement." Reviewed October. www.ahrq.gov/professionals/quality-patient-safety/quality-resources/tools/chtoolbx/understand/index.html.

Al-Abri, R., and A. Al-Balushi. 2014. "Patient Satisfaction Survey as a Tool Towards Quality Improvement." *Oman Medical Journal* 29 (1): 3–7.

Aluko, Y. 2017. "The Delicate Balance Between Cost and Quality in Value-Based Healthcare." *Becker's Healthcare*. Published February 20. www.beckershospitalreview.com/finance/the-delicate-balance-between-cost-and-quality-in-value-based-healthcare.html.

American Academy of Family Physicians (AAFP). 2016. "Value-Based Payment." Accessed June 16, 2020. www.aafp.org/about/policies/all/value-based-payment.html.

Bailey, Z., N. Krieger, M. Agenor, J. Graves, N. Linos, and M. Bassett. 2017. "Structural Racism and Health Inequities in the USA: Evidence and Interventions." *The Lancet* 389 (10077): 1453–63.

Batalden, M., P. Batalden, P. Margolis, M. Seid, G. Armstrong, L. Opipari-Arrigan, and H. Hartung. 2015. "Coproduction of Healthcare Services." *BMJ Quality & Safety* 25 (7): 509–17.

Burgener, A. 2017. "Enhancing Communication to Improve Patient Safety and to Increase Patient Satisfaction." *Health Care Manager* 36 (3): 238–43.

Carroll, A. 2015. "To Be Sued Less, Doctors Should Consider Talking to Patients More." *New York Times*. Published June 1. www.nytimes.com/2015/06/02/upshot/to-be-sued-less-doctors-should-talk-to-patients-more.html.

Castro, D., B. Miller, and A. Nager. 2014. "Unlocking the Potential of Physician-to-Patient Telehealth Services." Information technology & Innovation Foundation. Published May 12. https://itif.org/publications/2014/05/12/unlocking-potential-physician-patient-telehealth-services.

Centers for Medicare & Medicaid Services (CMS). 2020a. "Electronic Clinical Quality Measures Basics." Updated May 21. www.cms.gov/Regulations-and-Guidance/Legislation/EHRIncentivePrograms/ClinicalQualityMeasures.html.

————. 2020b. "What Are the Value-Based Programs?" Updated January 6. www.cms.gov/Medicare/Quality-Initiatives-Patient-Assessment-Instruments/Value-Based-Programs/Value-Based-Programs.html.

————. 2019a. "CMS-Approved Accrediting Organizations Contacts for Prospective Clients." Accessed June 16, 2020. www.cms.gov/Medicare/Provider-Enrollment-and-Certification/SurveyCertificationGenInfo/Downloads/Accrediting-Organization-Contacts-for-Prospective-Clients-.pdf.

————. 2019b. "Quality Initiatives—General Information." Updated November 17. www.cms.gov/Medicare/Quality-Initiatives-Patient-Assessment-Instruments/QualityInitiativesGenInfo/index.html.

Chassin, M. R., and E. C. Becher. 2002. "The Wrong Patient." *Annals of Internal Medicine*. Published June 4. http://annals.org/aim/fullarticle/715318/wrong-patient.

Chassin, M. R., and R. W. Galvin. 1998. "The Urgent Need to Improve Healthcare Quality." *JAMA* 280 (11): 1000–1005.

Christensen, C. M., R. M. J. Bohmer, and J. Kenagy. 2000. "Will Disruptive Innovations Cure Healthcare?" *Harvard Business Review* 78 (5): 102–12.

Christensen, C. M., and M. E. Raynor. 2003. *The Innovator's Solution: Creating and Sustaining Successful Growth*. Boston: Harvard Business School Press.

Damberg, C., M. Sorbero, S. Lovejoy, G. Martsolf, L. Raaen, and D. Mandel. 2014. "Measuring Success in Healthcare Value-Based Purchasing Programs: Findings from an Environmental Scan, Literature Review, and Expert Panel Discussions." *Rand Health Quarterly* 4 (3): 9.

Deloitte. 2017. *Transforming into a High Reliability Organization in Health Care*. Accessed June 16, 2020. https://www2.deloitte.com/content/dam/Deloitte/us/Documents/life-sciences-health-care/us-lshc-health-care-high-reliability-organization.pdf.

Dickman, S. L., D. U. Himmelstein, and S. Woolhandler. 2017. "Inequality and the Health-Care System in the USA." *The Lancet* 389: 1431–41.

Flavin, B. 2018. "7 Critical Factors That Impact Patient Experience." *Rasmussen College Health Sciences Blog*. Published July 10. www.rasmussen.edu/degrees/health-sciences/blog/patient-experience-factors/.

Gaffney, A., and D. McCormick. 2017. "The Affordable Care Act: Implications for Health-Care Equity." *The Lancet* 389: 1442–52.

Gift, R. G., and D. Mosel. 1994. *Benchmarking in Healthcare*. Chicago: American Hospital Publishing.

Godfrey, T. 2012. "What Is the Iron Triangle of Healthcare?" Penn Square Post. Published March 3. http://pennsquarepost.com/what-is-the-iron-triangle-of-health-care/.

Hughes, R. G., ed. 2008. *Patient Safety and Quality: An Evidence-Based Handbook for Nurses*, Rockville, MD: Agency for Healthcare Research and Quality.

Huntington, B., and N. Kuhn. 2003. "Communication Gaffes: A Root Cause of Malpractice Claims." *Baylor University Medical Center Proceedings* 16 (2): 157–61.

Institute for Healthcare Improvement (IHI). 2020a. "About Us." Accessed June 16. www.ihi.
org/about/Pages/default.aspx.

———. 2020b. "How to Improve." Accessed June 16. www.ihi.org/resources/Pages/
HowtoImprove/default.aspx.

———. 2020c. "The IHI Triple Aim Initiative: Better Care for Individuals, Better Health
for Populations, and Lower Per Capita Costs." Accessed June 16. www.ihi.org/Engage/
Initiatives/TripleAim/Pages/default.aspx.

———. 2017. "Quality Improvement Essentials Toolkit." Accessed June 16, 2020. www.ihi.
org/resources/Pages/Tools/Quality-Improvement-Essentials-Toolkit.aspx.

Institute of Medicine. 2001. *Crossing the Quality Chasm: A New Health System for the 21st
Century*. Washington, DC: National Academies Press.

———. 1999. *To Err Is Human: Building a Safer Health System*. Washington, DC: National
Academies Press.

———. 1996. *America's Health in Transition: Protecting and Improving Quality*. Washington, DC: National Academies Press.

Jha, B. 2018. "Accreditation, Quality, and Making Hospital Care Better." *JAMA* 320 (23):
2410–11.

Johns Hopkins Medicine. 2016. "Study Suggests Medical Errors Now Third Leading Cause of
Death in the U.S." News release, May 3. www.hopkinsmedicine.org/news/media/releases/
study_suggests_medical_errors_now_third_leading_cause_of_death_in_the_us.

The Joint Commission. 2020a. "About the Joint Commission." Accessed June 16. www.
jointcommission.org/about_us/about_the_joint_commission_main.aspx.

———. 2020b. "High Reliability in Health Care Is Possible." Accessed June 16. www.
centerfortransforminghealthcare.org/high-reliability-in-health-care.

————. 2019a. "Quality and Safety: Sentinel Events Statistics Released for 2018." Accessed June 17, 2020. www.jointcommission.org/resources/patient-safety-topics/sentinel-event/sentinel-event-data-summary/.

————. 2019b. "2019 National Patient Safety Goals." Accessed June 16, 2020. www.jointcommission.org/assets/1/6/2019_HAP_NPSGs_final2.pdf.

————. 2013. "Comprehensive Accreditation Manual for Hospital 2013: Sentinel Events." Published January. www.jointcommission.org/-/media/deprecated-unorganized/imported-assets/tjc/system-folders/topics-library/camh_2012_update2_24_sepdf.pdf.

Kanbanize. 2019. "7 Wastes of Lean: How to Optimize Resources." Accessed June 16, 2020. https://kanbanize.com/lean-management/value-waste/7-wastes-of-lean/.

Kaplan, M. 2016. "Co-production: A New Lens on Patient-Centered Care." Institute for Healthcare Improvement. Published April 1. www.ihi.org/communities/blogs/co-production-a-new-lens-on-patient-centered-care.

Kissick, W. 1994. *Medicine's Dilemmas: Infinite Needs Versus Finite Resources*. New Haven, CT: Yale University Press.

Lohr, K. N., ed. 1990. *Medicare: A Strategy for Quality Assurance*. Washington, DC: National Academies Press.

Medicare.gov. 2020. "Survey of Patients' Experiences (HCAHPS)." Accessed June 16. www.medicare.gov/hospitalcompare/about/survey-patients-experience.html.

Monk, J. 2002. "How a Hospital Failed a Boy Who Didn't Have to Die." *The State* (Columbia, SO), June 16, A1, A8–9.

National Committee for Quality Assurance (NCQA). 2020. "HEDIS and Performance Measurement." Accessed June 16. www.ncqa.org/hedis/.

National Quality Forum (NQF). 2020. "List of SREs." Accessed June 17. www.qualityforum.org/Topics/SREs/List_of_SREs.aspx.

Neilson, S. 2019. "The Gap Between Rich and Poor Americans' Health Is Widening." National Public Radio. Published June 28. www.npr.org/sections/health-shots/ 2019/06/28/736938334/the-gap-between-rich-and-poor-americans-health-is-widening.

O'Daniel, M., and A. Rosenstein. 2008. "Professional Communication and Team Collaboration." In *Patient Safety and Quality: An Evidence-Based Handbook for Nurses*, edited by R. G. Hughes, chapter 3. Rockville, MD: Agency for Healthcare Research and Quality.

Office of Disease Prevention and Health Promotion (ODPHP). 2014. *National Action Plan for Adverse Drug Event Prevention.* Accessed June 16, 2020. https://health.gov/sites/ default/files/2019-09/ADE-Action-Plan-508c.pdf.

Regula, C., J. Miller, and D. Mauger. 2007. "Quality of Care from a Patient's Perspective." *JAMA Dermatology* 143 (12): 1589–1603.

Rogers, S., A. Gawande, M. Kwann, A. Puopolo, C. Yoon, T. Brennan, and D. Studdert. 2006. "Analysis of Surgical Errors in Closed Malpractice Claims at 4 Liability Insurers." *Surgery* 140 (1): 25–33.

Saver, B., S. Martin, R. Adler, L. Candib, K. Deligiannidis, J. Golding, D. Mulling, M. Roberts, and S. Topolski. 2015. "Care That Matters: Quality Measurement and Health Care." PLOS Medicine 12(11): e1001902.

Schneider, E., D. Sarnak, D. Squires, A. Shah, and M. Doty. 2017. "Mirror, Mirror 2017: International Comparison Reflects Flaws and Opportunities for Better U.S. Healthcare." Commonwealth Fund. Published July. https://interactives.commonwealthfund.org/2017/ july/mirror-mirror.

Schuster, M., E. McGlynn, and R. Brook. 2005. "How Good Is the Quality of Healthcare in the United States?" *Milbank Quarterly* 83 (4): 843–95.

Spencer, C., D. Gaskin, and E. Roberts. 2013. "The Quality of Care Delivered to Patients Within the Same Hospital Varies by Insurance Type." *Health Affairs* 32 (10): 1731–39.

Sutcliffe, K., E. Lewton, and M. Rosenthal. 2004. "Communication Failures: An Insidious Contributor to Medical Mishaps." *Academy Medicine* 79 (2): 186–94.

W. Edwards Deming Institute. 2020. "PDSA Cycle." Accessed June 16. https://deming.org/explore/p-d-s-a.

Wallace, E., J. Lowry, S. M. Smith, and T. Fahey. 2013. "The Epidemiology of Malpractice Claims in Primary Care: A Systematic Review." *BMJ Open* 3(6): e002929.

Weiss, A., W. Freeman, K. Heslin, and M. Barrett. 2018. "Adverse Drug Events in U.S. Hospitals, 2010 versus 2014." Statistical Brief 234, Healthcare Cost and Utilization Project. Published January. www.hcup-us.ahrq.gov/reports/statbriefs/sb234-Adverse-Drug-Events.jsp.

Zimlich, R. 2017. "Value-Based Payment Update: Where We Are and Who Is Most Successful." *Managed Healthcare Executive*. Published November 16. http://managedhealthcareexecutive.modernmedicine.com/managed-healthcare-executive/news/value-based-payment-update-where-we-are-and-who-most-successful.

CHAPTER 11

HEALTH INFORMATION TECHNOLOGY

Medical records, once a stack of papers with hard-to-decipher notes, often duplicated for patients who visited a number of providers, now take the form of electronic health records. The Health Insurance Portability and Accountability Act of 1996, supported by initiatives of the Centers for Medicare & Medicaid Services, allowed for the portability, or sharing, of medical records among providers. Technology has also allowed for greater access to healthcare in the form of telemedicine as well as mobile apps that can assist in diagnostics, medication management, and health promotion.

The bottom line is that technology has created a variety of tools and resources that are now at the disposal of the healthcare community. These tools promise to improve patient care and outcomes (Jones 2018).

LEARNING OBJECTIVES

After reading this chapter, you will be able to

➤ Distinguish the components and value of an electronic health record.

➤ Perceive the advantages of cloud computing.

➤ Identify the challenges that the Health Insurance Portability and Accountability Act poses to interoperability.

➤ Recognize the emergence and value of telemedicine.

➤ Comprehend the opportunities of mobile application technology.

➤ Predict the future of health information technology.

289

ELECTRONIC HEALTH RECORDS

The **electronic health record (EHR)** provides an electronic platform for providers to document patient encounters as they occur over the life of an individual patient. Often, the term **electronic medical record (EMR)** is used interchangeably with *electronic health record*. However, there are some differences between the two. The EMR is the electronic version of a patient's medical record from one physician; it generally stays in the physician's office and is not shared. The EHR comprises a patient's records from many physicians, including primary care physicians and specialists, and provides a more comprehensive documentation of a patient's health. The EHR includes a patient's demographics, medical history, medications, immunizations, diagnostic information, and notes from multiple healthcare provider interactions. When used correctly, the EHR provides a complete record of all of the healthcare services provided to an individual. The benefits of EHRs include enhanced patient care, improved public health, ease of workflow, and lower costs of healthcare (Banova 2019; Nextgen 2019).

ENHANCED PATIENT CARE

Consider an individual who visits a primary care physician, a number of specialists, and possibly an emergency room. Not long ago, clinicians relied on written documents, copied and shared among physicians, and hoped that all of the patient's information was complete and accurate. The EHR gathers all of that information and provides valuable evidence. It can be used, for example, to warn of allergies to certain medications. It can aid in diagnosis, reduce errors, and support better patient outcomes (ONC 2017).

The Centers for Medicare & Medicaid Services (CMS) established the Electronic Health Record Incentive Program in 2011 to encourage clinicians and hospitals to demonstrate meaningful use of certified electronic health record technology. The first stage of the program created requirements for capturing clinical data. Stage 2 expanded on the first stage and supported the meaningful use of the data as a way to improve healthcare quality and patient outcomes. In 2017, CMS promoted this concept through the use of certified electronic health record technology (CEHRT). Today, this program is known as the Promoting Interoperability (PI) Programs. CMS is moving beyond the requirements of meaningful use to a new phase of EHR measurement that focuses on interoperability and giving patients greater access to their health records (CMS 2020).

Providers derive many benefits from the use of EHRs. EHRs allow for quick access to patient records even in remote locations. They enhance decision-making and medical information. EHRs allow providers to gather and report on real-time quality measurements and to interface with labs, registries, and other health information technology (IT). EHRs allow prescriptions to be sent electronically to pharmacies. EHRs should also reduce paperwork for physician offices. Physicians can make electronic referrals to specialists for follow-up care (ONC 2017). CMS has developed a quality payment program that rewards value and outcomes. Quality of care, efforts to promote interoperability, improvement activities, and cost all determine the amount that healthcare providers are paid (QPP 2020).

Patients also benefit from EHRs. Patient care is enhanced because patients are more involved in their care. Both doctors and patients have access to EHRs, allowing them to collaborate in decision-making about treatment. Patients can see the notes made about their medical evaluations, lab reports, and other diagnostic information. Instructions and follow-up care are noted in EHRs. Patients can interact with their physicians through online portals and other messaging tools, thereby enhancing communication (ONC 2017).

IMPROVED PUBLIC HEALTH

Public health addresses the overall health of a community and the individuals who live there. EHRs provide a set of data to clinical researchers and aid in developing responses to common health problems. One example might be identifying and responding to a viral or bacterial infection in a community. EHRs can paint a picture of how widespread the disease is (Banova 2019).

The first stage of the PI Programs, **meaningful use**, required providers to submit electronic data to immunization **registries** and electronic **syndromic surveillance** data to public health agencies (ONC 2019) (exhibit 11.1). While significant investment and progress has been made in the use of EHRs for clinical care, data collected for public health have been limited to syndromic surveillance, laboratory reporting, and registries. Some of these data include reportable diseases and conditions, vital records, and cancer registries. The potential of EHRs is much greater. They can also contribute to identifying disease,

meaningful use
The minimum US government standard for electronic health records, outlining how a patient's health information should be exchanged among clinicians or providers and insurance groups or payers.

registry
A tool for tracking the clinical care and outcomes collection of specific patient populations, such as patients with certain chronic diseases, types of cancer, or infections.

syndromic surveillance
The gathering, analysis, and interpretation of health data to diagnose and respond to population health and public health issues.

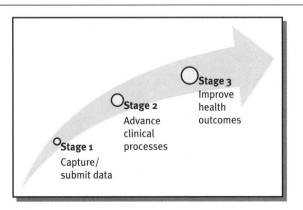

EXHIBIT 11.1
Promoting Interoperability Programs, Stage 1: Meaningful Use

functional status, and well-being of an entire population, but they are limited by a lack of standardization and linkage of data over time (Friedman et al. 2013).

Healthcare organizations that use electronic data effectively have a better chance of improving the health of their patient population. Electronic health information about the entire populations of patients served by such an organization can help providers better monitor, prevent, and manage disease (ONC 2019). In one study, researchers found that EHRs helped increase the number of opportunities to immunize children. These children were up to date on their immunizations earlier than the control group of patients (Fiks et al. 2007).

EASE OF WORKFLOW

One of the greatest benefits of EHRs is the reduction in the amount of time providers spend doing paperwork. Administrative tasks such as completing forms, coding, and billing can be streamlined. Electronic databases also allow for shortcuts in inquiries or searches about specific conditions (ONC 2017). The number of medical codes used to identify and bill for procedures is in the tens of thousands. The use of EHRs has made this process much easier, as entering data into a computerized system is faster and reduces the risk of error (Banova 2019).

LOWER HEALTHCARE COSTS

Medical practices save money with the use of EHRs. They report efficiencies in the form of reduced transcription costs, chart storage, improved documentation and coding, reduced medical errors, easy access to patient information, automated health insurance plan management, order and receipt of lab tests and diagnostic images, and links to public health registries and databases (ONC 2017). For example, a University of Michigan study reported that switching from paper records to EHRs reduced the cost of outpatient care by 3 percent (Adler-Milstein 2013).

CHALLENGES WITH EHRS

One of the biggest challenges facing the use of EHRs is the lack of interoperability, or the ability of different EHR systems to communicate with one another. Effective use of EHRs requires a standardized way of normalizing data, identifying patients, enforcing health IT interoperability standards, coordinating a variety of stakeholders, and removing information blocking (Monica 2017b).

The Regenstrief Institute's Center for Biomedical Informatics (CBMI) is a research organization focused on healthcare. The CBMI has more than 15 years of experience in patient health record matching. CBMI created the Indiana Network for Patient Care, which houses the largest interorganizational clinical database in the United States. CBMI director Shaun Grannis said in 2017,

> Matching the correct individual to his or her health data is critical to their medical care. Statistics show that up to one in five patient records are not accurately matched even within the same healthcare system. As many as half of patient records are mismatched when data is transferred between healthcare systems. (Monica 2017a)

Identical patient names, typographical errors, missing information, identity theft, changes of residency, and legal name changes all create challenges in correctly matching records with the right patient.

Health IT is used not only in hospitals and clinics but also in long-term care facilities, hospices, home health agencies, and other healthcare settings. While most agree that health IT standardization is important, organizations differ in how they interpret the standards. The CommonWell Health Alliance, an industry-led initiative represented by thousands of providers across the United States, is currently working on a vendor-neutral platform to increase interoperability. The group announced its "Carequality Framework," available to its members, in 2018. This framework allows some of the nation's largest EHR vendors to connect and exchange health data (CommonWell Health Alliance 2018).

Information blocking, defined by the Office of the National Coordinator for Health Information Technology, includes three criteria (ONC 2020):

1. Some act or course of conduct interferes with the exchange or use of electronic health information where permitted.

2. The actor knows or should know that the actions are likely to cause interference.

3. Under the circumstances, there is no reasonable justification for engaging in the act.

A 2017 national survey of health information exchange leaders reported that half of EHR vendors routinely engaged in information blocking, and one-quarter of respondents reported that hospitals and health systems routinely do so (Adler-Milstein and Pfeifer 2017). Yet information blocking is illegal, and the exchange of information is protected by the Health Insurance Portability and Accountability Act (HIPAA).

Another major challenge to the use of EHRs comes from the negative perception of the additional workloads that EHRs put on physicians. About 40 percent of physicians believe that EHRs bring more problems than benefits. Doctors feel that their needs have not been addressed in the design of EHRs and that inputting information takes too much time (Snell 2018).

Physicians complain about EHRs with too many boxes to check, forcing them to spend more time on tasks that do not directly benefit patients. An emergency room doctor, for example, may make 4,000 mouse clicks during the course of just one shift. In addition, doctors report having to spend an hour and a half daily outside of their normal work time to keep up on electronic paperwork. One study showed that clerical and administrative notes accounted for 44 percent of a physician's interactions with EHRs, not patient care. Even though more than $36 billion has been spent on EHRs and almost all hospitals use them, the promises of drastically improved healthcare as a result of EHRs have not yet been realized (Fry and Schulte 2019).

✳ PROTECTED HEALTH INFORMATION

HIPAA allows for the transmission of protected health information when it is needed for patient care. In general, a HIPAA-covered entity may disclose protected health information to another covered entity without needing patient consent for the following purposes (Irving 2018):

- Quality assessment and improvement
- Developing clinical guidelines
- Patient safety activities
- Improving health or reducing healthcare cost in populations
- Developing protocols
- Case management and care coordination
- Contacting healthcare providers and patients with information about treatment alternatives
- Reviewing qualifications of healthcare professionals
- Evaluating performance of healthcare providers and health plans
- Training programs or credentialing activities
- Fraud and abuse detection

HIPAA AND INTEROPERABILITY

The Health Insurance Portability and Accountability Act of 1996 (HIPAA) is often associated with keeping patient healthcare records private, not with sharing those records with others. Under HIPAA, patients are entitled to see and receive copies of information in their medical and other health records. Their families may also have access to some information related to an individual's care. In addition, HIPAA supports the sharing of health information among healthcare providers and health plans for the purposes of treatment, payment, and healthcare operations. HIPAA also supports the transmission of health information for research and public health purposes (Marchesini and Noonan 2018) (see sidebar).

CLOUD COMPUTING AND BIG DATA

Cloud computing allows users to access applications and data from anywhere on demand. Next-generation data centers and storage technologies provide the cloud infrastructure. These technologies are very robust and promise consumers reliable support and security (Buyya et al. 2009). In the case of healthcare, providers and patients can access information via the internet.

cloud computing
The use of a network of remote servers to store data accessed via the internet (i.e., the cloud).

Cloud computing allows for the storage of massive amounts of data at low cost. Healthcare professionals can use the cloud rather than purchase their own servers and other hardware. The cloud is a safer means of storing data because of its strong backup and recovery abilities (Banova 2019). Healthcare providers are increasingly using cloud services for health information exchange and patient engagement and empowerment tools. In addition, archived data, back-office solutions, and disaster recovery are based in the cloud (HIMSS Analytics 2016).

The emergence of EHRs and cloud computing has generated a high volume of data that is variable in its structure and nature. This is referred to as "big data." Big data in healthcare also includes diagnostic imaging, genomic sequencing, payer records, and research. Concerns about the privacy of health information, security, and cost have slowed the use of big data analysis in healthcare, but the push from CMS toward value-based payment is encouraging its adoption. Another push comes from providers making evidence-based decisions and efficiencies. "Undoubtedly, adopting the use of healthcare big data can transform the industry, driving it away from a fee-for-service model toward value-based care. In short, it can deliver on the promise of lowering healthcare costs while revealing ways to deliver superior patient experiences, treatments, and outcomes" (*NEJM Catalyst* 2018).

Yet the implementation of big data comes with challenges, such as data aggregation, policy and process, and management. Because healthcare data come from many sources, finding and gathering it requires a lot of effort. The challenges of EHRs and managing the data they produce are discussed earlier in this chapter. Format, accuracy, quality, and data cleaning are all challenges related to data aggregation. Some cloud providers have created products specific to health IT that are compliant with HIPAA regulations. Access control, authentication, security, and other rules make gathering big data difficult. The need for scientists and other experts who can manage and use the data collected poses another challenge (*NEJM Catalyst* 2018).

TELEMEDICINE

telemedicine

The use of two-way audio and video communication to facilitate communication between healthcare providers or between providers and patients.

The terms **telemedicine** and telehealth both describe a type of two-way audio and video communication used in healthcare. The two terms are often used interchangeably. In this section, we will refer to the concept as *telemedicine*. Telemedicine has been used for some time as a means of consultation between providers. In some cases, it has been used to facilitate communication between a specialist and a rural primary care provider who otherwise had limited access to specialized help (Banova 2019). Telemedicine also allows direct communication between patients and doctors (see sidebar).

(✳) **HEALTHCARE ON THE MOUNTAIN**

A local television advertisement portrays a backcountry skier who has hurt his ankle and is not sure what to do next. He pulls out his phone, connects with a healthcare provider, and shows the provider his ankle using the camera on his phone, and then gets advice on treatment.

This example not only illustrates remote access to care but also signals the possibility of greater healthcare access in rural America, allowing patients to save travel time and get a quicker response. Telemedicine can be provided at a much lower cost than care at an urgent care center or emergency room.

Many states recognize telemedicine as a cost-saving measure and cover it under their Medicaid program. Medicaid defines telemedicine as medicine that uses technologies such as the telephone, fax machine, e-mail, and remote patient monitoring devices to collect and transmit the health data (Medicaid.gov 2020).

One argument for the use of telemedicine is that it reduces costs. Telemedicine is designed to replace an in-person visit to a physician with a less expensive virtual visit. This was the case with pediatric patients whose parent or guardian calls the doctor in the evening or on weekends. Most parents reported they would have gone to an urgent care center or emergency department had they not had the option of telemedicine (Vyas,

Murren-Boering, and Solo-Josephson 2018). Telemedicine can also be used by those living in rural or remote areas, those who lack transportation, or individuals with limited mobility who have restricted access to physicians.

A 2017 study published in *Health Affairs*, however, suggested that a new group of consumers have emerged with the advent of telemedicine. According to this study, 88 percent of telemedicine visits represent individuals who are not just using technology as a substitute for visiting a physician or emergency department. These are instead new users and additional business from current users. Net annual spending in this case increased $45 per telehealth user (Ashwood et al. 2017). Exhibit 11.2 summarizes the growth of telehealth in recent years.

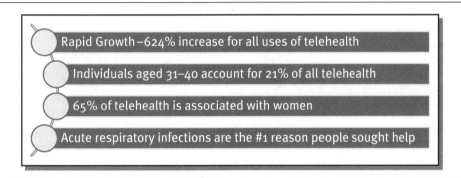

- Rapid Growth—624% increase for all uses of telehealth
- Individuals aged 31–40 account for 21% of all telehealth
- 65% of telehealth is associated with women
- Acute respiratory infections are the #1 reason people sought help

EXHIBIT 11.2
Telehealth Growth,
2014–2018

Source: Data from FAIR Health (2019).

Telemedicine has a number of benefits that complement more traditional care (Alvandi 2017):

- Providing specialized or even basic care in rural areas in the United States and globally

- Connecting patients virtually for quicker treatment, leading to better outcomes

- Allowing for better long-term care management and patient satisfaction as a result of increased interaction with providers

- Creating support across healthcare systems by sharing expertise within their organization

- Aiding health promotion and disease prevention and the management of chronic conditions

mHEALTH

A concept related to telehealth is **mHealth**, or mobile health, in which patients use a mobile phone, tablet, or other wireless device to monitor their health. Mobile health allows for greater mobility and portability for both the patient and the provider (Innovatemedtec 2020). A provider can use a smartphone or tablet to pull up the patient's EHR, look at the patient's medical history, communicate with the patient, and order other tests or complete prescriptions (Banova 2019).

mHealth
The use of mobile phones, tablets, or other wireless devices by patients to monitor their health.

(✱) SHARING OUR HEALTH DATA

Results of a 2018 Deloitte study (Betts and Korenda 2018) showed the following:

- More than half of all consumers are willing to share health data for emergency situations.

- About 40 percent are willing to share their health data to benefit research or to help improve the device they are using.

- Those with chronic disease are more willing to share their data.

The major benefit of mHealth is the convenience and the ability it gives patients and providers to communicate almost anywhere and at any time. Wearable devices and some mobile technology can monitor and report health data without the need for an office visit. It allows for easy communication, such as giving family members notice when their loved one is out of surgery or allowing clinicians to communicate about a patient who is currently in their care (SearchHealthIT 2020).

A 2018 Deloitte study of 4,530 healthcare consumers and 624 physicians reported that 42 percent of respondents used some kind of wearable device to keep track of their health information. Sixty percent said they were willing to share that information with their physician (Betts and Korenda 2018). Exhibit 11.3 shows how the use of mobile devices in monitoring health has increased since 2013.

However, mHealth also comes with some risks, including the opportunity for information to be hacked or inappropriately shared. Moreover, some applications do not work as advertised. A Johns Hopkins University study, for example, showed that an application for taking blood pressure readings was highly inaccurate (SearchHealthIT 2020).

EXHIBIT 11.3
Consumer Use of Technology for Health and Fitness Purposes

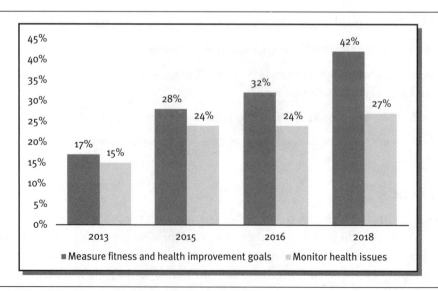

Source: Betts and Korenda (2018).

Mobile App Technology

Medicine is one of the services that has been most profoundly affected by mobile devices and applications. Mobile devices and apps not only keep track of physical activity levels, such as the number of steps taken or flights of stairs climbed, and sleep patterns; some also function as point-of-care tools. These devices store data in the cloud that supports clinical decision-making and improved patient outcomes (Divali, Camosso-Stefinovic, and Baker 2013; *NEJM Catalyst* 2018). These devices and apps assist physicians and patients with the following:

- Chronic care management
- Information management
- Medication management
- Medical reference
- Health record maintenance and access
- Patient monitoring
- Diagnostics
- Personal health records
- Women's health
- Fitness and weight loss
- Mental health

As of 2017, some 325,000 mHealth applications were available for download (Search-HealthIT 2020). However, many of these apps have not been rigorously tested. Some provide inaccurate data at best. Some are even dangerous (Hwang 2020). Many others show important benefits for clinicians and patients. They have shown a positive effect on patient care outcomes including a reduction of adverse events and shortened hospital length of stay (Divali, Camosso-Stefinovic, and Baker 2013; Mickan et al. 2013). Other proven benefits of mHealth applications include convenience, better clinical decision-making, improved accuracy, and enhanced productivity (Ventola 2014).

Patient Care

Mobile devices and applications are effective in patient documentation, patient care, and information seeking. Patient documentation is more complete, with fewer errors. Handheld devices also make it easier for physicians, nurses, and other caregivers to access clinical decision support systems (Mickan et al. 2013). Medical and nursing students note that the most beneficial mobile tools are drug references, medical textbooks, disease diagnosis apps, and medical calculators (Mosa, Yoo, and Sheets 2012). Physicians also report improved patient care using electronic resources. In one study, clinicians indicated that they made twice as many changes in patient management using mobile tools compared with paper resources (Prgomet, Georgiou, and Westbrook 2009).

IMPROVED ACCURACY

Clinicians spend much of their valuable time recording information related to the care and treatment of their patients. Mobile devices have been shown to improve the accuracy of that information, often because they are easier or more convenient to use (Ventola 2014). Accuracy includes more accurate diagnostic coding, more frequent documentation of side effects, and increased medication safety (Mickan et al. 2013).

ENHANCED PRODUCTIVITY

Hospitals and clinic executives who rely on physicians and others to complete all of the patient documentation needed for coding and billing have been creative and resourceful in motivating them to do that work. Research shows that mobile devices are helping with that challenge by streamlining workflow, enabling electronic prescribing, facilitating patient record maintenance and revision, and documenting the number of diagnoses. Mobile apps have also been shown to help with personal and professional time management (Ventola 2014).

SECONDARY USES OF HEALTH INFORMATION

Patient records have been gathered and used for years. While the primary use of these records is to support the delivery of healthcare to an individual, public health agencies, researchers, and government programs rely on this information for research and analysis to support health promotion and disease prevention. These are known as secondary uses of health information (Safran et al. 2007). Because of the ease of using EHRs to gather and share a tremendous amount of data, increased attention is being given to secondary uses of these records (Ramanathan et al. 2015).

HIPAA defines protections of health data acquired for primary uses, but it also allows secondary uses for public health and research. The Health Information Technology for Economic and Clinical Health Act of 2009 (HITECH) also supports the use of data for improving population health outcomes. CMS is working to standardize interoperable EHR technologies and data sharing for specific secondary uses (Ramanathan et al. 2015).

State laws related to the use of health information affect the role of public health. This, in turn, determines how health departments fulfill their essential functions. Early studies indicate that state laws vary widely in addressing health information. As the benefits and challenges of EHRs and electronic health data are better understood, states are updating laws that once supported paper health records to now include EHRs and secondary uses of data (Ramanathan et al. 2015).

 DEBATE TIME Will Telemedicine Lower Healthcare Costs?

A common argument for the use of telehealth is that it saves money. In many markets, the cost associated with a telehealth episode is less than the cost of a traditional office visit to a physician. However, some experts believe that the overall cost of healthcare will rise as the ease of access leads to increased use. In other words, people who otherwise would not seek care will now use telehealth visits for mild illnesses such as colds, ear infections, sinusitis, and bronchitis.

Will the overuse of healthcare cancel out the savings of telehealth? Is this overuse a bad thing, or are more people getting the care they need?

THE FUTURE OF HEALTH INFORMATION TECHNOLOGY

The prevalence of chronic disease continues to rise. The prevention and management of obesity, diabetes, and heart disease continue to challenge health professionals. Patient care management and compliance are also tough issues. Apps that successfully address these problems will significantly affect Americans' health and health costs (Tam and Sharma 2014). Mobile devices and apps will become more important for the education and provision of healthcare (see sidebar).

Research continues to identify the uses and benefits of health information technology. Big data provide millions of values and very large sample sizes. The term "data lake" is used to describe this collection of raw data. Events are underway that promise what one author describes as "data oceans," creating greater opportunities for analysis. Examples include collections of health records from

 THE RISE OF MOBILE DEVICES AND APPS

"The role played by mobile devices and apps in healthcare education is also expected to grow. Medical school healthcare providers and students predict that mobile devices and apps will become even more integrated into patient care and will eventually completely replace textbooks. As the use of medical devices and apps expands, more educational healthcare programs are expected to incorporate them into medical curricula" (Ventola 2014).

50 million Europeans as well as cohort data sets from researchers. A division of one Dutch company has more than 15 petabytes of data from 390 million medical records and other information. Healthcare experts can use these data for clinical decision-making (*NEJM Catalyst* 2018).

The Big Data to Knowledge (BD2K) initiative was launched by the National Institutes of Health in 2013 to support making data sets "FAIR"—findable, accessible, interoperable, and reusable. Data scientists have used these data sets to evaluate methods of diagnosing markers of bipolar disease and to identify drugs that can be repurposed to treat cancer (NIH 2020). The National Institutes of Health plans to launch a study known as the All of Us Research Program, which involves a cohort of at least 1 million volunteers. The goal is to study a wide range of diseases, better predict disease risk, understand how diseases occur, and find better ways to diagnose and treat them (US National Library of Medicine 2020).

SUMMARY

Electronic health records (EHRs) document patient encounters over the life of an individual patient. The EHR can provide a more comprehensive documentation of a patient's health. EHRs not only enhance patient care but also serve as a resource for public health agencies and health researchers.

If complete, EHRs can enhance patient care by allowing clinicians quick and complete access to the medical history of their patients at the point of care. They also enhance clinical decision-making. Physicians use EHRs to make electronic referrals to specialists and to send prescriptions directly to the pharmacy.

EHRs can alert public health officials by painting a picture of how widespread a disease or health problem is. Currently, however, the use of EHRs in public health is limited to surveillance, laboratory reporting, and registries. They have much greater potential.

One of the biggest challenges facing the use of EHRs is the variety of EHR systems or products on the market and their interoperability. Standardizing patient identities, enforcing health information technology (IT) interoperability standards, coordinating input from many stakeholders, and removing information blocking are issues that are still in the way of complete EHR interoperability.

The Centers for Medicare & Medicaid Services (CMS) introduced an initiative known as the Promoting Interoperability Programs with the goal of giving patients greater access to their health records. The Health Insurance Portability and Accountability Act of 1996 (HIPAA) supports this initiative.

EHRs gather massive amounts of patient data that are stored in the cloud, allowing users access to information anywhere on demand. Cloud computing allows for low-cost storage of data. Healthcare systems can save money by no longer needing to purchase their own servers and other hardware. The cloud is designed to provide strong backup and recovery systems.

Telemedicine is another aspect of health IT that has been in use for many years. Telemedicine and telehealth both describe a type of two-way video communication. Experts used cameras and computers for this purpose in the past. Today, most physicians and other clinicians use smartphones, tablets, and other mobile devices to do so. Rural healthcare is more robust because of telehealth. Hospital systems can support one another by sharing expertise. Telehealth has been shown to improve patient outcomes such as fewer hospital readmissions, improved patient compliance with recommended care plans, and faster recovery.

The use of mobile devices in healthcare, sometimes called "mHealth," has resulted in the development of applications that assist in chronic care management, information management, medication management, patient monitoring, diagnostics, access to personal health records, and health promotion. Hundreds of thousands of apps now exist, although not all of them have been tested or proven accurate.

Research continues to identify the uses and benefits of health IT. Big data provides millions of values and large sample sizes. The National Institutes of Health (NIH) launched the Big Data to Knowledge (BD2K) initiative to support ongoing research. The NIH plans to launch a study called the All of Us Research Program, to better understand and fight disease in the future.

QUESTIONS

1. How does the Centers for Medicare & Medicaid Services motivate hospitals and health systems to shift to electronic health records?
2. Name three benefits of electronic health records.
3. What does the term "interoperability" mean? What factors prevent the interoperability of electronic health records?
4. What does "portability" mean with respect to the Health Insurance Portability and Accountability Act of 1996?
5. How does cloud computing lower costs for healthcare organizations?
6. What is "big data"?
7. How has telemedicine changed over the past decade?
8. How has telehealth affected overall healthcare costs?
9. List two advantages and two disadvantages of mHealth or mobile health.
10. What is the difference between primary and secondary use of health information technology?

Assignments

1. Consider a patient who uses a Fitbit activity tracker or an Apple Watch to keep tabs on their physical activity levels. What happens to the data gathered by such a device, and how it might be used by physicians or health insurers to promote overall health and wellness programs?
2. Search for ten apps related to healthcare. Use keywords such as *obesity*, *diabetes*, *asthma*, and *heart disease*. Rank the ten apps based on their contributions to an individual's health and on the rankings given by the consumers using them.

Cases

Determining the Needs of the Community

Derek, chief information officer (CIO) of Acme Insurance, was contacted by two local university professors who wanted access to the patient records of everyone living in certain zip codes of the local community. With a population of 120,000, the community was home to two hospitals within the zip codes specified by the researchers and another in a nearby county. Acme Insurance represented patients served by most of the city's physicians and by one of the hospitals. Other health insurance groups paid for patients seen at the two other hospitals. The professors indicated they would be contacting those insurance companies with a similar request.

As CIO, Derek was familiar with the HIPAA regulations, but this was the first time he had been asked for these kinds of data. Electronic health records would allow him to easily gather data for the past five years. Older records would have to be accessed through the archives, which had not yet been indexed or added to the electronic system.

Discussion Questions

1. What do HIPAA regulations allow in the case of this research?
2. What other federal policy supports the secondary use (research) of health information? Hint: You might want to consult articles such as Ramanathan et al. (2015).
3. What role does the university's Institutional Review Board (IRB) have in the research the professors want to complete? You may have to do a little outside research to learn about IRBs.
4. What considerations should Derek make in regard to the privacy of the patients?

THE CHALLENGES OF INTEROPERABILITY

Susan was frustrated. As chair of the school of nursing at the local university, she wanted her students to get used to using electronic health records. Ideally, these students would leave her program and be able to use their employer's EHR system without any additional orientation. Other campus health profession leaders had similar concerns. However, the faculty found that within a 100-mile radius of the university, the area's many hospitals and three main healthcare systems all used different EHR vendors.

The local healthcare systems promoted electronic health information. They were all concerned about the safety and security of the records and the needs of their patients. They were also aware of the national push for system to integrate EHRs. In reality, however, the records housed in the variety of systems could not be shared. The software was too disconnected and dissimilar.

Susan wondered what her next step should be. Which system should she adopt, if any? How could she help move these groups toward better interoperability?

Discussion Questions

1. Who are the local stakeholders who might be involved in the challenge of interoperability?
2. What next step might these stakeholders take?
3. What are the barriers and reinforcements to taking this step?
4. Discuss how a local effort to implement interoperability might influence those at the national level.

REFERENCES

Adler-Milstein, J. 2013. "Effect of Electronic Health Records on Healthcare Costs: Longitudinal Comparative Evidence from Community Practices." *Annals of Internal Medicine* 159 (2): 97–104.

Adler-Milstein, J., and E. Pfeifer. 2017. "Information Blocking: Is It Occurring and What Policy Strategies Can Address It?" Milbank Quarterly 95 (1): 117–35.

Alvandi, M. 2017. "Telemedicine and Its Role in Revolutionizing Healthcare Delivery." *American Journal of Accountable Care*. Published March 10. www.ajmc.com/journals/ajac/2017/2017-vol5-n1/telemedicine-and-its-role-in-revolutionizing-healthcare-delivery.

Ashwood, J. S., A. Mehrotra, D. Cowling, and L. Uscher-Pines. 2017. "Direct-to-Consumer Telehealth May Increase Access to Care but Does Not Decrease Spending." *Health Affairs* 36 (3): 485–91.

Banova, B. 2019. "The Impact of Technology on Healthcare." American Institute of Medical Sciences and Education. Published June 2. www.aimseducation.edu/blog/the-impact-of-technology-on-healthcare.

Betts, D., and L. Korenda. 2018. "Inside the Patient Journey: Three Key Touch Points for Consumer Engagement Strategies." Deloitte Insights. Published September 25. https://www2.deloitte.com/insights/us/en/industry/health-care/patient-engagement-health-care-consumer-survey.html?id=us:2el:3pr:4di4632:5awa:6di:092418:&pkid=1005423.

Buyya, R., C. S. Yeo, S. Venugopal, J. Broberg, and I. Brandic. 2009. "Cloud Computing and Emerging IT Platforms: Vision, Hype, and Reality for Delivering Computing as the 5th Utility." *Future Generation Computer Systems* 25 (6): 599–616.

Centers for Medicare & Medicaid Services (CMS). 2020. "Promoting Interoperability Programs." Updated May 12. www.cms.gov/Regulations-and-Guidance/Legislation/EHRIncentivePrograms/index.html?redirect=/ehrincentiveprograms/30_Meaningful_Use.asp.

CommonWell Health Alliance. 2018. "CommonWell Health Alliance Announces General Availability of Carequality Connection." Published November 16. www.commonwellalliance.org/news-center/commonwell-news/commonwell-health-alliance-announces-general-availability-carequality-connection/.

Divali, P., J. Camosso-Stefinovic, and R. Baker. 2013. "Use of Personal Digital Assistants in Clinical Decision Making by Healthcare Professionals: A Systematic Review." *Health Informatics Journal* 19 (1): 16–28.

FAIR Health. 2019. "A Multilayered Analysis of Telehealth: How This Emerging Venue of Care Is Affecting the Healthcare Landscape." White Paper. Published July. https://

s3.amazonaws.com/media2.fairhealth.org/whitepaper/asset/A%20Multilayered%20 Analysis%20of%20Telehealth%20-%20A%20FAIR%20Health%20White%20Paper. pdf.

Fiks, A., R. Grundmeier, L. Biggs, A. Localio, and E. Alessandrini. 2007. "Impact of Clinical Alerts Within an Electronic Health Record on Routine Childhood Immunization in an Urban Pediatric Population." *Pediatrics* 120(4): 707–14.

Friedman, D., R. Parrish, and D. Ross. 2013. "Electronic Health Records and U.S. Public Health: Current Realities and Future Promise." *American Journal of Public Health* 103 (9): 1560–67.

Fry, E., and F. Schulte. 2019. "Death by a Thousand Clicks: Where Electronic Health Records Went Wrong." *Fortune*. Published March 18. https://fortune.com/longform/ medical-records/.

HIMSS Analytics. 2016. *The Cloud Evolution in Healthcare*. Accessed June 16, 2020. www. level3.com/~/media/files/ebooks/en_cloud_eb_healthcare.pdf.

Hwang, K. 2020. "Dangers of Defective Mobile Health Apps and Devices." Verywell Health. Updated March 20. www.verywellhealth.com/dangers-of-defective-mobile-health-apps-and-devices-1739151.

Innovatemedtec. 2020. "mHealth." Accessed June 18. https://innovatemedtec.com/ digital-health/mhealth.

Irving, F. 2018. "ONC Clarifies Health IT Interoperability Under HIPAA." EHR Intelligence. Accessed June 16, 2020. https://ehrintelligence.com/news/onc-clarifies health-it-interoperability-under-hipaa.

Jones, M. 2018. "Healthcare: How Technology Impacts the Healthcare Industry." Healthcare in America. Published December 26. https://healthcareinamerica.us/ healthcare-how-technology-impacts-the-healthcare-industry-b2ba6271c4b4.

Marchesini, K., and T. Noonan. 2018. "HIPAA & Health Information Portability: A Foundation for Interoperability." Health IT Buzz. Published August 30. www.healthit.gov/buzz-blog/privacy-and-security-of-ehrs/hipaa-health-information-portability-a-foundation-for-interoperability.

Medicaid.gov. 2020. "Telemedicine." Accessed June 16. www.medicaid.gov/medicaid/benefits/telemed/index.html.

Mickan, S., J. K. Tilson, H. Atherton, N. W. Roberts, and C. Heneghan. 2013. "Evidence of Effectiveness of Healthcare Professionals Using Handheld Computers: A Scoping Review of Systematic Reviews." *Journal of Medical Internet Research* 15 (10): e212.

Monica, K. 2017a. "Regenstrief to Develop Automated Patient EHR Matching Solution." EHR Intelligence. Published August 9. https://ehrintelligence.com/news/regenstrief-to-develop-automated-patient-ehr-matching-solution.

———. 2017b. "Top 5 Challenges to Achieving Healthcare Interoperability." EHR Intelligence. Published August 14. https://ehrintelligence.com/news/top-5-challenges-to-achieving-healthcare-interoperability.

Mosa, A. S., I. Yoo, and L. Sheets. 2012. "A Systematic Review of Healthcare Apps for Smartphones." *BMC Medical Informatics and Decision Making* 12: 67.

National Institutes of Health (NIH). 2020. "Big Data to Knowledge: Program Snapshot." Updated April 15. https://commonfund.nih.gov/bd2k.

NEJM Catalyst. 2018. "Healthcare Big Data and the Promise of Value-Based Care." Published Jan 1. https://catalyst.nejm.org/doi/full/10.1056/CAT.18.0290.

Nextgen. 2019. "Understanding EMR vs. EHR." Accessed June 16, 2020. www.nextgen.com/insights/emr-vs-ehr/emr-vs-ehr.

Office of the National Coordinator for Health Information Technology (ONC). 2020. "Information Blocking." Updated May 22. www.healthit.gov/topic/information-blocking.

————. 2019. "How Electronic Health Records Improve Public and Population Health Outcomes." Updated May 21. www.healthit.gov/faq/how-can-electronic-health-records-improve-public-and-population-health-outcomes.

————. 2017. "Benefits of EHRs." Updated October 5. www.healthit.gov/topic/health-it-basics/benefits-ehrs.

Prgomet, M., A. Georgiou, and J. I. Westbrook. 2009. "The Impact of Mobile Handheld Technology on Hospital Physicians' Work Practices and Patient Care: A Systematic Review." *Journal of the American Medical Informatics Association* 16 (6): 792–801.

Quality Payment Program (QPP). 2020. "MIPS Overview." Accessed June 16. https://qpp.cms.gov/mips/overview.

Ramanathan, T., C. Schmit, A. Menon, and C. Fox. 2015. "The Role of Law in Supporting Secondary Uses of Electronic Health Information." *Journal of Law, Medicine & Ethics* 43 (1): 48–51.

Safran, C., M. Bloomrosen, W. E. Hammond, et al. 2007. "Toward a National Framework for the Secondary Use of Health Data: An American Medical Informatics Association White Paper." *Journal of the American Medical Informatics Association* 14 (1): 1–9.

SearchHealthIT. 2020. "mHealth (Mobile Health)." Accessed June 18, 2020. https://searchhealthit.techtarget.com/definition/mHealth.

Snell, E. 2018. "40 Percent of Physicians See More EHR Challenges than Benefits." EHR Intelligence. Published June 5. https://ehrintelligence.com/news/40-of-physicians-see-more-ehr-challenges-than-benefits.

Tam, C., and A. Sharma. 2014. "Mobile Medical Apps: To Regulate or Not to Regulate?" American Pharmacists Association. Published December 1. www.pharmacist.com/article/mobile-medical-apps-regulate-or-not-regulate.

US National Library of Medicine. 2020. "What Is the Precision Medicine Initiative?" Published June 9. https://ghr.nlm.nih.gov/primer/precisionmedicine/initiative. Accessed Dec 31, 2018.

Ventola, C. L. 2014. "Mobile Devices and Apps for Healthcare Professionals: Uses and Benefits." *Pharmacy and Therapeutics* 39 (5): 356–64.

Vyas, S., J. Murren-Boezem, and P. Solo-Josephson. 2018. "Analysis of a Pediatric Telemedicine Program." *Telemedicine and e-Health* 24 (12). www.liebertpub.com/doi/10.1089/tmj.2017.0281.

CHAPTER 12

POPULATION HEALTH

A 2017 documentary titled *A Coalition of the Willing* describes a population health team in Doylestown, Pennsylvania, that has focused on the elderly since 2001 (Falk 2017). Health Quality Partners, made up of data analysts, social workers, nurses, and doctors, uses data to find extreme patterns of health needs in a population—a practice known as "hotspotting"—to identify those with the most need. They pull data from a vast database every night to identify areas of the community that are in need and then move into the area to care for the people there. Through this process the team has helped reduce mortality in this population by 25 percent. A testimonial on the group's website (www.hqp.org) reported, "At the time of starting the program, I was within 2–3 weeks of having a stroke because of my blood pressure. The care I received probably saved my life."

LEARNING OBJECTIVES

After reading this chapter, you will be able to

➤ Define population health.

➤ Differentiate between population health and public health.

➤ Evaluate the significance of determinants of health.

➤ Comprehend health disparities among individuals and groups.

➤ Understand "big data" in healthcare and the challenges associated with its use.

➤ Compare population health management tools and models.

➤ Analyze the role of healthcare in population health management.

WHAT IS POPULATION HEALTH?

population health
The health outcomes of a group of individuals, including the distribution of such outcomes within the group.

The term **population health** was first used in a report published in Canada in the early 1990s, although no precise definition was given (Evans, Barer, and Marmor 1994). Nearly a decade later, researchers David Kindig and Greg Stoddart (2003) defined population health as "the health outcomes of a group of individuals, including the distribution of such outcomes within the group." According to these authors, population health looks at the link between health outcomes, health determinants, and health policies and interventions. Likewise, the Centers for Disease Control and Prevention (CDC) views population health as a partnership among public health agencies, industry, academia, healthcare, and local government entities to achieve positive health outcomes (CDC 2019c). In 1998, Health Canada, that country's agency responsible for public health policy, defined the overall goal of population health: to improve the health of the entire population and to reduce inequalities among population groups.

public health
A field that is concerned with protecting and improving the health of people and communities.

Population health differs from **public health**. Public health is concerned with protecting and improving the health of people and communities. The American Public Health Association teaches that public health agencies conduct research, gather evidence, track disease outbreaks, prevent injury and illness, set standards to protect workers, and influence

EXHIBIT 12.1
Ten Essential Environmental Public Health Services

Source: PHIL (2017).

school nutrition, among other functions (APHA 2020). The CDC promotes three core functions of public health: assessment, policy development, and assurance. These three functions encompass ten essential environmental public health services: monitoring health, diagnosing and investigating health problems, educating and empowering people, mobilizing community partnerships, developing health policies, enforcing laws related to health and safety, linking people to health services, ensuring a competent environmental health workforce, evaluating population health services, and researching innovative solutions to health problems (CDC 2019b) (exhibit 12.1).

While public health experts play a vital role in the health of US states and communities, they partner with healthcare providers, community health workers, government agencies, schools, nonprofit agencies, researchers, business, community leaders, and others in the task of population health.

Determinants of Health

Determinants of health are factors that are drivers of health outcomes, and they are key to understanding the health of populations. Determinants of health are divided into five categories (Evans and Stoddart 1990). These include medical care, individual behavior, social environment, physical environment, and genetics. Medical care includes prevention, screening, treatment, and management of disease. Individual behaviors are lifestyle decisions that may include smoking, diet, and exercise. Social environment focuses on socioeconomic factors such as income, education, and occupation. Physical environment comprises clean air and water, opportunities to recreate, and even buildings in a community. Genetics are the characteristics that people inherited from their ancestors and their contribution to health outcomes (Kindig, Asada, and Booske 2008).

Social and physical environment together are commonly referred to as **social determinants of health** (CDC 2018). The Kaiser Family Foundation defines social determinants of health as encompassing economic stability, neighborhood and physical environment, education, food, community and social context, and the healthcare system. All of these factors affect the health outcomes of mortality, morbidity, life expectancy, healthcare expenditures, health status, and functional limitations (Artiga and Hinton 2018).

Studies have demonstrated that social determinants have a significant impact on health. For example, research has documented children's exposure to lead as a result of poor housing (Ahrens et al. 2016); the connection between food insecurity and kidney disease (Banerjee et al. 2017); disparities in the prevalence of diabetes (Beckles and Chou 2016); economic insecurity and its relationship to partner and sexual violence (Breiding et al. 2017); avoidable deaths from cardiovascular disease (Greer et al. 2016); and the relationship between socioeconomic status and cigarette smoking (Helms, King, and Ashley 2017).

Evidence gathered over the past 25 years has shed light on the significance of socioeconomic factors such as income, wealth, and education as causes of a variety of health

determinants of health
Factors that are drivers of health outcomes, including medical care, individual behavior, social environment, physical environment, and genetics.

social determinants of health
Factors in the social and physical environment that affect health outcomes, such as economic stability, neighborhood and physical environment, education, food, community and social context, and the healthcare system.

problems (Braveman and Gottlieb 2014). Exhibits 12.2, 12.3, and 12.4 illustrate three examples of the impact of social determinants on health.

Some researchers have attempted to identify the determinants of mortality. They suggest that 40 percent of deaths are caused by behavioral factors, 30 percent by genetics,

EXHIBIT 12.2
Years of Life
Remaining at Age
30 by Education,
2010

Education	Men	Women
Never been to college	43.2	48.8
Some college, no bachelor's degree	47.2	51.9
Bachelor's degree or higher	52.6	55.3

Source: Luy et al. (2019).

EXHIBIT 12.3
Infant Mortality
Rates by
Education, 2009

	Deaths per 1,000 Live Births
No high school diploma	7.65
High school diploma	7.15
Some college or technical school	5.82
Bachelor's degree or higher	3.73

Source: Mathews and MacDorman (2013).

EXHIBIT 12.4
Overall Health
Status by Income,
2018

Of those who make less than $35,000 per year, 54% report very good to excellent health and 18% report poor to fair health.

Of those who make more than $100,000 per year, 79% report very good to excellent health and 4% report poor to fair health.

Source: NCHS (2018).

15 percent by social circumstances, 10 percent by medical care, and 5 percent by physical environmental exposures (McGinnis, Williams-Russo, and Knickman 2002).

The determinants of health have significant and complex interactions with each other and with the outcomes themselves. Some outcomes have a reverse causality on determinants; for example, a lack of income may be a barrier to attaining higher education, eating a good diet, and living in an environment that allows for physical activity.

Health Disparities

The World Health Organization (WHO) uses fairness as a way to compare health systems around the world. The WHO (2000) argues that "it is not sufficient to protect or improve the average health of the population, if—at the same time—inequality worsens or remains high because the gain accrues disproportionately to those already enjoying better health." Good health, according to the WHO, represents the "best attainable average level" and the "smallest feasible differences among individuals and groups." *Health disparities* are preventable differences among population groups in the burden of disease or injury. Health disparities may also refer to differences among groups in terms of health insurance coverage, access to healthcare, or quality of healthcare. Health disparities occur when one population group is not afforded equal or fair treatment or the burden of disease or injury falls disproportionately on certain populations.

Data clearly identify health disparities in the areas of race/ethnicity, socioeconomic status, age, location, gender, disability status, and sexual orientation (Orgera and Artiga 2018). A CDC report went further, reviewing disparities in 29 areas within six broad categories: social determinants of health, environmental hazards, healthcare access and preventive services, behavioral risk factors, morbidity, and mortality. The CDC report was designed to assist public health, academia, and clinical experts; policymakers; community leaders (including healthcare leaders); researchers; and the general public in overcoming disparities (CDC 2013).

Health disparities affect the healthcare industry and US population as a whole, limiting the quality of care for all and imposing a huge financial burden on the entire population. A 2018 analysis estimated that health disparities resulted in $93 billion in excess medical care costs and $42 billion in lost productivity per year. The US economy also suffers as a result of premature deaths (Turner 2018).

Race/Ethnicity

People of color generally experience more barriers to accessing healthcare and use less healthcare than white Americans. According to a Kaiser Family Foundation study, among nonelderly adults, Hispanics/Latinos, African Americans, and American Indians and Alaska

Natives are more likely to go without care or delay care that they need. Whites tend to identify a personal primary care provider more often than Black or Hispanic/Latino adults (Orgera and Artiga 2018). Non-Hispanic/Latino Black adults are at least 50 percent more likely to die prematurely of heart disease or stroke than their non-Hispanic/Latino white counterparts. Adult diabetes is more prevalent in Hispanics/Latinos, non-Hispanic/Latino Blacks, and those of mixed race. The infant mortality rate is high for non-Hispanic/Latino Blacks—more than twice that of non-Hispanic/Latino white Americans (CDC 2013).

A 2017 report from the Agency for Healthcare Research and Quality supports this finding, indicating that Blacks, American Indians and Alaska Natives, and Native Hawaiians/Pacific Islanders experience worse access to healthcare compared with whites for 40 percent of the measures studied, such as access to care, patient safety, care coordination, effectiveness of care, and affordable care (AHRQ 2019).

SOCIOECONOMIC STATUS

Wide gaps exist between the richest and poorest households in the United States. A 2016 *JAMA* study found a gap in life expectancy of about 15 years for men and 10 years for women when comparing the richest 1 percent of individuals with the poorest 1 percent (Chetty, Stepner, and Abraham 2016). Exhibit 12.5 illustrates the income gaps between the nation's richest households, with an average income of $214,000 in 2016, and the poorest, which averaged only $13,000 (Semega, Fontenot, and Kollar 2017).

Americans living at or below the federal poverty level experienced worse access to care compared with higher-income people (incomes of 400 percent of the federal poverty

EXHIBIT 12.5

The Income Gap in the United States, 2016

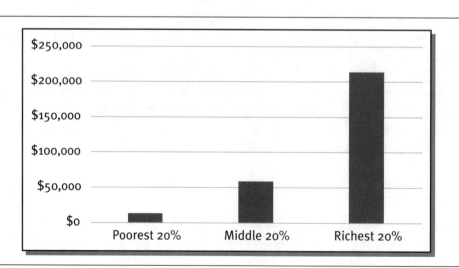

Source: Semega, Fontenot, and Kollar (2017).

level and higher) for all access measures except having a usual source of care with evening and weekend office hours. Even with this source of care, among low-income adults, visits to emergency departments in 2016 for asthma increased from 809 to 923 per 100,000 population, while the number of higher-income adults visiting the emergency department for the same reason decreased from 348 to 310 per 100,000 population. Significant disparities persist for low-income Americans who reported that they were unable to get the care they needed for financial reasons (AHRQ 2017).

Gender and Sexual Orientation

The National Institutes of Health (NIH) reports that women are twice as likely as men to experience depression and more likely to admit to negative mood states. Women also have a harder time quitting smoking. Nicotine replacement therapies such as patches and gum work better in men than in women, an effect that may be related to women's metabolism. Women are more susceptible to cardiovascular disease and experience osteoporosis more often. Finally, the NIH reports that sports injuries are more common in women and girls because of their knee and hip anatomy, imbalanced leg muscle strength, and looser tendons and ligaments (NIH 2019). A number of studies conducted by NIH offices and affiliates have placed women at higher risk of health problems related to alcohol use, breast and lung cancer, depression and other mental health disorders, and severe flu symptoms (NIH 2020). However, according to the CDC (2019a), men are about four times more likely to commit suicide than women, regardless of age or race/ethnicity.

LGBTQ (lesbian, gay, bisexual, transgender, and queer/questioning) individuals, according to the Office of Disease Prevention and Health Promotion, report higher rates of health disparities linked to social stigma and discrimination. These include psychiatric disorders, substance abuse, and suicide (ODPHP 2020d). Many LGBTQ individuals delay care or receive inferior care because of real or perceived homophobia or discrimination by healthcare providers (GLMA 2006). The National Health Interview Survey of 2013 identified a number of health indicators for which LGBTQ individuals are at higher risk (see exhibit 12.6): cigarette smoking, alcohol consumption, psychological distress, healthcare access (in defining a "usual place to go" for care), and failing to obtain needed medical care (Ward et al. 2014).

Geographic Location

Where a person chooses to live profoundly affects their health outcomes. In 2014, many southern and southwestern states (Arkansas, Kentucky, Louisiana, Mississippi, New Mexico, Oklahoma, Texas, and West Virginia), several western states (Nevada, Oregon, and Wyoming), and one midwestern state (Indiana) had the lowest overall quality scores (AHRQ 2017).

EXHIBIT 12.6
Selected Health-
Related Behavior
Indicators of US
Adults, by Sexual
Orientation and
Gender, 2013

25.8% of those who identify as gay or lesbian smoke, while 17.6% of those who identify as straight smoke.

10.8% of those identifying as bisexual expressed serious psychological distress, while 3.7% of those identifying as straight had similar issues.

39.5% of those who identified as bisexual had five or more drinks in one day, compared with 22.3% of their straight peers.

Source: Ward et al. (2014).

U.S. News & World Report and the Aetna Foundation assessed nearly 3,000 US counties across 81 metrics in ten categories. The analysis showed that substantial challenges among Black residents included homicide rates, low birth weight, and local access to food. The study found that nearly 700 communities had Black population segments larger than the national average, and only 30 of those communities were among the top 500 healthiest communities (McPhillips 2018).

POPULATION HEALTH MANAGEMENT

Gathering patient and community health data from a variety of sources, analyzing those data to create an understandable picture of the health of a population, and then taking action to improve the health of that group is *population health management*. A number of techniques and tools are used to create that picture. The tools covered here include community health needs assessments, County Health Rankings, the Healthy People initiative, Mobilizing for Action through Planning and Partnerships, the Association for Community Health Improvement's Community Health Assessment Toolkit, the Community Tool Box, and the Guide and Template for Comprehensive Health Improvement Planning.

big data
Large data sets that are used to analyze a population and find trends in individual or population health.

ANALYTICS AND POPULATION HEALTH

One study estimates that healthcare organizations had collected 150 exabytes—or 150 billion gigabytes—of data through 2011 (Terry 2013). Referred to as **big data**, these data take the form of electronic health records and financial billing systems. These data allow researchers to understand when an individual is likely to shift to a higher-risk category and allow a provider to intervene. The data sets provide the foundation for modeling patient populations by tracking the health risk status of a particular population (Bradley 2013).

Managing healthcare data poses a number of challenges. Finding employees with the skills to use the data can be difficult. Information technology investment in healthcare is among the lowest of all industries, even though the amount of data collected in healthcare exceeds that of manufacturing, financial services, or media. One study gave healthcare a score of 2.4 out of 5 in data management, use, and monetization—well below average according to some competency metrics (Kent 2018).

A 2019 study found that only one in five senior healthcare organizations use **analytics** for population health (Sucich 2019). The study, which surveyed 110 senior healthcare leaders, revealed the following:

◆   90 percent are using data analytics in clinical areas.

◆   Only about 22 percent are using analytics for population health.

◆   Among healthcare organizations that are not using analytics, only about 32 percent say that population health is a top priority.

Data-driven population health is an area of tremendous potential. Data exist in health and financial records, surveys, and public health records. However, the models for pulling data, and expert staff to analyze and use them, are not fully in place.

COMMUNITY HEALTH NEEDS ASSESSMENT

The Affordable Care Act (ACA) requires tax-exempt hospitals to complete a **community health needs assessment (CHNA)** every three years. This report is intended to assess the health needs of a community, prioritize those needs, and identify resources to address them. Under Internal Revenue Service rules, tax-exempt hospitals must solicit input from at least one state, local, tribal, or regional government public health department and members of medically underserved, low-income, and minority populations in the community. Hospitals must also consider written comments on their most recently conducted CHNA and outline how they plan to address the recommendations. These reports must be made available to the general public (IRS 2019). The sidebar presents an example of a CHNA partnership with Intermountain Healthcare, the Utah Department of Health, and several local health districts in that state.

Around the same time that the ACA was enacted, the Public Health Accreditation Board required a similar community health assessment of all local and state public health

analytics
The gathering and interpretation of data.

community health needs assessment (CHNA)
A report that assesses the health needs of a community, prioritizes those needs, and identifies resources to address them; under the Affordable Care Act (ACA), nonprofit hospitals are required to complete an assessment every three years.

✳ A CHNA PARTNERSHIP IN UTAH

Intermountain Healthcare, based in Utah, joined forces with state and local public health departments, community leaders, and representatives of local underserved populations to complete a CHNA in 2013 and another in 2016. Intermountain Healthcare's hospitals and local health departments, along with the Utah Department of Health, cohosted community input meetings. Participants included minority, low-income, and uninsured populations, as well as safety net clinic employees, school representatives, health advocates, mental health providers, local government leaders, and senior service providers.

In 2016, Intermountain worked with local health departments and the Utah Department of Health, along with some of Intermountain's clinical and operational leadership, to identify 100 health indicators representing 16 broad health issues (IMC 2016). These indicators become the drivers of action by Intermountain Healthcare in communities around the state. Priority health needs included the prevention of prediabetes, high blood pressure, depression, and prescription opioid misuse. Results of the CHNA were used to develop a three-year implementation strategy for Intermountain. Each of Intermountain Healthcare's 21 Utah hospitals developed its own CHNA report and implementation plan (see https://intermountainhealthcare.org/about/who-we-are/chna-reports). They have continued to monitor quarterly the outcome measures established in the CHNA.

The Utah Department of Health (2016) and each local health department established its own list of priorities, many of which were in line with those of Intermountain. The Utah Department of Health and the Weber-Morgan Health Department (2016) in northern Utah, for example, focused on preventing suicide, obesity, and adolescent substance abuse.

agencies that wished to be accredited (ASTHO 2017). The board's accreditation standards require public health departments to take the following steps:

- ◆ Be a part of or lead a collaborative process resulting in a community health assessment.

- ◆ Collect and maintain reliable data on public health conditions of the population served.

◆ Analyze these data and report on trends in health issues, environmental public health hazards, and social and economic health factors.

◆ Develop recommendations regarding public health policy, programs, and interventions.

The benefits and outcomes of community health assessments include the following:

◆ Improved organizational and community coordination and collaboration

◆ Stronger partnerships between healthcare and public health at the state and local levels

◆ Data-driven baselines against which implementation can be measured

◆ Identification of strengths and weaknesses related to improvement efforts

CHNAs are required of nonprofit hospitals and public health departments seeking accreditation. Many state and local health departments have chosen not to complete the accreditation process but are completing health assessments as part of their efforts to support the health of the populations they serve.

COUNTY HEALTH RANKINGS

Annually since 2010, the University of Wisconsin's Population Health Institute and the Robert Wood Johnson Foundation have produced the County Health Rankings for the nation's more than 3,000 counties. Data gathered from a number of US sources are analyzed and reported. The rankings take into account health factors such as health behaviors, clinical care, and social and economic factors; the physical environment; and health outcomes, measured by morbidity and mortality rates (Remington, Catlin, and Gennuso 2015). Exhibit 12.7 summarizes the County Health Rankings.

The County Health Rankings are widely used in the United States. The primary use of these and similar rankings is to help set goals and public health agendas. Local health departments can use them as part of their education efforts and to bring awareness to public health issues in a community. This can lead to motivation and debate over what needs to be done to help community populations. A second purpose is to establish responsibility for population health (Oliver 2010). However, some have criticized these rankings for what they view as the arbitrariness of the measures, the emphasis on insignificant differences, and the tendency to focus only on the data in the rankings (Arndt et al. 2013; Kanarek, Tasi, and Stanley 2011).

Exhibit 12.7
County Health
Rankings Model

Health Outcomes	Length of Life	
	Quality of Life	
Health factors		
	Health behaviors	Tobacco use
		Diet and exercise
		Alcohol and drug use
		Sexual activity
	Clinical care	Access to care
		Quality of care
	Social and economic factors	Education
		Employment
		Income
		Family and social support
		Community safety
	Physical environment	Air and water quality
		Housing and transit

Source: Remington, Catlin, and Gennuso (2015).

The 2019 County Health Rankings noted the following findings (Robert Wood Johnson Foundation 2019):

- More than one in ten households across the United States spend more than half of their income on housing costs. Renters spend a substantially higher percentage of their income on housing compared with homeowners. This is especially true for low-income households.

- Across the counties, households described as "severely cost burdened" are associated with more food insecurity, child poverty, and fair or poor health status.

- Black residents face greater barriers than white residents. Nearly one in four Black households spend more than half of their income on housing.

◆ About 13 percent of those living in the top-performing (10 percent) counties rate themselves in poor health, while 15 percent of those living in the bottom-performing counties (10 percent) do.

◆ The difference between the top- and bottom-performing counties is more pronounced for child poverty, with 15 percent reported in the top-performing counties and 22 percent in the bottom-performing counties.

◆ Across the counties, every 10 percent increase in the share of severely cost burdened households is linked to 29,000 more children in poverty, 86,000 more people who are food insecure, and 84,000 more people in fair or poor health.

The County Health Rankings show clearly that where people live makes a difference in their health outcomes.

HEALTHY PEOPLE

The Office of Disease Prevention and Health Promotion, an agency of the US Department of Health and Human Services, has spearheaded the development and implementation of the Healthy People initiative for four decades. Efforts are now underway for the introduction of Healthy People 2030 (ODPHP 2020c). The national health objectives set for the Healthy People 2020 initiative are based on evidence gathered before, during, and at the conclusion of the initiative. The overarching goals of Healthy People 2020 are as follows: (ODPHP 2020a):

◆ Attain high-quality, longer lives free of preventable disease, disability, injury, and premature death.

◆ Achieve health equity, eliminate disparities, and improve the health of all groups.

◆ Create social and physical environments that promote good health for all.

◆ Promote quality of life, health development, and healthy behaviors across all life stages.

Each Healthy People initiative establishes several topic areas and hundreds of objectives, supported by baseline national data and targets for improvement. In most cases, interventions and resources are offered to achieve the objectives. The sidebar features an example of how Healthy People 2020 made a difference in one Maryland community.

(✳) **HIGH INCIDENCE OF END-STAGE RENAL DISEASE IN MARYLAND'S LATINO POPULATION**

According to 2006–2010 data, the Maryland Department of Health learned that diabetic end-stage renal disease among Hispanics/Latinos was 10 percent to 20 percent higher than for non-Hispanic/Latino whites ages 55 and older. Related renal disease and obesity rates have increased over the last three decades. With funding from the Office of Disease Prevention and Health Promotion through the Healthy People 2020 Community Innovations Project, the department hired a Hispanic/Latino community member to reach out to the neighborhood to organize health screenings and education (ODPHP 2013). Before the introduction of the program, only 24 of 128 participants reported having their cholesterol checked in the past two years. After participating in the project, all of the participants were screened. Nearly one-third learned that they had elevated cholesterol. All were taught about exercise and healthy eating. In addition, many participants were connected with a primary care provider.

OTHER POPULATION HEALTH MANAGEMENT MODELS AND TOOLS

The CDC identifies common elements of assessment and planning frameworks and provides information about commonly used frameworks (CDC 2015). Mobilizing for Action through Planning and Partnerships (MAPP) is a tool that was developed to help communities prioritize public health issues and identify resources to address them. It is sometimes used to develop community health assessments and improvement plans. MAPP is broken down into six phases, illustrated in exhibit 12.8.

MAPP comprises four assessments: community themes and strengths, local public health system, community health status, and forces of change. MAPP focuses on the development of community partnerships and a continuous cycle of planning, implementation, and evaluation.

The Association for Community Health Improvement's Community Health Assessment Toolkit includes nine steps of strategizing engaging stakeholders, defining the community, collecting and analyzing data, prioritizing community health issues, documenting results, planning, implementation, and evaluation. It is designed as a resource for hospitals and public health agencies to conduct community health assessments (ACHI 2017).

The Community Tool Box, created by the University of Kansas, provides information on building healthy communities. One chapter of the tool box focuses on the health assessment process. It includes many of the steps listed in the other models, broken down into 24 sections (University of Kansas 2018).

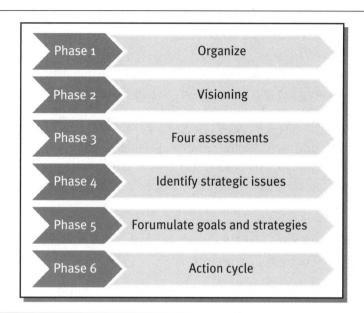

Exhibit 12.8
Phases of Mobilizing for Action through Planning and Partnerships (MAPP)

Source: NACCHO (2020).

The Guide and Template for Comprehensive Health Improvement Planning was developed by the Connecticut Department of Public Health. The department created the four-part plan prior to the passage of the ACA to facilitate the development of CDC-sponsored prevention and control plans. The first part of the template outlines the planning process. The second part contains examples of vision, mission, goals, objectives, strategies, and work plans. The third part focuses on criteria for setting priorities and focus areas. The last part contains a template for the health improvement plan. It is based on historically successful planning initiatives (Bower 2009).

The Association of State and Territorial Health Officials also created a booklet called *Developing a State Health Improvement Plan: Guidance and Resources: A Companion Document to ASTHO's State Health Assessment Guidance and Resources.* The ideas and principles in this guide are similar to those in the other resources discussed here. This 100-page booklet focuses on engaging stakeholders, creating a vision, gathering and leveraging data, establishing and communicating priorities, developing objectives and measures, and implementing and evaluating the state health improvement plan (ASTHO 2019).

HEALTHCARE'S ROLE IN POPULATION HEALTH

The Healthy People 2010 and 2020 initiatives included objectives specific to population health and health professions education. For example, several objectives promoted the inclusion of core disease prevention and population health content for students who will eventually care for patients (ODPHP 2020b). This emphasis applies to individual patients and clients cared for by healthcare workers and, by extension, to the education of the local population.

The Institute of Medicine reported in 2003 that true population health cannot be achieved until the entire US population has access to adequate healthcare. Some argue that it is the right of every citizen and the responsibility of the federal government to provide some sort of universal coverage. Access to care is key to achieving basic levels of health, including mental health, dental health, and care of chronic conditions. The ACA attempted to improve access to care for millions of Americans. A 2018 Commonwealth Fund survey (Collins, Bhupal, and Doty 2019) paints an evidenced-based picture of the outcomes of the ACA thus far:

◆ In 2018, 45 percent of US adults were inadequately insured, and the adult uninsured rate was 12.4 percent.

◆ Compared with 2010, however, fewer adults were uninsured, and the duration of coverage gaps was shorter.

◆ Employer plans provided less coverage in 2018 than they did in 2010, leading to more people with coverage being underinsured.

◆ More people had difficulty paying their medical bills.

One success of the ACA is that more adults, including those who are underinsured, are likely to have continuous care and to get regular preventive care. Healthcare plays a role in promoting health policy that influences the determinants of health and positively affects health outcomes.

The Commonwealth Fund report notes that prevention alone is not enough. Policy should expand Medicaid coverage without restrictions and ban insurance plans that do not comply with the provisions of the ACA. The report also argues for the importance of continued federal funding for healthcare navigators. Lifting the income cap to help some afford marketplace plans would bolster population health, as would offering tax credits for high out-of-pocket medical costs. Finally, policy should protect consumers from surprise medical bills and more.

The American Hospital Association (AHA) recognizes the role of healthcare in population health. In 2019, the organization implemented a strategic vision called the "AHA's Path Forward." The directive includes five areas of commitment from the AHA:

◆ Access to affordable, equitable health, behavioral, and social services

◆ Providing value to lives with given care

◆   Embracing the diversity of individuals and serving as their health partners

◆   Focusing on the well-being of individuals with community resources

◆   Coordinating seamless care

The AHA plan offers a picture of strategic priorities and what it calls "driving forces," such as payment for value, chronic care management, and population health management (AHA 2019). The effort is supported by ideas and resources from the Robert Wood Johnson Foundation in a "playbook" that fosters partnerships between hospitals and community partners (Health Research and Educational Trust 2017).

The American Medical Association includes in its tagline that it "promotes the art and science of medicine and the betterment of public health." Medical schools have only recently begun to include population health in their curricula. The idea of gathering evidence and then collaborating with community organizations to improve social determinants of health is a relatively new concept in most medical schools.

Changing the focus of the healthcare industry to emphasize population health is a slow process. Davis Nash, a physician and dean of the Jefferson College of Population Health in Philadelphia, gave the industry's effort a C grade in 2016, but in 2019, he upgraded his assessment to a B or B+. Nash indicates progress in those three years, noting that several schools and departments of population health have been established in medical schools (Squazzo 2019).

✱ DEBATE TIME The Healthcare Industry and Population Health

Some argue that the healthcare industry should be more involved with population health, even partnering with public health agencies and other stakeholders to keep their communities well. What do you think? Form two teams and debate the merits of such an idea. One team could focus on the positives of involving healthcare professionals as team members or even taking the lead on population health. Another team could argue that healthcare professionals should worry about the sick, not the well. Hospitals, for example, may not make a profit or even achieve a reasonable budget if too much is spent on community health.

Summary

Population health is defined as health outcomes of groups or individuals, including the distribution of those outcomes by social demographics, location, and other factors. Population health considers the links between health outcomes, determinants of health, and health policies and interventions. It differs from public health, which focuses on assessment, policy development, and assurance.

Determinants of health are factors that are drivers of health outcomes. They are key to understanding the health of populations. Determinants of health are divided into five categories: medical care, individual behavior, social environment, physical environment, and genetics. Social and physical environment together are referred to as social determinants of health. Evidence gathered over the past 25 years has demonstrated the significance of socioeconomic factors such as income, wealth, and education as causes of a variety of health problems.

Health disparities are preventable differences among population groups in the burden of disease or injury. Health disparities occur when one population group is not afforded equal or fair treatment or the burden of disease or injury falls disproportionately on certain populations. Data clearly identify health disparities in the areas of race/ethnicity, socioeconomic status, age, location, gender, disability status, and sexual orientation. Health disparities impose a financial burden on the entire population, resulting in $93 billion in excess medical care costs and $42 billion in lost productivity.

Big data and analytics are used to create models for improving population health. Healthcare organizations have billions of gigabytes of data at their disposal to analyze the needs of the populations they serve. Finding individuals with the skills to gather and analyze data and create analytical models, however, is a barrier to progress. For that reason, healthcare systems have been slow to use analytics to solve population health challenges.

The Affordable Care Act (ACA) requires tax-exempt hospitals to focus on population health by completing a community health needs assessment (CHNA) and improvement plan every three years. THE CHNA prioritizes the needs of the community and identifies resources to address them. Public health agencies that wish to be accredited must meet the same requirements.

Two other tools for population health management are the County Health Rankings produced by the University of Wisconsin's Population Health Institute and the Robert Wood Johnson Foundation and the Healthy People initiative of Office of Disease Prevention and Health Promotion, an agency of the US Department of Health and Human Services. These tools provide analysis and benchmark data to healthcare providers, public health agencies, and the general public. The County Health Rankings provide county-level data on life expectancy and quality of life (health outcomes) based on a set of health factors. Local data are compared with state data and top performers nationally to promote debate and set agendas for population health improvement.

Healthy People is a decades-old effort to set national population health objectives. Efforts are now underway for the introduction of Healthy People 2030. Each Healthy People initiative establishes several topic areas and hundreds of objectives, supported by baseline national data and targets for improvement.

Whether it is training healthcare workers to teach clients health promotion and disease prevention or taking care of their own employees, healthcare plays a major role in population health. That role extends to the communities served by these systems. Health policy and government are also key to population health improvement. The Institute of Medicine noted nearly two decades ago that true population health cannot be achieved until the entire US population has access to healthcare. Fewer people today are uninsured than before the enactment of the ACA, but more are underinsured.

The American Hospital Association, the American Medical Association, and other healthcare organizations support population health management. Medical schools include it as the "third pillar" of medical education. Moving healthcare toward an increased emphasis on population health is a slow process.

QUESTIONS

1. What is the difference between public health and population health?
2. What are some examples of determinants of health?
3. Give two examples of how social determinants of health affect health outcomes.
4. What are health disparities?
5. What are some examples of health disparities?
6. How do analysts use "big data" in healthcare?
7. What is the purpose of the community health needs assessment (CHNA)?
8. The study that compares health outcomes and health factors at a county level is called what?
9. What are the goals of the Healthy People 2020 initiative?
10. What is required for true population health, according to the Institute of Medicine?

ASSIGNMENTS

1. The 500 Cities Project is a collaboration between CDC, the Robert Wood Johnson Foundation, and the CDC Foundation. The project provides a variety of health data at the city or census tract level that may motivate stakeholders to take action. Visit the 500 Cities home page at www.cdc.gov/500cities/index.htm. Use the interactive map to find an area close to you. Zoom in on two or three small zones. Report at least one key measure (use the pulldown menu on the left side of the map to choose a measure).

2. Go to the Healthy People website at www.healthypeople.gov. Using the tools on the Healthy People home page, find a topic area of your choice. Identify two objectives within that topic. Report on the baseline data and the target reported for those objectives.

3. The County Health Rankings help identify social determinant needs at the county level. Go to www.countyhealthrankings.org and scroll down to identify a state on the interactive map. Choose a county in that state. How do the county's health outcomes (length of life and quality of life) compare with the rest of the state and the top US performers? Identify three health factors that you think the county should focus on improving.

Cases

Maternal Mortality in Louisiana

Officials at the Louisiana Department of Health are staring at the facts: Black women in the state are four times more likely to experience a pregnancy-related death than white women. Healthy People 2020 set a national goal of 11.4 maternal deaths per 100,000 live births. In 2018, Louisiana experienced 47.2 deaths per 100,000 among non-Hispanic/Latino Black women (AHR 2019).

As the department's experts looked more closely at the data, they found that the color of a woman's skin makes a difference when it comes to the care she receives, such as blood transfusions. The data made clear that bias and low-quality care are significant issues in Louisiana's healthcare systems (Donovan 2019).

Discussion Questions

1. What options are available to the Louisiana Department of Health in terms of population health directives or initiatives?
2. What specific steps could the Louisiana Department of Health take in working with the state's healthcare providers?

The Good Neighbor

Olivia, the new CEO of Mountain West Hospital, is taking time to meet local community leaders and show them that she wants to be a partner in making the community a great place to live. One of her key initiatives is to examine the general health of the community and learn how her organization can support the local health department and similar organizations. She knows that the Affordable Care Act requires nonprofit hospitals to complete a community health needs assessment, but Mountain West is part of a privately owned corporation, so it is not subject to that requirement. Clark has scheduled a meeting with her leadership team to discuss the hospital's role in the local population's health.

Discussion Questions

1. What steps should Clark take as she begins her efforts to improve the health of the community?
2. Find and describe some of the tools available to Clark that might help her analyze the needs of the community and prioritize the programs she puts in place.

REFERENCES

Agency for Healthcare Research and Quality (AHRQ). 2019. *2018 National Healthcare Quality and Disparities Report*. Published September. www.ahrq.gov/sites/default/files/wysiwyg/research/findings/nhqrdr/2018qdr.pdf.

———. 2017. *2016 National Healthcare Quality and Disparities Report*. Published October. www.ahrq.gov/research/findings/nhqrdr/nhqdr16/index.html.

Ahrens, K., B. Haley, L. Rossen, P. Lloyd, and Y. Aoki. 2016. "Housing Assistance and Blood Lead Levels: Children in the United States, 2005–2012." *American Journal of Public Health* 106 (11): 2049–56.

American Hospital Association (AHA). 2019. "Strategic Plan: AHA Path Forward." Accessed June 18, 2020. www.aha.org/2017-12-11-strategic-plan-aha-path-forward.

American Public Health Association (APHA). 2020. "What Is Public Health?" Accessed June 18. www.apha.org/what-is-public-health.

America's Health Rankings (AHR). 2019. "Maternal Mortality." Accessed June 22, 2020. www.americashealthrankings.org/explore/health-of-women-and-children/measure/maternal_mortality_a.

Arndt, S., L. Acion, K. Caspers, and P. Blood. 2013. "How Reliable Are County and Regional Health Rankings?" *Prevention Science* 14: 497–502.

Artiga, S., and E. Hinton. 2018. "Beyond Healthcare: The Role of Social Determinants in Promoting Health and Health Equity." Kaiser Family Foundation. Published May 10. www.kff.org/disparities-policy/issue-brief/beyond-health-care-the-role-of-social-determinants-in-promoting-health-and-health-equity/.

Association for Community Health Improvement (ACHI). 2017. "Community Health Assessment Toolkit." Accessed June 18, 2020. www.healthycommunities.org/Resources/toolkit.shtml#.XRZSUSBMGUk.

Association of State and Territorial Health Officials (ASTHO). 2019. *Developing a State Health Improvement Plan: Guidance and Resources: A Companion Document to ASTHO's State Health Assessment Guidance and Resources*. Accessed June 18, 2020. www.astho.org/WorkArea/DownloadAsset.aspx?id=6597.

————. 2017. "Community-Based Health Needs Assessment Activities: Opportunities for Collaboration Between Public Health Departments and Rural Hospitals." Accessed June 18, 2020. www.astho.org//uploadedFiles/Programs/Access/Primary_Care/Scan%20of%20Community-Based%20Health%20Needs%20Assessment%20Activities.pdf.

Banerjee, T., D. Crews, D. Wesson, S. Dharmarajan, R. Saran, N. Riso Burrows, S. Saydah, and N. Powe. 2017. "Food Insecurity, CKD, and Subsequent ESRD in U.S. Adults." *American Journal of Kidney Diseases* 70 (1): 38–47.

Beckles, G., and C. F. Chou. 2016. "Disparities in the Prevalence of Diagnosed Diabetes—United States, 1999–2002 and 2011–2014." *Morbidity and Mortality Weekly Report* 65 (45): 1265–69.

Bower, C. 2009. *Guide and Template for Comprehensive Health Improvement Planning: Version 2.1*. Connecticut Department of Public Health Planning Branch, Planning and Workforce Development Section. Published June. www.naccho.org/uploads/downloadable-resources/Programs/Public-Health-Infrastructure/CHIP-Guide.pdf.

Bradley, P. 2013. "Implications of Big Data Analytics on Population Health Management." *Big Data* 1 (3). https://doi.org/10.1089/big.2013.0019.

Braveman, P., and L. Gottlieb. 2014. "The Social Determinants of Health: It's Time to Consider the Cause of the Causes." *Public Health Reports* 129 (Suppl. 2): 19–31.

Breiding, M., K. Basile, J. Klevens, and S. Smith. 2017. "Economic Insecurity and Intimate Partner and Sexual Violence Victimization." *American Journal of Preventive Medicine* 53 (4): 457–64.

Centers for Disease Control and Prevention (CDC). 2019a. "CDC Research on SDOH." Updated December 12. www.cdc.gov/socialdeterminants/research/index.htm.

———. 2019b. "Resources Organized by Essential Services." Published March 7. www.cdc. gov/nceh/ehs/10-essential-services/resources.html.

———. 2019c. "What Is Population Health?" Published July 23. www.cdc.gov/ pophealthtraining/whatis.html.

———. 2018. "Social Determinants of Health: Know What Affects Health." Published January 29. www.cdc.gov/socialdeterminants/index.htm.

———. 2015. "Assessment & Planning Models, Frameworks & Tools." Published November 9. www.cdc.gov/publichealthgateway/cha/assessment.html.

———. 2013. "CDC Health Disparities and Inequalities Report—United States, 2013." *Morbidity and Mortality Weekly Report* 62 (3 Suppl.) www.cdc.gov/mmwr/pdf/other/ su6203.pdf.

Chetty, R., M. Stepner, and S. Abraham. 2016. "The Association Between Income and Life Expectancy in the United States, 2001–2014." *JAMA* 315 (16): 1750–66.

Collins, S., H. Bhupal, and M. Doty. 2019. "Health Insurance Coverage Eight Years After the ACA." Commonwealth Fund. Published February 7. www.commonwealthfund.org/ publications/issue-briefs/2019/feb/health-insurance-coverage-eight-years-after-aca.

Donovan, J. 2019. Speech delivered at the Association of University Programs in Health Administration Annual Conference, New Orleans, June 12.

Evans, R., M. Barer, and T. Marmor. 1994. *Why Are Some People Healthy and Others Not? The Determinants of Health of Populations*. New York: Aldine de Gruyter.

Evans, R., and G. Stoddart. 1990. "Producing Health, Consuming Healthcare." *Social Science & Medicine* 31 (12): 1347–63.

Falk, L. H. 2017. "Population Health Documentary Highlights Three Success Stories Transforming Healthcare." HealthCatalyst. Published Sept 29. www.healthcatalyst.com/population-health-documentary-showcases-success-stories.

Gay and Lesbian Medical Association (GLMA). 2006. *Guidelines for Care of Lesbian, Gay, Bisexual, and Transgender Patients*. http://glma.org/_data/n_0001/resources/live/GLMA%20guidelines%202006%20FINAL.pdf.

Greer, S., L. Schieb, M. Ritchey, M. George, and M. Casper. 2016. "County Health Factors Associated with Avoidable Deaths from Cardiovascular Disease in the United States, 2006–2010." *Public Health Reports* 131 (3): 438–48.

Health Canada. 1998. *Taking Action on Population Health*. Ottawa, Ontario: Health Canada.

Health Research and Educational Trust. 2017. *A Playbook for Fostering Hospital-Community Partnerships to Build a Culture of Health*. Published July. www.hpoe.org/Reports-HPOE/2017/A-playbook-for-fostering-hospitalcommunity-partnerships.pdf.

Helms, V., B. King, and P. Ashley. 2017. "Cigarette Smoking and Adverse Health Outcomes Among Adults Receiving Federal Housing Assistance." *Preventive Medicine* 99: 171–77.

Institute of Medicine. 2003. *The Future of the Public's Health in the 21st Century*. Washington, DC: National Academies Press.

Intermountain Medical Center (IMC). 2016. *2016 Community Health Needs Assessment*. Accessed June 19, 2020. https://intermountainhealthcare.org/about/who-we-are/chna-reports/-/media/37084070bfb24140acbddde5efc3d5cc.ashx.

Internal Revenue Service (IRS). 2019. "Community Health Needs Assessment for Charitable Hospital Organizations—Section 501(r)(3)." Updated September 20. www.irs.gov/

charities-non-profits/community-health-needs-assessment-for-charitable-hospital-
organizations-section-501r3.

Kanarek, N., H. L. Tsai, and J. Stanley. 2011. "Health Ranking of the Largest U.S. Counties
Using the Community Health Status Indicators Peer Strata and Database. *Journal of Public Health Management Practice* 17: 401–5.

Kent, J. 2018. "Big Data to See Explosive Growth, Challenging Healthcare Organizations."
Health IT Analytics. Published December 3. https://healthitanalytics.com/news/
big-data-to-see-explosive-growth-challenging-healthcare-organizations.

Kindig, D., and G. Stoddart. 2003. "What Is Population Health?" *American Journal of Public Health* 93 (3): 380–83.

Kindig, D., Y. Asada, and B. Booske. 2008. "A Population Health Framework for Setting
National and State Goals." *JAMA* 299 (17): 2081–83.

Luy, M., M. Zannella, C. Wegner-Siegmundt, Y. Minagawa, W. Lutz, and G. Caselli. 2019. "The
Impact of Increasing Education Levels on Rising Life Expectancy: A Decomposition for
Italy, Denmark, and the USA." *Genus: Journal Population Sciences* 75 (11). https://doi.
org/10.1186/s41118-019-0055-0.

Mathews, T. J., and M. F. MacDorman. 2013. "Infant Mortality Statistics from the 2009 Period
Linked Birth/Infant Death Dataset." *National Vital Statistics Report* 61: 1–28.

McGinnis, J., P. Williams-Russo, and J. Knickman. 2002. "The Case for More Active Policy
Attention to Health Promotion." *Health Affairs* 21 (2): 78–93.

McPhillips, D. 2018. "The Relationship of Race to Community Health." *U.S. News & World
Report*. Published September 25. www.usnews.com/news/healthiest-communities/
articles/2018-09-25/the-burden-of-race-on-community-health-in-america.

National Association of County and City Health Officials (NACCHO). 2020. "Mobilizing for Action through Planning and Partnerships (MAPP)." Accessed June 19. www.
naccho.org/programs/public-health-infrastructure/performance-improvement/
community-health-assessment/mapp.

National Center for Health Statistics (NCHS). 2018. "National Health Interview Survey, Table P-1: Respondent-Assessed Health Status, by Selected Characteristics: United States, 2018." Accessed June 19, 2020. https://ftp.cdc.gov/pub/Health_Statistics/NCHS/NHIS/SHS/2018_SHS_Table_P-1.pdf.

National Institutes of Health (NIH). 2020. "How Sex/Gender Influence Health & Disease (A–Z)." https://orwh.od.nih.gov/sex-gender/sexgender-influences-health-and-disease/how-sexgender-influence-health-disease-z.

———. 2019. "How Sex and Gender Influence Health and Disease." Accessed June 19, 2020. https://orwh.od.nih.gov/sites/orwh/files/docs/SexGenderInfographic11x17_508_Final_2.pdf.

Office of Disease Prevention and Health Promotion (ODPHP). 2020a. "About Healthy People." Accessed June 18. www.healthypeople.gov/2020/About-Healthy-People.

———.2020b. "Educational and Community-Based Programs." Accessed June 18. www.healthypeople.gov/2020/topics-objectives/topic/educational-and-community-based-programs/objectives.

———. 2020c. "History & Development of Healthy People." Accessed June 18. www.healthypeople.gov/2020/About-Healthy-People/History-Development-Healthy-People-2020.

———. 2020d. "Lesbian, Gay, Bisexual, and Transgender Health." Accessed June 18. www.healthypeople.gov/2020/topics-objectives/topic/lesbian-gay-bisexual-and-transgender-health#one.

———. 2013. "Healthy People 2020 at Work in the Community: Door-to-Door Program." Published March 29. www.healthypeople.gov/2020/healthy-people-in-action/story/healthy-people-2020-work-community-door-door-program.

Oliver, T. 2010. "Population Health Rankings as Policy Indicators and Performance Measures." *Preventing Chronic Disease* 7(5): A101.

Orgera, K., and S. Artiga. 2018. "Disparities in Health and Healthcare: Five Key Questions and Answers." Kaiser Family Foundation. August 8. www.kff.org/disparities-policy/issue-brief/disparities-in-health-and-health-care-five-key-questions-and-answers/.

Public Health Image Library (PHIL). 2017. "Image 22746." Accessed June 21, 2019. https://phil.cdc.gov/Details.aspx?pid=22746.

Remington, P., B. Catlin, and K. Gennuso. 2015. "The County Health Rankings: Rationale and Methods." *Population Health Metrics* 13: 11.

Robert Wood Johnson Foundation. 2019. *2019 County Health Rankings Key Findings Report*. Published March. www.countyhealthrankings.org/reports/2019-county-health-rankings-key-findings-report.

Semega, J., K. Fontenot, and M. Kollar. 2017. *Income and Poverty in the United States: 2016*. Current Population Reports, US Census Bureau. Published September. www.census.gov/content/dam/Census/library/publications/2017/demo/P60-259.pdf.

Squazzo, J. 2019. "Population Health Turned Inward: Employee Health Successes." *Healthcare Executive*, July/August, 8–14.

Sucich, K. 2019. "HIMSS Analytics Survey Sponsored by Dimensional Insight Finds Only 1 out of 5 Healthcare Organizations Using Analytics for Population Health." News release, June 28. www.prweb.com/releases/himss_analytics_survey_sponsored_by_dimensional_insight_finds_only_1_out_of_5_healthcare_organizations_using_analytics_for_population_health/prweb16271453.htm.

Terry, K. 2013. "Analytics: The Nervous System of IT-Enabled Healthcare." iHT². Published May 16. http://ihealthtran.com/iHT2analyticsreport.pdf.

Turner, A. 2018. "The Business Case for Racial Equity: A Strategy for Growth." W. K. Kellogg Foundation. Published April. https://altarum.org/sites/default/files/uploaded-publication-files/WKKellogg_Business-Case-Racial-Equity_National-Report_2018.pdf.

University of Kansas. 2018. "Assessing Community Needs and Resources." Community Tool Box, Center for Community Health and Development, University of Kansas. Accessed June 19, 2020. https://ctb.ku.edu/en/table-of-contents/assessment/assessing-community-needs-and-resources.

Utah Department of Health. 2016. *Utah Health Improvement Plan 2017–2020: A Healthier Tomorrow, Together.* https://ibis.health.utah.gov/pdf/opha/publication/UHIP.pdf.

Ward, B., J. J. Dahlhamer, A. Galinsky, and S. Joestl. 2014. "Sexual Orientation and Health Among U.S. Adults: National Health Interview Survey, 2013." *National Health Statistics Reports* 77. Published July 15. www.cdc.gov/nchs/data/nhsr/nhsr077.pdf.

Weber-Morgan Health Department. 2016. *Community Health Improvement Plan 2016–2020.* Accessed June 19, 2020. www.webermorganhealth.org/about/documents/CHIP_2017.pdf.

World Health Organization (WHO). 2000. "World Health Organization Assesses the World's Health Systems." Accessed June 19, 2020. www.who.int/whr/2000/media_centre/press_release/en/.

CHAPTER 13

THE US HEALTHCARE SYSTEM IN COMPARISON WITH OTHER COUNTRIES

In 2012, John Boehner, then Speaker of the US House of Representatives, articulated a long-held belief shared by many Americans: that the United States has the best healthcare system in the world (Jacobson 2012). Although this belief continues to be prevalent among one political party today, data do not support this assertion. The United States spends far more than other high-income and industrialized countries, gaps in the quality of care and access to healthcare persist, and Americans have worse health outcomes than people in other countries.

The United States ranks poorly on many measures of healthcare performance—last or near the bottom on most measures compared with other countries. The highest-ranked countries overall are the United Kingdom, Australia, and the Netherlands. The US healthcare system spends far more but falls short of the performance achieved by other high-income countries. The United States ranks lower than comparable high-income countries based on gross domestic product (GDP) and GDP per capita (per person). On some measures, such as the rates of mortality, premature death, and disease burden, the United States' performance is actually declining compared with similar nations (Sawyer and McDermott 2019; Schneider et al. 2017).

LEARNING OBJECTIVES

After reading this chapter, you will be able to

➤ Compare and contrast the four models of healthcare systems.

➤ Explain how the US healthcare system is a combination of the four models of healthcare.

➤ Appraise the benefits and disadvantages of making health insurance a requirement.

➤ Discuss why the United States has poorer healthcare outcomes than other countries.

➤ Compare and contrast the role of prices in healthcare costs and their effect on overall healthcare costs.

Beveridge model
Healthcare is paid for mostly by government taxes, with one primary healthcare insurer and healthcare services provided mainly by government employees; also called *socialized medicine.*

Bismarck model
Healthcare is paid for mostly by employees and employers, with many health insurers and healthcare services provided mainly by private providers; also called *all payer system.*

national health insurance model
Healthcare is paid for mostly by government taxes, with one health insurer and healthcare services provided mainly by private providers; also called *single payer system.*

out-of-pocket model
Healthcare is paid for mostly through individual funds, with a mix of private and government providers; also called *pay-to-play system.*

In the previous chapters, this book has examined many aspects of the US healthcare system. Healthcare in the United States differs from that in other developed nations in that it is a patchwork system comprising many different types of healthcare. All other developed countries primarily use one model for all citizens.

TYPES OF HEALTHCARE SYSTEMS

While each nation has adapted its own unique healthcare system to meet its needs, four general types of healthcare systems can be distinguished, as summarized in exhibit 13.1. These systems differ mainly in how healthcare is paid for and who provides healthcare services. In some countries, healthcare is paid for through taxes, whereas in other countries, healthcare is primarily paid for by employers, employees, or individuals. In some countries, healthcare providers are government employees or government-owned facilities, while others allow private practitioners and privately owned hospitals and clinics.

Four models of healthcare are used across the world. In almost all industrialized countries, healthcare is based on one of three models: the **Beveridge model**, the **Bismarck model**, or the **national health insurance model**. Nonindustrialized countries tend to use a fourth model, the **out-of-pocket model**. The United States has a mixed system that combines all four models.

The Beveridge model was designed in England by Lord William Beveridge to provide healthcare for all through taxes. The Bismarck model, named for the Prussian chancellor Otto von Bismarck, employs insurance companies that are funded by employees and employers. As exhibit 13.1 illustrates, the national health insurance model combines elements of the Beveridge and Bismarck models to create a single-payer, government-controlled insurance that generally pays private providers.

The United States does not fit into any one model described in exhibit 13.1. Rather, the US healthcare system is a patchwork of the four models. As a result, the US system is characterized by fragmented systems of care for different populations. For example,

◆ The US veterans healthcare system (discussed in chapter 3) is similar to socialized medicine (Beveridge model), as in the United Kingdom.

◆ Americans who get health insurance through their employer receive care from a system that is like Germany's all-payer system (Bismarck model).

EXHIBIT 13.1
Types of Healthcare Systems

Model	Type	How Expenses Are Paid	Providers	Description
Beveridge model	Socialized medicine	Mostly government taxes, one primary healthcare insurer	Mostly government employees	In this model, healthcare is provided and paid for by the government through taxes. The government owns many of the hospitals and clinics, and most physicians are employed by the government. Standardized health coverage is available to all citizens. Countries that use this model include the United Kingdom, Spain, New Zealand, and Cuba.
Bismarck model	All-payer system	Mostly by employers and employees, many healthcare insurers	Mostly by private providers	This model uses a health insurance system, often called "sickness funds," that is generally paid for by employers and employees. Insurance companies cannot make a profit. Sickness funds must provide a broad benefit package and must accept everyone. Physicians and hospitals are mostly private. The government closely regulates the healthcare system. Countries that use this model include France, Germany, Belgium, the Netherlands, Japan, and Switzerland.
National health insurance model	Single-payer system	Mostly government taxes, only one primary healthcare insurer	Mostly private providers	One health insurance company, controlled by the government, provides coverage to every citizen. Health insurance is funded by taxes. Physicians and hospitals tend to be privately owned. Countries using this system include Canada, Taiwan, and South Korea.
Out-of-pocket model	Pay-to-play system	Mostly by individual funds	Mix of private and government providers	This model is used primarily in non-industrialized countries that lack health insurance plans. Generally, only those who can afford to pay for healthcare receive it. Countries using this model include India, China, and others in Africa and South America.

Source: Reid (2010).

- ◆ The US Medicare program resembles Canada's single-payer system (national health insurance model).

- ◆ Americans without health insurance typically pay for healthcare costs out of pocket (pay-to-play model).

COMPARISON OF HEALTHCARE SYSTEMS

The US healthcare system differs dramatically from the systems of many other countries. To better understand the US healthcare system, it is helpful to compare it with the systems of other industrialized countries. The comparisons in this section focus on five aspects of healthcare systems: (1) the role of government in healthcare, (2) health insurance (who is covered and who pays for it), (3) health outcomes and costs by country, (4) healthcare administrative costs, and (5) how countries contain costs.

THE ROLE OF GOVERNMENT IN HEALTHCARE

As discussed in chapter 7, the US government is highly involved in the payment and provision of healthcare. However, unlike most other industrialized countries, the United States lacks a central government entity that regulates healthcare. Rather, many different federal agencies, as well as the states and private businesses, are involved in the regulation and operation of healthcare.

In France, the Ministry of Health dictates how much healthcare providers can charge and controls the budgets for hospitals. It also regulates the number of hospital beds, purchases of equipment, prices for procedures and drugs, and the number of doctors who are trained (Carroll and Frakt 2017). In the United Kingdom, the National Health Service has responsibility for promoting comprehensive health services and for monitoring and directing the quality, finances, and operational performance of most healthcare services provided in the country (NHS 2019).

One reason governments in other countries are more involved in regulating healthcare is that they pay for a much greater share of their country's healthcare costs. As shown in exhibits 13.2 and 13.3, the United States spends more than twice as much per capita than other countries. Although public expenditures (i.e., those paid by government) per capita are about the same as other countries, private expenditures are much higher. Less than half of healthcare costs in the United States are public expenditures, whereas in countries such as Germany, France, and Belgium, more than 80 percent of healthcare costs are public expenditures paid by government. Other countries pay up to 85 percent of healthcare costs. Because these governments pay such a large share of healthcare costs, they have a greater responsibility to monitor and manage their healthcare systems.

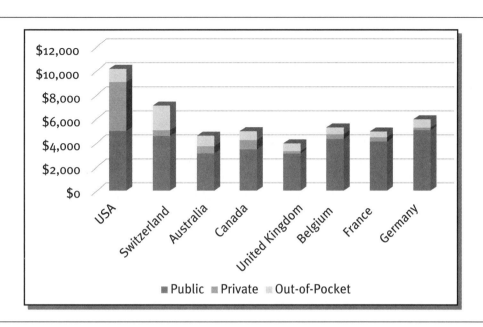

EXHIBIT 13.2
Public, Private, and Out-of-Pocket Healthcare Expenditures by Country, 2018 (per capita)

Source: Tikkanen and Abrams (2020).

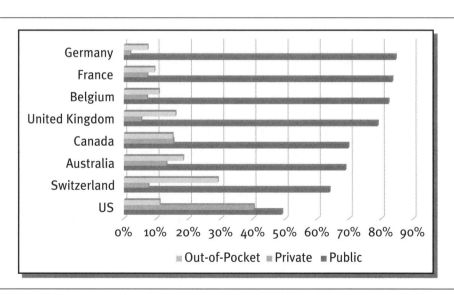

EXHIBIT 13.3
Shares of Public, Private, and Out-of-Pocket Expenditures by Country, 2018

Source: Tikkanen and Abrams (2020).

HEALTH INSURANCE: PAYMENT AND COVERAGE

Countries differ in the treatments and healthcare services that are covered and how those services are paid for. A few key differences are as follows (Carroll and Frakt 2017; Commonwealth Fund 2020; Seervai, Shah, and Osborn 2017):

◆ *United States.* Healthcare is provided and paid for by a mix of private and public sources. A majority of people receive health insurance through their employment. Older, disabled, and low-income people may have government health insurance through Medicare or Medicaid. Providers are primarily private hospitals and physicians, which may be not-for-profit or for-profit.

◆ *United Kingdom.* All residents are covered by comprehensive government health insurance. Insurance covers mental health care and some dental and eye care. There are no copays for services. About 10 percent of citizens have limited private insurance, generally through their employer, that gives them more rapid access to private care. Hospitals are primarily owned by the government, and the National Health Service is funded by national taxes.

◆ *Australia.* The country has a public and a private healthcare system. The public system, called Medicare, is funded by national taxes, and care is free or highly discounted. Public hospitals and community-based services are generally owned and governed by state and territorial governments. The private system includes privately owned hospitals and medical practices paid for by private insurance. About half of the population has private health insurance. Health insurance companies are both for-profit and not-for-profit.

◆ *The Netherlands.* All residents are required to purchase health insurance from private insurers. Most people also purchase supplemental private health insurance. The national government sets health priorities and monitors access, quality, and costs. Prevention and social support services are financed through general taxes. Adults have annual deductibles, except for general practice care. Payments to general practitioners consist of capitation fees and provider fees.

◆ *Belgium.* The government establishes health policy and regulates private insurance and services. Health insurance is mandatory through sickness funds. Many people also have supplemental health insurance. Patients can choose their providers. Hospitals are either public or not-for-profit organizations; clinical providers are mostly private practitioners with independent medical practices. Everyone is required to have health insurance with broad benefits. Copayments are required for healthcare services.

◆ *France.* Healthcare coverage is universal and compulsory. The federal government sets a national healthcare strategy and allocates funds among service sectors. Taxes support health insurance, and insurance companies negotiate with and pay providers. Citizens can also buy private insurance, and most receive government subsidies to do so. Health insurance is required for all. Government-provided insurance covers many services, including prescription drugs. Coinsurance is required for most services. General practitioners receive mostly fee-for-service payments.

◆ *Switzerland.* The Swiss health system is highly decentralized among the federal, cantonal, and municipal authorities. The 26 cantons (regions) separately license providers, coordinate hospital services, and subsidize care and health insurance premiums. The federal government regulates financing through mandatory health insurance. Municipalities are primarily responsible for long-term care and social support services. Government expenditures for healthcare come from general taxation, which pays for about three-quarters of healthcare costs. Residents must purchase mandatory health insurance. People can choose among general practitioners, who are paid according to a national fee-for-service scale, or specialists for care.

◆ *Canada.* Government taxes, mostly regional, pay for health insurance, which is mostly provided by the private sector. Universal health insurance is managed and administered by provinces. About two-thirds of Canadians also have supplemental private insurance, generally through their employer, to pay for prescription drugs, eye care, and dental care. The federal government shares the costs of healthcare with the provinces and sets standards for the services that are provided. There is no nationally defined benefit package; benefits are determined by the provinces. There is no cost sharing for publicly insured providers. Patients can choose their primary care physician.

◆ *Germany.* Most health insurance is paid for by employers and employees. Health insurance is required for all and provided through sickness funds, which are not-for-profit, nongovernmental insurance companies and private insurance. Government has a limited role in the direct financing and delivery of healthcare. However, mandated benefits are broad. Hospital stays and prescription drugs require copays. There is a maximum annual out-of-pocket limit, based on income. About 10 percent of the population (mainly those with high incomes and younger adults) choose to obtain private health insurance.

HEALTHCARE OUTCOMES AND COSTS

The US healthcare system performs quite poorly in comparison with other nations in terms of health outcomes and healthcare costs. As shown in exhibit 13.4, the United States ranks last overall among 11 industrialized countries on measures of equity, access, administrative efficiency, care delivery, and healthcare outcomes. Of the five factors listed in exhibit 13.4, the United States ranks last or next to last in all categories, except for care process, on which it ranks fifth. Thus, the United States has the highest costs and the lowest overall performance among these nations.

As exhibit 13.5 shows, the United States has a lower life expectancy and a much higher percentage of the population with chronic conditions than other countries. It also has a relatively small percentage (16 percent) of its population over the age of 65. Nevertheless, the United States is the only nation in which nearly all of the population does not have health insurance. In addition, the United States has the highest rate of obesity (40 percent), the highest suicide rate, and the fewest physicians per person.

Exhibit 13.4

Healthcare System Performance Rankings by Country, 2017

Country	Overall Ranking	Care Process	Access	Administrative Efficiency	Equity	Healthcare Outcomes
United Kingdom	1	1	3	3	1	10
Australia	2	2	4	1	7	1
Netherlands	3	4	1	9	2	6
New Zealand	4	3	7	2	8	7
Norway	5	10	5	4	5	2
Sweden	6	11	6	5	3	2
Switzerland	7	7	8	8	4	4
Germany	8	8	2	6	6	8
Canada	9	6	10	6	9	9
France	10	9	9	11	10	5
United States	11	5	11	10	11	11

Source: Data from Commonwealth Fund (2017).

EXHIBIT 13.5
Comparison of Healthcare Data by Country

Country	Life Expectancy at Birth (years) (2017)	Share of Adults with Chronic Conditions (2016)	Suicide Rate per 100,000 (2016)	Share of Population with Health Insurance (2016)	Obesity Rate (2017)	Physicians per 1,000 People (2018)	MRI Exams per 1,000 People (2017)	Share of Population over 65 (2020)
Switzerland	83.6	15%	11.2	100%	11.3%	4.3	74	18.3%
Australia	82.6	15%	11.9	100%	30.4%	3.7	45	15.8%
France	82.6	18%	n/a	99.9%	17.0%	3.2	114	20.3%
Sweden	82.5	18%	11.1	100%	13.1%	4.1	n/a	19.9%
Canada	82.0	22%	11.8	100%	26.3%	2.7	51	17.2%
Netherlands	81.8	14%	10.5	100%	13.4%	3.6	51	18.9%
United Kingdom	81.3	14%	7.3	100%	28.7%	2.9	62	18.3%
Germany	81.1	17%	10.2	100%	23.6%	4.3	143	21.4%
United States	78.6	28%	13.9	91.2%	40.0%	2.6	111	16.0%

Sources: Data from Gonzales and Sawyer (2017); Kamal, Cox, and Blumenkranz (2017); Population Reference Bureau (2020); Sawyer and Gonzales (2017); Sawyer and Sroczynski (2016); Sarnak, Squires, and Bishop (2017); Tikkanen and Abrams (2020) .

Studies have shown that higher healthcare costs in the United States are the result of higher prices. For instance, people in the United States spend more than $1,400 per year on prescription drugs, far more than other countries (Papanicolas, Woskie, and Jha 2018).

In addition, as displayed in exhibit 13.6, the average prices for common medical procedures are much higher in the United States. For instance, in 2017, the cost of cardiac (heart) bypass surgery in the United States was $78,100—more than six times the cost of the same surgery in the Netherlands, where the average charge was $11,670. The average charge for a magnetic resonance imaging (MRI) scan, a frequent radiological diagnostic procedure, was $1,430 in the United States, which was almost eight times the average charge of $190 in the Netherlands (Hargraves and Bloschichak 2019). High healthcare prices in the United States primarily reflect higher charges for prescription drugs, hospitals, physicians, and administration (Papanicolas, Woskie, and Jha 2018).

EXHIBIT 13.6
Healthcare Prices
in the United
States and Other
Countries, 2017

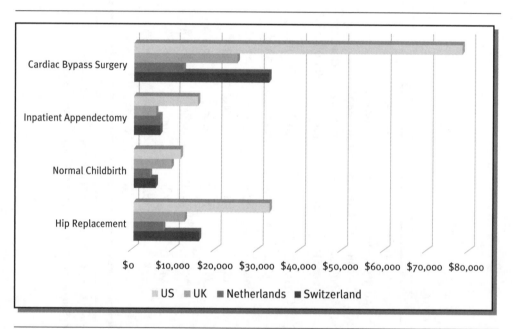

Source: Hargraves and Bloschichak (2019).

The same holds true of drug prices. One study showed that Americans spend 203 percent more per person on primary care prescription drugs than people in other countries; almost all of the difference is attributable to higher prices and more expensive treatment choices (Morgan et al. 2018). As shown in exhibits 13.7 and 13.8, individual drug prices are much higher in the United States than in other countries. Overall, most countries' drug prices are less than half the prices in the United States. For instance, Humira Pen, a drug used to treat rheumatoid arthritis and Crohn's disease, costs $4,481 in the United States but only $856 in the United Kingdom. Likewise, Victoza 3-Pak, an injection to treat type

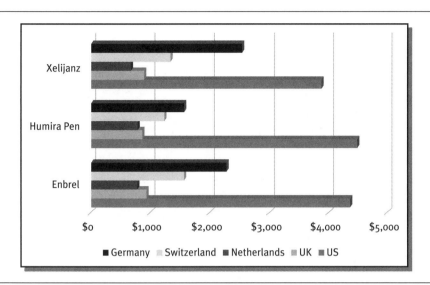

EXHIBIT 13.7
Drug Prices by
Country, 2017

Source: Hargraves and Bloschichak (2019).

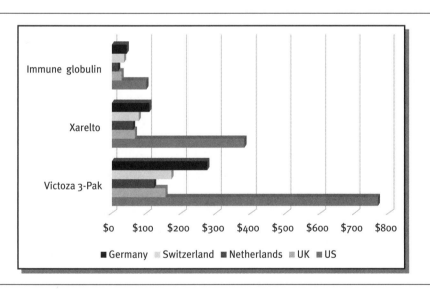

EXHIBIT 13.8
Drug Prices by
Country, 2017

Source: Hargraves and Bloschichak (2019).

2 diabetes, costs $766 in the United States but only $120 in the Netherlands (Hargraves and Bloschichak 2019).

Overall, people and businesses in the United States pay much more for healthcare. High prices make healthcare in the United States very expensive compared with the rest of the industrialized world. As John Hargraves, director of data strategy at the Health Care Cost Institute stated, "It is staggering how much the United States is more expensive" (Sanger-Katz 2019).

EXHIBIT 13.9
Physician
Compensation
by Country, 2019
(thousands)

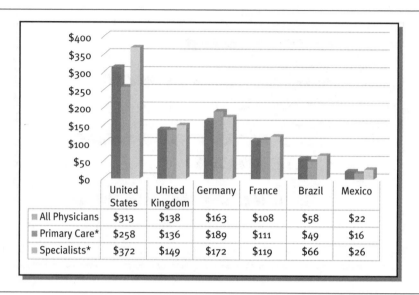

	United States	United Kingdom	Germany	France	Brazil	Mexico
■ All Physicians	$313	$138	$163	$108	$58	$22
■ Primary Care*	$258	$136	$189	$111	$49	$16
■ Specialists*	$372	$149	$172	$119	$66	$26

* Includes male salaries only.
Source: Kane et al. (2019).

Another factor that contributes to high healthcare prices in the United States is physician income. Exhibit 13.9 shows that physicians' income in the United States exceeds that of other countries. For example, primary care physicians in the United States earn an average of $258,000 per year, while primary care physicians in the United Kingdom make only $136,000 per year.

Physicians in the United States are highly trained, but they are also highly paid. In 2019, the top 10 percent of the US population earned $126,900, while physicians earned far more (Nunn, Parsons, and Shambaugh 2020).

HEALTHCARE ADMINISTRATIVE COSTS

Healthcare administrative expenses are an organization's overhead costs, including billing, management, adhering to regulations, cleaning, and maintenance. These costs vary dramatically across countries. Countries with more centralized decision-making tend to have lower healthcare administrative spending, whereas countries that allow more choice have higher administrative spending. For instance, in many countries, the choice of insurance plan and coverage is fairly limited. Yet in the United States, consumers can choose from many different private and public health insurance plans and levels of coverage.

In addition, many countries set standard prices for healthcare services. However, providers in the United States may be paid vastly different amounts for the same service.

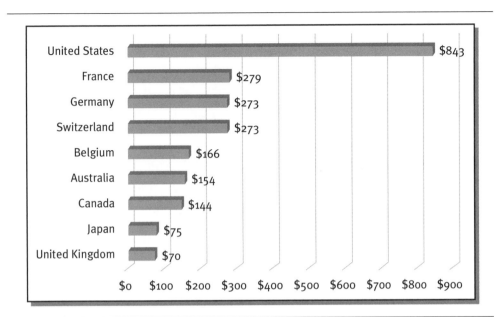

EXHIBIT 13.10
Healthcare
Administrative
Costs per Person,
2018

Source: Peterson Foundation (2019).

The fee-for-service payment model that is used in the United States requires enormous administrative spending for documentation, coding, billing, and rebilling for services that are charged individually.

Exhibit 13.10 shows the wide variation in healthcare administrative costs across countries. The United Kingdom spends only $70 per person per year on healthcare administrative costs, while the United States spends $843. Another study, whose results are displayed in exhibit 13.11, expanded these data by adding administrative costs for nursing homes, home health care, physician offices and insurance overhead and compared only the United States and Canada. The United States spent $2,497 per person per year compared with only $551 in Canada. Overall, the United States spent $812 billion in 2017 on healthcare administrative costs. These high costs are attributed to "the inefficiencies of the U.S. private insurance-based, multipayer system" (Himmelstein, Campbell, and Woolhandler 2020).

HOW COUNTRIES CONTAIN COSTS

Countries use different methods to contain healthcare costs. Although the United States employs some of the same cost-containment measures as other countries, it lacks the market power and leverage to effectively reduce costs. For instance, many countries with national health insurance coverage have a single entity that is responsible for negotiating and setting prices. In those countries, government purchasers have tremendous leverage to keep prices

EXHIBIT **13.11**
Expanded
Healthcare
Administrative
Costs per Person,
United States
Versus Canada,
2017

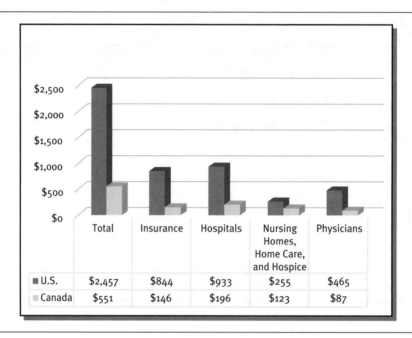

	Total	Insurance	Hospitals	Nursing Homes, Home Care, and Hospice	Physicians
■ U.S.	$2,457	$844	$933	$255	$465
▨ Canada	$551	$146	$196	$123	$87

Source: *Source:* Peterson Foundation (2019).

low. However, the United States has many different purchasers of healthcare—individuals, businesses, government—that lack the ability to negotiate lower prices.

The only exception in the United States is Maryland, which is the only state that has a commission to implement healthcare price controls. Everyone in Maryland pays the same price for healthcare coverage. The state has also shifted toward global budgets for inpatient and outpatient hospital services. Initially, Maryland's efforts appear to be improving care and moderating costs (RTI International 2018) (see sidebar).

As in Maryland, countries such as Germany have the power to mandate the prices that hospitals can charge for services. Like Germany, most industrialized countries have a single entity that is responsible for setting prices for prescription drugs, hospital services, and other healthcare providers. Even in small countries, government purchasers have enormous leverage to negotiate discounts and set prices. Because these governments negotiate prices for the entire country, nations such as Germany, Italy, and the United Kingdom can obtain price discounts of up to 50 percent (Coukell 2017; Morgan 2018).

Likewise, Canada controls costs principally by using single-payer purchasing, the use of mandatory global budgets for hospitals, negotiated fee schedules for physicians, drug formularies, and restrictions on the purchase of new equipment and technology. Canada has a Patented Medicine Review Board that regulates prices for new medications (Allin and Rudoler 2020).

✴ DEBATE TIME Maryland's Unique Healthcare System

The State of Maryland is unique in that it is the only state that has healthcare regulations like those in countries such as France, Japan, Switzerland, the Netherlands, and Germany. Since the 1970s, Maryland has set the prices that hospitals can charge. In 2014, the state implemented a maximum threshold for healthcare spending growth, called a *global budget*. In Maryland, hospitals' budgets are fixed, as are the amounts they can charge for services. Once a hospital hits its revenue cap, it does not make more money. This encourages hospitals to look outside their walls and try to improve community members' health. Although this system is not perfect, many believe that "Maryland is doing more and providing better incentives than any other state" (Golshan 2020).

Maryland hospitals have an incentive to keep patients out of hospitals. For example, in other states, a person who is readmitted to a hospital would traditionally generate more revenue for the hospital. However, in Maryland, readmissions are regarded as a problem and administrators try to understand why each readmission occurred. It might be that a diabetic patient lives too far from a grocery store to get healthy food or lacks transportation. Hospitals in Maryland have incentives to address these types of problems to keep people healthy.

Is Maryland's system working? Studies are inconclusive. Some hospitals have shown significant decreases in readmission rates and emergency room visits. However, primary care and pharmaceutical costs remain outside the purview of Maryland's global budgeting system. Nor does the state's system address the 6 percent of residents who do not have health insurance. Clearly, challenges persist, as healthcare costs continue to increase; however, Maryland's costs remain well below national averages.

Maryland claims that it is seeking to fix the broken incentives in America's healthcare system, but this is hard to do. As John Chessare, CEO of the Greater Baltimore Medical Center stated, "We don't like health planning in our country. . . . Let's design an efficient system to deliver better health and better care. In the United States, we don't want to have that conversation. And the rest of the world laughs at us because they cover all their citizens and their outcomes are as good as ours" (Mangum 2020).

Should we allow centralized planning in the states? What are the advantages of Maryland's regulations? What are the disadvantages?

France has taken additional steps to contain healthcare costs. These measures include reducing the number of hospital beds, eliminating about 600 prescription drugs from the federal formulary, greater use of generic and over-the-counter drugs, and reduction of fees to radiologists and laboratories. France has also centralized purchasing and increased the use of outpatient surgery (Durand-Zaleski 2020).

Even less developed countries such as India seek to regulate healthcare prices. For instance, India has a National Pharmaceutical Pricing Authority that sets drug prices and imposes price caps on 52 essential drugs (Siddiqui 2014). Australia also controls prescription drug prices based on the cost of other clinically comparable drugs, sharply reducing drug prices (Coukell 2017). However, in the United States, it is illegal for the government to negotiate with pharmaceutical companies to achieve lower prices, even though 88 percent of the population favor allowing the government to do so (Cubanski et al. 2019; Wasik 2018).

Although competition has not worked well in the United States, many politicians and government officials have not been willing to give up trying to make it work. Some believe that healthcare providers and patients should be given better information and stronger financial incentives to improve quality and to select better, more cost-effective services (Altman and Mechanic 2018). A number of countries have modified competition that is successful. Germany, the Netherlands, and Switzerland rely on private nonprofit health insurers that compete within a regulated environment. For example, Germany allows its sickness funds and associations to make their own rules on access and benefits coverage, Germans can choose to join any of the 109 competing sickness funds, and they have the ability to choose their doctor and hospital (Cheng 2020).

INNOVATIVE APPROACHES TO LOWER COSTS AND IMPROVE CARE

Many countries are using innovative approaches to lower their healthcare costs and provide better healthcare. The following are examples of these innovations:

◆ Using population health to target sicker populations so as to better manage expensive health services and improve the health of citizens. For example, China has implemented the Healthy China 2030 initiative to improve its health system and the health of its citizens (Tan, Liu, and Shao 2017).

◆ Increasing the use of smartphones and mobile devices to allow patients to interact remotely with their providers and to assess their own health. A British company, Babylon Health, along with Tencent, has more than 1.4 million people across Europe, Asia, and Africa using its mobile app (Sturman 2018).

◆ Coordinating patient care more effectively. For example, 59 percent of doctors in the Netherlands reported that they were always informed when a patient had been seen in the emergency room or discharged from a hospital. However, only 26 percent of US doctors reported that they received this information. In addition, 88 percent of doctors in the Netherlands and 84 percent in the United Kingdom made home visits, whereas only 6 percent of US doctors did so (Osborn et al. 2015).

◆ Changing how primary care is delivered by providing "health coaches," whose primary responsibility is to keep people healthy. IORA Health (www.iorahealth.com), based in Massachusetts, has partnered with some of the largest healthcare providers and insurers in the area, including Humana, UnitedHealthcare, Tufts, and Massachusetts Blue Cross/Blue Shield.

EFFICIENCY OF HEALTHCARE SYSTEMS

The overall efficiency of countries' healthcare systems can be compared according to the value that citizens receive for the amount of money spent. In one study, Bloomberg Business considered the relationship between a country's total health spending, life expectancy, and relative and absolute costs. As exhibit 13.12 shows, health systems in Asia and Europe far exceeded that of the United States in terms of healthcare efficiency.

EXHIBIT 13.12
Bloomberg Healthcare Efficiency Ranking

Rank	Economy	Efficiency Score	Life Expectancy (years)	Relative Cost	Absolute Cost
1	Hong Kong	87.3	84.3	5.7%	$2,222
2	Singapore	85.6	82.7	4.3%	$2,280
3	Spain	69.3	82.8	9.2%	$2,354
4	Italy	67.6	82.5	9%	$2,700
5	South Korea	67.4	82	7.4%	$2,013
8	Australia	62	82.4	9.4%	$4,934
16	Canada	55.5	82.1	10.4%	$4,508
16	France	55.5	82.3	11.1%	$4,026
35	United Kingdom	46.3	81	9.9%	$4,356
54	Azerbaijan	29.6	71.9	6.7%	$368
54	United States	29.6	78.7	16.8%	$9,536

Source: Data from Miller and Lu (2018).

Hong Kong and Singapore ranked as the first and second most efficient health systems, respectively, followed by Spain, Italy, and South Korea. Canada and France were tied for 16th place, and the United Kingdom ranked 36th. The US healthcare system ranked 54th, tied with Azerbaijan (Miller and Lu 2018). The takeaway is that although the United States spends more on healthcare than other countries, it achieves poorer health outcomes.

In light of the US healthcare system's poor efficiency rating, it is perhaps not surprising that only 16 percent of doctors in the United States believe that their healthcare system works well. In contrast, two-thirds (67 percent) of Norway's doctors believe that their healthcare system works well, followed by 57 percent in New Zealand and 36 percent in Canada (Osborn et al. 2015).

COMMON PROBLEMS IN ALL HEALTHCARE SYSTEMS

Healthcare across the world faces many similar challenges. Although other countries seem to perform better than the United States on many health outcome measures, most nations still struggle with rising costs and the challenge of maintaining high quality of and access to healthcare.

Industrialized countries in Europe, as in the United States, anticipate that healthcare costs will continue to increase. According to some projections, healthcare spending could increase from 8.8 percent of their GDP in 2015 to more than 10.2 percent in 2030. The extent of this growth will depend on what policy actions are taken through legislation and regulation to govern workforces, pharmaceuticals, new technologies, and health promotion and disease prevention (OECD 2019).

A report from the European Union (EU), which encompasses 28 member nations and about 513 million people, suggested the following solutions to key healthcare challenges (OECD and EU 2018):

◆ *More protection and prevention.* More than 1.2 million people die prematurely each year in the EU. This number could be reduced or eliminated by implementing better disease prevention policies.

◆ *More effective and people-centered health systems.* Wide disparities in survival rates exist among countries and among hospitals and healthcare providers within countries. Healthcare systems should focus more on patient satisfaction and management of chronic diseases.

◆ *Improved access to healthcare.* The poor continue to have difficulty accessing care. Poor Europeans experience five times more barriers to accessing care than richer ones.

◆   *More resilient healthcare systems.* Systems must be able to adapt to a rapidly
changing environment. Wasteful spending, which may account for 20 percent
of costs, must be addressed.

SUMMARY

While each nation has adapted its own unique healthcare system to meet its needs, four
general types of healthcare systems can be distinguished. These systems differ mainly in
how healthcare is paid for and who provides healthcare services. The four healthcare models
are (1) the Beveridge model, also known as socialized medicine, which is used in the United
Kingdom, Spain, New Zealand, and Cuba; (2) the Bismarck or all-payer model, which is used
in France, Germany, Belgium, the Netherlands, Japan, and Switzerland; (3) the national health
insurance or single-payer model, which is used in Canada, Taiwan, and South Korea; and
(4) the out-of-pocket or pay-to-play model, which is used mostly in developing countries in
Africa and South American and in China.

Healthcare in the United States, however, does not fit into any of these models. Rather,
it is a patchwork of the four models. The United States differs from other countries in terms
of the role of government in healthcare and who has health insurance and who pays for it.
Healthcare outcomes and costs vary widely by country, depending on the healthcare model
used and cost-containment measures taken.

Most countries, aside from the United States, have a central government entity that
regulates healthcare. Often, as in France, this is a ministry of health, which sets how much
insurance companies and hospitals can charge for services. Most countries pay for a greater
share of citizens' healthcare costs—often between 70 and 80 percent—whereas the US
government pays only about half of Americans' healthcare costs.

Many countries provide comprehensive health insurance that covers most healthcare
services. In some countries, such as the Netherlands, supplemental health insurance is available to cover services that are not covered under the national plan. Germany has a slightly
different system, in which health insurance is paid by a combination of taxes and employer
and employee contributions to not-for-profit, nongovernmental insurance companies, which
are heavily regulated by the German government.

Overall, the US health system compares poorly with those of other nations. Many
rankings place it last among industrialized nations, with the highest costs and lowest overall
performance.

High healthcare costs in the United States are driven by higher prices. Americans
pay about twice what people in other countries pay for prescription drugs and many times
more for other healthcare services.

Most countries set their national healthcare prices and therefore have the leverage
to negotiate substantially lower prices. In the United States, the negotiation of prices is

fragmented. An exception is Maryland, which has a commission that sets healthcare price controls statewide. Many countries are using population health targets to reduce healthcare costs and to improve the health of their citizens. Another cost-containment effort is the use of mobile apps to help people manage their healthcare.

Finally, US healthcare is inefficient when the costs of care are compared with health outcomes. Healthcare systems in Asia and Europe rank as the most efficient. The United States ranks 54th in terms of healthcare efficiency. Only 16 percent of doctors in the United States believe that the US healthcare system works well.

QUESTIONS

1. Compare and contrast the four healthcare models described in this chapter. What are the main differences among them?
2. What are some of the weaknesses of the out-of-pocket model of healthcare?
3. What are the advantages of the national health insurance or single-payer model of healthcare?
4. The veterans health system in the United States most resembles which healthcare system model?
5. In terms of the role of government in healthcare, what do most countries have that the United States does not?
6. What is the main reason costs in the US healthcare system are so high?
7. Canada, France, the United Kingdom, and the Netherlands raise money for most healthcare services through taxes. How does Germany raise funds for healthcare?
8. In which areas does the United States score more poorly in healthcare outcomes than other countries?
9. Which US state uses price controls?
10. Where does the United States rank in terms of healthcare efficiency?
11. What percent of doctors in the United States do not believe that the US healthcare system works well?

ASSIGNMENTS

1. Take the *New York Times* quiz "The Best Healthcare System in the World: Which One Would You Pick?" at www.nytimes.com/interactive/2017/09/18/upshot/best-health-care-system-country-bracket.html. Which country do you think has the best health system? Why?

2. Pick two countries not discussed in this chapter that are included in the Commonwealth Fund's International Profiles of Healthcare Systems, at www. commonwealthfund.org/publications/fund-reports/2017/may/international-profiles-health-care-systems. Answer the following questions:
   a. Which of the four healthcare models does each country use?
   b. How is healthcare paid for?
   c. What role do the private and public sectors play in providing healthcare?
   d. What are the pros and cons of each system?

CASES

LIVING IN SPAIN

Jackie moved to Spain to work for a public relations firm. She had health insurance from her previous employer, but she was surprised to learn that her new employer in Spain did not offer healthcare coverage. When she asked about this, she was told that more than 90 percent of Spaniards use the public healthcare system, which was mostly free. However, her new employer did provide supplementary private health insurance that would allow her to receive quicker care from a private hospital if she desired.

Jackie learned that she would be paying 4.7 percent of her salary and her employer would pay 23.6 percent of her salary to the government for health insurance. She was given a Tarjeta Sanitaria Individual health card to prove that she had health insurance. With this, she could get free care at public hospitals and doctors' offices. However, before seeing a doctor, she would need to register with a local primary care physician and decide whether she would use public or private payment. If she needed to see a specialist, she would need to get a referral from her primary care physician.

Jackie was excited to be living in Spain and hoped she would not need to use the healthcare system, but she was glad that she understood it better.

Discussion Questions

1. What other questions could Jackie ask about the Spanish healthcare system?
2. What advantage does Jackie gain by having supplemental private health insurance?
3. Would you use the private or public service? Why?

NARAYANA HEALTH

Narayana Health was established in India, where costs were 60 to 70 percent lower than equivalent services in the United States. After operating for many years in India, the company saw an opportunity to replicate its low costs and quality services just outside the United

States in the Cayman Islands. Narayana took the following actions to keep its prices low (Govindarajan and Ramamurti 2018):

- Spending only $700,000 per bed in the construction of the hospital versus about $2 million per bed in the United States
- Buying supplies from Indian vendors, at about one-tenth the cost for prescription drugs and one-half for equipment
- Outsourcing human resources, accounting, finance, medical transcription, and radiology to low-cost employees in India
- Using doctors from India who were paid 70 percent of US doctors' salaries

Narayana created a partnership with Ascension Health that helped funnel patients to the new hospital in the Cayman Islands. Ascension Health rotated its operating room staff to learn from Narayana. The new operating rooms ran 12 to 16 hours a day—nearly double the eight-hour shift in US operating rooms. The salaried Indian surgeons operated 12 hours a day, six days a week and performed 10 to 12 surgeries a week, compared with 2 to 4 surgeries done by a typical US surgeon. The hospital had infection and mortality rates comparable to hospitals in the United States. Productivity was enhanced by combining operating room and recovery functions and having nurses perform functions that are usually done by respiratory therapists and other clinicians in the United States (Goozner 2016).

Discussion Questions

1. How is the Narayana hospital in the Cayman Islands different from a hospital in the United States?
2. Why was the hospital more productive than a US hospital?
3. Do you think this type of hospital will come to the United States? Why?

REFERENCES

Allin, S., and D. Rudoler. 2020. "The Canadian Health Care System." Commonwealth Fund. Published June 5. https://international.commonwealthfund.org/countries/canada/.

Altman, S., and R. Mechanic. 2018. "Healthcare Costs Control: Where Do We Go from Here?" *Health Affairs Blog*. Published July 13. www.healthaffairs.org/do/10.1377/hblog20180705.24704/full/.

Carroll, A., and A. Frakt. 2017. "The Best Healthcare System in the World: Which One Would You Pick?" *New York Times*. Published September 18. www.nytimes.com/interactive/2017/09/18/upshot/best-health-care-system-country-bracket.html.

Cheng, T.-M. 2020. "Bending the Cost Growth Curve and Expanding Coverage: Lessons from Germany's All-Payer System." *Millbank Quarterly* 98 (2): 279–96.

Commonwealth Fund. 2020. "International Health Care Systems Profiles." Published June 5. https://international.commonwealthfund.org/.

———. 2017. "New 11-Country Study: U.S. Healthcare System Has Widest Gap Between People with Higher and Lower Incomes." Published July 13. www.commonwealthfund.org/press-release/2017/new-11-country-study-us-health-care-system-has-widest-gap-between-people-higher.

Coukell, A. 2017. "Other Countries Control Drug Prices; the U.S. Could, Too." The Hill. Published December 7. https://thehill.com/opinion/healthcare/363583-other-countries-control-drug-prices-the-us-could-too.

Cubanski, J., T. Neuman, S. True, and M. Freed. 2019. "What's the Latest on Medicare Drug Price Negotiations?" Kaiser Family Foundation. Published October 17. www.kff.org/medicare/issue-brief/whats-the-latest-on-medicare-drug-price-negotiations/.

Durand-Zalenski, I. 2020. "The French Health Care System." Commonwealth Fund. Published June 5. https://international.commonwealthfund.org/countries/france/.

Golshan, T. 2020. "The Answer to America's Health Care Cost Problem Might Be in Maryland." Vox. Published January 22. www.vox.com/policy-and-politics/2020/1/22/21055118/maryland-health-care-global-hospital-budget.

Gonzales, S., and B. Sawyer. 2017. "How Does U.S. Life Expectancy Compare to Other Countries?" Peterson-KFF Health System Tracker. Published December 23. www.healthsystemtracker.org/chart-collection/u-s-life-expectancy-compare-countries/?_sf_s=life#item-start.

Goozner, M. 2016. "Ascension Seeks Productivity Elixir from Its Joint Venture in Cayman Islands." *Modern Healthcare*. Published February 6. www.modernhealthcare.com/article/20160206/MAGAZINE/302069988.

Govindarajan V., and R. Ramamurti. 2018. "Is This the Hospital That Will Finally Push the Expensive U.S. Healthcare System to Innovate?" *Harvard Business Review*. Published June 22. https://hbr.org/2018/06/is-this-the-hospital-that-will-finally-push-the-expensive-u-s-health-care-system-to-innovate.

Hargraves, J., and A. Bloschichak. 2019. "International Comparisons of Health Care Prices from the 2017 iFHP Survey." Health Care Cost Institute. Published December 17. https://healthcostinstitute.org/in-the-news/international-comparisons-of-health-care-prices-2017-ifhp-survey.

Himmelstein, D., T. Campbell, and S. Woolhandler. 2020. "Health Care Administrative Costs in the United States and Canada, 2017." *Annals of Internal Medicine* 172 (2): 134–42.

Jacobson, L. 2012. "John Boehner Says U.S. Health Care System Is Best in the World." PolitiFact. Published July 5. www.politifact.com/truth-o-meter/statements/2012/jul/05/john-boehner/john-boehner-says-us-health-care-system-best-world/.

Kamal, R., C. Cox, and E. Blumenkranz. 2017. "What Do We Know About Social Determinants of Health in the U.S. and Comparable Countries? Peterson-KFF Health System Tracker. Published November 21. www.healthsystemtracker.org/chart-collection/know-social-determinants-health-u-s-comparable-countries/#item-start.

Kane, L., B. Schubsky, T. Locke, M. Kouimtzi, V. Duqueroy, C. Gottschling, M. Lopez, and L. Schwartz. 2019. "International Physician Compensation Report 2019: Do US Physicians Have It Best?" Medscape. Published September 19. www.medscape.com/slideshow/2019-international-compensation-report-6011814.

Mangum, A. 2020. "The Answer to America's Health Care Cost Problem Might Be in Maryland." Vox. Published January 22. www.vox.com/policy-and-politics/2020/1/22/21055118/maryland-health-care-global-hospital-budget.

Miller, L. J., and W. Lu. 2018. "These Are the Economies with the Most and Least Efficient Healthcare." Bloomberg News. Published September 19. www.bloomberg.com/news/ articles/2018-09-19/u-s-near-bottom-of-health-index-hong-kong-and-singapore-at-top.

Morgan, S. 2018. "What's Driving Prescription Drug Prices in the U.S.?" Commonwealth Fund. Published November 14. www.commonwealthfund.org/publications/ journal-article/2018/nov/whats-driving-prescription-drug-prices-us.

Morgan, S., C. Good, C. Leopold, A. Kaltenboeck, P. Bach, and A. Wagner. 2018. "An Analysis of the Expenditures on Primary Care Prescription Drugs in the United States Versus Ten Comparable Countries." *Health Policy* 122 (9): 1012–17.

National Health Service (NHS). 2019. "Our 2018/2019 Annual Report." Published July. www. england.nhs.uk/wp-content/uploads/2019/07/Annual-Report-Full-201819.pdf.

Nunn, R., J. Parsons, and J. Shambaugh. 2020. "A Dozen Facts About the Economics of the US Healthcare System." Brookings Institution. Published March 10. www.brookings.edu/ research/a-dozen-facts-about-the-economics-of-the-u-s-health-care-system/.

Organisation for Economic Co-operation and Development (OECD). 2019. "Health Spending Projections to 2030." Health Working Paper 110. Published May. www. oecd.org/officialdocuments/publicdisplaydocumentpdf/?cote=DELSA/HEA/WD/ HWP(2019)3&docLanguage=En.

Organisation for Economic Co-operation and Development (OECD) and European Commission (EU). 2018. *Health at a Glance: Europe 2018: State of Health in the EU Cycle.* Accessed June 22, 2020. https://ec.europa.eu/health/sites/health/files/state/ docs/2018_healthatglance_rep_en.pdf.

Osborn, R., D. Moulds, E. Schneider, M. Doty, D. Squires, and D. Sarnak. 2015. "Primary Care Physicians in Ten Countries Report Challenges Caring for Patients with Complex Health Needs." Commonwealth Fund. Published December 10. www. commonwealthfund.org/publications/journal-article/2015/dec/primary-care-physicians-ten-countries-report-challenges.

Papanicolas, I., L. Woskie, and A. Jha. 2018. "Healthcare Spending in the United States and Other High-Income Countries." *JAMA* 319 (10): 1024–39.

Peterson Foundation. 2019. "How Does the U.S. Healthcare System Compare to Other Countries?" Published July 22. www.pgpf.org/blog/2019/07/how-does-the-us-healthcare-system-compare-to-other-countries.

Population Reference Bureau. 2020. "Countries with the Oldest Populations in the World." Published March 23. www.prb.org/countries-with-the-oldest-populations/.

Reid, T. R. 2010. *The Healing of America: A Global Quest for Better, Cheaper and Fairer Care.* New York: Penguin.

RTI International. 2018. "Evaluation of the Maryland All-Payer Model: Third Annual Report." Report prepared for the Centers for Medicare & Medicaid. Published March. https://downloads.cms.gov/files/cmmi/md-all-payer-thirdannrpt.pdf.

Sanger-Katz, M. 2019. "In the US, an Angioplasty Costs $32,000. Elsewhere? Maybe $6,400." *New York Times.* Published December 27. www.nytimes.com/2019/12/27/upshot/expensive-health-care-world-comparison.html.

Sarnak, D., D. Squires, and S. Bishop. 2017. "Paying for Prescription Drugs Around the World: Why Is the U.S. an Outlier?" Commonwealth Fund. Published October 17. www.commonwealthfund.org/publications/issue-briefs/2017/oct/paying-prescription-drugs-around-world-why-us-outlier.

Sawyer, B., and S. Gonzales. 2017. "How Does Infant Mortality in the U.S. Compare to Other Countries?" Peterson-KFF Health System Tracker. Published October 18. www.healthsystemtracker.org/chart-collection/infant-mortality-u-s-compare-countries/#item-start.

Sawyer, B., and D. McDermott. 2019. "How Does the Quality of the U.S. Healthcare System Compare to Other Countries?" Peterson-KFF Health System Tracker. Published March 28. www.healthsystemtracker.org/chart-collection/quality-u-s-healthcare-system-compare-countries/#item-start.

Sawyer, B., and N. Sroczynski. 2016. "How Do U.S. Healthcare Resources Compare to Other Countries?" Peterson-KFF Health System Tracker. Published September 30. www.healthsystemtracker.org/chart-collection/u-s-health-care-resources-compare-countries/.

Schneider, E., D. Sarnak, D. Squires, A. Shah, and M. Doty. 2017. "Mirror, Mirror 2017: International Comparison Reflects Flaws and Opportunities for Better U.S. Healthcare." Commonwealth Fund. Published July 14. www.commonwealthfund.org/publications/fund-reports/2017/jul/mirror-mirror-2017-international-comparison-reflects-flaws-and.

Seervai, S., A. Shah, and R. Osborn. 2017. "How Other Countries Achieve Universal Coverage." Commonwealth Fund. Published October 27. www.commonwealthfund.org/blog/2017/how-other-countries-achieve-universal-coverage.

Siddiqui, Z. 2014. "India Extends Price Caps to 52 More Essential Drugs." Reuters. Published December 12. www.reuters.com/article/us-india-pharmaceuticals-prices-idUSKBN0JQ0KY20141212.

Sturman, C. 2018. "Top Healthcare Innovations for 2019." Healthcare Global. Published December 10. www.healthcareglobal.com/top-10/top-10-healthcare-innovations-2019.

Tan, X., X. Liu, and H. Shao. 2017. "Health China 2030: A Vision for Healthcare." *Value in Health Regional Issues* 12C: 112–14.

Tikkanen, R., and M. Abrams. 2020. "US Health Care from a Global Perspective, 2019: Higher Spending, Worse Outcomes?" Commonwealth Fund. Published January 30. www.commonwealthfund.org/publications/issue-briefs/2020/jan/us-health-care-global-perspective-2019.

Wasik, J. 2018. "Why Medicare Can't Get the Lowest Drug Prices." *Forbes*. Published August 10. www.forbes.com/sites/johnwasik/2018/08/10/why-medicare-cant-get-the-lowest-drug-prices/#1e623770302b.

CHAPTER 14

THE FUTURE OF HEALTHCARE IN THE UNITED STATES

What is the future of healthcare in the United States? Some believe that meaningful healthcare reform will occur only when we change the way healthcare is paid for. "If you look across the healthcare system today, the same services vary significantly in cost and quality at different providers. To close that gap and improve the delivery of care for every provider, we need . . . [to] transition to policies that better reward coordinated, quality care. We also need to provide more opportunities for primary care providers to practice the way they think is best. As one example, . . . Comprehensive Primary Care . . . offers up-front primary care payments to allow doctors to deliver care more flexibly, such as providing enhanced access to care out of the office or outside of regular office hours, supported by monthly care management fees that allow primary care doctors and clinicians to spend more time with their patients, serve their patients' needs outside of the office visit, and coordinate with specialists" (Burwell 2016).

LEARNING OBJECTIVES

After reading this chapter, you will be able to

➤ Describe the many challenges facing healthcare in the United States.

➤ Compare and contrast the arguments on whether healthcare is a right or a privilege.

➤ Evaluate the disadvantages of focusing on treatment rather than prevention.

➤ Explain the problems of addiction in the United States and potential solutions.

➤ Argue why US healthcare should be more integrated and less fragmented and suggest possible solutions.

➤ Compare social determinants of health and describe healthcare reforms to better address them.

➤ Identify technology that may significantly change healthcare.

Healthcare in the United States faces many challenges. Like all governments across the world, the United States struggles with organizing, providing, and paying for healthcare services. The United States faces many of the same problems as other countries, but they are exacerbated by wide political and philosophical divides regarding healthcare. The two major political parties in the United States seem to be deadlocked on healthcare reform, disagreeing strongly on the role of the government in healthcare and the way healthcare should be delivered and paid for (Irwin 2017).

One thing that the parties agree on is that the United States spends a lot on healthcare. The United States spends about 18 percent of its gross domestic product (GDP) on healthcare, whereas other industrialized countries spend an average of 10 percent. In addition, almost 25 percent of the US federal budget is allocated to healthcare (Davis 2018). Despite these challenges, many efforts are underway in the United States to improve healthcare.

FOCUS ON PREVENTION VERSUS TREATMENT

The prevention of disease needs to become a higher priority. Healthcare in the United States faces a key challenge to shift emphasis from acute care and treatment of disease to the prevention of disease. The US healthcare model has long emphasized acute care over prevention and public health. Just three diseases—heart disease, cancer, and diabetes—account for almost three-quarters of US healthcare expenditures. The frequency and severity of these and other diseases could be moderated if more resources were dedicated to preventing them. The United States has an opportunity to reduce disease and improve people's health, if only the country would change its focus to prevention (Marvasti and Stafford 2012).

As discussed in chapters 3 and 7, the main factor that sustains the focus on acute care and treatment rather than prevention is the fee-for-service payment model. Most healthcare payments are made through a fee-for-service arrangement, which promotes the overuse of services and discourages prevention (Salmond and Echevarria 2017). Fee-for-service payment for healthcare has been likened to paying carpenters by the inch of lumber they use, or plumbers by each foot of pipe installed. Clearly, if carpenters and plumbers were paid this way, their use of lumber and pipe would skyrocket. Under fee-for-service payment, physicians are rewarded for ordering more tests and performing surgeries. They are paid more when they provide more services. As a result, they may provide more care than is needed (Burwell 2016).

Most healthcare policymakers believe that healthcare providers should be given financial incentives to promote health and wellness and provide preventive interventions. Providers who deliver more cost-effective treatment and keep their patients healthy should also share in the savings of healthcare dollars (Davis 2018). Some healthcare systems, such as Kaiser Permanente, already practice this type of medicine (see sidebar). This model could be replicated across the United States.

✳ KAISER PERMANENTE CREATES INCENTIVES TO FOCUS ON PREVENTIVE CARE

Kaiser Permanente is an example of a healthcare system that focuses on preventive care. With patients in eight states, Kaiser owns hospitals and clinics and operates a nonprofit health insurance plan. Kaiser receives a fixed annual payment to care for each person it covers, so the company has incentives to keep members healthy and out of the hospital. These incentives improve the lives of members and, at the same time, lower the costs for payers and providers and increase Kaiser's efficiency (Davis 2018). Because healthy people avoid expensive healthcare, Kaiser has sought to improve community members' health through obesity reduction, healthy eating, and housing initiatives (Lee 2019). However, providing integrated care and accepting capitation has been difficult for most healthcare providers.

IS HEALTHCARE A RIGHT OR A PRIVILEGE?

The United States is the only industrialized country that has not determined whether healthcare is a right for everyone or a privilege only for those who can afford it (Gawande 2017). This debate over healthcare deeply divides Americans. If healthcare is a right, then the government has a responsibility to ensure that each citizen has access to a certain level of healthcare. Citizens should reasonably receive equal levels in terms of quality and access to healthcare services. However, if healthcare is a privilege, then the government should have a limited role and allow the marketplace to provide different levels of care to those who can afford it.

Calls for greater equality in healthcare have grown more insistent. Today, almost 60 percent of Americans and 85 percent of Democrats believe that the government should ensure the provision of healthcare to all citizens. However, about 40 percent of the US population and around 68 percent of Republicans oppose greater government involvement in healthcare, and many of those in opposition seek to stop what they regard as the intrusion of government in aspects of healthcare (Bialik 2017; Jones 2018).

In 2008, the year President Barack Obama was elected, more than 50 million Americans, or 16.3 percent of the population, lacked health insurance. President Obama declared that year that "healthcare should be a right for every American" and pushed for the passage of the Affordable Care Act (ACA) of 2010. That law reduced the number of uninsured to 12.7 percent by 2016. However, as a result of changes in the ACA implemented under President Donald Trump, the number of uninsured began to rise, and by 2018, the share had reached 15.5 percent (Collins et al. 2018; Maruthappu, Ologunde, and Gunarajasingam 2013).

The Democratic Party promotes healthcare as a right, and a common Democratic campaign theme since 2018 has been "Medicare for All"—but what exactly Medicare for All means remains uncertain. Medicare for All could be enacted as a single-payer system supported by taxes, totally eliminating private health insurance, or it could be structured to allow people to buy into the existing Medicare system, among many other options (Scott 2018).

THE IMPACT OF HEALTHCARE COSTS

Over the past several decades, increasing healthcare costs have placed a greater burden on patients and employees. As exhibit 14.1 shows, the percentage of healthcare expenditures that are paid out of pocket dropped from 34 percent to 10 percent of total costs between 1970 and 2018. However, because of the *overall* increase in healthcare costs, out-of-pocket costs in dollar terms increased nearly tenfold, from $119 per person in 1970 to $1,093 in 2016. This increase occurred even though employers and insurance plans have borne significantly higher costs (Kamal, McDermott, and Cox 2019). In 1970, total US healthcare expenditures amounted to $75.6 billion; by 2018, that number stood at more than $3.6

Category	1970	2018
Total per capita healthcare spending	$355	$10,207
Share of out-of-pocket spending	34%	10%
Share of private insurance spending	21%	37%
Share of public insurance spending	22%	45%

EXHIBIT 14.1
Total US Health Expenditures by Percentages and Dollars, 1970 and 2018

Source: Data from Kamal, McDermott, and Cox (2019); Tikkanen and Abrams (2020).

trillion. Likewise, per capita (per person) total healthcare spending jumped from $355 in 1970 to $10,207 in 2018. Adjusted for inflation, individual out-of-pocket healthcare cost rose from $121 per year in 1970 to $1,035 in 2016 (Kamal, McDermott, and Cox 2019; Rosenberg 2018).

As a reflection of how costs have been shifted to employees and patients, the average deductible increased from $303 to more than $1,200 between 2006 and 2016 (Claxton et al. 2018). Because of high out-of-pocket costs, many people are delaying or choosing not to seek needed healthcare. One study showed that about 10 percent of the US population did not seek medical care and 25 percent lacked dental care in 2016 because of high costs (Cox and Sawyer 2018).

Employees and employers often choose high-deductible plans to lower their monthly healthcare premiums. In 2018, 70 percent of all large businesses offered high-deductible plans. Many employees choose high-deductible plans because their premiums are about 42 percent lower than health insurance coverage with lower deductibles. Many annual deductibles for family coverage are now more than $4,300 (Miller 2018).

High healthcare costs impose hardships on families that lack the financial resources to obtain healthcare services. According to a Federal Reserve survey, more than 40 percent of families reported that they could not afford a $400 emergency expense without borrowing money or selling a possession (Tozzi and Tracer 2018). Only about 30 percent of US employees feel that they can afford healthcare without experiencing financial hardship. In addition, almost 80 percent of workers are unhappy with the cost of their health insurance, and many have begun to contribute less to their retirement accounts and other savings to cover healthcare costs (Miller 2018).

Although almost 40 percent of large companies in the United States offer *only* high-deductible health insurance plans to their employees, many large businesses are now considering lowering their healthcare insurance deductibles. For example, CVS, which moved its 200,000 employees to high-deductible plans a decade ago, is reconsidering high deductibles after seeing the hardships imposed on employees when they became ill (Tozzi and Tracer 2018).

WASTE IN HEALTHCARE

Financial waste in healthcare occurs far too often. Estimates suggest that about 30 percent of total healthcare expenditures, or about $765 billion—more than the United States spends on defense—may be wasted (Allen 2017; Mercola 2018). Waste occurs in the following areas:

◆ *Unnecessary services.* Unnecessary services occur as a result of nonstandardized clinical protocols. A lack of proper protocols leads physicians to order low-value tests and services that provide little or no value to the patient (Haefner 2018).

◆ *Excess administrative costs.* About one-quarter of medical spending goes toward administrative costs (Cutler 2018). The United States spends about 8 percent on administration, whereas most nations spend only 1 to 3 percent (Knox 2018).

◆ *Inflated prices.* Prices for prescription drugs, doctors, and hospitals are dramatically higher in the United States than in other countries. For instance, the average cost of a CT scan in the United States is $896 compared with $97 in Canada (Knox 2018).

◆ *Fraud.* Healthcare fraud exceeds $68 billion each year in the United States, with the federal government winning fraud judgments of over $2.6 billion in 2019 (McGrail 2020).

◆ *Avoidable errors.* Medical errors increase healthcare costs and injure many people every year. Research suggests that 250,000 to 440,000 people per year die in the United States from a medical error, making it the third-leading cause of death in the nation (Sipherd 2018).

A focus on preventive care over acute care may not reduce short-term healthcare costs. In the long run, it may actually increase costs as people live longer. However, patients' quality of life could certainly be improved.

✳ DOES PREVENTIVE CARE SAVE MONEY?

Prevention may not save healthcare costs in the long run. Although the reasoning is counterintuitive, a number of studies have shown that most preventive healthcare efforts do not save healthcare costs. Aside from childhood immunizations and the use of low-dose aspirin, most preventive efforts, such as smoking cessation programs, actually increase long-term healthcare costs because people live longer. Prevention still improves people's quality of life, but it may not reduce healthcare spending over a person's lifetime (Carroll 2018).

HEALTHCARE COSTS AND OUTCOMES COMPARED WITH OTHER COUNTRIES

In a global economy, the efficiency and costs of a country's healthcare system affect the competitiveness of its businesses and products. As mentioned earlier in this book, US expenditures on healthcare far exceed those of other countries. As Warren Buffet stated,

Exhibit 14.2

Comparison of Healthcare Expenditures and Health Outcomes

	US	Sweden	Switzerland	Germany	France	Japan	Canada	UK
Total healthcare spending as a share of national GDP	17.8%	11.9%	12.4%	11.3%	11%	10.9%	10.3%	9.7%
Public spending as a share of national GDP	8.3%	10.0%	7.7%	8.7%	8.7%	8.6%	7.4%	7.6%
Mean spending on health per capita ($USD)	$9,403	$6,808	$6,787	$5,182	$3,661	$3,727	$4,641	$3,377
Life expectancy	78.8	82.3	83	80.7	82.4	83.9	81.7	81
Maternal mortality (deaths per 100,000 live births)	26.4	4.4	5.8	9	7.8	6.4	7.3	9.2
Infant mortality (deaths per 1,000 live births)	5.8	2.5	3.9	3.3	3.8	2.1	5.1	3.9

Source: Data from Papanicolas, Woskie, and Jha (2018).

"The ballooning costs of healthcare act as a hungry tapeworm on the American economy" (Sahadi 2018). High healthcare costs are built into American products, making US exports less competitive.

Unfortunately, despite the higher level of spending, the US healthcare outcomes are worse than those of other countries that spend far less. As shown in exhibit 14.2, the United States spends almost 40 percent more per capita than the next-closest country—$9,403 compared with Sweden's $6,808. At the same time, however, life expectancy and maternal and infant mortality are much worse than in other countries.

THE CHALLENGE OF SUBSTANCE ABUSE

Many Americans experience substance abuse disorders. Drug misuse costs the United States more than $1 trillion per year. Although illegal drugs remain a problem, about 60 percent of overdose deaths involve prescription drugs (Cidambi 2017). In the past decade, misuse of opioids has become a crisis. In 2017, almost 45,000 deaths were attributed to opioid overdoses (Bruder 2018). To combat substance abuse, the following measures have been recommended:

◆ *Decriminalize some drug possession.* About 1.5 million arrests are made annually for drug violations. Decriminalization would keep many people out of prison and better facilitate treatment.

◆ *Increase funding for treatment.* Many people with substance abuse disorders lack the resources to obtain treatment. Outpatient treatment services may not be accessible because of financial or transportation barriers.

◆ *Increase education to diminish substance abuse.* Patients especially need to understand the addictive potential of some prescription drugs (Cidambi 2017).

FRAGMENTED DELIVERY OF HEALTHCARE

Healthcare in the United States is delivered through a fragmented system. Patients often seek care from both specialists and primary care physicians who frequently do not communicate with each other (see sidebar). Solutions to increase coordination among providers include the following (Mate and Compton-Phillips 2014):

◆ Change the payment system to pay for integrated care. Pay providers a lump sum for overall care for a period of time under some form of capitated payment model.

◆ Standardize work and clarify the roles of providers.

◆ Create universal electronic health records to allow better communication across providers.

◆ Reduce dependence on specialty care by increasing the number of primary care physicians to coordinate care.

(✱) A FRAGMENTED SYSTEM

"We have this discombobulated, fragmented system that leads [the] U.S. to have very high administrative costs, and everything is disconnected. You have to go from one system to another when you go from one provider to another. Some health [information] gets lost with the transfer from one provider to the next. And there's a private healthcare system that funds you when you are under 65, and when you're over 65, you get funded by Medicare. And maybe most of your problems occur when you're on Medicare, so our private healthcare system doesn't have a lot of incentive to keep you healthy when you're over 65, because they're not on the hook for it."

—*Dan Polsky, Executive Director, University of Pennsylvania Leonard Davis Institute of Health Economics (Wharton School of Business 2017)*

Some integrated multispecialty care clinics are working to reduce fragmentation and improve care. For example, the Virginia Mason Health System in Seattle, Washington, has been recognized as a pioneer in integrating patient care, increasing quality, and reducing costs. Its efforts have led to more standardized treatments, elimination of unnecessary care, and lower costs (Blackmore, Mecklenburg, and Kaplan 2011).

Other efforts aim to integrate behavioral health and medical treatment. Patients with mental illness are at high risk of medical problems, which dramatically lowers their life expectancy. For instance, about 25 percent of patients admitted to a hospital for a medical or surgical diagnosis also suffer with a behavioral health problem. Many health systems are developing stronger community partnerships with mental health clinics, health centers, churches, and other agencies to better address mental health needs. As shown in the list below, there are many things that need to be done to improve mental health treatment (AHA 2019):

♦ Screenings and prevention services

♦ Coordination and integration

♦ Community partnerships

♦ Workforce development

♦ Infrastructure development

♦ De-stigmatizing behavioral health

Experts believe that integrating mental health care, coupled with a focus on preventive and physical care, can improve patient outcomes and provide a better life for patients (Schuster et al. 2018).

In an attempt to address fragmentation and increase competitiveness, hospitals, health systems, and medical practices have consolidated over the past 30 years, creating ever-larger organizations. By 2017, in most areas, a single health system controlled more than 50 percent of hospital admissions. More physicians now work for hospital systems, and the concentration of hospitals in markets has increased substantially. As shown in exhibit 14.3, population areas with highly concentrated hospital markets and health insurance availability increased significantly between 2003 and 2017. This consolidation trend continued in 2018 and 2019, with many mega-mergers occurring. Although consolidation may facilitate greater integration, it may ultimately be bad for consumers, as markets with high concentrations appear to drive up prices and profits (Hiltzik 2020; MedPAC 2020).

Many healthcare leaders believe that continued consolidation of healthcare providers will occur, triggered by the need for capital to invest heavily in technology and prepare for an uncertain future. Mergers and acquisitions and consolidation of markets

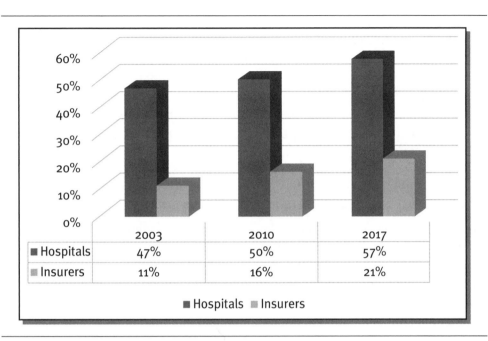

Source: MedPAC (2020).

EXHIBIT 14.3
Markets with High
Concentrations
of Hospitals and
Healthcare Insurers,
2003–2017

are expected to continue in all segments of healthcare, but primarily in the following (Herschman et al. 2020):

◆ Long-term care

◆ Physician practices

◆ Healthcare information technology and software

◆ Pharmaceuticals

◆ Hospitals and healthcare systems

◆ Medical device firms

◆ Home care and hospices

EXPANSION OF HEALTHCARE COMPETITION TO TECH COMPANIES

The traditional healthcare system also faces greater competition. In many ways, the nature of healthcare competition is changing. Rather than just hospitals, health systems, doctors, and insurance companies competing for business, technology giants and large companies, such as Amazon, Google, and Apple, have entered the healthcare market. Most healthcare leaders feel vulnerable to these efforts, and they are concerned as healthcare expands more into digital health; meanwhile, traditional healthcare providers continue to focus on the construction of new facilities. The COVID-19 pandemic may provide a new impetus for the use of digital healthcare. Studies have shown that consumers are interested in using digital healthcare, but health systems have been slow to offer such options. For example, in 2019, almost 90 percent of healthcare systems did not offer voice-activated assistants, half used some wearable devices and in-home monitoring, and about 40 percent offered smartphone apps (KaufmanHall 2019). Yet, telemedicine use exploded in 2020 during the pandemic, increasing more than 8,000 percent from 2019 to 2020 (Gelburd 2020).

INTEGRATING SOCIAL DETERMINANTS OF HEALTH

Most healthcare and governmental leaders agree that to truly improve healthcare in the United States and the health of Americans, healthcare must extend beyond the walls of hospitals and clinics and address social determinants of health. Social determinants of health are factors in the social and physical environment that influence a person's health. These include socioeconomic status, education, food security, housing, employment and social support functions. Chapter 13 discusses social determinants of health and population health, which have a significant impact on today's healthcare outcomes. Efforts are underway across the country to address social determinants of health. Medicaid and Medicare are now giving providers the ability to meet patients' needs outside their medical offices by paying for services that address social determinant of health needs. For instance, Oregon and Colorado have implemented Medicaid delivery models that integrate medical, physical, behavioral, and social services (Artiga and Hinton 2018).

A wide majority of people want more collaboration between their providers and community resources. One study indicated that more than 70 percent of respondents wanted

 DEBATE TIME Potential Savings Because of Social Factors

Addressing social determinants of health may be the answer to greater healthcare savings. These factors may include access to transportation, healthy food, a safe environment, education, and housing. Greater attention to social determinants could save up to $102 billion in annual medical costs. Many providers are starting to broaden "their care teams to include nutritionists, behavioral health specialists, social workers, and community health workers trained in nonmedical health-related issues" (PwC 2018). Why has the traditional provision of healthcare mostly ignored social factors? What could be done to change this?

more cooperation among their community, providers, payers, and employers. Billions of dollars could be saved in doing so (PwC 2018).

HEALTH DISPARITIES

Health disparities persist in the areas of race/ethnicity, socioeconomic status, age, location, gender, disability status, and sexual orientation, resulting in poorer quality of care and healthcare outcomes. These disparities create an additional $93 billion in unnecessary healthcare costs and $42 billion in lost productivity (Orgera and Artiga 2018). In addition, the number of minorities in the United States continues to grow rapidly: By 2045, the white population is expected to account for less than half of the total population (Frey 2018). Without action to reduce health disparities, these inequities may be exacerbated as the demographics of the US population change.

Minority racial/ethnic populations have been shown to receive lower-quality care because they tend to go to poorer-quality institutions (hospitals and clinics) that have higher proportions of Medicaid patients and receive less financial support. However, many of the differences could be eliminated if these populations had stable health insurance and primary care medical homes (Beal 2018).

AGING AND CHRONIC CONDITIONS

As in most countries, the US population continues to age as birthrates fall and people live longer lives. The US Census Bureau predicts that more than 20 percent of the population will be over the age of 65 by the mid-2030s, and for the first time there will be more older people than children in the United States (see sidebar).

✱ A MAJORITY OF ELDERLY

The United States, like most developed countries, is growing older. "The aging of baby boomers means that within just a couple decades, older people are projected to outnumber children for the first time in U.S. history," said Jonathan Vespa, a demographer with the US Census Bureau. "By 2035, there will be 78.0 million people 65 years and older compared to 76.4 million under the age of 18" (US Census Bureau 2018). As people age and live longer, they experience more chronic diseases and use more healthcare services. An aging population puts more pressure on already stressed healthcare providers and increases healthcare costs.

Exhibit 14.4

Americans with
Two or More
Chronic Diseases
by Age, 2014

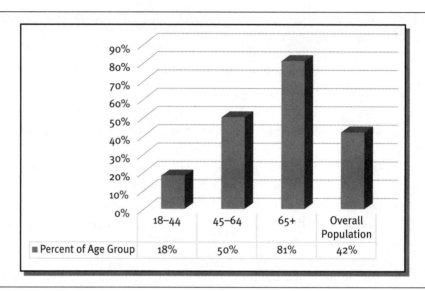

	18–44	45–64	65+	Overall Population
▪ Percent of Age Group	18%	50%	81%	42%

Source: Data from Buttorff, Ruder, and Bauman (2017).

About 60 percent of all people in the United States suffer from at least one chronic illness. As shown in exhibit 14.4, 42 percent of the US population, or just over 100 million people, have two or more chronic diseases. The incidence of multiple chronic disease increases with age, rising from 18 percent among 18- to 44-year-olds to 81 percent for people over the age of 65. As would be expected, the more chronic conditions a person has, the more health services they will use. For instance, a person with five or more chronic diseases will be eight times more likely to be hospitalized. Furthermore, although Americans with five or more chronic illnesses account for only 12 percent of the US population, they account for 41 percent of total healthcare expenditures (Buttorff, Ruder, and Bauman 2017). In addition, older people with multiple chronic diseases experience greater rates of depression (Wilson-Genderson, Heid, and Pruchno 2017).

However, research has demonstrated that higher levels of exercise among older adults dramatically reduce the likelihood of having chronic diseases and increase their ability to live healthfully (Wilson-Genderson, Heid, and Pruchno 2017).

LACK OF TRANSPARENCY AND VARIATION OF PRICES

Little financial transparency exists in healthcare pricing. Most patients do not know—and cannot find out—the costs of healthcare services until long after the service has been received. Providers typically charge different payers, such as Medicare, insurance companies, and private payers, different prices for the same services. Many including federal legislators are seeking solutions to increase transparency and reduce variation in healthcare prices (see sidebar).

> (✳) **DEBATE TIME** Transparency in Healthcare
>
> In 2018, a bipartisan group of senators asked for recommendations to improve transparency in healthcare. They noted that "in virtually every other industry, consumers are able to price shop, compare quality, and then decide what product best fits their needs. In healthcare, the lack of information and the inability to access it hurts patients and prevents normal market forces from driving competition, lowering prices, and improving quality" (Cassidy et al. 2018).
>
> Why is price transparency a problem in healthcare? How would price transparency help reduce costs or improve the quality of services? Are there some people who are not sensitive to healthcare costs? Why?

Price transparency in healthcare has become more important as the number of high-deductible plans has grown from 3 million enrollees in 2006 to 20 million in 2016 and patients become responsible for a greater share of their healthcare bills (AHIP 2017). Price transparency is regarded as essential for competitive, functioning healthcare markets.

However, just knowing healthcare prices might not be enough, as people often do not use the information effectively (Desai et al. 2016). Merely publishing the prices of goods and services does not help patients understand what they will be charged. To help, some have suggested implementing reference pricing, which would set maximum prices that insurance companies would pay for services (Gudiksen 2018). Others have recommended the following actions (Gustafsson and Bishop 2019):

◆ Focus transparency efforts on goods and services that can be compared, such as prescription drugs and diagnostic imaging.

◆ Group costs into episodes of care, procedures, or annual costs of care.

◆ Combine prices with quality and outcomes.

◆ Use the same format and provide information in a centralized, convenient location that people can access.

◆ Provide price information to doctors and other healthcare providers.

◆ Encourage shared decision-making regarding treatment options.

New Technology

New technology will certainly change the future of medicine. In less than a decade, experts expect to see a shift from traditional physician office visits to frequent virtual visits and online doctor–patient interactions. As discussed in chapter 10, telemedicine uses smartphones and mobile devices to facilitate communication between doctors and patients. Telemedicine is expected to become common to treat mild illnesses such as colds, flu, and minor injuries and to better manage chronic illnesses. Very soon, a majority of patient interactions with healthcare facilities may occur through mobile devices, thereby improving doctors' efficiency and making primary care more accessible (Costantini 2018; Quora 2018).

Advances in artificial intelligence (AI)—the use of computer systems to perform tasks that normally require human intelligence—may also change healthcare dramatically. AI has been used in combination with surgical robots for more than a decade, but now its use is becoming more common. The number of robot-assisted procedures performed in hospitals jumped from 1.5 percent of all procedures in 2003 to 27 percent in 2015 (Zimmerman 2018). In addition, AI has the ability to better diagnose many illnesses better than humans and could be especially useful in specialties such as radiology and pathology (Loh 2018). AI could save healthcare billions of dollars through more effective diagnostics, improved drug discovery, and better treatment for diseases (Rosso 2018).

Many other technological advances may have significant impacts on healthcare in the near future, including the following:

- *3D printing* could allow for low-cost, custom-built implants, joints, bones, and blood vessels, greatly lowering costs and improving outcomes.

- *Drones* could be used to facilitate deliveries of medical supplies and testing samples, drastically reducing wait times.

- *Wearable health monitoring devices* could transmit information about patients' conditions and tests to providers for continuous monitoring.

- *Virtual and augmented reality* could be used for treatment in physical and occupational therapy, in addition to pain management and medical training.

- *Medical tricorders* (palm-sized health tools) could be used measure ECGs (electrocardiograms), heart rate, oxygen saturation, temperature, blood pressure, and other functions.

- *Genome sequencing* could be used to provide data on drug sensitivity, medical conditions, better diets, and vitamin needs at a low cost.

- *Nanotechnology* could be use for precise drug delivery, wound monitoring, and diagnoses (The Medical Futurist 2020; Palmer 2018).

Many healthcare providers find it difficult to keep up with new technology. New technology drives change in healthcare, but it is often costly and may require significant training. Investments in new technology account for 40 to 50 percent of total healthcare cost increases (Clemens 2017).

New technology may work well, but it also may be difficult to integrate into existing systems. For instance, sometimes electronic health records require extensive integration to link with new technology.

Technology can automate and refine tasks and actions that normally are performed by humans. For instance, before infusion pumps were invented, nurses had to give patients injections on a regular basis. Infusion pumps eliminated this task and automated the delivery of medications. Keeping up with technology will continue to be a major challenge for all healthcare providers.

US healthcare organizations need to be adaptable, nimble, and prepared for change to keep up with technological advances. Some have suggested that successful healthcare systems will make care convenient and personalized and that hospitals will become more like luxury hotels (Morgan 2018). Others believe that healthcare providers must quickly shift their operations to support value-based payment and to build multisystem, clinically integrated accountable care networks (AHA 2017). Whatever the future holds for healthcare in the United States, strong leaders will be needed to guide organizations through these troubled waters to reposition and improve this vital aspect of our society.

SUMMARY

Healthcare in the United States faces many challenges, including rising costs and contentions among political parties regarding the direction of healthcare in the future. The current focus on treatment of illness, rather than preventive care, remains a critical factor that has yet to be addressed. Current payments for healthcare providers encourage treatment for acute illnesses and provision of invasive procedures. Instead, medical professionals should be given financial incentives to promote health and wellness and provide preventive interventions.

The United States is the only industrialized country without a nationwide healthcare system and some level of guaranteed healthcare for citizens. Americans remain divided as to whether healthcare is a right or a privilege.

The rising costs of healthcare affect individuals and businesses. Average out-of-pocket costs have jumped almost tenfold since the 1970s, and per capita spending has increased almost 30-fold. More employees are choosing high-deductible health plans, which pose significant financial burdens on families.

Waste in healthcare fuels some of the cost increases. Some suggest that waste accounts for 30 percent of healthcare expenditures. Waste in healthcare includes unnecessary services, excess administrative costs, inflated prices, fraud, and avoidable medical errors.

The United States spends far more on healthcare than other industrialized countries, but it has worse healthcare outcomes. Expenditures for healthcare in the United States are 40 percent higher than in similar countries, but outcomes such as life expectancy and maternal and infant mortality rates compare poorly with those of other countries.

Substance abuse remains a challenge in the United States, costing more than $1 trillion per year. The misuse of opioids in the past decade has become a crisis, resulting in almost 45,000 deaths in 2017.

One major problem with the US healthcare system is the fragmented delivery of healthcare services. Patients often see multiple specialists and primary care physicians who fail to communicate with each other. Integration of care is needed, which is now occurring in some clinics.

Integrating the social determinants of health into healthcare also remains a challenge. Social determinants of health include the social and physical environment, such as housing, employment, and food security, that directly affect a person's health. A number of states are seeking to integrate social determinants into their Medicaid and Medicare programs. Billions of dollars could be saved by emphasizing and integrating social determinants of health into the US healthcare system.

Healthcare disparities exist in the United States in the areas of race/ethnicity, socioeconomic status, age, location, gender, disability status, and sexual orientation. These disparities result in poorer quality of care and health outcomes. These populations are expected to see the highest growth in the future. The challenge is to improve the hospitals and clinics where these populations obtain healthcare services.

Aging will also affect the future of US healthcare. By the mid-2030s, more than 20 percent of the US population is expected to be over 65 years old. Older people suffer more from chronic diseases, which dramatically increase the use and cost of healthcare.

The lack of transparency and wide variation in healthcare prices are also major issues in the United States. Little transparency exists in healthcare pricing. In addition, prices for healthcare services can range widely. The wide variance in prices has become more important as patient deductibles have increased.

The future of healthcare will also be affected by advances in technology. New technology that furthers the use of telemedicine, such as artificial intelligence, robotics, 3D printing, drones, wearable health-monitoring devices, and virtual reality, will be important to the future provision of healthcare in the United States.

QUESTIONS

1. Why is it important to spend more on preventive care rather than merely treatment of illness?
2. If healthcare is a "right," should everyone have access to the same services? Should people who can afford to purchase higher-quality services be allowed to do so?

3. The share of out-of-pocket healthcare costs dropped from 34 percent to 10 percent for individuals, yet actual expenses increased almost ten times. How can that be so?
4. What are some of the causes of waste in healthcare?
5. How would decriminalization of drug possession help address the substance abuse problem in the United States?
6. What are four solutions to integrate the fragmented US healthcare system?
7. How does addressing social determinants of health impact healthcare?
8. Why do minority populations have worse health outcomes than white populations?
9. If a person has five or more chronic diseases, how likely is he or she to be admitted to a hospital?
10. What segment of insured patients should be most concerned about price transparency in healthcare?
11. How might 3D printing change healthcare?

Assignments

1. President George W. Bush stated that the United States already has universal healthcare because anyone can "just go to an emergency room." However, emergency room treatment is very different from care received at a clinic of your choice (Johnson 2017).
    a. How is the option of going to an emergency room different from universal healthcare coverage?
    b. Why is emergency room service a poor alternative to having a primary care provider?
2. Read the opinion piece about the role of technology in healthcare in the future: "How Technology Can Change the Future of Health in America," The Hill, March 21, 2018, at https://thehill.com/opinion/healthcare/379572-how-technology-can-change-the-future-of-health-in-america. Write a one-page paper describing the technologies you perceive as most important and how they might affect your life.

Cases

The Hospital CEO Dilemma

Josephine is CEO of Natten Community Hospital. She would very much like to focus more on promoting preventive care, which the hospital does by sponsoring health clinics in different neighborhoods four times a year. However, providing free preventive services to low-income residents does not earn revenue for the hospital. In fact, increasing the number of low-income patients causes the hospital to lose more money. The hospital makes money when sick people come to the hospital for treatment—especially people with insurance. Basically, the sicker the community is, the better the hospital does, and Josephine gets rewarded through bonuses.

Discussion Questions

1. Why does the hospital makes more money when people are sick?
2. What could Josephine do to encourage integration of social determinants of care?
3. Would a program like Medicare for All change the hospitals' incentives?

HEALTHCARE WASTE

Sam runs a health insurance company that has faced many challenges. He is certain that he can lower costs by focusing on areas that have been identified as wasted resources. He has read that many doctors and hospitals order unnecessary and low-value tests, that too much fraud occurs in healthcare, and that prices are too high. His company has collected a lot of data, as its customers span a large regional area. He wonders what he could do to address waste in healthcare. At the same time, he wants to maintain the good relationships that his company has established with local healthcare providers.

Discussion Questions

1. Which area of waste might be the best for Sam to address? Why?
2. Would it be appropriate for an insurance company to investigate fraud? Why?

REFERENCES

Allen, M. 2017. "A Prescription to Reduce Waste in Healthcare Spending." National Public Radio. Published December 21. www.npr.org/sections/health-shots/2017/12/21/572329335/a-prescription-to-reduce-waste-in-health-care-spending.

American Hospital Association (AHA). 2019. "Increasing Access to Behavioral Health Care Advances Value for Patients, Providers and Communities." *Trendwatch*. Published May. www.aha.org/system/files/media/file/2019/05/aha-trendwatch-behavioral-health-2019.pdf.

———. 2017. "Hospitals and Health Systems Prepare for Value-Driven Future." *Trendwatch*. Published December. www.aha.org/system/files/research/reports/tw/tw2017-valuebasedpayments.pdf.

America's Health Insurance Plans (AHIP). 2017. *2016 Survey of Health Savings Account–High Deductible Health Plans*. Published February. www.ahip.org/wp-content/uploads/2017/02/2016_HSASurvey_Draft_2.14.17.pdf.

Artiga, S., and E. Hinton. 2018. "Beyond Healthcare: The Role of Social Determinants in Promoting Health and Health Equity." Issue Brief, Kaiser Family Foundation. Published May 10. www.kff.org/disparities-policy/issue-brief/beyond-health-care-the-role-of-social-determinants-in-promoting-health-and-health-equity/.

Beal, A. 2018. "Reframing a National Dialogue About Healthcare Disparities." Commonwealth Fund. Published April 27. www.commonwealthfund.org/blog/2018/reframing-national-dialogue-about-health-care-disparities.

Bialik, K. 2017. "More Americans Say Government Should Ensure Healthcare Coverage." Pew Research Center. Published January 13. www.pewresearch.org/fact-tank/2017/01/13/more-americans-say-government-should-ensure-health-care-coverage/.

Blackmore, C., R. Mecklenburg, and G. Kaplan. 2011. "At Virginia Mason, Collaboration Among Providers, Employers, and Health Plans to Transform Care Cut Costs and Improve Quality." *Health Affairs* 30 (9): 1680–87.

Bruder, J. 2018. "The Worst Drug Crisis in American History." *New York Times*. Published July 31. www.nytimes.com/2018/07/31/books/review/beth-macy-dopesick.html.

Burwell, S. M. 2016. "Building a System That Works: The Future of Healthcare." *Health Affairs Blog*. Published December 12. www.healthaffairs.org/do/10.1377/hblog20161212.057877/full/.

Buttorff, C., T. Ruder, and M. Bauman. 2017. *Multiple Chronic Conditions in the United States*. RAND Corporation. Accessed June 22, 2020. www.fightchronicdisease.org/sites/default/files/TL221_final.pdf.

Carroll, A. 2018. "Preventive Care Saves Money? Sorry, It's Too Good to Be True." *New York Times*. Published January 29. www.nytimes.com/2018/01/29/upshot/preventive-health-care-costs.html.

Cassidy B., C. Grassley, T. Young, M. F. Bennet, T. Carper, and C. McCaskill. 2018. "Letter to Stakeholders." Published February 28. www.cassidy.senate.gov/imo/media/doc/Cassidy%20Price%20Transparency%20Letter.pdf.

Cidambi, I. 2017. "Actual Cost of Drug Abuse in U.S. Tops $1 Trillion Annually." *Psychology Today*. Published August 10. www.psychologytoday.com/us/blog/sure-recovery/201708/actual-cost-drug-abuse-in-us-tops-1-trillion-annually.

Claxton, G., L. Levitt, M. Rae, and B. Sawyer. 2018. "Increases in Cost-Sharing Payments Continue to Outpace Wage Growth." Peterson-KFF Health System Tracker. Published June 15. www.healthsystemtracker.org/brief/increases-in-cost-sharing-payments-have-far-outpaced-wage-growth/#item-start.

Clemens, M. 2017. "Technology and Rising Healthcare Costs." *Forbes*. Published October 26. www.forbes.com/sites/forbestechcouncil/2017/10/26/technology-and-rising-health-care-costs/#67235bb8766b.

Collins, S., M. Gunja, M. Doty, and H. Bhupal. 2018. "First Look at Health Insurance Coverage in 2018 Finds ACA Gains Beginning to Reverse." Commonwealth Fund. Published May 1. www.commonwealthfund.org/blog/2018/first-look-health-insurance-coverage-2018-finds-aca-gains-beginning-reverse?redirect_source=/publications/blog/2018/apr/health-coverage-erosion.

Costantini, R. 2018. "Telehealth Integrated with Hospitals and Retail Health Is the Wave of the Future." *Becker's Hospital Review*. Published May 17. www.beckershospitalreview.com/healthcare-information-technology/telehealth-integrated-with-hospitals-and-retail-health-is-the-wave-of-the-future.html.

Cox, C., and B. Sawyer. 2018. "How Does Cost Affect Access to Care?" Peterson-KFF Health System Tracker. Published January 17. www.healthsystemtracker.org/chart-collection/cost-affect-access-care/#item-start.

Cutler, D. 2018. "What Is the U.S. Health Spending Problem?" *Health Affairs* 37 (3): 493–97.

Davis, K. 2018. "The Real Reason Healthcare Is Bankrupting America." CNBC. Published January 11. www.cnbc.com/2018/01/11/the-real-reason-health-care-is-bankrupting-america.html.

Desai, S., L. Hatfield, A. Hicks, M. Chernew, and A. Mehrotra. 2016. "Association Between Availability of a Price Transparency Tool and Outpatient Spending." *JAMA* 315 (17): 1874–81.

Frey, W. 2018. "The U.S. Will Become 'Minority White' in 2045, Census Projects." Brookings Institution. Published March 14. www.brookings.edu/blog/the-avenue/2018/03/14/the-us-will-become-minority-white-in-2045-census-projects/.

Gawande, A. 2017. "Is Healthcare a Right?" *The New Yorker*. Published October 2. www.newyorker.com/magazine/2017/10/02/is-health-care-a-right.

Gelburd, R. 2020. "Telehealth Growth in April Suggests Continuing Impact of COVID-19." *American Journal of Managed Care*. Published July 7. www.ajmc.com/view/telehealth-growth-in-april-suggests-continuing-impact-of-covid19.

Gudiksen, K. 2018. "Reference Pricing: When Transparency Is Not Enough." *The Source Blog*. Published June 12. http://sourceonhealthcare.org/reference-pricing-when-transparency-is-not-enough/.

Gustafsson, L., and S. Bishop. 2019. "Hospital Price Transparency: Making It Useful for Patients." Commonwealth Fund. Published February 12. www.commonwealthfund.org/blog/2019/hospital-price-transparency-making-it-useful-patients.

Haefner, M. 2018. "Healthcare Has a Waste Problem. Here's What Hospitals Can Do About It." *Becker's Hospital Review*. Published May 29. www.beckershospitalreview.com/quality/healthcare-has-a-waste-problem-here-s-what-hospitals-can-do-about-it.html.

Herschman, G., A. Patel, L. Kocot, and H. Torres. 2020. "Insight: Healthcare Consolidation Strong in 2019—Expect Even Stronger 2020." Bloomberg Law. Published January 27. https://news.bloomberglaw.com/health-law-and-business/insight-health-care-consolidation-strong-in-2019-expect-even-stronger-2020.

Hiltzik, M. 2020. "Hospital Mergers Reduce Patient Care and Drive Up Prices, New Data Show." *Los Angeles Times*. Published January 2. www.latimes.com/business/story/2020-01-02/hospital-mergers-reduce-patient-care.

Irwin, N. 2017. "The Health Debate Shows What Both Parties Care About Most." *New York Times*. Published June 23. www.nytimes.com/2017/06/23/upshot/the-health-debate-shows-what-both-parties-care-about-most.html.

Johnson, T. 2017. "Analysis: Healthcare Should Be a Right, but the U.S. Doesn't Have a System." ABC News. Published November 23. https://abcnews.go.com/Health/analysis-health-care-us-system/story?id=51281693.

Jones, K. 2018. "It's Time to Recognize Healthcare as a Right." *Washington Post*. Published January 17. www.washingtonpost.com/news/made-by-history/wp/2018/01/17/its-time-to-recognize-health-care-as-a-right/?utm_term=.20b59c0ce667.

Kamal, R., D. McDermott, and C. Cox. 2019. "How Has U.S. Spending on Healthcare Changed over Time?" Peterson-KFF Health System Tracker. Published December 20. www.healthsystemtracker.org/chart-collection/u-s-spending-healthcare-changed-time/#item-start.

KaufmanHall. 2019. *2019 State of Consumerism in Healthcare: The Bar Is Rising*. Accessed June 22, 2020. www.kaufmanhall.com/sites/default/files/documents/2019-06/2019_state_of_consumerism_in_healthcare_kaufmanhall_0.pdf.

Knox, R. 2018. "Why Are the U.S. Health Costs the World's Highest? Study Affirms 'It's the Prices, Stupid.'" WBUR. Published March 13, www.wbur.org/commonhealth/2018/03/13/us-health-costs-high-jha.

Lee, B. 2019. "What Kaiser Permanente Sees in the Community." *Forbes*. Published May 5. www.forbes.com/sites/brucelee/2019/05/05/what-kaiser-permanente-sees-in-the-community/#1ccdfb347b11.

Loh, E. 2018. "Medicine and the Rise of the Robots: A Qualitative Review of Recent Advances of Artificial Intelligence in Health." *BMJ Leader* 2 (2): 59–63.

Maruthappu, M., R. Ologunde, and A. Gunarajasingam. 2013. "Is Healthcare a Right? Health Reforms in the U.S.A. and Their Impact upon the Concept of Care." *Annals of Medicine and Surgery* 2 (1): 15–17.

Marvasti, F., and R. Stafford. 2012. "From 'Sick Care' to Healthcare: Reengineering Prevention into the U.S. System." *New England Journal of Medicine* 367 (10): 889–91.

Mate, K., and A. Compton-Phillips. 2014. "The Antidote to Fragmented Healthcare." *Harvard Business Review*. Published December 15. https://hbr.org/2014/12/the-antidote-to-fragmented-health-care.

McGrail, S. 2020. "DoJ Recovered $2.6B from Healthcare Fraud Cases in 2019." Revcycle Intelligence. Published January 20. https://revcycleintelligence.com/news/doj-recovered-2.6b-from-healthcare-fraud-cases-in-2019.

The Medical Futurist. 2020. "10 Ways Technology Is Changing Healthcare." Published March 3. https://medicalfuturist.com/ten-ways-technology-changing-healthcare/.

Medicare Payment Advisory Commission (MedPAC). 2020. *Congressional Request on Health Care Provider Consolidation*. Published March. www.medpac.gov/docs/default-source/reports/mar20_medpac_ch15_sec.pdf?sfvrsn=0.

Mercola, J. 2018. "U.S. Healthcare System Wastes More Money than the Entire Pentagon Budget Annually." Health Impact News. Published August 13. http://healthimpactnews.com/2013/us-health-care-system-wastes-more-money-than-the-entire-pentagon-budget-annually/.

Miller, S. 2018. "High-Deductible Plans More Common, but So Are Choices." Society for Human Resource Management. Published February 9. www.shrm.org/resourcesandtools/hr-topics/benefits/pages/high-deductible-plans-more-common-but-so-are-choices.aspx.

Morgan, B. 2018. "A Healthcare Wake-Up Call: Prepare for the Patient Experience of the Future." *Forbes*. Published December 11. www.forbes.com/sites/blakemorgan/2018/12/11/a-healthcare-wake-up-call-prepare-for-the-patient-experience-of-the-future/#13d8f59c20d6.

Orgera, K., and S. Artiga. 2018. "Disparities in Health and Healthcare: Five Key Questions and Answers." Issue Brief, Kaiser Family Foundation. Published August 8. www.kff.org/disparities-policy/issue-brief/disparities-in-health-and-health-care-five-key-questions-and-answers/.

Palmer, B. 2018. "6 Technological Breakthroughs That Will Change Healthcare." PCMA. Published February 13. www.pcmaconvene.org/features/new-healthcare-technology/.

Papanicolas, I., L. Woskie, and A. Jha. 2018. "Healthcare Spending in the United States and Other High-Income Countries." *JAMA* 319 (10): 1024–39.

PricewaterhouseCoopers (PwC). 2018. "Top Health Industry Issues of 2018: Social Determinants Come to the Forefront." Accessed June 24, 2020. www.pwc.com/us/en/health-industries/top-health-industry-issues/social-determinants.html.

Quora. 2018. "What Are the Latest Trends in Telemedicine in 2018?" *Forbes*. Published July 31. www.forbes.com/sites/quora/2018/07/31/what-are-the-latest-trends-in-telemedicine-in-2018/#1f4dca4f6b9e.

Rosenberg, J. 2018. "How U.S. Spending on Healthcare Has Changed over Time." *American Journal of Managed Care Blog*. Published January 2. www.ajmc.com/focus-of-the-week/how-us-spending-on-healthcare-has-changed-over-time.

Rosso, C. 2018. "The Future of AI in Healthcare." *Psychology Today*. Published June 13. www.psychologytoday.com/us/blog/the-future-brain/201806/the-future-ai-in-health-care.

Sahadi, J. 2018. "Warren Buffet Is Right. Healthcare Costs Are Swallowing the Economy." CNN. Published January 30. https://money.cnn.com/2018/01/30/news/economy/health-care-costs-eating-the-economy/index.html.

Salmond, S., and M. Echevarria. 2017. "Healthcare Transformation and Changing Roles for Nursing." *Orthopedic Nursing* 36 (1): 12–25.

Schuster, J., C. Nikolajski, J. Kogan, C. Kang, P. Schake, T. Carney, S. Morton, and C. Reynolds. 2018. "A Payer-Guided Approach to Widespread Diffusion of Behavioral Health Homes in Real World Settings." *Health Affairs* 37 (2): 248–56.

Scott, D. 2018. "The 'Pleasant Ambiguity' of Medicare-for-All in 2018, Explained." Vox. Published July 2. www.vox.com/policy-and-politics/2018/7/2/17468448/medicare-for-all-single-payer-health-care-2018-elections.

Sipherd, R. 2018. "The Third-Leading Cause of Death in U.S. Most Doctors Don't Want You to Know About." CNBC. Published February 28. www.cnbc.com/2018/02/22/medical-errors-third-leading-cause-of-death-in-america.html.

Tikkanen, R., and M. Abrams. 2020. "US Health Care from a Global Perspective, 2019." Commonwealth Fund. Published January 30. www.commonwealthfund.org/publications/issue-briefs/2020/jan/us-health-care-global-perspective-2019.

Tozzi, J., and Z. Tracer. 2018. "Some Big Employers Moving Away from High Deductible Health Plans." *Insurance Journal*. Published June 26. www.insurancejournal.com/news/national/2018/06/26/493273.htm.

US Census Bureau. 2018. "Older People Projected to Outnumber Children for the First Time in U.S. History." News release, March 13. www.census.gov/newsroom/press-releases/2018/cb18-41-population-projections.html.

Wharton School of Business. 2017. "Is Canada the Right Model for a Better U.S. Healthcare System?" Knowledge at Wharton. Published May 19. http://knowledge.wharton.upenn.edu/article/lessons-can-u-s-learn-canadian-health-care-system/.

Wilson-Genderson, M., A. Heid, and R. Pruchno. 2017. "Onset of Multiple Chronic Conditions and Depressive Symptoms: A Life Events Perspective." *Innovation in Aging* 1 (2): 1–10.

Zimmerman, B. 2018. "To Robot or Not to Robot—How Community Hospitals Can Get the Best Robot-Assisted Surgery Without Breaking the Bank." *Becker's Hospital Review*. Published March 13. www.beckershospitalreview.com/quality/to-robot-or-not-to-robot-how-community-hospitals-can-get-the-best-robot-assisted-surgery-without-breaking-the-bank.html.

GLOSSARY

academic medical center (AMC): An organization whose mission is to provide care for the poor, train medical students and healthcare professionals, and conduct research.

activities of daily living (ADLs): Routine activities that people do every day, such as eating, bathing, getting dressed, toileting, transferring, and continence.

actuary: A professional with advanced training in mathematics and statistics who analyzes the risks and costs associated with different populations, levels of healthcare access, quality, delivery, and financing.

acute care: Immediate, short-term treatment for conditions or injuries that may be life-threatening or require constant monitoring by healthcare professionals.

adverse selection: A situation in healthcare that occurs when sicker (or potentially sicker) people buy health insurance, while healthier people do not, thus increasing the overall risk of the pool.

Affordable Care Act (ACA): A federal law passed in 2010 to reform the US healthcare system.

allopathic medicine: A system of medical practice that focuses on treating disease through medication, surgery, or other interventions; also called *conventional medicine* or *mainstream medicine*.

almshouse: A house originally built by an organization or person to take care of the poor.

American Medical Association (AMA): The largest professional association of physicians and medical students in the United States, founded in 1847.

analytics: The gathering and interpretation of data.

assisted living facility: A living arrangement designed to provide basic personal care needs, assistance with activities of daily living (ADLs), limited administration of medications, and services such as laundry and housekeeping; also known as a *residential care community*.

asymmetric information: The knowledge gap that exists between two parties.

bad debt: Charges for services that are billed but uncollectible and are not charity care.

balance billing: The practice of billing patients for the difference between what their health insurance pays and what the healthcare provider charges; also known as *surprise billing*.

Balanced Budget Act of 1997: A federal law that authorized Medicare Part C, expanding managed care Medicare programs and the State Children's Health Insurance Program.

benchmarking: A quality improvement tool in which an organization compares itself to some standard, often industry best practices.

Beveridge model: A type of healthcare system in which healthcare is paid for mostly by government taxes, with one primary healthcare insurer and healthcare services provided mainly by government employees; also called *socialized medicine.*

big data: Large data sets that are used to analyze a population and find trends in individual or population health.

biosimilar: A drug that has the same clinical effect as a generic drug but a different chemical composition.

Bismarck model: A type of healthcare system in which healthcare is paid for mostly by employees and employers, with many health insurers and healthcare services provided mainly by private providers; also called *all payer system.*

blockbuster drug: A prescription drug that has annual sales greater than $1 billion.

bundled payments: A payment method in which healthcare providers are paid a set amount for an episode or cycle of care (e.g., hip surgery).

capitation: A payment method in which hospitals, physicians, and other healthcare providers receive a fixed payment per person for providing services for a fixed time period.

caregiver: Any person who helps care for an older individual or person with a disability who lives at home.

cause-and-effect diagram: A graphical depiction of the strategy for achieving a specific outcome (effect) and the factors that influence that outcome (causes); also known as a *fishbone diagram.*

chronic disease: A disease that persists for three months or longer that generally cannot be prevented by vaccines or cured by medication.

clinical trial: A research study in which human subjects are used to evaluate the effects of a medication, medical device, or intervention to determine its effectiveness and safety.

cloud computing: The use of a network of remote servers to store data accessed via the internet (i.e., the cloud).

community health center: A neighborhood health center that generally serves low-income and uninsured populations.

community health needs assessment (CHNA): A report that assesses the health needs of a community, prioritizes those needs, and identifies resources to address them; under the Affordable Care Act (ACA), nonprofit hospitals are required to complete an assessment every three years.

community rating: A method of setting insurance premiums that uses the general community population (e.g., a metropolitan area) as the risk pool.

concierge medicine: A model of healthcare in which patients pay an annual fee or retainer to be a part of a primary care physician's practice. Patients receive greater physician access and enhanced services. The physician may bill the patient's health insurance.

continuing care retirement community (CCRC): A retirement complex that offers a range of services and levels of care.

contractual allowances: The difference between the amount that healthcare providers bill for services and the amount they are paid, based on their contracts with third-party insurers and government programs such as Medicare and Medicaid; also called *contractual adjustments.*

coproduction of healthcare: Collaboration between patients, families, and healthcare providers to co-create and co-deliver care.

determinants of health: Factors that are drivers of health outcomes, including medical care, individual behavior, social environment, physical environment, and genetics.

diminishing return: A progressively smaller increase in outputs with each incremental increase in inputs.

direct primary care (DPC): A model of healthcare in which patients pay a flat membership fee for a package of primary care services. The physician does not bill the patient's health insurance.

drug tiers: Groups of prescription drugs that have different costs and copays for consumers.

dual diagnosis: The diagnosis of both a mental illness and a substance abuse disorder.

econometrics: The branch of economics focused on using statistics to describe economic systems.

elasticity of demand: The change in the demand for or quality of a product or service in response to an increase or decrease in price.

electronic health record (EHR): A comprehensive electronic record of an individual's health information across multiple healthcare providers; ideally, it includes a patient's demographics, medical history, medications, immunizations, diagnostic information, and notes from multiple healthcare provider interactions.

electronic medical record (EMR): The electronic version of a patient's medical record from one physician; it generally stays in the physician's office and is not shared.

Emergency Medical Treatment and Labor Act: A federal law passed in 1986 to prevent "patient dumping," the practice of emergency rooms refusing to treat people who lack the financial resources to pay for their care.

experience rating: A method of setting insurance premiums that clusters people into smaller risk pools determined by their health history, age, gender, and other factors to set premiums.

external reference pricing: A method that countries use to set and negotiate the prices they will pay for prescription drugs.

externality: A side effect or an involuntary cost or benefit imposed on a third party.

fee-for-service: A payment method in which hospitals, physicians, and other healthcare providers are paid for each service provided.

Flexner Report: A study published in 1910 by the Carnegie Foundation that evaluated medical education in the United States and prompted major changes in the way physicians were educated.

flowchart: A graphical depiction of a process that allows for the identification of problems and bottlenecks.

formulary: A list of approved prescription drugs that an insurance plan covers; also called a *drug list*.

for-profit hospital: A hospital that is organized to create a profit for its owners; also called an *investor-owned hospital*. For-profit hospitals must pay state and federal taxes and can distribute profits to their investors and raise money from investors and stock offerings.

full capitation: A payment method in which a fixed amount is paid to an organization to provide a comprehensive package of healthcare services for a set period of time.

fully insured company: A company that pays a set annual premium to a health insurance firm to provide healthcare coverage to its employees; in this arrangement, the health insurance company assumes the financial risk.

generic drug: A copy of a brand-name drug that has the same dosage, intended use, administration, and strength as the original drug.

health disparities: Differences in health outcomes and their causes among groups of people.

Health Insurance Portability and Accountability Act (HIPAA): A federal law passed in 1996 that set national standards to protect the privacy and security of patients' health information.

hospice care: Short-term supportive and sometimes palliative care for terminally ill patients.

hospital: A healthcare facility that provides medical and surgical treatment and nursing care for patients who are sick or injured.

indemnity healthcare plan: A health insurance plan that allows individuals to choose their own healthcare providers, providing the greatest amount of flexibility for users. These plans generally use fee-for-service payment.

Indian Health Service: The federal government health system that provides healthcare services to Native Americans.

inelastic demand: Little change in the consumption of a product or service when prices increase or decrease.

inpatient care: Care that requires at least an overnight stay in a medical facility, usually a hospital.

inputs: Resources that are combined to produce outputs; in healthcare, inputs include personnel, equipment, buildings, land, and supplies.

insurance: The pooling of financial resources by groups of people (called risk pools) to share risk.

Iron Triangle of Healthcare: A concept introduced by William Kissick describing three competing dimensions of healthcare: access, cost, and quality.

The Joint Commission: The largest accrediting organization in the United States, which accredits about 88 percent of all US hospitals.

Lean: A method used to reduce waste and to increase value to the consumer by identifying what adds value, enhancing this, and seeking to reduce other actions and processes that do not add value.

life expectancy: The average number of years a person is expected to live.

long-term care: Care that is provided for an extended period of time to patients with chronic illness or disability.

managed care: A system used by health insurance companies to reduce the costs and improve the quality of healthcare.

marginal benefit: The gain or benefit that a patient receives from consuming an additional unit of service; also referred to as *marginal utility*.

marginal cost: The cost of consuming the next unit of service.

meaningful use: The minimum US government standard for electronic health records, outlining how a patient's health information should be exchanged among clinicians or providers and insurance groups or payers.

medical device industry: An industry that is regulated by the US Food and Drug Administration (FDA) and encompasses a wide range of equipment and products that are critical to healthcare delivery, such as surgical gloves, artificial joints, crutches, and imaging equipment.

medical loss ratio: The percentage of health premium dollars that a health insurance plan spends on provider payments (e.g., medical and surgical costs) as opposed to administrative costs.

mHealth: The use of mobile phones, tablets, or other wireless devices by patients to monitor their health.

micro-hospital: A small hospital with 8 to 50 beds that can provide locally needed services, such as exercise facilities, laboratory testing, imaging services, and pharmacies.

Military Health System (MHS): A system of military healthcare facilities and providers focused on maintaining the health of active-duty military and reserve personnel.

moral hazard: A situation in which people have an incentive to increase their risk when they do not bear the full cost of the risk.

morbidity: The rate of disease or injury in a population.

national health insurance model: A type of healthcare system in which healthcare is paid for mostly by government taxes, with one health insurer and healthcare services provided mainly by private providers; also called *single payer system*.

not-for-profit hospital: A hospital that is legally organized as a nonprofit corporation and must invest all of its profits back into the organization. Because of the community benefits they provide, not-for-profit hospitals are exempt from paying federal and state taxes.

opportunity cost: The benefits that are given up by choosing an alternative; in other words, the value of a resource when it is employed in its next-best use.

osteopathic medicine: A system of medicine that originated in the manipulation of the musculoskeletal system and that emphasizes preventive medicine while taking a holistic approach to health.

out-of-pocket model: A type of healthcare system in which healthcare is paid for mostly through individual funds, with a mix of private and government providers; also called *pay-to-play system*.

outpatient care: Care that does not require an overnight stay in a medical facility, such as a hospital; also called *ambulatory care*.

outpatient psychiatric treatment: Psychiatric services offered on an ambulatory basis that do not require a continuous stay of 24 hours or longer in a treatment facility.

outputs: Goods and services that are produced from a combination of inputs (resources).

over-the-counter (OTC) drug: A drug that can be purchased without a prescription; often sold in pharmacies, grocery stories, and convenience stores.

Pareto chart: A bar or line graph that allows for the identification of the causes that contribute to an overall effect.

partial capitation: A payment method in which an organization is paid a fixed amount to provide a select set of healthcare services for a set period of time.

patent medicines: Nonprescription drugs made of proprietary, or secret, compounds that were sold to the public in the early 1900s.

patented brand-named drug: A drug that is marketed under the manufacturer's name and protected by a patent, usually for 20 years.

patient day: A unit of measure of the time of one day that a patient remains in a hospital or other overnight facility; also known as an *inpatient day, census day,* or *bed occupancy day.*

pharmacy benefit manager (PBM): A company that manages prescription drug benefits for health insurers to control drug spending and provide more effective drugs to consumers.

physician extender: A healthcare provider who is not a physician but performs medical activities typically done by a physician; most physician extenders are nurse practitioners or physician assistants.

Plan-Do-Study-Act: A four-step quality improvement process; also known as the *Deming Wheel.*

poorhouse: A home or residential institution where people were required to live if they could not financially support themselves.

population health: The health outcomes of a group of individuals, including the distribution of such outcomes within the group.

preexisting condition: An illness or condition that an individual has prior to enrollment in health insurance coverage.

premium: The amount that is paid (typically monthly or annually) for an insurance policy.

primary care: Basic care, usually provided by doctors, nurse practitioners, and physician assistants in an ambulatory care setting.

primary care physician (PCP): A physician who typically serves as the first contact for patients with basic medical needs; treats acute and chronic ailments and illnesses; and focuses on health promotion, disease prevention, health maintenance, and counseling. PCPs primarily practice family medicine, internal medicine, and pediatrics.

production function: The conversion of inputs into outputs.

psychiatric unit: A unit (department) within a community hospital that is dedicated to the inpatient treatment of mental illness.

public health: A field that is concerned with protecting and improving the health of people and communities.

quality-adjusted life year (QALY): A measure of the burden of disability or morbidity; ranges from 1, perfect health, to 0, death.

quaternary care: Highly specialized healthcare services offered at large hospitals; quaternary care may involve experimental treatments and procedures.

registry: A tool for tracking the clinical care and outcomes collection of specific patient populations, such as patients with certain chronic diseases, types of cancer, or infections.

residential treatment center: A mental health facility where psychiatric treatment is provided in a home-like environment with less medical involvement.

respite care: Care that offers family and other caregivers the opportunity to allow someone else to take care of their loved one or client for a short time, often just for the day; also called *adult day services*.

risk pool: A cluster of people whose medical costs are combined to determine health premiums.

safety-net hospital: A hospital that is committed by mission or mandate to care for those with limited or no access to healthcare services because they lack financial resources.

scarce resources: Resources that are limited and may not be sufficient to meet demand.

secondary care: Care that focuses on the prevention, diagnosis, and treatment of more serious illnesses and injuries for short periods of time. Secondary care includes childbirth services, emergency services, and general surgery.

self-insured company: A company that offers its own healthcare coverage and retains financial responsibility for all employee healthcare costs; in this arrangement, the company assumes the financial risk.

senior center: A community-based center that provides services to the elderly. Programs at these centers address the individual needs of functionally or cognitively impaired adults as well as those who simply want to socialize with others their age.

sentinel event: An event that results in death or serious physical or psychological injury to a patient.

single-payer system: A healthcare payment system that has a single entity that pays healthcare providers.

Six Sigma: A business processes improvement method that uses qualitative and quantitative techniques to increase performance and reduce variation.

skilled nursing facility (SNF): A licensed facility that provides general nursing care to those who are chronically ill or unable to take care of their daily living needs; also called a *skilled nursing center*.

social determinants of health: Factors in the social and physical environment that affect health outcomes, such as economic stability, neighborhood and physical environment, education, food, community and social context, and the healthcare system.

stakeholder: An individual or group that has some investment in an organization or obtains some benefit from it.

stop-loss insurance: An insurance policy that provides protection against large losses for companies that self-fund their employee benefit plans; the policy pays out after a certain threshold of healthcare costs is reached.

syndromic surveillance: The gathering, analysis, and interpretation of health data to diagnose and respond to population health and public health issues.

telemedicine: The use of two-way audio and video communication to facilitate communication between healthcare providers or between providers and patients.

tertiary care: Care that encompasses complicated services and results from referrals from primary or secondary providers.

third-party administrator (TPA): A company that provides claims processing and employee benefits management without assuming any financial risk.

third-party payer: An entity (a company or individual) that pays for medical services on behalf of a patient.

Triple Aim: A modified version of the Iron Triangle that highlights the interdependencies of population health, quality of care, and cost; it refers to the simultaneous pursuit of three goals: improving the health of populations, improving the patient experience of care, and reducing the per capita cost of healthcare.

value-based payment: A payment system in which provider payments are linked to the cost and quality of care.

Veterans Health Administration (VHA): A healthcare system run by the US federal government that provides hospital services to current and past military members.

INDEX

Note: Italicized page locators refer to exhibits.

ABOUT THE AUTHORS

Stephen L. Walston, PhD, has worked as both a professor and a healthcare administrator. He currently serves as Director of the University of Utah's Master of Healthcare Administration (MHA) program. Previously, he served as Vice President for Academic Affairs at the University of Utah Asia Campus (UAC), located at the Incheon Global Campus in Songdo, Korea. He has also been Associate Dean for Academic Affairs at the University of Oklahoma's College of Public Health, MHA Program Director at Indiana University, and faculty member at Cornell University. Before his academic career, he was an executive for 14 years in hospitals in the western United States. During this time, he was a CEO for ten years. He became a fellow of the American College of Healthcare Executives in 1993. He holds a PhD in healthcare systems and management from the University of Pennsylvania's Wharton School.

Dr. Walston has been active internationally and has worked in many Middle Eastern and Central American countries helping organizations to improve their strategic direction and leadership capabilities. He served on the Saudi Arabian Ministry of Health's International Advisory Board for five years. He currently serves on the Gardner Policy Institute Health Care Advisory Board. He has published in many prestigious journals in the United States and Europe, in addition to authoring five books. He is fluent in Spanish. In his free time, he enjoys woodworking, beekeeping, reading, bicycling, gardening, and spending time with his children and grandchildren.

Ken Johnson, PhD, FACHE, serves as associate dean and professor in the Dumke College of Health Professions at Weber State University in Ogden, Utah. He holds a doctorate in health education and has primarily taught in the areas of healthcare administration and population health. He is a past chair of the Association of University Programs in Healthcare Administration (AUPHA) and past president of the National Association of Local Boards of Health (NALBOH). He is a fellow of both the American College of Healthcare Executives and the Association of Schools of Allied Health Professions. He represents the latter as a member of the Healthy People Curriculum Task Force. Prior to his appointment at Weber State, Ken worked for 15 years in healthcare, holding positions in hospital administration and medical group management.